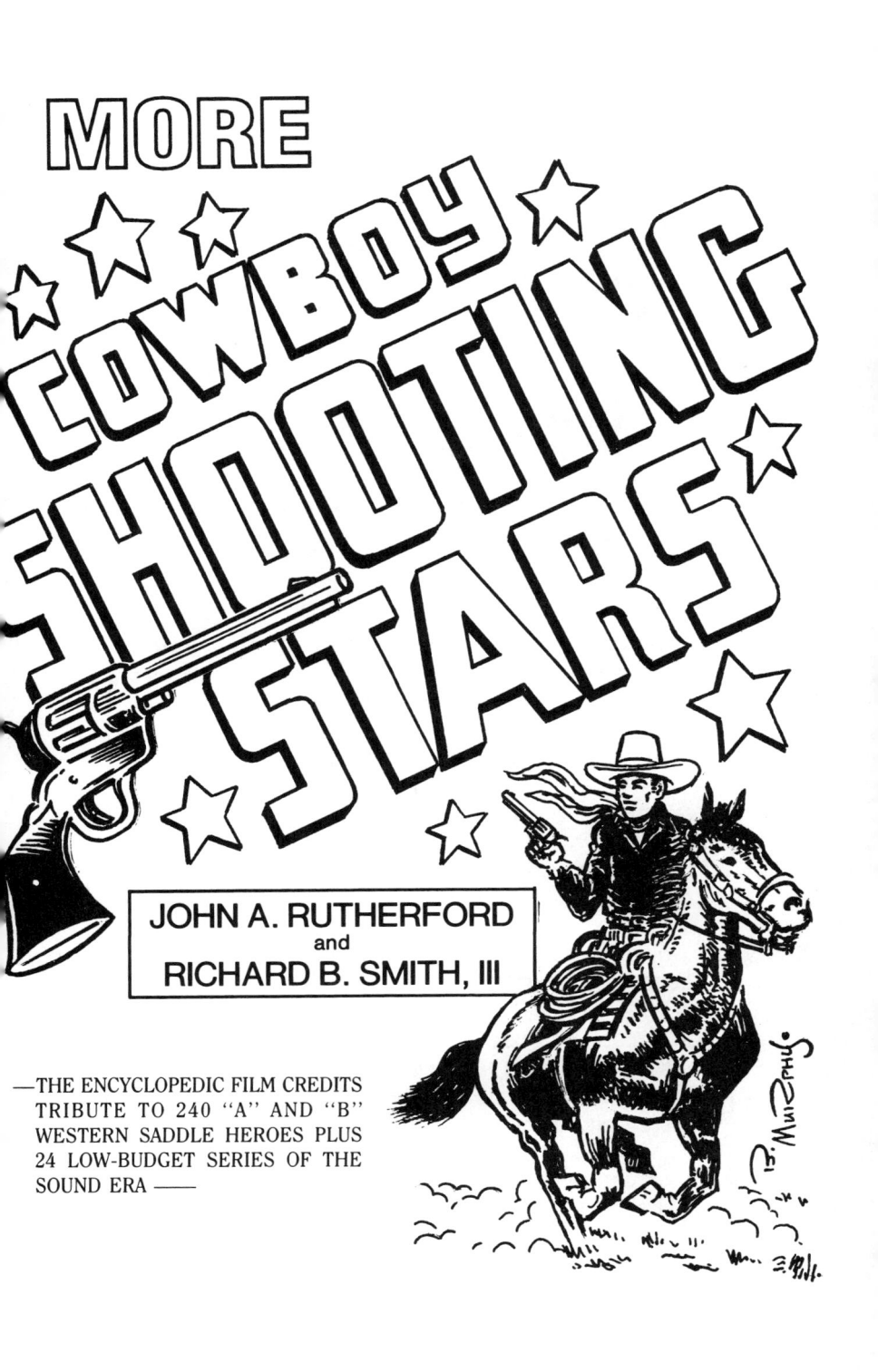

MORE COWBOY SHOOTING STARS

JOHN A. RUTHERFORD
and
RICHARD B. SMITH, III

—THE ENCYCLOPEDIC FILM CREDITS TRIBUTE TO 240 "A" AND "B" WESTERN SADDLE HEROES PLUS 24 LOW-BUDGET SERIES OF THE SOUND ERA—

Other books by Empire Publishing:
   The Roy Rogers Reference-Trivia-Scrapbook Book by David Rothel
   The Gene Autry Reference-Trivia-Scrapbook Book by David Rothel
   Iron Eyes Cody, The Proud American by Iron Eyes Cody and Marietta Thompson
   Cowboy Shooting Stars by John A. Rutherford and Richard B. Smith, III
   Allan "Rocky" Lane, Republic's Action Ace by Chuck Thornton and David Rothel
   Tom Mix Highlights by Andy Woytowich
   Don't Look Up! by Danny Gordon and Paul Dellinger
   An Ambush of Ghosts by David Rothel

Empire Publishing, Inc.
3130 U.S. 220
Madison, NC 27025
(919) 427-5850

More Cowboy Shooting Stars © copyright 1992 by John A. Rutherford and Richard B. Smith, III

All rights reserved under International and Pan American copyright convention. No part of this book may be reproduced in any manner whatsoever without written permission from the publisher, except in the case of brief quotations embodied in reviews and articles.

Library of Congress Catalog Number 92-074737
ISBN Number 0-944019-11-0

Published and printed in The United States of America

1 2 3 4 5 6 7 8 9 10

This book is dedicated to the memory of talented western directors

LAMBERT HILLYER (1893 - 1969)

and

JOSEPH "JOE" KANE (1894 - 1975)

whose technical expertise with their craft, starting in the silent era, enriched the very quality of films for stars as well as movie and television audiences alike. Such skills are much appreciated even many years later by endless admirers of the oater genre.

ACKNOWLEDGMENTS

MORE COWBOY SHOOTING STARS is the culmination of a many-years' objective on the part of each author initially having pursued different paths which eventually merged into one for this book.

Both of us have been life-long admirers of "A" and "B" westerns and their stars. We observed a genre which gradually transferred, starting in 1950, from the once awe-inspiring panorama of the 35mm theater screen that showed such features produced by numerous Hollywood movie studios to the much smaller picture image on television with its own 30- and 60-minute presentations. Current hour-and-a-half or longer TV releases are distributed through national and cable network production facilities.

Of course, western fans can still watch their favorite films of yesteryear via TV showings, 16mm prints, and videotapes. Monthly film clubs and annual film conventions are positive outlets which assure the genre's maintaining its popularity.

It has been our privilege to know enlightened individuals who continue observing the western today with its ever-changing trends and steadfastly maintain their devotion accompanied by undiminished enthusiasm. Often sought personally from them are advice, assistance, and observations which they share always. Such generosity has been immeasurable for this publication's finality.

We thank and are very grateful to Craig Allison, Lewis Bagwell, Tom Betts, Paul Dellinger, Linda Downey, Ron Downey, Joe Fair, Mack A. Houston, Boyd Magers, Jack Mathis, Merrill T. McCord, Ray Nielsen, Patrick J. Sheehan, John D. Stone, and Edward A. Wall.

Michael Chapin, John Kimbrough, and James Warren provided generous insight on various stages of their careers.

The authors extend special thanks to Donald Key and Rhonda Lemons of Empire Publishing, Inc., for the typesetting, printing, and distribution of this book that involved endless hours of production time. Their continued faith and support since 1987 for our projects—starting with the edition of *COWBOY SHOOTING STARS*—has been especially gratifying.

John A. Rutherford
Richard B. Smith, III

INTRODUCTION

MORE COWBOY SHOOTING STARS is a super film reference book of "A" and "B" western saddlers' sound credits from 1928—involving both lead and support roles in movie and television features—which is intended as an available guide for film collectors, film fans, and film historians who are personally devoted to the oater genre.

It is a vast expansion over the 100-page handbook *COWBOY SHOOTING STARS* published in 1988. That publication contained basically the starring films of 110 "B" saddlers, including a few series, with some entries carrying a number of support roles. The current book contains more personalities than have ever been spotlighted in any other printed edition—240 individuals and 24 series—covering the subject of individual western stars and their oater credits in single-line format.

As with the 1988 version, *MORE COWBOY SHOOTING STARS* has the subjects in alphabetical order with their films listed according to chronological release. Studio abbreviations are included again as well as a separate index of corporation names to identify those acronyms. The majority of films have running times with some given an additional range where applicable (56-58 minutes). Westerns in color are designated with a (C) before the year of release. Features two reels or less have been omitted. TV movies where a studio or network can't be identified are so noted with the abbreviation TVM.

New additions and revisions within the credits include more identified series (several will be new to the reader), when a star started/ended a particular series, and these symbols: (s) support for fourth billing down in a film; (cs) co-star for third billing; (so) song; (vo) voice role; (ho) host; (gs) guest star; (nr) narrator. Wherever possible, alternate titles including those from Great Britain have been inserted.

Many western movies did not take the straight shoot-em-up themes of the hero after a usual assortment of villains who were robbers, rustlers, land grabbers, smugglers, etc. This held most true for "A" features that carried adult themes of romance, heavy plot, period-oriented storylines, and a goodly amount of majestic scenery—the last category prevailing when a motion picture company went on location sometimes thousands of miles away from Hollywood. Some features listed are not westerns in the strictest sense, but they carry enough basics to qualify for inclusion.

An additional highlight preceding the credits is a brief biographical piece on each individual along with a year of birth. The year of death is added if it pertains. Series receive the same treatment. Persons known to have acted under other names are mentioned.

For "B" stars where appropriate, the years they were included in the Top Money-Making Western Stars list (1936-54), as conducted by the *Motion Picture Herald* of theatre exhibitors, are added in the profile. Such a poll was an annual barometer measuring their box-office success. Had the poll started in 1930, cowboys Tom Mix, Buck Jones, Ken Maynard, Hoot Gibson, Bob Steele, George O'Brien, Tim McCoy, and John Wayne surely would have been listed practically every year through 1935.

Compilation of *MORE COWBOY SHOOTING STARS* through final production took almost two years. A project of such magnitude can take many twists and turns when additional research is involved. A movie-television video guide was located that inadvertently contained only alternate titles of the abbreviated Jimmy Ellison-Russell Hayden series for Lippert Pictures. Such a fluke was the equivalent of a mother-lode gold strike when matched with *Variety* reviews of the original monickers.

For an individual who aspired to be a western movie star, it turned out as a monumental undertaking and was the *toughest* part of the acting profession. A cowboy not only had to learn his dialogue, but he also had to possess endless stamina in order to ride, rope, shoot, and fight (possibly sing, too, if that were a forte), along with steering cattle and horse herds, as well as driving stagecoaches, covered wagons, and supply carriers. There was the task as well of keeping an alert eye out on location during exteriors' photography for poisonous snakes, the ability to make sure his horse didn't fall or step into a hole on the open range which varied in terrain, and patiently contending with showers of dust from camera trucks and other riders. Finally, he had to battle Mother Nature's tempestuous elements of wind, rain, snow, heat, and cold.

Each person spotlighted garnered lots of appreciation for accomplishments in the western film, regardless of whether it involved a bunch of credits or just a few. Some were multi-talented individuals who also spent a great deal of time in other genres of the American movie industry, as well as overseas filming, performing comedy and drama. Whatever trails these western heroes followed, we remember not only their charm, grace, style, and wit but also their courage, daring, dignity, and professionalism.

ABOUT THE PUBLISHERS

Empire Publishing, Inc. of North Carolina began its publishing operation in the spring of 1974 where in a small basement recreation room, the internationally-known movie collector's newspaper, The *Big Reel* was born.

Each and every month since 1974, The *Big Reel* has grown to be one of the world's best sources for movie collectors to buy, trade and sell movie collectors to buy, trade and sell movie related material. Donald Key, creator and founder of The *Big Reel*, along with his lifetime companion, Noreen, still remain very active in the business servicing their more than 4,000 enthusiastic subscribers around the globe. The tabloid size monthly newspaper usually contains more than 128 pages and is crammed with ads from collectors; nostalgia merchants and readers' personal remembrances of the old time stars. It also consists of special articles and feature stories of interest to the movie fan-collector.

The Keys did business as a mom and pop operation for the first several years. Presently, five additional employees are working with the company—daughters Rhonda and Doneen, Debra DeLancey, Jan Fulcher, and Octola Currin.

In March 1986, the corporation was moved from a residence operation to new spacious office quarters just outside of Madison, NC. Because of the additional office space now available, other publishing ventures have been launched. Empire has published several books by well-known western author, David Rothel: *The Roy Rogers Reference-Trivia-Scrapbook, The Gene Autry Reference-Trivia-Scrapbook,* and *An Ambush of Ghosts—A Personal Guide to Western Film Locations.* Other publications by Empire include *Allan "Rocky" Lane, Republic's Action Ace* by Chuck Thornton and David Rothel, *Iron Eyes Cody, the Proud American* by Iron Eyes Cody and Marietta Thompson, and *Tom Mix Highlights* by Andy Woytowich. All books may be ordered directly from the publisher.

And now you are holding in your hands their latest publication, *MORE COWBOY SHOOTING STARS* compiled by film historians John A. Rutherford and Richard B. Smith, III. Within its pages, we believe, you will quickly discover one of the handiest little books ever made available to the oater genre movie buff. We sincerely hope that you will enjoy this "A" and "B" western reference and information book and find it to be very useful for many years to come.

Staff and Management
Empire Publishing, Inc.

TABLE OF CONTENTS

ACTION WESTERNS series 12
JOHN AGAR 12
BOB ALLEN 13
REX ALLEN 13
DANA ANDREWS 14
RICHARD ARLEN 14
JAMES ARNESS 15
GENE AUSTIN 16
GENE AUTRY 16
BOB BAKER 18
SMITH BALLEW 19
JIM BANNON 19
LEX BARKER 20
DON "RED" BARRY 20
BUZZ BARTON 22
SAMMY BAUGH 23
WARNER BAXTER 23
NOAH BEERY, JR. 23
WALLACE BEERY 24
REX BELL 25
BRUCE BENNETT 26
WILLIAM BISHOP 26
RICHARD BOONE 27
WILLIAM BOYD 27
SCOTT BRADY 29
MARLON BRANDO 29
GEORGE BRENT 30
DAVID BRIAN 30
LLOYD BRIDGES 30
CHARLES BRONSON 31
JAMES BROWN 32
JIM BROWN 32
JOHNNY MACK BROWN 32
YUL BRYNNER 35
JACK BUETEL 35
BUFFALO BILL, JR. 35
JAMES CAAN 37
JAMES CAGNEY 37
RORY CALHOUN 37
ROD CAMERON 38
ROCKY CAMRON 39
JUDY CANOVA 40
HARRY CAREY 40
HARRY CAREY, JR. 41

MacDONALD CAREY 42
PHIL CAREY 43
JOHNNY CARPENTER 43
LEO CARRILLO 44
JOHN CARROLL 44
LIGHTNIN' BILL CARSON series 45
BILLY THE KID/BILLY CARSON series 45
SUNSET CARSON 47
HOPALONG CASSIDY series .. 47
JEFF CHANDLER 49
LANE CHANDLER 50
MICHAEL CHAPIN 52
THE CISCO KID series 53
DANE CLARK 54
JAMES COBURN 54
STEVE COCHRAN 54
BILL CODY 55
CHUCK CONNORS 55
ROBERT CONRAD 56
GARY COOPER 56
WENDELL COREY 57
JOSEPH COTTEN 57
BUSTER CRABBE 57
JAMES CRAIG 59
BRODERICK CRAWFORD 59
KEN CURTIS 60
BOB CUSTER 60
JIM DAVIS 61
EDDIE DEAN 62
YVONNE DE CARLO 63
RICHARD DENNING 64
JOHN DEREK 64
EDDIE DEW 65
RICHARD DIX 65
BRIAN DONLEVY 66
KIRK DOUGLAS 66
HOWARD DUFF 67
THE DURANGO KID series 67
DAN DURYEA 69
CLINT EASTWOOD 69
NELSON EDDY 70
RICHARD EGAN 70

BILL ELLIOTT	71
SAM ELLIOTT	72
JIMMY ELLISON	73
JOHN ERICSON	73
FAMOUS WESTERNS series	74
TEX FLETCHER	75
ERROL FLYNN	75
HENRY FONDA	75
DICK FORAN	76
GLENN FORD	77
STEVE FORREST	77
PRESTON FOSTER	78
THE FRONTIER MARSHALS series	78
ROBERT FULLER	79
CLARK GABLE	79
JAMES GARNER	79
HOOT GIBSON	80
STEWART GRANGER	81
KIRBY GRANT	81
PETER GRAVES	82
MONTE HALE	82
JON HALL	83
RICHARD HARRIS	83
RICHARD HARRISON	83
RUSSELL HAYDEN	84
STERLING HAYDEN	85
VAN HEFLIN	86
CHARLTON HESTON	86
WILD BILL HICKOK series	87
TERENCE HILL	87
JOHN HODIAK	88
WILLIAM HOLDEN	88
JACK HOLT	88
TIM HOLT	89
BOB HOPE	90
GEORGE HOUSTON	90
JACK HOXIE	91
ROCK HUDSON	91
JEFFREY HUNTER	91
TAB HUNTER	92
WALTER HUSTON	92
JOHN IRELAND	93
THE IRISH COWBOYS series	93
ART JARRETT	93
BEN JOHNSON	94
BUCK JONES	95
HOWARD KEEL	97
TOM KEENE	97
BRIAN KEITH	98
PAUL KELLY	99
GEORGE KENNEDY	100
JOHN KIMBROUGH	100
FRED KOHLER, JR.	100
KRIS KRISTOFFERSON	101
ALAN LADD	102
BURT LANCASTER	102
MICHAEL LANDON	103
ALLAN "ROCKY" LANE	103
KEITH LARSEN	104
LASH LaRUE	114
REX LEASE	114
ROBERT LIVINGSTON	117
ROBERT LOGAN	119
THE LONE RIDER series	119
JACK LUDEN	119
JOHN LUND	120
JEANETTE MacDONALD	120
FRED MacMURRAY	120
GUY MADISON	121
JOCK MAHONEY	122
DEAN MARTIN	123
LEE MARVIN	123
VICTOR MATURE	124
KEN MAYNARD	124
KERMIT MAYNARD	126
TIM McCOY	130
JOEL McCREA	131
NEVADA JACK McKENZIE series	132
STEPHEN McNALLY	133
STEVE McQUEEN	133
RAY MILLAND	134
ROBERT MITCHUM	134
TOM MIX	135
DOCTOR MONROE series	135
MONTIE MONTANA	135
GEORGE MONTGOMERY	136
CLAYTON MOORE	137
DENNIS MOORE	138
DENNIS MORGAN	140
CHESTER MORRIS	140

WAYNE MORRIS	141
AUDIE MURPHY	141
DON MURRAY	142
WILLIE NELSON	142
FRANCO NERO	143
JAMES NEWILL	143
PAUL NEWMAN	143
JACK NICHOLSON	144
NORTHWEST MOUNTIE series	144
HUGH O'BRIAN	145
DAVE O'BRIEN	145
EDMOND O'BRIEN	147
GEORGE O'BRIEN	147
MAUREEN O'HARA	148
DOROTHY PAGE	149
JACK PALANCE	149
FESS PARKER	150
WILLARD PARKER	150
JOHN PAYNE	150
GREGORY PECK	151
GEORGE PEPPARD	151
JACK PERRIN	152
LEE POWELL	154
TYRONE POWER	154
ELVIS PRESLEY	154
ROBERT PRESTON	155
ANTHONY QUINN	155
VERA RALSTON	156
JACK RANDALL	156
THE RANGE BUSTERS series	157
THE RANGE RIDER series	158
RONALD REAGAN	158
ROBERT REDFORD	159
DUNCAN RENALDO	159
RENFREW OF THE ROYAL MOUNTED series	160
JOHN PAUL REVERE series	160
BURT REYNOLDS	160
RIN-TIN-TIN	161
TEX RITTER	161
DALE ROBERTSON	163
KENNY ROGERS	163
ROY ROGERS	164
GILBERT ROLAND	166
CESAR ROMERO	167
BUDDY ROOSEVELT	167
THE ROUGH RIDERS series	169
ROUGH-RIDIN' KIDS series	169
JANE RUSSELL	169
REB RUSSELL	170
ROBERT RYAN	170
RED RYDER series	170
WILD BILL SAUNDERS series	171
FRED SCOTT	172
RANDOLPH SCOTT	172
FRANK SINATRA	174
ROBERT STACK	174
BARBARA STANWYCK	174
CHARLES STARRETT	175
BOB STEELE	178
ANTHONY STEFFEN	181
MARK STEVENS	181
JAMES STEWART	181
BARRY SULLIVAN	182
KENT TAYLOR	182
ROBERT TAYLOR	183
ROD TAYLOR	183
THE TEXAS RANGERS series	184
THE THREE MESQUITEERS series	184
SPENCER TRACY	186
THE TRAIL BLAZERS series	186
TOM TRYON	187
FORREST TUCKER	187
TOM TYLER	188
LEE VAN CLEEF	190
ROBERT WAGNER	192
JIMMY WAKELY	192
WALLY WALES	193
CLINT WALKER	197
JAMES WARREN	197
JOHN WAYNE	197
RICHARD WIDMARK	199
BILL WILLIAMS	200
GUINN "BIG BOY" WILLIAMS	201
FRED WILLIAMSON	202
WHIP WILSON	202
MONTGOMERY WOOD	203
ROBERT WOODS	203
LORETTA YOUNG	203
ROBERT YOUNG	204

ACTION WESTERNS series (1944 - 1945)

These six thrill-a-minute "B" westerns at Republic Pictures launched Allan Lane as a major oats star for 1940s Saturday matinee theater attendees. The fourth entry, THE TOPEKA TERROR, found Lane exclaiming he'd been after land grabber Roy Barcroft for three years. Little did the saddler realize that such a snippet of dialogue prophetically meant he'd still be chasing down the studio contract villain for another eight years in 36 more gallopers.

(ALLAN LANE, WALLY VERNON)
SILVER CITY KID .... 1944 ... REP .... 55 ____
STAGECOACH TO MONTEREY .... 1944 ... REP .... 55 ____

(ALLAN LANE, MAX TERHUNE, DUNCAN RENALDO)
SHERIFF OF SUNDOWN .... 1944 ... REP .... 57 ____

(ALLAN LANE, EARLE HODGINS)
THE TOPEKA TERROR .... 1945 ... REP .... 55 ____

(ALLAN LANE)
CORPUS CHRISTI BANDITS .... 1945 ... REP ..... 55-57 ____
TRAIL OF KIT CARSON .... 1945 ... REP .... 55 ____

JOHN AGAR (1921 -   )

Leading man whose most famous western role was that of the young cavalry lieutenant who courted Shirley Temple in the John Ford epic, FORT APACHE. At the time Agar was the real life husband of Temple.

FORT APACHE (s) .... 1948 ... RKO .... 127 ____
SHE WORE A YELLOW RIBBON (s) .... (C) .. 1949 ... RKO .... 104 ____
ALONG THE GREAT DIVIDE (cs) .... 1951 ... WB .... 88 ____
WOMAN OF THE NORTH COUNTRY (s) .... (C) .. 1952 ... REP .... 90 ____
THE LONESOME TRAIL .... 1955 ... LIP .... 73 ____
TARANTULA .... 1955 ... UI .... 80 ____
STAR IN THE DUST .... (C) .. 1956 ... UI .... 80 ____
FLESH AND THE SPUR .... (C) .. 1956 ... AI .... 80 ____
RIDE A VIOLENT MILE .... 1957 ... 20T .... 70 ____
FRONTIER GUN .... 1958 ... 20T .... 70 ____
CAVALRY COMMAND .... (C) .. 1963 ... PAD .... 86 ____
LAW OF THE LAWLESS .... (C) .. 1964 ... PAR .... 87 ____
   (aka INVITATION TO A HANGING) (s)
STAGE TO THUNDER ROCK (s) .... (C) .. 1964 ... PAR .... 82 ____
   (aka STAGECOACH TO HELL)
YOUNG FURY (s) .... (C) .. 1965 ... PAR ..... 79-80 ____
JOHNNY RENO (s) .... (C) .. 1966 ... PAR .... 83 ____
WACO (s) .... (C) .. 1966 ... PAR .... 85 ____
THE UNDEFEATED (s) .... (C) .. 1969 ... 20T .... 119 ____
CHISUM (s) .... (C) .. 1970 ... WB .... 111 ____
BIG JAKE (s) .... (C) .. 1971 ... NG .... 110 ____

BOB ALLEN (1906 -   )

He concentrated an acting career during the 1930s with moderate-budgeted drawing room dramas and mysteries; however, Allen starred in the 1936-37 "B" western series for Columbia Pictures as a ranger. Bob has been a frequent guest at film conventions in recent years.

LAW BEYOND THE RANGE (s)	1935	COL	56-60
THE REVENGE RIDER (s)	1935	COL	57-60
FIGHTING SHADOWS (s)	1935	COL	58
THE UNKNOWN RANGER	1936	COL	58
RIO GRANDE RANGER	1936	COL	54
RANGER COURAGE	1937	COL	58
LAW OF THE RANGER	1937	COL	57
RECKLESS RANGER	1937	COL	56
THE RANGERS STEP IN	1937	COL	58

REX ALLEN (1920 -   )

"The Arizona Cowboy," possessing a beautiful singing voice, became the last Republic Pictures "B" saddler who mainlined 19 oatuners (1950-54). Rex's best was COLORADO SUNDOWN. A Top Money-Making Western Star (1951-54), Allen filmed 39 half-hour segments of the "Frontier Doctor" TV series for Republic in the mid-1950s. He narrated 150 episodes of "Wonderful World of Color" for Disney on NBC-TV. Rex was honored by Gov. Rose Mofford in August 1989 for "dedication" to Arizona. Has the Rex Allen Arizona Cowboy Museum at Willcox.

THE ARIZONA COWBOY		1950	REP	67
HILLS OF OKLAHOMA		1950	REP	67
REDWOOD FOREST TRAIL		1950	REP	67
UNDER MEXICALI STARS		1950	REP	67
(aka UNDER MEXICALI SKIES)				
TRAIL OF ROBIN HOOD (gs)	(C)	1950	REP	67
SILVER CITY BONANZA		1951	REP	67
THUNDER IN GOD'S COUNTRY		1951	REP	67
RODEO KING AND THE SENORITA		1951	REP	67
UTAH WAGON TRAIN		1951	REP	67
COLORADO SUNDOWN		1952	REP	67
THE LAST MUSKETEER		1952	REP	67
BORDER SADDLEMATES		1952	REP	67
I DREAM OF JEANIE (s)	(C)	1952	REP	90
OLD OKLAHOMA PLAINS		1952	REP	60
SOUTH PACIFIC TRAIL		1952	REP	60
OLD OVERLAND TRAIL		1953	REP	60
IRON MOUNTAIN TRAIL		1953	REP	54
SWEETHEARTS ON PARADE (s)	(C)	1953	REP	90
DOWN LAREDO WAY		1953	REP	54
SHADOWS OF TOMBSTONE		1953	REP	54
RED RIVER SHORE		1953	REP	54
PHANTOM STALLION		1954	REP	54
FOR THE LOVE OF MIKE	(C)	1960	20T	90
(aka NONE BUT THE BRAVE) (s)				
TOMBOY AND THE CHAMP (s)	(C)	1961	UI	92
THE LEGEND OF LOBO (nr)	(C)	1962	BV	67
THE INCREDIBLE JOURNEY (nr)	(C)	1963	BV	80
RUN APPALOOSA RUN (nr)	(C)	1966	BV	48
CHARLIE, THE LONESOME COUGAR	(C)	1967	BV	75

13

14 / REX ALLEN, continued

BORN TO BUCK (nr)	(C)	1968...CTI	94
VANISHING WILDERNESS (nr)	(C)	1974...PIE	93
THE SECRET OF NAVAJO CAVE (nr)	(C)	1976...KI	87
THE LEGEND OF COUGAR CANYON (nr)	(C)	1980...FA	87

DANA ANDREWS (1909 -)

Mostly a tough-guy-type leading man whose most memorable western role was that of the mule train leader in the mining story, CANYON PASSAGE, by Ernest Haycox.

LUCKY CISCO KID		1940...20T	68
KIT CARSON		1940...UA	97
THE WESTERNER (s)		1940...UA	94
BELLE STARR	(C)	1941...20T	87
THE OX-BOW INCIDENT		1943...20T	75
(aka STRANGE INCIDENT)			
CANYON PASSAGE	(C)	1946...UNI	90
THREE HOURS TO KILL	(C)	1954...COL	77
SMOKE SIGNAL	(C)	1955...UI	88
STRANGE LADY IN TOWN	(C)	1955...WB	112
COMANCHE	(C)	1956...UA	87
TOWN TAMER	(C)	1965...PAR	89
JOHNNY RENO	(C)	1966...PAR	89
TAKE A HARD RIDE (s)	(C)	1975...20T	102

RICHARD ARLEN (1900 - 1976)

Leading man of second features who starred in numerous western films from early 1930s Zane Grey stories at Paramount to Screen Guild oaters in the late 1940s. Best-known role was as the ill-fated pal of Gary Cooper in the classic western, THE VIRGINIAN. Arlen's straightforward values were his forte.

THE VIRGINIAN (s)	1929...PAR	87
THE LIGHT OF WESTERN STARS	1930...PAR	69
THE SANTA FE TRAIL	1930...PAR	65
(aka THE LAW RIDES WEST)		
THE BORDER LEGION	1930...PAR	68
THE CONQUERING HORDE	1931...PAR	73
GUN SMOKE	1931...PAR	65
CAUGHT	1931...PAR	68
HELLDORADO	1934...FOX	75
THE MINE WITH THE IRON DOOR	1936...COL	66
SECRET VALLEY (aka GANGSTER'S BRIDE)	1937...20T	57
SILENT BARRIERS	1937...G-B	84
(aka THE GREAT BARRIER)		
CALL OF THE YUKON	1938...REP	70
MUTINY ON THE BLACKHAWK	1939...UNI	68
LEGION OF LOST FLYERS	1939...UNI	63
MAN FROM MONTREAL	1939...UNI	60
MUTINY IN THE ARCTIC	1941...UNI	68
MEN OF THE TIMBERLAND	1941...UNI	61
WILDCAT	1942...PAR	70-75
ALASKA HIGHWAY	1943...PAR	66
TIMBER QUEEN	1944...PAR	70-75
THE BIG BONANZA	1944...REP	68
BUFFALO BILL RIDES AGAIN	1947...SG	70

RICHARD ARLEN, continued / 15

THE RETURN OF WILDFIRE	(C)	1948	SG	83	
(aka BLACK STALLION)					
GRAND CANYON		1949	SG	69	
KANSAS RAIDERS (s)	(C)	1950	UI	80	
SILVER CITY (aka HIGH VERMILION) (cs)	(C)	1951	PAR	90	
FLAMING FEATHER (s)	(C)	1952	PAR	78	
THE BLAZING FOREST (s)	(C)	1952	PAR	90	
HIDDEN GUNS		1956	REP	66	
WARLOCK (s)	(C)	1959	20T	121	
THE SHEPHERD OF THE HILLS	(C)	1964	HI	110	
(aka THUNDER MOUNTAIN)					
LAW OF THE LAWLESS	(C)	1964	PAR	87	
(aka INVITATION TO A HANGING) (s)					
YOUNG FURY (s)	(C)	1965	PAR	79-80	
BLACK SPURS (s)	(C)	1965	PAR	81	
THE BOUNTY KILLER (s)	(C)	1965	EMB	92	
TOWN TAMER (s)	(C)	1965	PAR	89	
APACHE UPRISING (s)	(C)	1966	PAR	90	
JOHNNY RENO (s)	(C)	1966	PAR	83	
WACO (s)	(C)	1966	PAR	85	
RED TOMAHAWK (s)	(C)	1967	PAR	82	
FORT UTAH (s)	(C)	1967	PAR	83	
HOSTILE GUNS (s)	(C)	1967	PAR	91	
BUCKSKIN (s)	(C)	1968	PAR	97	

JAMES ARNESS (1923 -   )
Once a protege of John Wayne, he is television's most enduring adult western star having performed 20 years (1955-75) as Matt Dillon on CBS-TV's famous "Gunsmoke" series (233 half-hour segments, 400 hour segments) in addition to helming "How the West Was Won" for MGM-TV (1977-79) during 26 hour-long shows. Arness today makes 100-minute "Gunsmoke" TV movies.

THE MAN FROM TEXAS (s)		1947	EL	71	
WAGON MASTER (s)		1950	RKO	86	
STARS IN MY CROWN (s)		1950	MGM	89	
SIERRA (s)	(C)	1950	UI	83	
WYOMING MAIL (s)	(C)	1950	UI	87	
BELLE LE GRAND (s)		1951	REP	90	
CAVALRY SCOUT (s)	(C)	1951	MON	78	
HELLGATE (s)		1952	LIP	87	
HORIZONS WEST (s)	(C)	1952	UI	81	
LONE HAND (s)	(C)	1953	UI	80	
HONDO (s)	(C)	1954	WB	84	
MANY RIVERS TO CROSS (s)	(C)	1955	MGM	92	
THE FIRST TRAVELING SALESLADY (s)	(C)	1956	RKO	92	
GUN THE MAN DOWN		1956	UA	78	
(aka ARIZONA MISSION)					
ALIAS JESSE JAMES (gs)	(C)	1959	UA	92	
THE MACAHANS	(C)	1976	MGM-TV	125	
THE ALAMO: 13 DAYS TO GLORY	(C)	1987	NBC-TV	145	
GUNSMOKE: RETURN TO DODGE	(C)	1987	CBS-TV	100	
RED RIVER	(C)	1988	MGM-UA/TV	100	
GUNSMOKE: THE LAST APACHE	(C)	1990	CBS-TV	100	
GUNSMOKE: TO THE LAST MAN	(C)	1992	CBS-TV	100	

GENE AUSTIN (1900 - 1972)

His starring role in a musical western for Colony Pictures apparently did not generate sufficient box-office receipts for the studio to continue with more oatuners.

BELLE OF THE NINETIES (s)	1934	PAR	73
KLONDIKE ANNIE (s)	1936	PAR	80
SONGS AND SADDLES	1938	CLY	65
MY LITTLE CHICKADEE (s)	1940	UNI	85
MOON OVER LAS VEGAS (s)	1944	UNI	69

GENE AUTRY (1907 -   )

Autry's life has been extraordinary—from radio, movie and TV cowboy to multimillionaire businessman. Gene was Republic Pictures' first official singing cowboy in 1935 with TUMBLING TUMBLEWEEDS. By 1953, he had completed 88 horse operas, including 32 for Columbia Studios. His top "B" westerns were DOWN MEXICO WAY and the two Cinecolor features THE STRAWBERRY ROAN and THE BIG SOMBRERO. A Top Money-Making Western Star (1936-42, 1946-54), Autry had 91 half-hour CBS-TV shows (1950-56) under his Flying A Pictures that also turned out "The Range Rider" and "Annie Oakley" among others. Hosting "Melody Ranch Theater" on TNN in the late 1980s, Gene's main activities now are ownership of the California Angels baseball team, which he offered for sale during 1992, and the highly-acclaimed Gene Autry Western Heritage Museum in Los Angeles.

IN OLD SANTA FE (s)	1934	MAS	63
MYSTERY MOUNTAIN (s) (SER)	1934	MAS	12CH
THE PHANTOM EMPIRE (SER)	1935	MAS	12CH
(aka RADIO RANCH)			
TUMBLING TUMBLEWEEDS	1935	REP	57
MELODY TRAIL	1935	REP	60
THE SAGEBRUSH TROUBADOUR	1935	REP	54
THE SINGING VAGABOND	1936	REP	52
RED RIVER VALLEY	1936	REP	56
(aka MAN OF THE FRONTIER)			
COMIN' 'ROUND THE MOUNTAIN	1936	REP	55
THE SINGING COWBOY	1936	REP	56
GUNS AND GUITARS	1936	REP	60
OH, SUSANNA!	1936	REP	59
RIDE RANGER RIDE	1936	REP	54-59
THE BIG SHOW (aka HOME IN OKLAHOMA)	1936	REP	70
THE OLD CORRAL (aka TEXAS SERENADE)	1936	REP	56-60
ROUND-UP TIME IN TEXAS	1937	REP	58
GIT ALONG LITTLE DOGIES	1937	REP	62
(aka SERENADE OF THE WEST)			
ROOTIN' TOOTIN' RHYTHM	1937	REP	60
(aka RHYTHM ON THE RANCH)			
YODELIN' KID FROM PINE RIDGE	1937	REP	60
(aka THE HERO OF PINE RIDGE)			
PUBLIC COWBOY NO. 1	1937	REP	59
BOOTS AND SADDLES	1937	REP	59
SPRINGTIME IN THE ROCKIES	1937	REP	60
THE OLD BARN DANCE	1938	REP	60
GOLD MINE IN THE SKY	1938	REP	60
MAN FROM MUSIC MOUNTAIN	1938	REP	58
PRAIRIE MOON	1938	REP	58
RHYTHM OF THE SADDLE	1938	REP	58

GENE AUTRY, continued / 17

Title	Year	Studio	#
WESTERN JAMBOREE	1938	REP	56
HOME ON THE PRAIRIE	1939	REP	58
MEXICALI ROSE	1939	REP	58
BLUE MONTANA SKIES	1939	REP	56
MOUNTAIN RHYTHM	1939	REP	59
COLORADO SUNSET	1939	REP	64
IN OLD MONTEREY	1939	REP	73
ROVIN' TUMBLEWEEDS	1939	REP	64
(aka WASHINGTON COWBOY)			
SOUTH OF THE BORDER (aka SOUTH OF TEXAS)	1939	REP	71
RANCHO GRANDE	1940	REP	68
SHOOTING HIGH	1940	20T	65
MEN WITH STEEL FACES	1940	TIM	70
(feature version of THE PHANTOM EMPIRE serial)			
GAUCHO SERENADE	1940	REP	66-70
CAROLINA MOON	1940	REP	65
RIDE, TENDERFOOT, RIDE	1940	REP	65
MELODY RANCH	1940	REP	84
RIDIN' ON A RAINBOW	1941	REP	79
BACK IN THE SADDLE	1941	REP	71
THE SINGING HILL	1941	REP	75
SUNSET IN WYOMING	1941	REP	65
UNDER FIESTA STARS	1941	REP	64
DOWN MEXICO WAY	1941	REP	78
SIERRA SUE	1941	REP	64
COWBOY SERENADE	1942	REP	66
HEART OF THE RIO GRANDE	1942	REP	70
HOME IN WYOMIN'	1942	REP	67
STARDUST ON THE SAGE	1942	REP	65
CALL OF THE CANYON	1942	REP	71
BELLS OF CAPISTRANO	1942	REP	73
SIOUX CITY SUE	1946	REP	69
TRAIL TO SAN ANTONE	1947	REP	67
TWILIGHT ON THE RIO GRANDE	1947	REP	71
SADDLE PALS	1947	REP	72
ROBIN HOOD OF TEXAS	1947	REP	71
THE LAST ROUND-UP	1947	COL	77
THE STRAWBERRY ROAN (C)	1948	COL	76
(aka FOOLS AWAKE)			
LOADED PISTOLS	1949	COL	79
THE BIG SOMBRERO (C)	1949	COL	78
RIDERS OF THE WHISTLING PINES	1949	COL	70
RIM OF THE CANYON	1949	COL	70
THE COWBOY AND THE INDIANS	1949	COL	70
RIDERS IN THE SKY	1949	COL	70
SONS OF NEW MEXICO (aka THE BRAT)	1950	COL	71
MULE TRAIN	1950	COL	70
COW TOWN	1950	COL	70
BEYOND THE PURPLE HILLS	1950	COL	70
INDIAN TERRITORY	1950	COL	70
THE BLAZING SUN (aka THE BLAZING HILLS)	1950	COL	70
GENE AUTRY AND THE MOUNTIES	1951	COL	70
TEXANS NEVER CRY	1951	COL	70
WHIRLWIND	1951	COL	70
SILVER CANYON	1951	COL	70
HILLS OF UTAH	1951	COL	70

18 / GENE AUTRY, continued

VALLEY OF FIRE	1951	COL	63
THE OLD WEST	1952	COL	61
NIGHT STAGE TO GALVESTON	1952	COL	61
APACHE COUNTRY	1952	COL	62
BARBED WIRE (aka FALSE NEWS)	1952	COL	61
WAGON TEAM (aka WAGON TRAIN)	1952	COL	61
BLUE CANADIAN ROCKIES	1952	COL	58
WINNING OF THE WEST	1953	COL	57
ON TOP OF OLD SMOKY	1953	COL	59
GOLDTOWN GHOST RIDERS	1953	COL	57
PACK TRAIN	1953	COL	57
SAGINAW TRAIL	1953	COL	56
LAST OF THE PONY RIDERS	1953	COL	59
ALIAS JESSE JAMES (gs) (C)	1959	UA	92

BOB BAKER (1911 - 1975)

He warbled for a two-season series of Universal Pictures "B" oaters (1937-39) and entered the Top Money-Making Western Star ranks in 1939. Baker was seriously injured on location for THE PHANTOM STAGE, then paired with Johnny Mack Brown during six features. After early 1940s supports, he left the screen.

COURAGE OF THE WEST	1937	UNI	57
SINGING OUTLAW	1938	UNI	57
BORDER WOLVES	1938	UNI	57
THE LAST STAND	1938	UNI	57
WESTERN TRAILS	1938	UNI	58
OUTLAW EXPRESS	1938	UNI	57
THE BLACK BANDIT	1938	UNI	57-60
GUILTY TRAILS	1938	UNI	57
PRAIRIE JUSTICE	1938	UNI	57
GHOST TOWN RIDERS	1938	UNI	54
HONOR OF THE WEST	1939	UNI	58-60
THE PHANTOM STAGE	1939	UNI	58
DESPERATE TRAILS	1939	UNI	58
OKLAHOMA FRONTIER	1939	UNI	58
CHIP OF THE FLYING U	1939	UNI	55
WEST OF CARSON CITY	1940	UNI	55
RIDERS OF PASCO BASIN	1940	UNI	56
BAD MAN FROM RED BUTTE	1940	UNI	58
ALONG THE RIO GRANDE (s)	1941	RKO	64
ARIZONA BOUND (s)	1941	MON	57
FORBIDDEN TRAILS (s)	1941	MON	59
RIDE 'EM COWBOY (s)	1942	UNI	86
OVERLAND MAIL (s) (SER)	1942	UNI	15CH
WILD HORSE STAMPEDE (cs)	1943	MON	59
OKLAHOMA RAIDERS	1944	UNI	56
(aka MIDNIGHT RAIDERS; RIDERS OF OKLAHOMA) (s)			
MYSTERY MAN (s)	1944	UA	58

SMITH BALLEW (1902 - 1984)

He made just a few starring "B" oaters in the late 1930s. Ballew did have one unique western with RAWHIDE—his sidekick was none other than New York Yankees baseball great Lou Gehrig. In 1938, Smith became a Top Money-Making Western Star. Was a talented, melodious singer.

WESTERN GOLD		1937	20T	56
(aka THE MYSTERIOUS STRANGER)				
ROLL ALONG COWBOY		1937	20T	55
HAWAIIAN BUCKAROO		1938	20T	61
RAWHIDE		1938	20T	59
PANAMINT'S BAD MAN		1938	20T	60
GAUCHO SERENADE (s)		1940	REP	66
DRIFTING ALONG (s)		1946	MON	60
UNDER ARIZONA SKIES (s)		1946	MON	59
TEX GRANGER (s)	(SER)	1948	COL	15CH
THE CARIBOO TRAIL (s)	(C)	1950	20T	81
I KILLED GERONIMO (s)		1950	UA	62
THE RED BADGE OF COURAGE (s)		1951	MGM	69

JIM BANNON (1911 - 1984)

Best remembered as concluding star of the *Red Ryder* series whose four 1949 Cinecolor releases for Eagle-Lion required tinted hair, Bannon and co-star Don Reynolds abruptly ended the films when they refused to hand over a larger percentage of earnings to the owner of the "Red Ryder" character. He mainlined "The Adventures of Champion" half-hour TV show (26 episodes) for 1955-56.

RIDERS OF THE DEADLINE (s)		1943	UA	70
RENEGADES (s)	(C)	1946	COL	87
THE GAY SENORITA		1946	COL	69
DANGERS OF THE CANADIAN MOUNTED. (SER)		1948	REP	12CH
(aka R.C.M.P. & THE TREASURE OF GENGHIS KHAN)				
TRAIL TO LAREDO (aka SIGN OF THE DAGGER) (s)		1948	COL	54
FRONTIER REVENGE (s)		1948	SG	55
THE MAN FROM COLORADO (s)	(C)	1948	COL	99
RIDE, RYDER, RIDE!	(C)	1949	EL	59
(starts *Red Ryder* series)				
ROLL, THUNDER, ROLL!	(C)	1949	EL	58
THE FIGHTING REDHEAD	(C)	1949	EL	55
COWBOY AND THE PRIZEFIGHTER	(C)	1949	EL	55
(ends *Red Ryder* series)				
JIGGS AND MAGGIE OUT WEST (s)		1950	MON	66
SIERRA PASSAGE (s)		1951	MON	81
RIDIN' THE OUTLAW TRAIL (s)		1951	COL	56
THE REDHEAD AND THE COWBOY (s)		1951	PAR	82
CANYON RAIDERS		1951	MON	54
NEVADA BADMEN		1951	MON	58
THE TEXAS RANGERS (s)	(C)	1951	COL	74
STAGECOACH DRIVER		1951	MON	52
WANTED: DEAD OR ALIVE		1951	MON	59
LAWLESS COWBOYS		1951	MON	58
THE BLACK LASH (s)		1952	WA	55
RODEO (s)	(C)	1952	MON	70
THE GREAT JESSE JAMES RAID (s)	(C)	1953	LIP	73
JACK SLADE (aka SLADE) (s)		1953	AA	90

JIM BANNON, continued

THE COMMAND (s)	(C)..1954	WB	88
WAR ARROW (s)	(C)..1954	UI	78
ONE MASK TOO MANY (s)	(C)..1956	WRA-TV	75
THE TRUTH (s)	(C)..1956	WRA-TV	75
VENGEANCE VOW (s)	(C)..1956	WRA-TV	75
THEY CAME TO CORDURA (s)	(C)..1959	COL	123

LEX BARKER (1919 - 1973)

Ex-Tarzan actor who became successful in European western films, especially as the character, Shatterhand.

UNDER THE TONTO RIM (s)		1947...RKO	61
UNCONQUERED (s)	(C)..1948	PAR.	146-147
RETURN OF THE BAD MEN (s)		1948...RKO	90
THE BATTLES OF CHIEF PONTIAC		1952...REA	72
THUNDER OVER THE PLAINS	(C)..1953	WB	82
THE YELLOW MOUNTAIN	(C)..1954	UI	78
THE MAN FROM BITTER RIDGE	(C)..1955	UI	80
DUEL ON THE MISSISSIPPI	(C)..1955	COL	72
WAR DRUMS	(C)..1957	UA	75
THE DEERSLAYER	(C)..1957	20T	76
APACHE GOLD	(C)..1965	COL	91-111
(aka WINNETOU THE WARRIOR; WINNETOU)			
THE TREASURE OF SILVER LAKE	(C)..1965	COL	82-106
TREASURE OF THE AZTECS	(C)..1965	CCC/FK	102
A PLACE CALLED GLORY	(C)..1966	EMB	92
THE LAST OF THE RENEGADES	(C)..1966	COL	93-104
WHO KILLED JOHNNY R?	(C)..1966	CCC/FK	91
THE DESPERADO TRAIL	(C)..1967	COL	93
(aka WINNETOU III; VINETU III)			
OLD SHATTERHAND	(C)..1967	GFE	89
(aka APACHES LAST BATTLE; SHATTERHAND)			
WINNETOU AND SHATTERHAND IN THE VALLEY OF DEATH	(C)..1968	CCC/FK	90
THE HALF BREED	(C)..1973	HAM	90

DON "RED" BARRY (1912 - 1980)
(aka DONALD BARRY)

Short in height but a rip-snorting action ace for Republic Pictures (1940-44) with 29 "B" mustangers, Don was outstanding in OUTLAWS OF PINE RIDGE. A Top Money-Making Western Star (1942-44), Barry leaped into oaters for Lippert (1949-50). His last years in acting were devoted to top-notch movie and television character roles.

WYOMING OUTLAW (s)		1939...REP	56
SAGA OF DEATH VALLEY (s)		1939...REP	58
DAYS OF JESSE JAMES (s)		1939...REP	63
GHOST VALLEY RAIDERS		1940...REP	57
ADVENTURES OF RED RYDER	(SER)..1940	REP	12CH
ONE MAN'S LAW		1940...REP	57
THE TULSA KID		1940...REP	57
FRONTIER VENGEANCE		1940...REP	57
TEXAS TERRORS		1940...REP	57
WYOMING WILDCAT		1941...REP	56

DON "RED" BARRY, continued / 21

Title	Year	Studio	Page
THE PHANTOM COWBOY	1941	REP	56
TWO-GUN SHERIFF	1941	REP	56
DESERT BANDIT	1941	REP	56
KANSAS CYCLONE	1941	REP	58
THE APACHE KID	1941	REP	56
DEATH VALLEY OUTLAWS	1941	REP	56
A MISSOURI OUTLAW	1941	REP	58
ARIZONA TERRORS	1942	REP	56
STAGECOACH EXPRESS	1942	REP	57
JESSE JAMES, JR. (aka SUNDOWN FURY)	1942	REP	56
THE CYCLONE KID	1942	REP	56
THE SOMBRERO KID	1942	REP	56
OUTLAWS OF PINE RIDGE	1942	REP	57
THE SUNDOWN KID	1942	REP	55
DEAD MAN'S GULCH	1943	REP	56
CARSON CITY CYCLONE	1943	REP	57
DAYS OF OLD CHEYENNE	1943	REP	55
FUGITIVE FROM SONORA	1943	REP	55
THE BLACK HILLS EXPRESS	1943	REP	55
THE MAN FROM THE RIO GRANDE	1943	REP	55
CANYON CITY	1943	REP	55
CALIFORNIA JOE	1943	REP	55
OUTLAWS OF SANTA FE	1944	REP	54
BELLS OF ROSARITA (gs)	1945	REP	68
PLAINSMAN AND THE LADY (s)	1946	REP	87
OUT CALIFORNIA WAY (gs) (C)	1946	REP	67
MADONNA OF THE DESERT	1948	REP	60
THE DALTON GANG (aka OUTLAW GANG)	1949	LIP	58
SQUARE DANCE JUBILEE	1949	LIP	79
RED DESERT	1949	LIP	60
TOUGH ASSIGNMENT	1949	LIP	64
GUNFIRE	1950	LIP	59
TRAIN TO TOMBSTONE	1950	LIP	56
BORDER RANGERS (aka OUTLAW FURY)	1950	LIP	57
I SHOT BILLY THE KID	1950	LIP	57
UNTAMED HEIRESS	1954	REP	70
JESSE JAMES' WOMEN (C)	1954	UA	83
THE TWINKLE IN GOD'S EYE (s)	1955	REP	73
SEVEN MEN FROM NOW (s) (C)	1956	WB	78
GUN DUEL IN DURANGO (aka DUEL IN DURANGO) (s)	1957	UA	73
WARLOCK (s) (C)	1959	20T	121
BORN RECKLESS (s)	1959	WB	79
WALK LIKE A DRAGON (s)	1960	PAR	95
BUFFALO GUN (s)	1961	GLB	72
LAW OF THE LAWLESS (aka INVITATION TO A HANGING) (s) (C)	1964	PAR	87
WAR PARTY	1965	20T	72
FORT COURAGEOUS	1965	20T	72
CONVICT STAGE	1965	20T	71
TOWN TAMER (s) (C)	1965	PAR	89
APACHE UPRISING (s) (C)	1966	PAR	90
ALVAREZ KELLY (s) (C)	1966	COL	116
RED TOMAHAWK (s) (C)	1967	PAR	82
HOSTILE GUNS (s) (C)	1967	PAR	91
FORT UTAH (s) (C)	1967	PAR	83

DON "RED" BARRY, continued

Title		Year	Studio	#
THE SHAKIEST GUN IN THE WEST (s)	(C)	1968	UNI	101
BANDOLERO! (s)	(C)	1968	20T	106
SHALAKO (s)	(C)	1968	CRC	113
THE COCKEYED COWBOYS OF CALICO COUNTY (aka A WOMAN FOR CHARLEY) (s)	(C)	1970	UNI	97
DIRTY DINGUS MAGEE (s)	(C)	1970	MGM	91
RIO LOBO (s)	(C)	1970	NG	114
ONE MORE TRAIN TO ROB (s)	(C)	1971	UNI	108
JUNIOR BONNER (s)	(C)	1972	CRC	100
THE GATLING GUN (s)	(C)	1972	EE	93
SHOWDOWN (s)	(C)	1973	UNI	99
BOSS NIGGER (aka BOSS; THE BLACK BOUNTY KILLER) (s)	(C)	1974	DP	87
BLAZING STEWARDESSES (aka TEXAS LAYOVER) (cs)	(C)	1975	II	85
FROM NOON TILL THREE (s)	(C)	1976	UA	99
HOOPER (s)	(C)	1978	WB	100
HOT LEAD AND COLD FEET (s)	(C)	1978	BV	90
SHAME, SHAME ON THE BIXBY BOYS (s)	(C)	1978	CAL	90
KATE BLISS AND THE TICKER-TAPE KID (s)	(C)	1978	ASP-TV	120
BACK ROADS (s)	(C)	1981	WB	94

BUZZ BARTON (1914 - 1980)

Following appearances in silents as a juvenile, Barton made low-budget oaters for independent film outfits during the early 1930s, but then was confined for almost 10 years afterwards with support roles in "B" westerns.

Title		Year	Studio	#
PALS OF THE PRAIRIE		1929	FBO	50
CANYON HAWKS		1930	B4	60
BREED OF THE WEST		1930	B4	60
THE APACHE KID'S ESCAPE (s)		1930	RJH	51
WILD WEST WHOOPEE		1931	ALL	57
RIDERS OF THE CACTUS		1931	B4	60
FLYING LARIATS		1931	B4	60
THE CYCLONE KID		1931	B4	60
THE MYSTERY TROOPER	(SER)	1931	SYN	10CH
HUMAN TARGETS		1932	B4	55
GUNFIRE (cs)		1935	RES	56
FIGHTING PIONEERS (cs)		1935	RES	60
SADDLE ACES (cs)		1935	RES	56
THE TONTO KID (cs)		1935	RES	61
POWDERSMOKE RANGE (s)		1935	RKO	71
FEUD OF THE WEST (cs)		1936	GN	62
THE RIDING AVENGER (cs)		1936	GN	58
ROMANCE RIDES THE RANGE (s)		1936	SPE	59
ROLLING CARAVANS (s)		1938	COL	55
STAGECOACH DAYS (s)		1938	COL	58
PHANTOM GOLD (s)		1938	COL	56
THE MEXICALI KID (s)		1938	MON	51
IN EARLY ARIZONA (s)		1938	COL	53
FRONTIERS OF '49 (s)		1939	COL	54
LONE STAR PIONEERS (s)		1939	COL	56
SILVER ON THE SAGE (s)		1939	PAR	68
THE LAW COMES TO TEXAS (s)		1939	COL	58

WILD HORSE VALLEY (cs)	1940	MET	57
LAND OF THE SIX GUNS (s)	1940	MON	54
WHITE EAGLE (s) (SER)	1941	COL	15CH
COME ON DANGER (s)	1942	RKO	58

SAMMY BAUGH (1913 -   )

He was a famous quarterback with the Washington Redskins in 1941 when Republic Pictures tapped him to helm its 12-chapter serial KING OF THE TEXAS RANGERS. Now retired at Rotan, Texas, Sammy was photo-featured in *The Washington Post Magazine* (September 1, 1991 edition).

KING OF THE TEXAS RANGERS (SER)	1941	REP	12CH

WARNER BAXTER (1892 - 1951)

Although mainly a dramatic actor, Baxter won an Oscar for his portrayal of the Cisco Kid in the early sound western, IN OLD ARIZONA. He continued this role in several other films. Warner wrapped up "A" oater participation by 1939.

RAMONA	1928	UA	78
IN OLD ARIZONA	1929	FOX	91
ROMANCE OF THE RIO GRANDE	1929	FOX	90
THE ARIZONA KID	1930	FOX	79
THE SQUAW MAN (aka THE WHITE MAN)	1931	MGM	106-120
THE CISCO KID	1931	FOX	60-61
UNDER THE PAMPAS MOON	1935	FOX	78
THE PRISONER OF SHARK ISLAND	1936	20T	95
THE ROBIN HOOD OF EL DORADO	1936	MGM	86
THE RETURN OF THE CISCO KID	1939	20T	70

NOAH BEERY, JR. (1913 -   )

A fine character actor from a famous film acting family, Noah's main starring roles in westerns were a series of second features for Hal Roach. Better known for his support of many western stars in "A" features, Beery mainlined 49 half-hour NBC-TV shows (1956-57) for "Circus Boy" and was Ralph Taeger's pal during the 60-minute "Hondo" MGM-TV show (1967) in 17 episodes.

HEROES OF THE WEST (cs) (SER)	1932	UNI	12CH
THE RUSTLERS' ROUNDUP (cs)	1933	UNI	56-60
FIGHTING WITH KIT CARSON (s) (SER)	1933	MAS	12CH
THE TRAIL BEYOND	1934	LMO	55
STORMY	1935	UNI	70
DEVIL'S CANYON	1935	SUN	
FIVE BAD MEN	1935	SUN	
TROUBLE AT MIDNIGHT	1937	UNI	68
FORBIDDEN VALLEY	1938	UNI	67
BAD LANDS (s)	1939	RKO	70
OF MICE AND MEN (s)	1940	UA	107
THE LIGHT OF WESTERN STARS (s)	1940	PAR	67
20 MULE TEAM	1940	MGM	83-84
THE CARSON CITY KID (s)	1940	REP	57
RIDERS OF DEATH VALLEY (s) (SER)	1941	UNI	15CH
DUDES ARE PRETTY PEOPLE (cs)	1942	UA	42
OVERLAND MAIL (s) (SER)	1942	UNI	15CH

NOAH BEERY, JR., continued

Title	Year	Studio	Page
CALABOOSE (cs)	1943	UA	45
PRAIRIE CHICKENS (cs)	1943	UA	46
FRONTIER BADMEN (s)	1943	UNI	77
UNDER WESTERN SKIES	1945	UNI	57
THE DALTONS RIDE AGAIN (s)	1945	UNI	71
RED RIVER (s)	1948	UA	125-133
INDIAN AGENT	1948	RKO	65
THE DOOLINS OF OKLAHOMA (aka THE GREAT MANHUNT) (s)	1949	COL	90
DAVY CROCKETT INDIAN SCOUT (aka INDIAN SCOUT) (s)	1950	UA	71
THE SAVAGE HORDE (s)	1950	REP	90
TWO FLAGS WEST (s)	1950	20T	92
THE LAST OUTPOST (s) (C)	1951	PAR	89
THE TEXAS RANGERS (s) (C)	1951	COL	74
THE CIMARRON KID (s) (C)	1952	UI	65-84
THE STORY OF WILL ROGERS (s) (C)	1952	WB	109
WAGONS WEST (C)	1952	MON	70
WINGS OF THE HAWK (s) (C)	1953	UI	80
WAR ARROW (s) (C)	1954	UI	78
THE YELLOW TOMAHAWK (cs) (C)	1954	UA	82-83
THE BLACK DAKOTAS (s) (C)	1954	COL	65
WHITE FEATHER (s) (C)	1955	20T	102
JUBAL (s) (C)	1956	COL	101
THE FASTEST GUN ALIVE (s)	1956	MGM	89
DECISION AT SUNDOWN (s) (C)	1957	COL	77
ESCORT WEST (s)	1959	UA	75
GUNS OF THE TIMBERLAND (aka STAMPEDE) (s) (C)	1960	WB	91
7 FACES OF DR. LAO (s) (C)	1964	MGM	100
CALL TO GLORY (s) (C)	1965	COL	90
INCIDENT AT PHANTOM HILL (s) (C)	1966	UNI	88
HONDO AND THE APACHES (s) (C)	1967	MGM	85
JOURNEY TO SHILOH (s) (C)	1968	UNI	101
HEAVEN WITH A GUN (s) (C)	1969	MGM	101
THE COCKEYED COWBOYS OF CALICO COUNTY (aka A WOMAN FOR CHARLEY) (s) (C)	1970	UNI	97
SIDEKICKS (s) (C)	1974	WB-TV	90
THE SPIKES GANG (s) (C)	1974	UA	96
SAVAGES (cs) (C)	1974	S/GP-TV	90
THE BASTARD (s) (C)	1978	UNI-TV	200
THE CAPTURE OF GRIZZLY ADAMS (s) (C)	1982	NBC-TV	90
THE BEST LITTLE WHOREHOUSE IN TEXAS (s) (C)	1982	RKO/UNI	114
WALTZ ACROSS TEXAS (s) (C)	1982	ATL	99

WALLACE BEERY (1889 - 1949)
Despite a noticeably raspy voice interwoven with his rough-hewn comic nature, Beery was able to mainline numerous MGM "A" westerns for 20 years with the best features probably being BILLY THE KID, VIVA VILLA!, and A MESSAGE TO GARCIA, the latter film for 20th Century-Fox.

Title	Year	Studio	Page
BILLY THE KID (aka THE HIGHWAYMAN RIDES)	1930	MGM	90-98
VIVA VILLA!	1934	MGM	90-115
AH, WILDERNESS!	1935	MGM	98

WALLACE BEERY, continued / 25

A MESSAGE TO GARCIA	1936	20T	85-90
THE BAD MAN OF BRIMSTONE	1937	MGM	89
STAND UP AND FIGHT	1939	MGM	.97-105
THE MAN FROM DAKOTA	1940	MGM	74-75
(aka AROUSE AND BEWARE)			
20 MULE TEAM	1940	MGM	84
WYOMING	1940	MGM	88-89
(aka MAN FROM WYOMING; BAD MAN OF WYOMING)			
THE BAD MAN (aka TWO-GUN CUPID)	1941	MGM	70
JACKASS MAIL	1942	MGM	80
BARBARY COAST GENT	1944	MGM	87
BAD BASCOMB	1946	MGM	112
BIG JACK	1949	MGM	85-95

REX BELL (1903 - 1962)

He rode in the saddle from 1932 through 1936 for studios like Monogram, Resolute, and Colony, then did very rare supports into 1961. Later years found Rex as Nevada's lieutenant governor. Bell was campaigning for the top state office in 1962 when he suffered a fatal heart attack.

LIGHTNIN' (s)	1930	FOX	94
BATTLING WITH BUFFALO BILL (SER)	1931	UNI	12CH
BROADWAY TO CHEYENNE	1932	MON	60
(aka FROM BROADWAY TO CHEYENNE)			
THE MAN FROM ARIZONA	1932	MON	58
LUCKY LARRIGAN	1932	MON	58-62
DIAMOND TRAIL	1932	MON	61
FIGHTING TEXANS (aka RANDY STRIKES OIL)	1933	MON	58-60
CRASHING BROADWAY	1933	MON	55
THE FUGITIVE	1933	MON	56
RAINBOW RANCH	1933	MON	55
GUNFIRE	1935	RES	59
FIGHTING PIONEERS	1935	RES	60
SADDLE ACES	1935	RES	56
THE TONTO KID	1935	RES	61
TOO MUCH BEEF	1936	CLY	60
WEST OF NEVADA	1936	CLY	57-59
THE IDAHO KID	1936	CLY	59
MEN OF THE PLAINS	1936	CLY	62
LAW AND LEAD	1936	CLY	60
STORMY TRAILS	1936	CLY	58
TOMBSTONE, THE TOWN TOO TOUGH TO DIE (s)	1942	PAR	79
DAWN ON THE GREAT DIVIDE (cs)	1942	MON	66
LONE STAR (s)	1952	MGM	90-94
SKY FULL OF MOON (s)	1952	MGM	73
THE MISFITS (s)	1961	UA	121

BRUCE BENNETT (1906 -   )
(aka HERMAN BRIX)

His career skyrocketed in the late 1930s with four superb Republic cliffhangers. One famous role was that of a Texas ranger in THE LONE RANGER serial for 1938. Bennett's star had dimmed by 1940, but he had meaty assignments doing support work at major studios like Columbia, Paramount, and Warner Brothers.

Title	Year	Studio	#
LAND OF FIGHTING MEN	1938	MON	53
THE LONE RANGER (cs) (SER)	1938	REP	15CH
HAWK OF THE WILDERNESS (SER)	1938	REP	12CH
(aka LOST ISLAND OF KIOGA)			
BLAZING SIX SHOOTERS	1940	COL	63
(aka STOLEN WEALTH) (s)			
HI-YO-SILVER	1940	REP	69
(feature version of THE LONE RANGER serial) (cs)			
THE MAN FROM TUMBLEWEEDS (s)	1940	COL	59
WEST OF ABILENE (aka THE SHOWDOWN) (cs)	1940	COL	57
CHEYENNE (aka THE WYOMING KID) (s)	1947	WB	100
THE TREASURE OF THE SIERRA MADRE (s)	1948	WB	126
SILVER RIVER (s)	1948	WB	110
THE YOUNGER BROTHERS (cs) (C)	1949	WB	77
THE GREAT MISSOURI RAID (s) (C)	1951	PAR	85
THE LAST OUTPOST (cs) (C)	1951	PAR	89
ROBBERS' ROOST (s) (C)	1955	UA	82
THE BOTTOM OF THE BOTTLE (s) (C)	1956	20T	88
HIDDEN GUNS	1956	REP	66
THE THREE OUTLAWS	1956	AFR	74
DANIEL BOONE, TRAIL BLAZER (C)	1956	REP	76
LOVE ME TENDER (s)	1956	20T	89
THREE VIOLENT PEOPLE (s) (C)	1957	PAR	100
FLAMING FRONTIER	1958	20T	70
THE OUTSIDER (cs)	1961	UI	108

WILLIAM BISHOP (1918 - 1959)

He was a low-key but serious actor who appeared in numerous "A" westerns at Columbia Pictures through the early 1950s. Bishop's career prematurely ended by death from cancer. The great actress Helen Hayes was his aunt.

Title	Year	Studio	#
ADVENTURES IN SILVERADO	1948	COL	75
(aka ABOVE ALL LAWS)			
CORONER CREEK (s) (C)	1948	COL	90
THUNDERHOOF (aka FURY) (cs)	1948	COL	77
BLACK EAGLE	1948	COL	76
THE UNTAMED BREED (s) (C)	1948	COL	79
THE WALKING HILLS (cs)	1949	COL	78
THE TOUGHER THEY COME (cs)	1950	COL	69
THE TEXAS RANGERS (s) (C)	1951	COL	74
CRIPPLE CREEK (s) (C)	1952	COL	78
THE RAIDERS (C)	1952	UI	80
(aka RIDERS OF VENGEANCE) (s)			
THE REDHEAD FROM WYOMING (s) (C)	1953	UI	80
GUN BELT (s) (C)	1953	UA	77
OVERLAND PACIFIC (s) (C)	1954	UA	73
WYOMING RENEGADES (s) (C)	1955	COL	73
TOP GUN	1955	UA	73

THE WHITE SQUAW (cs)	1956	COL	73
THE PHANTOM STAGECOACH	1957	COL	69
THE OREGON TRAIL (C)	1959	20T	86

RICHARD BOONE (1917 - 1981)

He was a fine actor whose properly measured dialogue delivery proved a major asset for those personal performances rendered in 1950s-1970s dramas and "A" westerns at 20th Century-Fox and other big studios. Boone's greatest prominence came on CBS-TV's "Have Gun—Will Travel" (1957-63) for 156 half-hour segments where he portrayed the intelligent, hired sharpshooter Paladin. He also was "Hec Ramsey" for that 90-minute NBC-TV show (1972-74) with 10 episodes.

KANGAROO (s)	(C)	1952	20T	84
RED SKIES OF MONTANA (s)	(C)	1952	20T	96
RETURN OF THE TEXAN (s)	(C)	1952	20T	88
WAY OF A GAUCHO (cs)	(C)	1952	20T	91
CITY OF BAD MEN (cs)	(C)	1953	20T	82
SIEGE AT RED RIVER	(C)	1954	20T	86
(aka THE SIEGE OF RED RIVER) (cs)				
THE RAID (cs)	(C)	1954	20T	83
TEN WANTED MEN (cs)	(C)	1955	COL	80
MAN WITHOUT A STAR (s)	(C)	1955	UI	88-89
ROBBERS' ROOST	(C)	1955	UA	82
STAR IN THE DUST (cs)	(C)	1956	UI	80
THE TALL T	(C)	1957	COL	78
THE ALAMO (s)	(C)	1960	UA	190
A THUNDER OF DRUMS	(C)	1961	MGM	97
RIO CONCHOS	(C)	1964	20T	107
HOMBRE (cs)	(C)	1967	20T	110
MADRON	(C)	1970	4ST	92-93
BIG JAKE	(C)	1971	NG	110
A HARD ROAD TO VENGEANCE	(C)	1973	NBC-TV	98
AGAINST A CROOKED SKY	(C)	1975	DD	100
THE SHOOTIST (gs)	(C)	1976	PAR	99-100
GOD'S GUN (cs)	(C)	1977	IYC	93

WILLIAM BOYD (1898 - 1972)

He became millions of youngsters' *Hopalong Cassidy* series favorite in 66 features for Paramount (1935-41) and United Artists (1942-44; 1946-48). Boyd was a Top Money-Making Western Star (1936-45, 1947-50) in addition to doing 52 half-hour episodes of the Clarence Mulford character (1952-54) for TV syndication.

THE PAINTED DESERT	1931	RKO	80-83
CARNIVAL BOAT	1932	RKO	62
MEN OF AMERICA	1932	RKO	75
(aka THE GREAT DECISION)			
HOP-A-LONG CASSIDY	1935	PAR	59-62
(aka HOPALONG CASSIDY ENTERS) (starts *Hopalong Cassidy* series)			
THE EAGLE'S BROOD	1935	PAR	60
BAR 20 RIDES AGAIN	1935	PAR	63
CALL OF THE PRAIRIE	1936	PAR	67
THREE ON THE TRAIL	1936	PAR	67
HEART OF THE WEST	1936	PAR	65-78

WILLIAM BOYD, continued

Title	Year	Studio	Pages
HOPALONG CASSIDY RETURNS	1936	PAR	75
TRAIL DUST	1936	PAR	74-77
BORDERLAND	1937	PAR	82
HILLS OF OLD WYOMING	1937	PAR	79
NORTH OF THE RIO GRANDE	1937	PAR	70
RUSTLERS' VALLEY	1937	PAR	60
HOPALONG RIDES AGAIN	1937	PAR	65
TEXAS TRAIL	1937	PAR	63
PARTNERS OF THE PLAINS	1938	PAR	68
CASSIDY OF BAR 20	1938	PAR	56
HEART OF ARIZONA	1938	PAR	68
BAR 20 JUSTICE	1938	PAR	70
PRIDE OF THE WEST	1938	PAR	55
IN OLD MEXICO	1938	PAR	62
SUNSET TRAIL	1938	PAR	60
THE FRONTIERSMEN	1938	PAR	74
SILVER ON THE SAGE	1939	PAR	68
THE RENEGADE TRAIL	1939	PAR	58
RANGE WAR	1939	PAR	66
LAW OF THE PAMPAS	1939	PAR	74
SANTA FE MARSHAL	1940	PAR	68
THE SHOWDOWN	1940	PAR	63
HIDDEN GOLD	1940	PAR	61
STAGECOACH WAR	1940	PAR	63
THREE MEN FROM TEXAS	1940	PAR	76
DOOMED CARAVAN	1941	PAR	61
IN OLD COLORADO	1941	PAR	67
BORDER VIGILANTES	1941	PAR	62
PIRATES ON HORSEBACK	1941	PAR	69
WIDE OPEN TOWN	1941	PAR	78
STICK TO YOUR GUNS	1941	PAR	63
SECRET OF THE WASTELANDS	1941	PAR	70
OUTLAWS OF THE DESERT	1941	PAR	66
RIDERS OF THE TIMBERLINE	1941	PAR	59
TWILIGHT ON THE TRAIL	1941	PAR	58
UNDERCOVER MAN	1942	UA	68
LOST CANYON	1942	UA	63
HOPPY SERVES A WRIT	1943	UA	67
BORDER PATROL	1943	UA	67
LEATHER BURNERS	1943	UA	58
COLT COMRADES	1943	UA	67
BAR 20	1943	UA	54
FALSE COLORS	1943	UA	65
RIDERS OF THE DEADLINE	1943	UA	70
TEXAS MASQUERADE	1944	UA	59
LUMBERJACK	1944	UA	63
MYSTERY MAN	1944	UA	58
FORTY THIEVES	1944	UA	60
THE DEVIL'S PLAYGROUND	1946	UA	62
FOOL'S GOLD	1947	UA	63
UNEXPECTED GUEST	1947	UA	61
DANGEROUS VENTURE	1947	UA	59
HOPPY'S HOLIDAY	1947	UA	60
THE MARAUDERS	1947	UA	63-68
SILENT CONFLICT	1948	UA	61
THE DEAD DON'T DREAM	1948	UA	68

WILLIAM BOYD, continued / 29

SINISTER JOURNEY	1948	UA	59	____
BORROWED TROUBLE	1948	UA	60	____
FALSE PARADISE	1948	UA	61	____
STRANGE GAMBLE	1948	UA	62	____

(ends *Hopalong Cassidy* series)

SCOTT BRADY (1924 - 1985)

The ex-lumberjack brother of film star Lawrence Tierney who played his western roles with a brashness that also allowed him to play villains. Outstanding examples were those fine outlaw parts Scott did in Republic's superb JOHNNY GUITAR and THE MAVERICK QUEEN. Brady became "Shotgun Slade" during 78 episodes of the half-hour syndicated show (1959-60).

THE GAL WHO TOOK THE WEST (cs)	(C)	1949	UI	84	____
KANSAS RAIDERS (s)	(C)	1950	UI	80	____
BRONCO BUSTER	(C)	1952	UI	80	____
UNTAMED FRONTIER (cs)	(C)	1952	UI	75	____
MONTANA BELLE (cs)	(C)	1952	RKO	81	____
A PERILOUS JOURNEY (cs)		1953	REP	90	____
THE LAW VS. BILLY THE KID	(C)	1954	COL	73	____
JOHNNY GUITAR (cs)	(C)	1954	REP	110	____
THE VANISHING AMERICAN		1955	REP	90	____
MOHAWK	(C)	1956	20T	79-80	____
THE MAVERICK QUEEN (cs)	(C)	1956	REP	92	____
THE STORM RIDER		1957	20T	70	____
THE RESTLESS BREED	(C)	1957	20T	81-86	____
AMBUSH AT CIMARRON PASS		1958	20T	87	____
BLOOD ARROW		1958	20T	78	____
STAGE TO THUNDER ROCK	(C)	1964	PAR	82	____

(aka STAGECOACH TO HELL) (cs)

BLACK SPURS (s)	(C)	1965	PAR	81	____
RED TOMAHAWK (cs)	(C)	1967	PAR	82	____
FORT UTAH (cs)	(C)	1967	PAR	83	____
ARIZONA BUSHWHACKERS (s)	(C)	1968	PAR	86	____
THEY RAN FOR THEIR LIVES (s)	(C)	1969	CV	92	____
THE GUN RIDERS	(C)	1969	II	98	____

(aka FIVE BLOODY GRAVES; LONELY MAN; FIVE BLOODY GRAVES TO TOMBSTONE) (cs)

| CAIN'S WAY | (C) | 1970 | MDA | 95 | ____ |

(aka CAIN'S CUTTHROATS; THE BLOOD SEEKERS)

| THE LAST RIDE OF THE DALTON GANG (s) | (C) | 1979 | NBC-TV | 150 | ____ |

MARLON BRANDO (1924 -   )

Major film actor whose few western films have been rather off-beat. Best known in the genre for his excellent portrayal of the ill-fated Mexican bandit leader who rose to become a revolutionary in VIVA ZAPATA!

VIVA ZAPATA!		1952	20T	113	____
ONE-EYED JACKS	(C)	1961	PAR	141	____
THE CHASE	(C)	1966	COL	135	____
THE APPALOOSA	(C)	1966	UNI	98	____

(aka SOUTHWEST TO SONORA)

| THE MISSOURI BREAKS | (C) | 1976 | UA | 126 | ____ |

GEORGE BRENT (1904 - 1979)

He was a suave, debonair Irish actor with Warner Brothers into the early 1940s who later made appearances in several rugged adventure westerns. Among them was MONTANA BELLE where he teamed with Jane Russell.

LIGHTNING WARRIOR	(SER)	1931	MAS	12CH
GOD'S COUNTRY AND THE WOMAN	(C)	1937	WB	85
GOLD IS WHERE YOU FIND IT	(C)	1938	WB	97
JEZEBEL (cs)		1938	WB	104
SILVER QUEEN		1942	UA	80
RED CANYON	(C)	1949	UI	82
MONTANA BELLE	(C)	1952	RKO	81

DAVID BRIAN (1914 -   )

His forte was as the villainous, smooth, yet tough-talking type of he-man in "A" westerns for major studios during the 1950s. Warner Brothers, Republic, and Columbia used Brian's extensive dramatic talents. He was great as Randolph Scott's nemesis in FORT WORTH.

BEYOND THE FOREST (cs)		1949	WB	96
INSIDE STRAIGHT		1951	MGM	89
FORT WORTH	(C)	1951	WB	80
SPRINGFIELD RIFLE (cs)	(C)	1952	WB	93
A PERILOUS JOURNEY		1953	REP	90
AMBUSH AT TOMAHAWK GAP (cs)	(C)	1953	COL	73
DAWN AT SOCORRO (cs)	(C)	1954	UI	80
TIMBERJACK (cs)	(C)	1955	REP	94
FURY AT GUNSIGHT PASS		1956	COL	68
THE FIRST TRAVELING SALESLADY (s)	(C)	1956	RKO	92
THE WHITE SQUAW		1956	COL	73
HOW THE WEST WAS WON (s)	(C)	1963	MGM	155-165
CALL TO GLORY (cs)	(C)	1965	COL-TV	90
THE RARE BREED (s)	(C)	1966	UNI	97-108

LLOYD BRIDGES (1913 -   )

Beginning his film career as bit character actor in Columbia "B" westerns, he is best remembered in "A" oaters as the calculating but immature deputy to Marshal Gary Cooper in the classic HIGH NOON. Bridges starred in CBS-TV's "The Loner" for 26 hour-long shows (1965-66).

THE MEDICO OF PAINTED SPRINGS		1941	COL 59
(aka DOCTOR'S ALIBI) (s)			
THE SON OF DAVY CROCKETT (aka BLUE CLAY) (s)		1941	COL 59
SHUT MY BIG MOUTH (s)		1942	COL 71
NORTH OF THE ROCKIES (aka FALSE CLUES) (s)		1942	COL 60
RIDERS OF THE NORTHLAND		1942	COL 58
(aka NEXT IN LINE) (s)			
PARDON MY GUN (s)		1942	COL 57
HAIL TO THE RANGERS (aka ILLEGAL RIGHTS) (s)		1943	COL 57
SADDLE LEATHER LAW		1944	COL 55
(aka THE POISONER) (s)			
ABILENE TOWN (s)		1946	UA 89
CANYON PASSAGE (s)	(C)	1946	UNI 90
RAMROD (s)		1947	UA 94

LLOYD BRIDGES, continued

UNCONQUERED (s)	(C)	1948	PAR	146-147
RED CANYON (s)	(C)	1949	UI	82
CALAMITY JANE AND SAM BASS (s)	(C)	1949	UI	85
COLT .45 (aka THUNDERCLOUD) (s)	(C)	1950	WB	74
LITTLE BIG HORN (aka THE FIGHTING SEVENTH)		1951	LIP	86
HIGH NOON (cs)		1952	UA	85
LAST OF THE COMANCHES	(C)	1953	COL	85
(aka THE SABRE AND THE ARROW) (s)				
THE TALL TEXAN		1953	LIP	81
CITY OF BAD MEN (s)	(C)	1953	20T	82
WICHITA (cs)	(C)	1955	AA	81
APACHE WOMAN	(C)	1955	ARC	83
WETBACKS	(C)	1956	BAN	89
THE RAINMAKER (s)	(C)	1957	PAR	121
RIDE OUT FOR REVENGE (cs)		1957	UA	78-79
THE SILENT GUN	(C)	1969	PAR-TV	90
RUNNING WILD	(C)	1973	GC	85
(aka DELIVER US FROM EVIL)				
BEAR ISLAND (s)	(C)	1980	COL	118
THE BLUE AND THE GRAY (s)	(C)	1982	CBS-TV	295

CHARLES BRONSON (1921 -   )
(aka CHARLES BUCHINSKI, CHARLES BUCHINSKY)

A dark and muscular actor who rose from character roles in American films to become a super international star as a result of his European westerns. Outstanding as the chief outlaw who bullies banker Victor Buono in 4 FOR TEXAS.

RED SKIES OF MONTANA (s)	(C)	1952	20T	98
RIDING SHOTGUN (s)	(C)	1954	WB	75
APACHE (s)	(C)	1954	UA	91
DRUM BEAT (s)	(C)	1954	WB	111
VERA CRUZ (s)	(C)	1954	UA	94
JUBAL (s)	(C)	1956	COL	101
RUN OF THE ARROW (aka HOT LEAD) (s)	(C)	1957	RKO	85
SHOWDOWN AT BOOT HILL		1958	20T	72
THE MAGNIFICENT SEVEN (s)	(C)	1960	UA	120
A THUNDER OF DRUMS (s)	(C)	1961	MGM	97
THE MEANEST MEN IN THE WEST	(C)	1962	NBC-TV	92
4 FOR TEXAS (s)	(C)	1963	WB	124
GUNS OF DIABLO	(C)	1964	MGM-TV	79
GUNS FOR SAN SEBASTIAN (cs)	(C)	1968	MGM	111
VILLA RIDES (s)	(C)	1968	PAR	125
ONCE UPON A TIME IN THE WEST (s)	(C)	1969	PAR	165
THE RUGGED LAND	(C)	1970	UNI	60
CHATO'S LAND	(C)	1972	UA	92
RED SUN	(C)	1972	NG	112
THE BULL OF THE WEST	(C)	1975	UNI	120
BREAKOUT	(C)	1975	COL	96
BREAKHEART PASS	(C)	1976	UA	95
FROM NOON TILL THREE	(C)	1976	UA	99
CHINO	(C)	1976	IRC	98
(aka VALDEZ, THE HALFBREED; THE VALDEZ HORSES)				
THE WHITE BUFFALO (aka HUNT TO KILL)	(C)	1977	UA	97
BORDERLINE	(C)	1980	AFD	106
DEATH HUNT	(C)	1981	20T	97

JAMES BROWN (1920 - 1992)

He garnered character parts in "A" westerns into the early 1950s, then had great success as Lt. Rip Masters with the "Adventures of Rin-Tin-Tin" on ABC-TV (1954-59) for 164 half-hour episodes. Brown then starred in several early 1960s westerns released by United Artists. Highly respected by film industry peers.

THE FOREST RANGERS (s)	(C)	1942	PAR	87
THE FABULOUS TEXAN (s)		1947	REP	98
THE GALLANT LEGION (s)		1948	REP	88
THE YOUNGER BROTHERS (s)	(C)	1949	WB	76
BRIMSTONE (s)	(C)	1949	REP	90
MONTANA (s)	(C)	1950	WB	76
THE GROOM WORE SPURS (s)		1951	UI	81
SPRINGFIELD RIFLE (s)	(C)	1952	WB	93
THE MAN BEHIND THE GUN (s)	(C)	1953	WB	82
WOMAN THEY ALMOST LYNCHED (s)		1953	REP	90
THE CHARGE AT FEATHER RIVER (s)	(C)	1953	WB	96
THUNDER OVER THE PLAINS (s)	(C)	1953	WB	82
WINGS OF CHANCE	(C)	1961	UI	76
FIVE GUNS TO TOMBSTONE		1961	UA	71
THE GAMBLER WORE A GUN		1961	UA	68
GUN FIGHT		1961	UA	68
GUN STREET		1961	UA	67
BLACK SPURS (s)	(C)	1965	PAR	81
ADIOS AMIGO (s)	(C)	1975	AP	87

JIM BROWN (1936 -)

A famous professional football star with the Cleveland Browns who became a black film lead in action films, several of which are westerns. Among the standouts are 20th Century-Fox's RIO CONCHOS and 100 RIFLES.

RIO CONCHOS (s)	(C)	1964	20T	107
100 RIFLES	(C)	1969	20T	110
EL CONDOR	(C)	1970	NG	98-102
TAKE A HARD RIDE	(C)	1975	20T	108
KID VENGEANCE	(C)	1977	IYC	94

JOHNNY MACK BROWN (1904 - 1974)
(aka JOHN MACK BROWN)

This gracious Alabama gentleman made many thrilling low-budget hayburners through 1952, especially for Universal and Monogram Studios where he shot straight and fought like a tiger in punching out screen baddies such as Tris Coffin, Jack Ingram, Marshall Reed, and Eddie Parker. Brown was a Top Money-Making Western Star (1940-50) with such "B" gems as LAW AND ORDER, FLAME OF THE WEST, and THE GENTLEMAN FROM TEXAS. An outstanding horseman, Johnny excelled as well with gun-trick acrobatics.

MONTANA MOON		1930	MGM	88
BILLY THE KID		1930	MGM	90-98
(aka THE HIGHWAYMAN RIDES)				
THE GREAT MEADOW		1931	MGM	81
LASCA OF THE RIO GRANDE		1931	UNI	60
THE VANISHING FRONTIER		1932	PAR	70
FIGHTING WITH KIT CARSON	(SER)	1933	MAS	12CH

JOHNNY MACK BROWN, continued / 33

BELLE OF THE NINETIES (cs)		1934...PAR	73
THE RUSTLERS OF RED DOG	(SER)	1935...UNI	12CH
BRANDED A COWARD		1935...SUP	57
BETWEEN MEN		1935...SUP	57-59
THE COURAGEOUS AVENGER		1935...SUP	58
VALLEY OF THE LAWLESS		1936...SUP	58
DESERT PHANTOM		1936...SUP	55-60
ROGUE OF THE RANGE		1936...SUP	58
EVERYMAN'S LAW		1936...SUP	62
THE CROOKED TRAIL		1936...SUP	60
UNDER COVER MAN		1936...REP	56
LAWLESS LAND		1936...REP	55
BAR-Z BAD MEN		1937...REP	51
THE GAMBLING TERROR		1937...REP	53
TRAIL OF VENGEANCE		1937...REP	54
GUNS IN THE DARK		1937...REP	56
A LAWMAN IS BORN		1937...REP	61
WILD WEST DAYS	(SER)	1937...UNI	13CH
BOOTHILL BRIGADE		1937...REP	53
BORN TO THE WEST (aka HELL TOWN) (cs)		1937...PAR	66
WELLS FARGO (s)		1937...PAR	94-115
FLAMING FRONTIERS	(SER)	1938...UNI	15CH
THE OREGON TRAIL	(SER)	1939...UNI	15CH
DESPERATE TRAILS		1939...UNI	60
OKLAHOMA FRONTIER		1939...UNI	59
CHIP OF THE FLYING U		1939...UNI	55
WEST OF CARSON CITY		1940...UNI	56
RIDERS OF PASCO BASIN		1940...UNI	56
BAD MAN FROM RED BUTTE		1940...UNI	58
SON OF ROARING DAN		1940...UNI	60-63
RAGTIME COWBOY JOE		1940...UNI	58
LAW AND ORDER (aka THE LAW)		1940...UNI	57
PONY POST		1940...UNI	59
BOSS OF BULLION CITY		1941...UNI	61
BURY ME NOT ON THE LONE PRAIRIE		1941...UNI	61
LAW OF THE RANGE		1941...UNI	59
RAWHIDE RANGERS		1941...UNI	57
MAN FROM MONTANA (aka MONTANA JUSTICE)		1941...UNI	57
THE MASKED RIDER		1941...UNI	58
ARIZONA CYCLONE		1941...UNI	57
STAGECOACH BUCKAROO		1942...UNI	58
FIGHTING BILL FARGO		1942...UNI	57-59
RIDE 'EM COWBOY (s)		1942...UNI	86
THE SILVER BULLET		1942...UNI	61
BOSS OF HANGTOWN MESA		1942...UNI	59
* DEEP IN THE HEART OF TEXAS		1942...UNI	62
* LITTLE JOE, THE WRANGLER		1942...UNI	60-64
* THE OLD CHISHOLM TRAIL		1942...UNI	61
* TENTING TONIGHT ON THE OLD CAMP GROUND		1943...UNI	62
(aka TENTING TONIGHT)			
THE GHOST RIDER		1943...MON	52-58
(starts *Nevada Jack McKenzie* series for Monogram)			
* CHEYENNE ROUNDUP		1943...UNI	59
* RAIDERS OF SAN JOAQUIN		1943...UNI	59
(aka RIDERS OF SAN JOAQUIN)			
THE STRANGER FROM PECOS		1943...MON	56
* THE LONE STAR TRAIL		1943...UNI	58
SIX-GUN GOSPEL		1943...MON	55

* co-starred with Tex Ritter

JOHNNY MACK BROWN, continued

OUTLAWS OF STAMPEDE PASS	1943...MON	55
THE TEXAS KID	1943...MON	57
RAIDERS OF THE BORDER	1944...MON	53-59
PARTNERS OF THE TRAIL	1944...MON	54
LAW MEN	1944...MON	57
RANGE LAW	1944...MON	57
WEST OF THE RIO GRANDE	1944...MON	57
LAND OF THE OUTLAWS	1944...MON	55
LAW OF THE VALLEY	1944...MON	52
GHOST GUNS	1944...MON	60
THE NAVAJO TRAIL	1945...MON	60
GUN SMOKE	1945...MON	57
FLAME OF THE WEST	1945...MON	60-70
(aka FLAMING FRONTIER) (non-series)		
STRANGER FROM SANTA FE	1945...MON	56
THE LOST TRAIL	1945...MON	53
FRONTIER FEUD	1945...MON	54
BORDER BANDITS	1946...MON	58
(ends *Nevada Jack McKenzie* series)		
DRIFTING ALONG	1946...MON	60
THE HAUNTED MINE	1946...MON	51
UNDER ARIZONA SKIES	1946...MON	59
THE GENTLEMAN FROM TEXAS	1946...MON	55
SHADOWS ON THE RANGE	1946...MON	57
TRIGGER FINGERS	1946...MON	56
SILVER RANGE	1946...MON	53
RAIDERS OF THE SOUTH	1947...MON	55
VALLEY OF FEAR	1947...MON	54
TRAILING DANGER	1947...MON	58
LAND OF THE LAWLESS	1947...MON	59
THE LAW COMES TO GUNSIGHT	1947...MON	56-58
CODE OF THE SADDLE	1947...MON	53
FLASHING GUNS	1947...MON	59
PRAIRIE EXPRESS	1947...MON	55
GUN TALK	1947...MON	58
OVERLAND TRAILS	1948...MON	58
CROSSED TRAILS	1948...MON	53-57
FRONTIER AGENT	1948...MON	57
TRIGGERMAN	1948...MON	56
BACK TRAIL	1948...MON	54
THE FIGHTING RANGER	1948...MON	57
THE SHERIFF OF MEDICINE BOW	1948...MON	55
GUNNING FOR JUSTICE	1948...MON	55
HIDDEN DANGER	1948...MON	55
LAW OF THE WEST	1949...MON	54
TRAIL'S END	1949...MON	55-57
STAMPEDE	1949...AA	77
WEST OF EL DORADO	1949...MON	58
RANGE JUSTICE	1949...MON	54-57
WESTERN RENEGADES	1949...MON	56
WEST OF WYOMING	1950...MON	57
OVER THE BORDER	1950...MON	58
SIX GUN MESA	1950...MON	57
LAW OF THE PANHANDLE	1950...MON	55
OUTLAW GOLD	1950...MON	51
SHORT GRASS	1950...AA	82-84

JOHNNY MACK BROWN, continued / 35

COLORADO AMBUSH	1951	MON	51
MAN FROM SONORA	1951	MON	54-59
BLAZING BULLETS	1951	MON	51
MONTANA DESPERADO	1951	MON	51
OKLAHOMA JUSTICE	1951	MON	56
WHISTLING HILLS	1951	MON	58
TEXAS LAWMEN (aka LONE STAR LAWMAN)	1951	MON	54
TEXAS CITY	1952	MON	54
MAN FROM THE BLACK HILLS	1952	MON	51
DEAD MAN'S TRAIL	1952	MON	59
CANYON AMBUSH	1952	MON	53
THE MARSHAL'S DAUGHTER (gs)	1953	UA	71
THE BOUNTY KILLER (s)	(C) 1965	EMB	92
REQUIEM FOR A GUNFIGHTER (s)	(C) 1966	EMB	91
APACHE UPRISING (s)	(C) 1966	PAR	90

YUL BRYNNER (1915 - 1985)

A Russian-born, bald-headed actor who became an unusual western type hero. His excellent portrayal as the chief gunfighter in the classic feature, THE MAGNIFICENT SEVEN, allowed him to be successful in other western films.

THE MAGNIFICENT SEVEN	(C) 1960	UA	125-126
KINGS OF THE SUN	(C) 1963	UA	108
INVITATION TO A GUNFIGHTER	(C) 1964	UA	92
RETURN OF THE SEVEN	(C) 1966	UA	96
VILLA RIDES	(C) 1968	PAR	125
THE BOUNTY HUNTERS	(C) 1970	PEACF	106
ADIOS, SABATA	(C) 1971	UA	104
CATLOW	(C) 1971	MGM	101-103
WESTWORLD	(C) 1973	MGM	87-88

JACK BUETEL (1915 - 1989)

In THE OUTLAW for producer Howard Hughes, he portrayed Billy the Kid for a western debut but only had occasional screen credits thereafter through the 1950s. Buetel co-starred with Edgar Buchanan on "Judge Roy Bean" for 39 TV episodes of the 1956 syndicated show.

THE OUTLAW	1943	UA	121
BEST OF THE BADMEN (cs)	(C) 1951	RKO	84
ROSE OF CIMARRON	(C) 1952	20T	72
THE HALF-BREED (cs)	(C) 1952	RKO	81
JESSE JAMES' WOMEN	(C) 1954	UA	83
MUSTANG	1959	UA	73

BUFFALO BILL, JR. (1895 - 1961)
(aka JAY WILSEY)

Mainlining silent oaters in the 1920s, he then starred in independent mustangers during the early 1930s, but by 1936, Wilsey found work only with support roles to other "B" stars. In the early 1940s, he did good stunt work in features like SADDLE LEATHER LAW.

BEYOND THE RIO GRANDE	1930	B4	60
SOUTH OF SONORA	1930	B4	60

BUFFALO BILL, JR., continued

Title	Year	Studio	No.
BAR L RANCH	1930	B4	60
WAY OUT WEST (s)	1930	MGM	70
THE CHEYENNE KID	1930	WC	
WESTWARD BOUND	1931	SYN	60
TRAILS OF THE GOLDEN WEST	1931	COS	58
THE PUEBLO TERROR	1931	COS	61
RIDERS OF THE GOLDEN GULCH	1932	WC	52
THE TEXAN	1932	PA	64
HIDDEN GOLD (s)	1932	UNI	56
THE FIGHTING COWBOY	1933	SPR	58
TERROR TRAIL (s)	1933	UNI	56
DEADWOOD PASS (s)	1933	FM	62
RUSTY RIDES ALONE (s)	1933	COL	58
THE THRILL HUNTER (s)	1933	COL	58-60
LIGHTNING BILL	1934	SPR	46
PALS OF THE PRAIRIE	1934	IMP	20
RAWHIDE ROMANCE	1934	SPR	47
RIDING SPEED	1934	SPR	50
ADVENTURES OF TEXAS JACK (s)	1934	SEC	17
WHEELS OF DESTINY (s)	1934	UNI	64
THE LAWLESS FRONTIER (s)	1934	LMO	54-59
'NEATH THE ARIZONA SKIES (s)	1934	LMO	52
TRAILS OF ADVENTURE	1935	AME	57
THE WHIRLWIND RIDER	1935	AME	50
CIRCLE CANYON	1935	AME	48
TEXAS TERROR (s)	1935	LMO	51
THE PHANTOM EMPIRE (SER) (aka RADIO RANCH) (s)	1935	MAS	12CH
RAINBOW VALLEY (s)	1935	LMO	52
THE ROARING WEST (s) (SER)	1935	UNI	15CH
POWDERSMOKE RANGE (s)	1935	RKO	71
FIVE BAD MEN (cs)	1935	SUN	
THE MIRACLE RIDER (s) (SER)	1935	MAS	15CH
HEROES OF THE RANGE (s)	1936	COL	58
AVENGING WATERS (s)	1936	COL	57
THE PHANTOM RIDER (s) (SER)	1936	UNI	15CH
RANGER COURAGE (s)	1937	COL	58
WAY OUT WEST (s)	1937	MGM	65
LAW OF THE RANGER (s)	1937	COL	57
RECKLESS RANGER (s)	1937	COL	56
FORLORN RIVER (s)	1937	PAR	56
THE RANGERS STEP IN (s)	1937	COL	58
BLUE MONTANA SKIES (s)	1939	REP	56
PIONEERS OF THE FRONTIER (aka THE ANCHOR) (s)	1940	COL	56
BEYOND THE SACRAMENTO (aka POWER OF JUSTICE) (s)	1940	COL	58
THE LONE RIDER RIDES ON (s)	1941	PRC	64
THE LONE RIDER CROSSES THE RIO (s)	1941	PRC	63
NORTH FROM THE LONE STAR (s)	1941	COL	58
THE LONE RIDER IN GHOST TOWN (s)	1941	PRC	64
LAWLESS PLAINSMEN (aka ROLL ON) (s)	1942	COL	59
SADDLE LEATHER LAW (aka THE POISONER) (s)	1944	COL	55

JAMES CAAN (1939 -   )
A contemporary leading man of the 1970s-1980s who has made a few western films. Better known for his non-oaters. Good in EL DORADO.

THE GLORY GUYS (s)	(C)	1965	UA	112
EL DORADO (cs)	(C)	1967	PAR	126
JOURNEY TO SHILOH	(C)	1968	UNI	101
ANOTHER MAN, ANOTHER CHANCE	(C)	1977	UA	132
(aka ANOTHER MAN, ANOTHER WOMAN)				
COMES A HORSEMAN	(C)	1978	UA	110
LITTLE MOON AND JUD McGRAW	(C)	1979	COU	80
(aka GONE WITH THE WEST; BRONCO BUSTERS)				

JAMES CAGNEY (1899 - 1986)
Superstar actor who was best known for his hard-hitting Warner Brothers gangster dramas of the 1930s-1950s. This multi-talent great made a few western films and was as equally successful in the "A" oater genre. Cagney is a howl with his coyote imitation in THE BRIDE CAME C.O.D.

FRISCO KID		1935	WB	77
THE OKLAHOMA KID		1939	WB	85
TORRID ZONE		1940	WB	88
THE BRIDE CAME C.O.D.		1941	WB	92
RUN FOR COVER	(C)	1955	PAR	92-93
TRIBUTE TO A BAD MAN	(C)	1956	MGM	95
ARIZONA BUSHWHACKERS (nr)	(C)	1968	PAR	86

RORY CALHOUN (1923 -   )
This ex-firefighter became a leading man who starred in numerous western films for the major studios—20th Century-Fox, Universal, Columbia, and Paramount. Calhoun's pleasant manner found him starring in "The Texan" TV series for CBS (1958-60) with 30-minute shows. Much danger for Rory in APACHE TERRITORY.

NOB HILL (s)	(C)	1945	20T	95
MASSACRE RIVER		1949	AA	78
SAND (aka WILL JAMES' SAND) (cs)	(C)	1949	20T	77-78
A TICKET TO TOMAHAWK (cs)	(C)	1950	20T	90
RETURN OF THE FRONTIERSMAN	(C)	1950	WB	74
ROGUE RIVER	(C)	1950	EL	84
WAY OF A GAUCHO	(C)	1952	20T	91
THE SILVER WHIP		1953	20T	73
POWDER RIVER	(C)	1953	20T	77-78
RIVER OF NO RETURN (cs)	(C)	1954	20T	91
THE YELLOW TOMAHAWK	(C)	1954	UA	82-83
A BULLET IS WAITING	(C)	1954	COL	82
DAWN AT SOCORRO	(C)	1954	UI	80
FOUR GUNS TO THE BORDER	(C)	1954	UI	82-83
THE LOOTERS		1955	UI	87
THE TREASURE OF PANCHO VILLA	(C)	1955	RKO	92-96
THE SPOILERS (cs)	(C)	1956	UI	84
RED SUNDOWN	(C)	1956	UI	81-86
RAW EDGE	(C)	1956	UI	76
UTAH BLAINE		1957	COL	75

38 / RORY CALHOUN, continued

THE HIRED GUN	1957	MGM	63-64
THE DOMINO KID	1957	COL	73-74
RIDE OUT FOR REVENGE	1957	UA	78-79
APACHE TERRITORY	(C).. 1958	COL	75
THE SAGA OF HEMP BROWN	(C).. 1958	UI	79-80
THE GUN HAWK	(C).. 1963	AA	92
YOUNG FURY	(C).. 1965	PAR	79-80
BLACK SPURS	(C).. 1965	PAR	81
FINGER ON THE TRIGGER	(C).. 1965	AA	87
APACHE UPRISING	(C).. 1966	PAR	90
NIGHT OF THE LEPUS (cs)	(C).. 1972	MGM	88
KINO, THE PADRE ON HORSEBACK	(C).. 1977	KI	116
(aka MISSION TO GLORY) (s)			
THE REBELS (s)	(C).. 1979	OPT-TV	200
THE BLUE AND THE GRAY (s)	(C).. 1982	CBS-TV	295
BAD JIM (s)	(C).. 1990	21T	90

ROD CAMERON (1910 - 1983)

A tall, rugged Canadian who early on was briefly a "B" western star, but who quickly moved into "A" western features by the late 1940s with both Republic and Universal. Previously he had been a stunt double for Buck Jones and a stand-in for Fred MacMurray. Rod strutted toughness in such features as PANHANDLE, THE PLUNDERERS, STAMPEDE, and RIDE THE MAN DOWN.

RANGERS OF FORTUNE (s)	1940	PAR	80
NORTH WEST MOUNTED POLICE (s)	(C).. 1940	PAR	125
THE PARSON OF PANAMINT (s)	1941	PAR	84
THE FOREST RANGERS (s)	(C).. 1942	PAR	87
THE KANSAN (s)	1943	UA	79
FRONTIER LAW (s)	1943	UNI	55
RIDING HIGH (aka MELODY INN) (s)	(C).. 1943	PAR	88
BOSS OF BOOMTOWN	1944	UNI	56
TRIGGER TRAIL	1944	UNI	59
RIDERS OF THE SANTA FE (aka MILE A MINUTE)	1944	UNI	60
THE OLD TEXAS TRAIL (aka STAGECOACH LINE)	1944	UNI	60
BEYOND THE PECOS	1945	UNI	59
SALOME, WHERE SHE DANCED	(C).. 1945	UNI	90
RENEGADES OF THE RIO GRANDE	1945	UNI	56
(aka BANK ROBBERY)			
FRONTIER GAL	(C).. 1945	UNI	84
(aka THE BRIDE WASN'T WILLING)			
PIRATES OF MONTEREY	(C).. 1947	UI	77
BELLE STARR'S DAUGHTER	(C).. 1948	20T	85
PANHANDLE	1948	AA	84
RIVER LADY	(C).. 1948	UI	78
THE PLUNDERERS	(C).. 1948	REP	87
STRIKE IT RICH	1949	AA	81
STAMPEDE	1949	AA	78
BRIMSTONE	(C).. 1949	REP	90
DAKOTA LIL	(C).. 1950	20T	88
SHORT GRASS	1950	AA	82
STAGE TO TUCSON	(C).. 1951	COL	82
(aka LOST STAGE VALLEY)			
OH! SUSANNA	(C).. 1951	REP	90
CAVALRY SCOUT	(C).. 1951	MON	78

ROD CAMERON, continued / 39

FORT OSAGE	(C) .. 1952 ... MON	72	____
WAGONS WEST	(C) .. 1952 ... MON	70	____
WOMAN OF THE NORTH COUNTRY	(C) .. 1952 ... REP	90	____
RIDE THE MAN DOWN	(C) .. 1953 ... REP	90	____
SAN ANTONE	1953 ... REP	90	____
SOUTHWEST PASSAGE (aka CAMELS WEST)	(C) .. 1954 ... UA	82	____
HELL'S OUTPOST	1954 ... REP	90	____
SANTA FE PASSAGE	(C) .. 1955 ... REP	90	____
YAQUI DRUMS	1956 ... AA	71	____
SPOILERS OF THE FOREST	(C) .. 1957 ... REP	68	____
GUNFIGHT AT BLACK HORSE CANYON (s)	1962 ... REV	100	____
THE GUN HAWK	1963 ... AA	92	____
THE TWO FROM RIO BRAVO	(C) .. 1963 ... CTJ	93	____
(aka GUNS DON'T ARGUE; BULLETS DON'T ARGUE)			
PATHS OF HATE	(C) .. 1964 ... UHC	85-95	____
(aka BULLET IN THE FLESH; BULLET AND THE FLESH)			
THE BOUNTY KILLER	(C) .. 1965 ... EMB	92	____
REQUIEM FOR A GUNFIGHTER	(C) .. 1965 ... EMB	91	____
RIDE THE WIND (s)	(C) .. 1966 ... NBC-TV	100	____
THUNDER AT THE BORDER	(C) .. 1969 ... COL	98	____
(aka OLD FIREHAND)			
JESSIE'S GIRLS (aka WANTED WOMEN) (s)	(C) .. 1975 ... MAP	86	____

ROCKY CAMRON (1903 - 1967)
(aka GENE ALSACE, BUCK COBURN)

He had a high time menacing western heroes during the 1930s-1940s but came over to the side of the law long enough for a straight role in two of *The Trail Blazers* series in 1944 as well as HARMONY TRAIL which starred Ken Maynard.

WHOOPEE (s)	(C) .. 1930 ... UA	94	____
GUNS FOR HIRE (s)	1932 ... KEN	58	____
RANGE WARFARE (s)	1935 ... KEN	55	____
GUNSMOKE ON THE GUADALUPE	1935 ... KEN	57	____
(aka GUNSMOKE OVER THE GUADALUPE)			
MOONLIGHT ON THE PRAIRIE (s)	1935 ... WB	63	____
TREACHERY RIDES THE RANGE (s)	1936 ... WB	56	____
TRAILIN' WEST (aka ON SECRET SERVICE) (s)	1936 ... WB	56	____
CALIFORNIA MAIL (s)	1936 ... WB	56-60	____
GUNS OF THE PECOS (s)	1937 ... WB	65	____
RANGER COURAGE (s)	1937 ... COL	58	____
LAND BEYOND THE LAW (s)	1937 ... WB	54	____
BLAZING SIXES (s)	1937 ... WB	55	____
THE OVERLAND EXPRESS (s)	1938 ... COL	55	____
THE OKLAHOMA KID (s)	1939 ... WB	85	____
PALS OF THE SILVER SAGE (s)	1940 ... MON	52	____
ADVENTURES OF RED RYDER (s)	(SER) .. 1940 ... REP	12CH	____
THE GOLDEN TRAIL (aka GOLD TRAIL) (s)	1940 ... MON	52	____
RAINBOW OVER THE RANGE (s)	1940 ... MON	58	____
ARIZONA FRONTIER (s)	1940 ... MON	55	____
TAKE ME BACK TO OKLAHOMA	1940 ... MON	64	____
(aka OKLAHOMA BOUND) (s)			
ROLLING HOME TO TEXAS	1940 ... MON	62	____
(aka RIDIN' HOME TO TEXAS) (s)			
WINNERS OF THE WEST (s)	(SER) .. 1940 ... UNI	13CH	____

ROCKY CAMRON, continued

RIDIN' THE CHEROKEE TRAIL	1941	MON	62
(aka THE CHEROKEE TRAIL) (s)			
THE PIONEERS (s)	1941	MON	61
WANDERERS OF THE WEST (s)	1941	MON	58
DYNAMITE CANYON (s)	1941	MON	58
THE GUNMAN FROM BODIE (s)	1941	MON	62
THE DRIFTIN' KID (s)	1941	MON	55-57
RIDING THE SUNSET TRAIL (s)	1941	MON	56
LONE STAR LAW MEN (s)	1941	MON	58-61
WESTERN MAIL (s)	1942	MON	54
ARIZONA ROUNDUP (s)	1942	MON	56
WHERE TRAILS END (s)	1942	MON	55
OUTLAW TRAIL (starts *The Trail Blazers* series)	1944	MON	55
SONORA STAGECOACH	1944	MON	61
(ends *The Trail Blazers* series)			
HARMONY TRAIL (aka THE WHITE STALLION) (cs)	1944	MAT	57
WILDFIRE	(C) 1945	SG	60
(aka WILDFIRE: THE STORY OF A HORSE) (s)			
SONG OF OLD WYOMING (s)	(C) 1945	PRC	65
ROMANCE OF THE WEST (s)	(C) 1946	PRC	58
THE FIGHTING STALLION (s)	(C) 1950	EL	63
CALLAWAY WENT THATAWAY	1951	MGM	81
(aka THE STAR SAID NO) (s)			

JUDY CANOVA (1916 - 1983)

A female hillbilly type musical star who appeared in comedy western roles during the 1940s and 1950s. Republic Pictures was her primary movie studio.

CHATTERBOX	1943	REP	76
SINGIN' IN THE CORN (aka GIVE AND TAKE)	1946	COL	65-68
HONEYCHILE	(C) 1951	REP	89-90
OKLAHOMA ANNIE	(C) 1952	REP	90
UNTAMED HEIRESS	1954	REP	70
CAROLINA CANNONBALL	1955	REP	74
LAY THAT RIFLE DOWN	1955	REP	71
ADVENTURES OF HUCKLEBERRY FINN (s)	(C) 1960	MGM	107

HARRY CAREY (1878 - 1947)

He began a distinguished career with silent films in the 1910s, and went on for the next 30 years to mix oaters like POWDERSMOKE RANGE and THE LAST OUTLAW with straight dramas, comedies, and serials. Closing out the 1940s doing supports in such super "A" westerns as ANGEL AND THE BADMAN and RED RIVER, Carey was posthumously honored in 1949 when John Ford dedicated 3 GODFATHERS to him and again during 1991 with a Golden Boot Award in Los Angeles.

THE TRAIL OF '98	1929	MGM	94
THE VANISHING LEGION	(SER) 1931	MAS	12CH
CAVALIER OF THE WEST	1931	ART	75
WITHOUT HONORS	1932	ART	66
BORDER DEVILS	1932	ART	65
THE LAST OF THE MOHICANS	(SER) 1932	MAS	12CH
THE NIGHT RIDER	1932	ART	72

HARRY CAREY, continued

THE DEVIL HORSE	(SER).. 1932	MAS	12CH
LAW AND ORDER (aka GUNS A'BLAZING)	1932	UNI	75
SUNSET PASS (s)	1933	PAR	61
MAN OF THE FOREST (s)	1933	PAR	62
THE THUNDERING HERD	1933	PAR	59
(aka BUFFALO STAMPEDE; IN THE DAYS OF THE THUNDERING HERD) (s)			
WAGON TRAIL	1935	AJA	55
RUSTLERS' PARADISE	1935	AJA	61
POWDERSMOKE RANGE	1935	RKO	71
BARBARY COAST (s)	1935	UA	91
THE LAST OF THE CLINTONS	1935	AJA	59
WILD MUSTANG	1935	AJA	62
ACES WILD	1936	COM	57
GHOST TOWN	1936	COM	60
THE PRISONER OF SHARK ISLAND (s)	1936	20T	95
SUTTER'S GOLD (s)	1936	UNI	95
THE LAST OUTLAW	1936	RKO	62
BORDER CAFE	1937	RKO	67
THE LAW WEST OF TOMBSTONE	1938	RKO	73
THE SHEPHERD OF THE HILLS (s)	(C).. 1941	PAR	95-98
THE SPOILERS (s)	1942	UNI	87
ANGEL AND THE BADMAN (cs)	1947	REP	100
DUEL IN THE SUN (s)	(C).. 1947	SEL	130-138
THE SEA OF GRASS (s)	1947	MGM	131
RED RIVER (s)	1948	UA	125-133

HARRY CAREY, JR. (1921 -)

The son of the adult western great, he, too, has become a screen legend performing fine support work in many highly-acclaimed "A" westerns such as RED RIVER, 3 GODFATHERS, SHE WORE A YELLOW RIBBON, RIO GRANDE, and THE SEARCHERS. Carey teamed well with fellow actor Ben Johnson.

PURSUED (s)	1947	WB	101
RED RIVER (s)	1948	UA	125-133
BLOOD ON THE MOON (s)	1948	RKO	88
3 GODFATHERS (cs)	(C).. 1949	MGM	106
SHE WORE A YELLOW RIBBON (s)	(C).. 1949	RKO	104
WAGON MASTER	1950	RKO	86
COPPER CANYON (s)	(C).. 1950	PAR	83
RIO GRANDE (s)	1950	REP	105
CATTLE DRIVE (s)	(C).. 1951	UI	77
WARPATH (s)	(C).. 1951	PAR	95
SAN ANTONE (s)	1953	REP	90
SWEETHEARTS ON PARADE (s)	(C).. 1953	REP	90
SILVER LODE (s)	(C).. 1954	RKO	80
THE OUTCAST (s)	(C).. 1954	REP	90
THE SEARCHERS (s)	(C).. 1956	WB	119
THE GREAT LOCOMOTIVE CHASE	(C).. 1956	BV	85
(aka ANDREWS' RAIDERS) (s)			
7TH CAVALRY (s)	(C).. 1956	COL	75
THE RIVER'S EDGE (s)	(C).. 1957	20T	87
FROM HELL TO TEXAS (aka MANHUNT) (s)	(C).. 1958	20T	100
ESCORT WEST (s)	1959	UA	75
RIO BRAVO (s)	(C).. 1959	WB	141
NOOSE FOR A GUNMAN (s)	1960	UA	69

HARRY CAREY, JR., continued

TWO RODE TOGETHER (s)	(C)	1961	COL	91-109
THE RAIDERS (aka THE PLAINSMAN) (s)	(C)	1964	UNI	75
CHEYENNE AUTUMN (s)	(C)	1964	WB	145-160
TAGGART (s)	(C)	1964	UNI	85
SHENANDOAH (s)	(C)	1965	UNI	105
THE RARE BREED (s)	(C)	1966	UNI	97-108
BILLY THE KID VS. DRACULA (s)	(C)	1966	EMB	72
ALVAREZ KELLY (s)	(C)	1966	COL	116
THE WAY WEST (s)	(C)	1967	UA	122
THE BALLAD OF JOSIE (s)	(C)	1968	UNI	102
BANDOLERO! (s)	(C)	1968	20T	106
DEATH OF A GUNFIGHTER (aka THE LAST GUNFIGHTER) (s)	(C)	1969	UNI	94
THE UNDEFEATED (s)	(C)	1969	20T	119
RIDE A NORTHBOUND HORSE (s)	(C)	1969	BV	79
DIRTY DINGUS MAGEE (s)	(C)	1970	MGM	79-90
BIG JAKE (s)	(C)	1971	NG	110
ONE MORE TRAIN TO ROB (s)	(C)	1971	UNI	108
SOMETHING BIG (s)	(C)	1971	NG	108
TRINITY IS STILL MY NAME (cs)	(C)	1972	AE	121
MAN OF THE EAST (cs)	(C)	1972	AE	122
WHITE FANG (s)	(C)	1972	AC	97
CAHILL UNITED STATES MARSHAL (aka CAHILL) (s)	(C)	1973	WB	103
TAKE A HARD RIDE (s)	(C)	1975	20T	103
KATE BLISS AND THE TICKER-TAPE KID (s)	(C)	1978	ASP-TV	120
THE LONG RIDERS (s)	(C)	1980	UA	100
WILD TIMES (s)	(C)	1980	GC-TV	200
THE SHADOW RIDERS (aka LOUIS L'AMOUR'S SHADOW RIDERS) (s)	(C)	1982	CBS-TV	100
ONCE UPON A TEXAS TRAIN (aka TEXAS GUNS) (s)	(C)	1988	CBS-TV	100
CHERRY 2000 (cs)	(C)	1988	ORI	93
BACK TO THE FUTURE PART III (s)	(C)	1990	UNI	118
BAD JIM (s)	(C)	1990	21T	90
LEGENDS OF THE AMERICAN WEST (ho)	(C)	1992	CFE-TV	96

MacDONALD CAREY (1913 -   )

A Broadway actor who starred in several western films during the 1950s, among them Republic's highly-praised STRANGER AT MY DOOR. Better known for his dramas, Carey has been a TV mainstay on NBC's popular soap opera "Days of Our Lives" since 1965. Spokesman for the American Association of Retired Persons.

STREETS OF LAREDO (cs)	(C)	1949	PAR	92
COMANCHE TERRITORY	(C)	1950	UI	76
THE LAWLESS (aka THE DIVIDING LINE)		1950	PAR	83
COPPER CANYON (cs)	(C)	1950	PAR	83
THE GREAT MISSOURI RAID	(C)	1951	PAR	83-85
CAVE OF OUTLAWS	(C)	1951	UI	75-78
COUNT THE HOURS		1953	RKO	74
HANNAH LEE (aka OUTLAW TERRITORY)	(C)	1953	REA	79
STRANGER AT MY DOOR		1956	REP	85
MAN OR GUN		1958	REP	79
ORDEAL (s)	(C)	1973	TVM	74
THE REBELS (s)	(C)	1979	UNI-TV	200

PHIL CAREY (1925 -   )

A Broadway actor who starred in several Columbia western films in the 1950s. Better known to oater fans as the Ranger Captain on the television series "Laredo" for NBC (1965-67) which was headed by the late Neville Brand.

CATTLE TOWN (s)	1952	WB	71
SPRINGFIELD RIFLE (s)	(C).. 1952	WB	93
THE MAN BEHIND THE GUN (s)	(C).. 1953	WB	83
CALAMITY JANE (s)	(C).. 1953	WB	101
GUN FURY (cs)	(C).. 1953	COL	83
THE NEBRASKAN	(C).. 1953	COL	68
MASSACRE CANYON	1954	COL	64-66
THE OUTLAW STALLION	(C).. 1954	COL	64
THEY RODE WEST (cs)	(C).. 1954	COL	84
WYOMING RENEGADES	(C).. 1955	COL	73
COUNT THREE AND PRAY (cs)	(C).. 1955	COL	102
RETURN TO WARBOW	(C).. 1958	COL	67
TONKA (aka A HORSE NAMED COMANCHE)	(C).. 1958	BV	97
BLACK GOLD	1963	WB	76
THE GREAT SIOUX MASSACRE	(C).. 1965	COL	91
(aka CUSTER MASSACRE; THE MASSACRE AT THE ROSEBUD) (cs)			
THREE GUNS FOR TEXAS (s)	(C).. 1968	UNI	99
BACKTRACK (s)	(C).. 1969	UNI	95
HARD DAY AT BLUE NOSE (cs)	(C).. 1974	MPCS	66

JOHNNY CARPENTER (1914 -   )
(aka JOSH CARPENTER, JOHN FORBES)

He did support work as a cowhand or gunman in "B" westerns through 1951. Then Carpenter starred in several independent horse operas during the 1950s. Since the early 1940s, the basic thrust of Johnny's life has been the operation of a ranch for handicapped children. Carpenter received praise for this non-stop humanitarian effort from former President Ronald Reagan in 1990.

THUNDERING TRAILS (s)	1943	REP	56
THE NAVAJO TRAIL (s)	1945	MON	60
SANTA FE SADDLEMATES (s)	1945	REP	56
TRAIL OF KIT CARSON (s)	1945	REP	55
SONG OF OLD WYOMING (s)	(C). 1945	PRC	65
NORTHWEST TRAIL (s)	(C). 1945	SG	64
ROMANCE OF THE WEST (s)	(C). 1946	PRC	58
THE EL PASO KID (s)	1946	REP	54
SONG OF THE WASTELAND (s)	1947	MON	56
THE STRANGER FROM PONCA CITY (s)	1947	COL	56
RELENTLESS (s)	(C). 1948	COL	93
RED CANYON (s)	(C). 1949	UI	82
THE KID FROM TEXAS	(C). 1950	UI	78
(aka TEXAS KID, OUTLAW) (s)			
THE FIGHTING STALLION (s)	(C). 1950	EL	73
COMANCHE TERRITORY (s)	(C). 1950	UI	76
BORDER OUTLAWS	1950	EL	59
(aka THE PHANTOM HORSEMAN) (s)			
BADMAN'S GOLD	1951	UA	56
CAVE OF OUTLAWS (s)	(C). 1951	UI	75
THE VANISHING OUTPOST (s)	1951	WA	56

43

44 / JOHNNY CARPENTER, continued

CATTLE QUEEN (aka QUEEN OF THE WEST) (s)	1951	UA	72
THE DUEL AT SILVER CREEK (s) (C)	1952	UI	77
SON OF THE RENEGADE	1953	UA	57
LAW AND ORDER (s) (C)	1953	UI	80
THE LAWLESS RIDER	1954	UA	62
OUTLAW TREASURE	1955	ARC	67
RED SUNDOWN (s) (C)	1956	UI	82
I KILLED WILD BILL HICKOK	1956	WCP	63
TOMBOY AND THE CHAMP (s)	1961	UI	92

LEO CARRILLO (1880 - 1961)

A roguish, Mexican bandit type in "A" westerns is better known for his sidekick role in "The Cisco Kid" television series (1950-56) as Pancho.

LASCA OF THE RIO GRANDE	1931	UNI	60-65
GIRL OF THE RIO (aka THE DOVE)	1932	RKO	69
VIVA VILLA! (cs)	1934	MGM	90-115
IN CALIENTE (s)	1935	WB	84
THE GAY DESPERADO	1936	UA	86
THE BARRIER	1937	PAR	90-91
THE GIRL OF THE GOLDEN WEST (s)	1938	MGM	120
THE ARIZONA WILDCAT	1939	20T	69
THE GIRL AND THE GAMBLER	1939	RKO	63
RIO (s)	1939	UNI	77
20 MULE TEAM	1940	MGM	83-84
WYOMING	1940	MGM	89
(aka MAN FROM WYOMING; BAD MAN OF WYOMING)			
RIDERS OF DEATH VALLEY (cs) (SER)	1941	UNI	15CH
ROAD AGENT (aka TEXAS ROAD AGENT)	1941	UNI	60
MEN OF TEXAS (aka MEN OF DESTINY) (s)	1942	UNI	82
TIMBER	1942	UNI	60
SIN TOWN (s)	1942	UNI	73
AMERICAN EMPIRE (aka MY SON ALONE)	1942	UA	81
FRONTIER BADMEN (cs)	1943	UNI	77
MOONLIGHT AND CACTUS	1944	UNI	60
UNDER WESTERN SKIES	1945	UNI	56-60
MEXICANA (aka BEYOND THE BORDER) (cs)	1945	REP	83
THE FUGITIVE (s)	1947	RKO	104
THE VALIANT HOMBRE (starts The Cisco Kid series)	1949	UA	60
THE GAY AMIGO	1949	UA	60
THE DARING CABALLERO	1949	UA	60
SATAN'S CRADLE	1949	UA	60
THE GIRL FROM SAN LORENZO	1950	UA	59
(ends The Cisco Kid series)			
PANCHO VILLA RETURNS	1950	HCF	95-96

JOHN CARROLL (1907 - 1979)

A tall, dark singer who starred in several western films on the big-budget scale at Republic Pictures during the late 1940s - early 1950s. He portrayed Zorro in the serial ZORRO RIDES AGAIN. Carroll's roles emphasized much romance.

HI, GAUCHO!	1935	RKO	48-59
ZORRO RIDES AGAIN (SER)	1937	REP	12CH
ROSE OF THE RIO GRANDE	1938	MON	60

JOHN CARROLL, continued / 45

WOLF CALL	1939	MON	60-67
GO WEST (s)	1940	MGM	81
RIO RITA (s)	1942	MGM	91
PIERRE OF THE PLAINS	1942	MGM	57-66
FIESTA (s) (C)	1947	MGM	104
WYOMING (cs)	1947	REP	84
THE FABULOUS TEXAN (cs)	1947	REP	98
OLD LOS ANGELES (aka CALIFORNIA OUTPOST)	1948	REP	88
ANGEL IN EXILE	1948	REP	90
THE AVENGERS	1950	REP	90
SURRENDER	1950	REP	90
HIT PARADE OF 1951 (aka SONG PARADE)	1950	REP	85
BELLE LE GRAND	1951	REP	90
DECISION AT SUNDOWN (C)	1957	COL	77
ZORRO RIDES AGAIN	1959	REP	65-68

(feature version of ZORRO RIDES AGAIN serial)

PLUNDERERS OF PAINTED FLATS	1959	REP	70-77

LIGHTNIN' BILL CARSON series (1936; 1938 - 1939)

Tim McCoy starred as various types of lawmen in this cheaply-made series for Victory Pictures, sometimes disguising himself as a Mexican to defeat the adversaries.

(TIM McCOY)

LIGHTNIN' BILL CARSON	1936	PUR	57-75

(TIM McCOY, BEN CORBETT)

LIGHTNING CARSON RIDES AGAIN	1938	VIC	59
SIX-GUN TRAIL	1938	VIC	59
CODE OF THE CACTUS	1939	VIC	56
TEXAS WILDCATS	1939	VIC	57
OUTLAW'S PARADISE	1939	VIC	62
TRIGGER FINGERS	1939	VIC	60
THE FIGHTING RENEGADE	1939	VIC	58
STRAIGHT SHOOTER	1939	VIC	54

BILLY THE KID / BILLY CARSON series (1940 - 1946)

Originally set in 1939 by PDC (later PRC), as "Tales of Billy the Kid" for cowboy George Houston to helm eight features which never materialized for him, this series finally got underway when Bob Steele played the outlaw gone straight in six low-budgeters during the 1940-41 season. Then Buster Crabbe took over the remaining five years through 1946. The "B" screenplays were only fair but for a few exceptions.

(BOB STEELE, AL ST. JOHN, CARLETON YOUNG)

BILLY THE KID OUTLAWED	1940	PRC	52-60
BILLY THE KID IN TEXAS	1940	PRC	52-63
BILLY THE KID'S GUN JUSTICE	1940	PRC	57-63
BILLY THE KID'S RANGE WAR	1941	PRC	57-60
BILLY THE KID'S FIGHTING PALS	1941	PRC	62

(BOB STEELE, AL ST. JOHN, REX LEASE)

BILLY THE KID IN SANTA FE	1941	PRC	66

46 / BILLY THE KID / BILLY CARSON series, continued

(BUSTER CRABBE, AL ST. JOHN, DAVE O'BRIEN)
BILLY THE KID WANTED .... 1941 ... PRC .... 64 ____

(BUSTER CRABBE, AL ST. JOHN, CARLETON YOUNG)
BILLY THE KID'S ROUND-UP .... 1941 ... PRC .... 58 ____

(BUSTER CRABBE, AL ST. JOHN, BUD McTAGGART)
BILLY THE KID TRAPPED .... 1942 ... PRC .... 59 ____

(BUSTER CRABBE, AL ST. JOHN, DAVE O'BRIEN)
BILLY THE KID'S SMOKING GUNS .... 1942 ... PRC .... 58 ____
LAW AND ORDER .... 1942 ... PRC ..... 56-58 ____

(BUSTER CRABBE, AL ST. JOHN)
THE MYSTERIOUS RIDER .... 1942 ... PRC .... 56 ____

(BUSTER CRABBE, AL ST. JOHN, DAVE O'BRIEN)
SHERIFF OF SAGE VALLEY .... 1942 ... PRC .... 60 ____
  (aka BILLY THE KID, SHERIFF OF SAGE VALLEY)

(BUSTER CRABBE, AL ST. JOHN)
THE KID RIDES AGAIN .... 1943 ... PRC .... 60 ____
FUGITIVE OF THE PLAINS .... 1943 ... PRC .... 57 ____
WESTERN CYCLONE .... 1943 ... PRC .... 56 ____
THE RENEGADES .... 1943 ... PRC .... 58 ____
CATTLE STAMPEDE .... 1943 ... PRC ..... 58-60 ____
BLAZING FRONTIER (ends *Billy the Kid*) .... 1943 ... PRC .... 59 ____
THE DEVIL RIDERS (starts *Billy Carson*) .... 1943 ... PRC .... 58 ____
THE DRIFTER .... 1943 ... PRC ..... 60-62 ____
FRONTIER OUTLAWS .... 1944 ... PRC .... 58 ____
THUNDERING GUN SLINGERS .... 1944 ... PRC .... 60 ____
VALLEY OF VENGEANCE (aka VENGEANCE) .... 1944 ... PRC ..... 56-58 ____
FUZZY SETTLES DOWN .... 1944 ... PRC .... 61 ____
RUSTLERS' HIDEOUT .... 1944 ... PRC .... 60 ____
WILD HORSE PHANTOM .... 1944 ... PRC .... 56 ____
OATH OF VENGEANCE .... 1944 ... PRC .... 57 ____
HIS BROTHER'S GHOST .... 1945 ... PRC .... 54 ____
SHADOWS OF DEATH .... 1945 ... PRC .... 60 ____
GANGSTER'S DEN .... 1945 ... PRC .... 55 ____
STAGECOACH OUTLAWS .... 1945 ... PRC .... 59 ____
BORDER BADMEN .... 1945 ... PRC .... 59 ____
FIGHTING BILL CARSON .... 1945 ... PRC .... 51 ____
PRAIRIE RUSTLERS .... 1945 ... PRC .... 56 ____
LIGHTNING RAIDERS .... 1946 ... PRC .... 61 ____
GHOST OF HIDDEN VALLEY .... 1946 ... PRC .... 56 ____
GENTLEMEN WITH GUNS .... 1946 ... PRC .... 52 ____
PRAIRIE BADMEN .... 1946 ... PRC .... 55 ____
TERRORS ON HORSEBACK .... 1946 ... PRC .... 55 ____
OVERLAND RIDERS .... 1946 ... PRC .... 54 ____
OUTLAWS OF THE PLAINS .... 1946 ... PRC .... 58 ____

SUNSET CARSON (1922 - 1990)
An action "B" western cowboy star for Republic Pictures (1944-46) with crackerjack oaters like SHERIFF OF CIMARRON and SANTA FE SADDLEMATES, Sunset left the studio in 1946 while a Top Money-Making Western Star and made several highly-criticized color Yucca sagas in the late 1940s. He spent the next 40 years of his life with rodeos, personal appearance tours, and film conventions. Carson hosted 52 hour-long episodes of PBS' "Six-Gun Heroes" (1982-84).

Title	Year	Studio	Min
CALL OF THE ROCKIES	1944	REP	54
BORDERTOWN TRAIL	1944	REP	55
CODE OF THE PRAIRIE	1944	REP	56
FIREBRANDS OF ARIZONA	1944	REP	55
SHERIFF OF CIMARRON	1945	REP	53
SANTA FE SADDLEMATES	1945	REP	56
BELLS OF ROSARITA (gs)	1945	REP	68
OREGON TRAIL	1945	REP	55
BANDITS OF THE BADLANDS	1945	REP	55
ROUGH RIDERS OF CHEYENNE	1945	REP	56
THE CHEROKEE FLASH	1945	REP	55-58
DAYS OF BUFFALO BILL	1946	REP	56
ALIAS BILLY THE KID	1946	REP	56
THE EL PASO KID	1946	REP	54
RED RIVER RENEGADES	1946	REP	55
RIO GRANDE RAIDERS	1946	REP	57
SUNSET CARSON RIDES AGAIN	(C) 1948	YUC	60
DEADLINE	(C) 1948	YUC	57
FIGHTING MUSTANG	(C) 1948	YUC	56
BATTLING MARSHAL	(C) 1948	YUC	53-55
RIO GRANDE	1950	AST	70

HOPALONG CASSIDY series (1935-1944; 1946-1948)
It was the longest running trio series of quality "B" westerns for 11 seasons with William Boyd having various sidekicks—Jimmy Ellison, George Hayes, Russell Hayden, Andy Clyde, Rand Brooks, etc.—to assist him in tracking down every type of old West crook. Highly rated are THREE MEN FROM TEXAS, WIDE OPEN TOWN, and HOPPY SERVES A WRIT.

(WILLIAM BOYD, JIMMY ELLISON, GEORGE HAYES)

Title	Year	Studio	Min
HOP-A-LONG CASSIDY	1935	PAR	59-62
(aka HOPALONG CASSIDY ENTERS)			
THE EAGLE'S BROOD	1935	PAR	60
BAR 20 RIDES AGAIN	1935	PAR	63
CALL OF THE PRAIRIE	1936	PAR	67
THREE ON THE TRAIL	1936	PAR	67
HEART OF THE WEST	1936	PAR	65-78

(WILLIAM BOYD, GEORGE HAYES, WILLIAM JANNEY)

Title	Year	Studio	Min
HOPALONG CASSIDY RETURNS	1936	PAR	75

(WILLIAM BOYD, JIMMY ELLISON, GEORGE HAYES)

Title	Year	Studio	Min
TRAIL DUST	1936	PAR	77
BORDERLAND	1937	PAR	82

48 / HOPALONG CASSIDY series, continued

(WILLIAM BOYD, GEORGE HAYES, RUSSELL HAYDEN)
HILLS OF OLD WYOMING .... 1937 ... PAR .... 79 ____
NORTH OF THE RIO GRANDE .... 1937 ... PAR .... 70 ____
RUSTLERS' VALLEY .... 1937 ... PAR .... 60 ____
HOPALONG RIDES AGAIN .... 1937 ... PAR .... 65 ____
TEXAS TRAIL .... 1937 ... PAR .... 63 ____

(WILLIAM BOYD, RUSSELL HAYDEN, HARVEY CLARK)
PARTNERS OF THE PLAINS .... 1938 ... PAR .... 68 ____

(WILLIAM BOYD, RUSSELL HAYDEN, FRANK DARIEN)
CASSIDY OF BAR 20 .... 1938 ... PAR .... 56 ____

(WILLIAM BOYD, GEORGE HAYES, RUSSELL HAYDEN)
HEART OF ARIZONA .... 1938 ... PAR .... 68 ____
BAR 20 JUSTICE .... 1938 ... PAR .... 70 ____
PRIDE OF THE WEST .... 1938 ... PAR .... 55 ____
IN OLD MEXICO .... 1938 ... PAR .... 62 ____
SUNSET TRAIL .... 1938 ... PAR .... 60 ____
THE FRONTIERSMEN .... 1938 ... PAR .... 74 ____
SILVER ON THE SAGE .... 1939 ... PAR .... 68 ____
THE RENEGADE TRAIL .... 1939 ... PAR .... 58 ____

(WILLIAM BOYD, RUSSELL HAYDEN, BRITT WOOD)
RANGE WAR .... 1939 ... PAR .... 66 ____

(WILLIAM BOYD, RUSSELL HAYDEN, SIDNEY TOLER)
LAW OF THE PAMPAS .... 1939 ... PAR .... 74 ____

(WILLIAM BOYD, RUSSELL HAYDEN, BRITT WOOD)
SANTA FE MARSHAL .... 1940 ... PAR .... 68 ____
THE SHOWDOWN .... 1940 ... PAR .... 63 ____
HIDDEN GOLD .... 1940 ... PAR .... 61 ____
STAGECOACH WAR .... 1940 ... PAR .... 63 ____

(WILLIAM BOYD, RUSSELL HAYDEN, ANDY CLYDE)
THREE MEN FROM TEXAS .... 1940 ... PAR .... 76 ____
DOOMED CARAVAN .... 1941 ... PAR .... 61 ____
IN OLD COLORADO .... 1941 ... PAR .... 67 ____
BORDER VIGILANTES .... 1941 ... PAR .... 62 ____
PIRATES ON HORSEBACK .... 1941 ... PAR .... 69 ____
WIDE OPEN TOWN .... 1941 ... PAR .... 78 ____

(WILLIAM BOYD, ANDY CLYDE, BRAD KING)
STICK TO YOUR GUNS .... 1941 ... PAR .... 63 ____
SECRET OF THE WASTELANDS .... 1941 ... PAR .... 70 ____
OUTLAWS OF THE DESERT .... 1941 ... PAR .... 66 ____
RIDERS OF THE TIMBERLINE .... 1941 ... PAR .... 59 ____
TWILIGHT ON THE TRAIL .... 1941 ... PAR .... 58 ____

HOPALONG CASSIDY series, continued /49

(WILLIAM BOYD, ANDY CLYDE, JAY KIRBY)
UNDERCOVER MAN	1942	UA	68
LOST CANYON	1942	UA	63
HOPPY SERVES A WRIT	1943	UA	67
BORDER PATROL	1943	UA	67
LEATHER BURNERS	1943	UA	58
COLT COMRADES	1943	UA	67

(WILLIAM BOYD, ANDY CLYDE, GEORGE REEVES)
BAR 20	1943	UA	54

(WILLIAM BOYD, ANDY CLYDE, JIMMY ROGERS)
FALSE COLORS	1943	UA	65
RIDERS OF THE DEADLINE	1943	UA	70
TEXAS MASQUERADE	1944	UA	59
LUMBERJACK	1944	UA	63
MYSTERY MAN	1944	UA	58
FORTY THIEVES	1944	UA	60

(WILLIAM BOYD, ANDY CLYDE, RAND BROOKS)
THE DEVIL'S PLAYGROUND	1946	UA	62
FOOL'S GOLD	1947	UA	63
UNEXPECTED GUEST	1947	UA	61
DANGEROUS VENTURE	1947	UA	59
HOPPY'S HOLIDAY	1947	UA	60
THE MARAUDERS	1947	UA	63-68
SILENT CONFLICT	1948	UA	61
THE DEAD DON'T DREAM	1948	UA	68
SINISTER JOURNEY	1948	UA	59
BORROWED TROUBLE	1948	UA	60
FALSE PARADISE	1948	UA	61
STRANGE GAMBLE	1948	UA	62

JEFF CHANDLER (1918 - 1961)
Began in western films playing Cochise, the Apache chief, in BROKEN ARROW. He made numerous "A" oaters throughout the 1950s that included another version of Rex Beach's THE SPOILERS.

BROKEN ARROW	(C)	1950	20T	92
TWO FLAGS WEST (cs)		1950	20T	92
THE BATTLE AT APACHE PASS	(C)	1952	UI	85
THE GREAT SIOUX UPRISING	(C)	1953	UI	80
WAR ARROW	(C)	1954	UI	78
TAZA, SON OF COCHISE (s)	(C)	1954	UI	79
FOXFIRE	(C)	1955	UI	91-93
THE SPOILERS	(C)	1956	UI	84
PILLARS OF THE SKY	(C)	1956	UI	95
(aka THE TOMAHAWK AND THE CROSS)				
DRANGO		1957	UA	92-96
MAN IN THE SHADOW (aka PAY THE DEVIL)		1958	UI	80
THUNDER IN THE SUN	(C)	1959	PAR	81
THE JAYHAWKERS	(C)	1959	PAR	100
THE PLUNDERERS		1960	AA	94

LANE CHANDLER (1899 - 1972)

He lost out to Gary Cooper for stardom at Paramount Pictures, then mainlined independent oaters during the early 1930s. Chandler eventually established his reputation as a solid character player in a vast array of "A" and "B" westerns for the next several decades.

Title	Year	Studio	Length
FIREBRAND JORDAN (aka FIREBRAND JOHNSON)	1930	B4	60
BEYOND THE LAW	1930	SYN	50
UNDER TEXAS SKIES (s)	1930	SYN	57
HURRICANE HORSEMAN (aka THE MEXICAN)	1931	KEN	50
RIDERS OF RIO (aka LAW OF THE RIO)	1931	RP	
THE CHEYENNE CYCLONE	1932	KEN	57
BATTLING BUCKAROO (aka HIS LAST ADVENTURE)	1932	KEN	
GUNS FOR HIRE	1932	KEN	58
LAWLESS VALLEY	1932	KEN	
THE RECKLESS RIDER	1932	KEN	
TEXAS TORNADO	1932	KEN	55
WYOMING WHIRLWIND	1932	KEN	55
THE DEVIL HORSE (s) (SER)	1932	MAS	12CH
VIA PONY EXPRESS (cs)	1933	MAJ	60
TROUBLE BUSTERS	1933	MAJ	55
THE FIDDLIN' BUCKAROO (s)	1933	UNI	62
FIGHTING WITH KIT CARSON (s) (SER)	1933	MAS	12CH
WAR OF THE RANGE (cs)	1933	FM	60
SAGEBRUSH TRAIL (cs)	1933	LMO	58
BEYOND THE LAW (cs)	1934	COL	58
THE LONE BANDIT	1934	EMP	60
OUTLAW TAMER	1934	EMP	60
COYOTE TRAILS (s)	1935	COM	63
NORTH OF ARIZONA (aka BORDER RAIDERS) (cs)	1935	COM	60
RIO RATTLER (s)	1935	COM	63
THE LAWLESS NINETIES (s)	1936	REP	55
WINDS OF THE WASTELAND (s)	1936	REP	58
THE IDAHO KID (s)	1936	CLY	59
LAW AND LEAD (s)	1936	CLY	60
STORMY TRAILS (s)	1936	CLY	58
THE PLAINSMAN (s)	1937	PAR	113
LAW OF THE RANGER (s)	1937	COL	57
RECKLESS RANGER (s)	1937	COL	56
WELLS FARGO (s)	1937	PAR	115
ZORRO RIDES AGAIN (s) (SER)	1937	REP	12CH
HEROES OF THE ALAMO	1938	COL	75
LAND OF FIGHTING MEN (s)	1938	MON	53
THE LONE RANGER (cs) (SER)	1938	REP	15CH
HEART OF ARIZONA (s)	1938	PAR	68
TWO GUN JUSTICE (s)	1938	MON	57
COME ON, RANGERS (s)	1938	REP	58
HAWK OF THE WILDERNESS (SER) (aka LOST ISLAND OF KIOGA) (s)	1938	REP	12CH
NORTH OF THE YUKON (s)	1939	COL	64
THE LAW COMES TO TEXAS (s)	1939	COL	58
UNION PACIFIC (s)	1939	PAR	125
MAN OF CONQUEST (s)	1939	REP	97-99
SOUTHWARD, HO! (s)	1939	REP	58
OUTPOST OF THE MOUNTIES (aka ON GUARD) (s)	1939	COL	63
OKLAHOMA FRONTIER (s)	1939	UNI	58

LANE CHANDLER, continued / 51

SAGA OF DEATH VALLEY (s)	1939	REP	58
THE TAMING OF THE WEST (s)	1939	COL	55
MAN FROM MONTREAL (s)	1939	UNI	60
MY LITTLE CHICKADEE (s)	1940	UNI	85
VIRGINIA CITY (s)	1940	WB	121
PIONEERS OF THE WEST (s)	1940	REP	56
HI-YO-SILVER	1940	REP	69
(feature version of THE LONE RANGER serial) (cs)			
DARK COMMAND (s)	1940	REP	94
WAGONS WESTWARD (s)	1940	REP	69
DEADWOOD DICK (s) ......(SER)	1940	COL	15CH
PONY POST (s)	1940	UNI	59
SANTA FE TRAIL (s)	1940	WB	110
THE HOWARDS OF VIRGINIA	1940	COL	122
(aka TREE OF LIBERTY) (s)			
NORTH WEST MOUNTED POLICE (s)......(C)	1940	PAR	125
THE ROUND-UP (s)	1941	PAR	90
LADY FROM LOUISIANA (s)	1941	REP	82
SIX-GUN GOLD (s)	1941	RKO	57
LAST OF THE DUANES (s)	1941	20T	55-57
THEY DIED WITH THEIR BOOTS ON (s)	1942	WB	140
SUNDOWN JIM (s)	1942	20T	58
THE VALLEY OF VANISHING MEN (s)......(SER)	1942	COL	15CH
TENTING TONIGHT ON THE OLD CAMP GROUND	1943	UNI	61
(aka TENTING TONIGHT) (s)			
WILD HORSE RUSTLERS (s)	1943	PRC	55
LAW OF THE SADDLE (s)	1943	PRC	57
RIDING HIGH (aka MELODY INN) (s)......(C)	1943	PAR	88
IN OLD OKLAHOMA (aka WAR OF THE WILDCATS) (s)	1943	REP	102
OKLAHOMA RAIDERS	1944	UNI	57
(aka MIDNIGHT RAIDERS; RIDERS OF OKLAHOMA) (s)			
TRIGGER TRAIL (s)	1944	UNI	58
SILVER CITY KID (s)	1944	REP	54
RUSTLERS' HIDEOUT (s)	1944	PRC	60
TRIGGER LAW (s)	1944	MON	56
LIGHTS OF OLD SANTA FE (s)	1944	REP	78
RIDERS OF THE SANTA FE (aka MILE A MINUTE) (s)	1944	UNI	63
SAGEBRUSH HEROES (s)	1945	COL	54
ALONG CAME JONES (s)	1945	RKO	90
SENORITA FROM THE WEST (s)	1945	UNI	63
SAN ANTONIO (s)......(C)	1945	WB	112
SARATOGA TRUNK (s)	1946	WB	135
GUNNING FOR VENGEANCE (aka JAIL BREAK) (s)	1946	COL	53-56
TWO-FISTED STRANGER (aka HIGH STAKES) (s)	1946	COL	50
TERROR TRAIL (aka HANDS OF MENACE) (s)	1946	COL	55
CALIFORNIA (s)......(C)	1947	PAR	98
PURSUED (s)	1947	WB	100
THE VIGILANTES RETURN......(C)	1947	UI	67
(aka THE RETURN OF THE VIGILANTES) (s)			
DUEL IN THE SUN (s)......(C)	1947	SEL	130-138
THE ARIZONA RANGER (s)	1948	RKO	63
UNCONQUERED (s)......(C)	1948	PAR	146-147
RETURN OF THE BAD MEN (s)	1948	RKO	96
NORTHWEST STAMPEDE (s)......(C)	1948	EL	76
RED RIVER (s)	1948	UA	125-133
A SOUTHERN YANKEE (aka MY HERO!) (s)	1948	MGM	90

52 / LANE CHANDLER, continued

Title	Year	Studio	Page
BELLE STARR'S DAUGHTER (s) (C)	1948	20T	85
THE PALEFACE (s) (C)	1948	PAR	91
TULSA (s) (C)	1949	EL	90
RIDERS OF THE WHISTLING PINES (s)	1949	COL	70
AMBUSH (s)	1950	MGM	89
MONTANA (s) (C)	1950	WB	76
OUTCASTS OF BLACK MESA (aka THE CLUE) (s)	1950	COL	54
JIGGS AND MAGGIE OUT WEST (s)	1950	MON	66
PRAIRIE ROUNDUP (s)	1951	COL	53
SANTA FE (s) (C)	1951	COL	89
ALONG THE GREAT DIVIDE (s)	1951	WB	88
CATTLE QUEEN (aka QUEEN OF THE WEST) (s)	1951	UA	72
THE HAWK OF WILD RIVER (s)	1952	COL	54
THE BIG TREES (s) (C)	1952	WB	89
RANCHO NOTORIOUS (s) (C)	1952	RKO	89
THE LION AND THE HORSE (s) (C)	1952	WB	83
THE SAN FRANCISCO STORY (s)	1952	WB	80
THE LUSTY MEN (s)	1952	RKO	113
COW COUNTRY (s)	1953	AA	82
TAKE ME TO TOWN (s) (C)	1953	UI	81
THE CHARGE AT FEATHER RIVER (s) (C)	1953	WB	96
CALAMITY JANE (s) (C)	1953	WB	101
THUNDER OVER THE PLAINS (s) (C)	1953	WB	82
BORDER RIVER (s) (C)	1954	UI	81
THE COMMAND (s) (C)	1954	WB	88
SILVER LODE (s) (C)	1954	RKO	80
SHOTGUN (s) (C)	1955	AA	80
TALL MAN RIDING (s) (C)	1955	WB	83
APACHE AMBUSH (s)	1955	COL	68
THE INDIAN FIGHTER (s) (C)	1955	UA	88
THE LONE RANGER (s) (C)	1956	WB	86
GREAT DAY IN THE MORNING (s) (C)	1956	RKO	92
THE FIRST TEXAN (s) (C)	1956	AA	82
THE FIRST TRAVELING SALESLADY (s) (C)	1956	RKO	92
THE STORM RIDER (s)	1957	20T	70
QUANTRILL'S RAIDERS (s) (C)	1958	AA	75
NOOSE FOR A GUNMAN (s)	1960	UA	69
LITTLE SHEPHERD OF KINGDOM COME (s) (C)	1961	20T	108
REQUIEM FOR A GUNFIGHTER (s) (C)	1965	EMB	91
ONE MORE TRAIN TO ROB (s) (C)	1971	UNI	108

MICHAEL CHAPIN (1936 -   )

He did outstanding support work while a young juvenile, especially with UNDER CALIFORNIA STARS as the crippled boy needing a leg operation, and headed the *Rough-Ridin' Kids* series for Republic Pictures (1951-52). Gary Cooper's son in SPRINGFIELD RIFLE.

Title	Year	Studio	Page
SONG OF ARIZONA (s)	1946	REP	68
UNDER CALIFORNIA STARS (C)	1948	REP	70
(aka UNDER CALIFORNIA SKIES) (s)			
BUCKAROO SHERIFF OF TEXAS	1951	REP	60
(starts *Rough-Ridin' Kids* series)			
WELLS FARGO GUNMASTER (non-series) (s)	1951	REP	60
THE DAKOTA KID	1951	REP	60

ARIZONA MANHUNT .... 1951 ... REP .... 60 ____
WILD HORSE AMBUSH .... 1952 ... REP .... 54 ____
  (ends *Rough-Ridin' Kids* series)
WAGONS WEST (s) .... (C) .. 1952 ... MON .... 70 ____
SPRINGFIELD RIFLE (s) .... (C) .. 1952 ... WB .... 93 ____

THE CISCO KID series (1929; 1931; 1939 - 1941; 1945 - 1947; 1949 - 1950)
The author O. Henry's famous "Robin Hood of the Old West" caballero was extremely happy and carefree. He loved to romance and dazzle beautiful senoritas with unending charm when his energies weren't diverted into capturing desperadoes. Warner Baxter, Cesar Romero, Gilbert Roland, and Duncan Renaldo each did the role with the latter carrying it into TV for six years (1950-56).

(WARNER BAXTER)
IN OLD ARIZONA .... 1929 ... FOX .... 95 ____

(WARNER BAXTER, CHRIS-PIN MARTIN)
THE CISCO KID .... 1931 ... FOX .... 61 ____
THE RETURN OF THE CISCO KID .... 1939 ... 20T .... 70 ____

(CESAR ROMERO, CHRIS-PIN MARTIN)
THE CISCO KID AND THE LADY .... 1939 ... 20T .... 73 ____
VIVA CISCO KID .... 1940 ... 20T .... 70 ____
LUCKY CISCO KID .... 1940 ... 20T .... 68 ____
THE GAY CABALLERO .... 1940 ... 20T .... 57 ____
ROMANCE OF THE RIO GRANDE .... 1941 ... 20T .... 73 ____
RIDE ON VAQUERO .... 1941 ... 20T .... 64 ____

(DUNCAN RENALDO, MARTIN GARRALAGA)
THE CISCO KID RETURNS .... 1945 ... MON .... 64 ____
IN OLD NEW MEXICO .... 1945 ... MON .... 62 ____
SOUTH OF THE RIO GRANDE .... 1945 ... MON .... 62 ____

(GILBERT ROLAND, MARTIN GARRALAGA)
THE GAY CAVALIER .... 1946 ... MON .... 65 ____
SOUTH OF MONTEREY .... 1946 ... MON .... 63 ____
BEAUTY AND THE BANDIT .... 1946 ... MON .... 77 ____
RIDING THE CALIFORNIA TRAIL .... 1947 ... MON .... 59 ____

(GILBERT ROLAND, CHRIS-PIN MARTIN)
ROBIN HOOD OF MONTEREY .... 1947 ... MON .... 55 ____
KING OF THE BANDITS .... 1947 ... MON .... 66 ____

(DUNCAN RENALDO, LEO CARRILLO)
VALIANT HOMBRE .... 1949 ... UA .... 60 ____
THE GAY AMIGO .... 1949 ... UA .... 62 ____
THE DARING CABALLERO .... 1949 ... UA .... 60 ____
SATAN'S CRADLE .... 1949 ... UA .... 60 ____
THE GIRL FROM SAN LORENZO .... 1950 ... UA .... 59 ____

DANE CLARK (1915 -   )

A tough guy leading man of the 1940s-1950s, primarily with Warner Brothers, who made only a few westerns when branching away from movie dramas.

TENNESSEE JOHNSON		1942	MGM 100-103
(aka THE MAN ON AMERICA'S CONSCIENCE) (s)			
DEEP VALLEY		1947	WB 104
BARRICADE	(C)	1950	WB 75
FORT DEFIANCE	(C)	1951	UA 81
THUNDER PASS		1954	LIP 76-80
MASSACRE	(C)	1956	20T 76
OUTLAW'S SON		1957	UA 87
THE McMASTERS	(C)	1970	CHE 89-97
(aka THE BLOOD CROWD) (s)			

JAMES COBURN (1928 -   )

A tall, lean, cool actor whose knife-throwing gunfighter in THE MAGNIFICENT SEVEN helped elevate him to stardom. Coburn was a participant in "Klondike" on NBC-TV (1960-61) for 18 half-hour episodes. Great in WATERHOLE #3.

RIDE LONESOME (s)	(C)	1959	COL 73
FACE OF A FUGITIVE (s)	(C)	1959	COL 81
THE MAGNIFICENT SEVEN (s)	(C)	1960	UA 125-126
THE MAN FROM GALVESTON (cs)	(C)	1964	WB 57
MAJOR DUNDEE (s)	(C)	1965	COL 124
WATERHOLE #3	(C)	1967	PAR 95-100
THE HONKERS	(C)	1972	UA 101-110
A FISTFUL OF DYNAMITE	(C)	1972	UA 121-158
(aka DUCK YOU SUCKER)			
PAT GARRETT AND BILLY THE KID	(C)	1973	MGM 106-122
A REASON TO LIVE, A REASON TO DIE	(C)	1974	KTI 92
(aka MASSACRE AT FORT HOLMAN)			
BITE THE BULLET (cs)	(C)	1975	COL 131
THE LAST HARD MEN	(C)	1976	20T 103
DRAW!	(C)	1984	HBO-TV 98
YOUNG GUNS II (s)	(C)	1990	20T 109

STEVE COCHRAN (1917 - 1965)

He was a rugged star with Warner Brothers in the early 1950s who had to be rated tops for THE LION AND THE HORSE. Cochran's tender concern for young child actress Sherry Jackson shines through in this spirited "A" outdoor drama.

THE GAY SENORITA (s)		1946	COL 69
DALLAS (cs)	(C)	1950	WB 94
RATON PASS (aka CANYON PASS)		1951	WB 84
JIM THORPE—ALL AMERICAN		1951	WB 107
(aka MAN OF BRONZE) (cs)			
THE LION AND THE HORSE	(C)	1952	WB 83
SHARK RIVER	(C)	1953	UA 80
BACK TO GOD'S COUNTRY	(C)	1953	UI 78
QUANTRILL'S RAIDERS	(C)	1958	AA 75
THE DEADLY COMPANIONS	(C)	1961	PAT 90
(aka TRIGGER HAPPY) (cs)			

BILL CODY (1891 - 1948)
He starred in a minor series of low budgeters for Monogram and Spectrum through 1936. Cody's son, Bill, Jr., made numerous appearances.

UNDER TEXAS SKIES	1930	SYN	57
DUGAN OF THE BADLANDS	1931	MON	60
THE MONTANA KID	1931	MON	60
OKLAHOMA JIM	1931	MON	60
LAND OF WANTED MEN	1931	MON	62
GHOST CITY	1932	MON	60
MASON OF THE MOUNTED	1932	MON	58
LAW OF THE NORTH	1932	MON	55
TEXAS PIONEERS (aka THE BLOOD BROTHER)	1932	MON	58
FRONTIER DAYS	1934	SPE	61
THE BORDER MENACE	1934	AYW	55
BORDER GUNS	1934	AYW	55
SIX GUN JUSTICE	1935	SPE	57
THE CYCLONE RANGER	1935	SPE	60
THE TEXAS RAMBLER	1935	SPE	59
THE VANISHING RIDERS	1935	SPE	58
LAWLESS BORDERS (aka BORDER PATROL)	1935	SPE	58
THE RECKLESS BUCKAROO	1935	CRE	57
WESTERN RACKETEERS	1935	AYW	48
BLAZING JUSTICE	1936	SPE	60
OUTLAWS OF THE RANGE	1936	SPE	59
STAGECOACH (s)	1939	UA	96
THE FIGHTING GRINGO (s)	1939	RKO	59

CHUCK CONNORS (1921 - 1992)
A former baseball star whose athletic build and ability made him a good lead for westerns. Better known as rancher Lucas McCain of the hit ABC television series "The Rifleman" (1958-63) with 168 half-hour shows. Connors headed the abbreviated "Branded" for NBC-TV in 1966.

NAKED ALIBI (s)		1954...UI	86
THE HIRED GUN (s)		1957...MGM	63-64
TOMAHAWK TRAIL (aka MARK OF THE APACHE)		1957...UA	60
OLD YELLER (s)	(C)	1958...BV	83
THE BIG COUNTRY (s)	(C)	1958...UA	166
GERONIMO	(C)	1962...UA	101
RIDE BEYOND VENGEANCE	(C)	1966...COL	95
(aka THE NIGHT OF THE TIGER)			
KILL THEM ALL AND COME BACK HOME	(C)	1970...FAN	93-98
(aka KILL THEM ALL AND COME BACK ALONE)			
THE DESERTER (aka RIDE TO GLORY) (cs)	(C)	1970...PAR	99
SUPPORT YOUR LOCAL GUNFIGHTER (s)	(C)	1971...UA	92
THE PROUD AND THE DAMNED	(C)	1972...COL	94-97
(aka PROUD, DAMNED AND DEAD)			
PANCHO VILLA (s)	(C)	1973...SI	92
BANJO HACKETT: ROAMIN' FREE (s)	(C)	1976...COL-TV	100
STANDING TALL (s)	(C)	1978...QMP-TV	100
THE CAPTURE OF GRIZZLY ADAMS (cs)	(C)	1982...NBC-TV	100
ONCE UPON A TEXAS TRAIN	(C)	1988...CBS-TV	100
(aka TEXAS GUNS) (s)			

CHUCK CONNORS, continued

HIGH DESERT KILL	(C) .. 1989 ... USA-TV .. 100		
THE GAMBLER, PART IV— THE LUCK OF THE DRAW (gs)	(C) .. 1991 ... NBC-TV .. 200		

ROBERT CONRAD (1935 -   )

He was the best action star of any TV western series when it came to staging those outstanding fight scenes in the superior "Wild Wild West" (1965-69) during 104 hour-long shows for CBS. Conrad reprised his James West role for two TV feature movies in 1979 and 1980.

THE LAST DAY (cs)	(C) .. 1975 ... PAR-TV .. 100	
THE BANDITS	(C) .. 1979 ... CZ 89	
THE WILD WILD WEST REVISITED	(C) .. 1979 ... CBS-TV .. 100	
MORE WILD WILD WEST	(C) .. 1980 ... CBS-TV .. 100	
CROSSFIRE	(C) .. 1986 ... ACA 82	
HIGH MOUNTAIN RANGERS	(C) .. 1987 ... CBS-TV .. 100	

GARY COOPER (1901 - 1961)

Superstar of the 1930s-1950s who made one of the earliest sound westerns, THE VIRGINIAN, in 1929 and continued as the major "A" genre film star throughout his career. In 1952 Gary won his second Oscar in a western role for HIGH NOON. Just before dying in 1961, Cooper was awarded a third Oscar for his contributions to the film industry. This Montanan became a true "man of the west."

WOLF SONG	1929 ... PAR 70-80	
THE VIRGINIAN	1929 ... PAR 90	
ONLY THE BRAVE	1930 ... PAR 71	
THE TEXAN	1930 ... PAR 71-79	
THE SPOILERS	1930 ... PAR 81	
FIGHTING CARAVANS (aka BLAZING ARROWS)	1931 ... PAR 91	
I TAKE THIS WOMAN	1931 ... PAR 74	
OPERATOR 13	1934 ... MGM 86	
THE PLAINSMAN	1937 ... PAR . 113-115	
THE COWBOY AND THE LADY	1938 ... UA 90-91	
THE WESTERNER	1940 ... UA 99-100	
NORTH WEST MOUNTED POLICE	(C) .. 1940 ... PAR 125	
ALONG CAME JONES	1945 ... RKO 90	
SARATOGA TRUNK	1946 ... WB 135	
UNCONQUERED	(C) .. 1948 ... PAR . 146-147	
BRIGHT LEAF	1950 ... WB 110	
DALLAS	(C) .. 1950 ... WB 94	
DISTANT DRUMS	(C) .. 1951 ... WB 101	
IT'S A BIG COUNTRY (cs)	1952 ... MGM 89	
HIGH NOON	1952 ... UA 85	
SPRINGFIELD RIFLE	(C) .. 1952 ... WB 93	
BLOWING WILD	1953 ... WB 90	
GARDEN OF EVIL	(C) .. 1954 ... 20T 100	
VERA CRUZ	(C) .. 1954 ... UA 94	
FRIENDLY PERSUASION	(C) .. 1956 ... AA ... 137-140	
MAN OF THE WEST	(C) .. 1958 ... UA 100	
THE HANGING TREE	(C) .. 1959 ... WB 106	
ALIAS JESSE JAMES (gs)	(C) .. 1959 ... UA 92	
THEY CAME TO CORDURA	(C) .. 1959 ... COL 123	

WENDELL COREY (1914 - 1968)
A sophisticated Paramount comedy and drama lead who held his own in a number of sporadic starring roles with "A" westerns through the 1960s.

DESERT FURY (s)	(C)	1947	PAR	95
THE FURIES (cs)		1950	PAR	109
THE GREAT MISSOURI RAID	(C)	1951	PAR	85
THE WILD NORTH (aka THE BIG NORTH) (cs)(C)		1952	MGM	97
THE RAINMAKER (cs)	(C)	1957	PAR	121
THE LIGHT IN THE FOREST (s)	(C)	1958	BV	93
ALIAS JESSE JAMES (cs)	(C)	1959	UA	92
BLOOD ON THE ARROW (cs)	(C)	1964	AA	91
WACO (s)	(C)	1966	PAR	85
RED TOMAHAWK (s)	(C)	1967	PAR	82
BUCKSKIN (cs)	(C)	1968	PAR	97

JOSEPH COTTEN (1905 -   )
Soft-spoken, Virginia born actor who was better known with his dramatic roles made for Orson Welles and Alfred Hitchcock than performing western parts.

DUEL IN THE SUN	(C)	1947	SEL	130-138
BEYOND THE FOREST		1949	WB	96
TWO FLAGS WEST		1950	20T	92
UNTAMED FRONTIER	(C)	1952	UI	75
THE BOTTOM OF THE BOTTLE	(C)	1956	20T	88
THE HALLIDAY BRAND		1957	UA	77-79
TOUCH OF EVIL (s)		1958	UI	95-105
THE LAST SUNSET (s)	(C)	1961	UI	112
THE GREAT SIOUX MASSACRE	(C)	1965	COL	91
(aka CUSTER MASSACRE; THE MASSACRE AT THE ROSEBUD)				
THE TRAMPLERS (aka SHOW DOWN)	(C)	1966	EMB	90-105
THE HELLBENDERS	(C)	1967	EMB	92
BRIGHTY OF THE GRAND CANYON	(C)	1967	FFC	89-92
WHITE COMANCHE	(C)	1968	IPC	90
CUTTER'S TRAIL (cs)	(C)	1970	CBS-TV	100
CARAVAN (s)	(C)	1978	UNI	123
HEAVEN'S GATE (s)	(C)	1980	UA	149

BUSTER CRABBE (1908 - 1983)
(aka LARRY "BUSTER" CRABBE)
He is known best as Universal's "Flash Gordon" and "Buck Rogers" in those late 1930s serials, but did western film star work with PRC's very low-budgeted *Billy the Kid / Billy Carson* series (1941-46). Crabbe was a Top Money-Making Western Star in 1936.

MAN OF THE FOREST (s)	1933	PAR	63
TO THE LAST MAN (aka LAW OF VENGEANCE) (s)	1933	PAR	70
THE THUNDERING HERD	1933	PAR	59
(aka BUFFALO STAMPEDE; IN THE DAYS OF THE THUNDERING HERD) (s)			
THE WANDERER OF THE WASTELAND	1935	PAR	62-66
NEVADA	1935	PAR	59-60
DRIFT FENCE (aka TEXAS DESPERADOES)	1936	PAR	56
DESERT GOLD	1936	PAR	58

58 / BUSTER CRABBE, continued

Title	Year	Studio	Page
THE ARIZONA RAIDERS	1936	PAR	58
ARIZONA MAHONEY	1936	PAR	58
FORLORN RIVER	1937	PAR	56
COLORADO SUNSET (s)	1939	REP	64
BILLY THE KID WANTED	1941	PRC	64
(starts *Billy the Kid* series for PRC)			
BILLY THE KID'S ROUND-UP	1941	PRC	58
BILLY THE KID TRAPPED	1942	PRC	58
BILLY THE KID'S SMOKING GUNS	1942	PRC	58
LAW AND ORDER	1942	PRC	56-58
THE MYSTERIOUS RIDER	1942	PRC	56
WILDCAT (cs)	1942	PAR	70-75
SHERIFF OF SAGE VALLEY	1942	PRC	60
(aka BILLY THE KID, SHERIFF OF SAGE VALLEY)			
THE KID RIDES AGAIN	1943	PRC	60
FUGITIVE OF THE PLAINS	1943	PRC	57
WESTERN CYCLONE	1943	PRC	56
THE RENEGADES	1943	PRC	58
CATTLE STAMPEDE	1943	PRC	58-60
BLAZING FRONTIER (ends *Billy the Kid* series)	1943	PRC	59
THE DEVIL RIDERS (starts *Billy Carson* series)	1943	PRC	58
THE DRIFTER	1943	PRC	60-62
FRONTIER OUTLAWS	1944	PRC	58
THUNDERING GUN SLINGERS	1944	PRC	60
VALLEY OF VENGEANCE (aka VENGEANCE)	1944	PRC	56-58
FUZZY SETTLES DOWN	1944	PRC	61
RUSTLERS' HIDEOUT	1944	PRC	60
WILD HORSE PHANTOM	1944	PRC	56
OATH OF VENGEANCE	1944	PRC	57
HIS BROTHER'S GHOST	1945	PRC	54
SHADOWS OF DEATH	1945	PRC	60
GANGSTER'S DEN	1945	PRC	55
STAGECOACH OUTLAWS	1945	PRC	59
BORDER BADMEN	1945	PRC	59
FIGHTING BILL CARSON	1945	PRC	51
PRAIRIE RUSTLERS	1945	PRC	56
LIGHTNING RAIDERS	1946	PRC	61
GHOST OF HIDDEN VALLEY	1946	PRC	56
GENTLEMEN WITH GUNS	1946	PRC	52
PRAIRIE BADMEN	1946	PRC	55
TERRORS ON HORSEBACK	1946	PRC	55
OVERLAND RIDERS	1946	PRC	54
OUTLAWS OF THE PLAINS (ends *Billy Carson* series)	1946	PRC	58
THE LAST OF THE REDMEN (C)	1947	COL	77
(aka LAST OF THE REDSKINS) (s)			
GUN BROTHERS	1956	UA	79
THE LAWLESS EIGHTIES	1957	REP	70
BADMAN'S COUNTRY	1958	WB	68
GUNFIGHTERS OF ABILENE	1960	UA	67
THE BOUNTY KILLER (s)	(C) 1965	EMB	92
ARIZONA RAIDERS (s)	(C) 1965	COL	88
THE COMEBACK TRAIL	(C) 1982	DER	76

JAMES CRAIG (1911 - 1985)
An outdoor leading man known for his western roles in the 1940s-1950s. A distinctive voice added to Craig's characterizations.

Title	Year	Studio	Pages
THUNDER TRAIL (aka THUNDER PASS; ARIZONA AMES)	1937	PAR	56
BORN TO THE WEST (aka HELL TOWN) (s)	1937	PAR	66
PRIDE OF THE WEST (s)	1938	PAR	55
OVERLAND WITH KIT CARSON (s) (SER)	1939	COL	15CH
THE TAMING OF THE WEST (s)	1939	COL	55
TWO-FISTED RANGERS (s)	1940	COL	62
WINNERS OF THE WEST (cs) (SER)	1940	UNI	13CH
LAW AND ORDER (aka THE LAW) (s)	1940	UNI	57
VALLEY OF THE SUN	1942	RKO	79-84
THE OMAHA TRAIL	1942	MGM	62-64
NORTHWEST RANGERS	1942	MGM	64-69
GENTLE ANNIE	1944	MGM	80
BOYS' RANCH	1946	MGM	97
THE MAN FROM TEXAS	1947	EL	71
NORTHWEST STAMPEDE (C)	1948	EL	76-79
DRUMS IN THE DEEP SOUTH (C)	1951	RKO	87
FORT VENGEANCE (C)	1953	AA	75
LAST OF THE DESPERADOS	1956	ASC	70
MASSACRE (C)	1956	20T	76
SHOOT-OUT AT MEDICINE BEND (C)	1957	WB	87
THE PERSUADER	1957	AA	72
NAKED IN THE SUN (C)	1957	AA	78
MAN OR GUN (cs)	1958	REP	79
FOUR FAST GUNS	1960	UI	72
FORT UTAH (s) (C)	1967	PAR	83
HOSTILE GUNS (s) (C)	1967	PAR	91
ARIZONA BUSHWHACKERS (s) (C)	1968	PAR	86

BRODERICK CRAWFORD (1911 - 1986)
An aggressive leading man whose tough-guy roles made him known in all types of films. During the mid-1950s, he became a television star with the 30-minute "Highway Patrol" as Dan Matthews who verbally barked orders to subordinates.

Title	Year	Studio	Pages
WHEN THE DALTONS RODE (s)	1940	UNI	80
TRAIL OF THE VIGILANTES (cs)	1940	UNI	75
TEXAS RANGERS RIDE AGAIN (s)	1940	PAR	67
BADLANDS OF DAKOTA (s)	1941	UNI	74
NORTH TO THE KLONDIKE	1942	UNI	58-60
MEN OF TEXAS (aka MEN OF DESTINY)	1942	UNI	82-87
SIN TOWN	1942	UNI	74-75
BAD MEN OF TOMBSTONE (cs)	1949	AA	75
LONE STAR (cs)	1952	MGM	90-94
LAST OF THE COMANCHES (C) (aka THE SABRE AND THE ARROW)	1953	COL	85
THE LAST POSSE	1953	COL	73-84
THE FASTEST GUN ALIVE (cs)	1956	MGM	92
MUTINY AT FORT SHARP (C)	1966	WME	90-91
KID RODELO (cs)	1966	PAR	91
THE TEXICAN (aka THE TEXAS KID) (C)	1966	COL	91
RED TOMAHAWK (cs) (C)	1967	PAR	82

KEN CURTIS (1916 - 1991)

Starting out as star of a Columbia Pictures "B" musical western series in the mid-1940s, Curtis became a member of The Sons of the Pioneers with his rich, melodious voice and did a variety of character parts in "A" oaters until landing the famed role of crusty deputy Festus Hagen in the "Gunsmoke" CBS-TV show (1964-75).

Title	Year	Studio	Page
SWING IN THE SADDLE (aka SWING AND SWAY)	1944	COL	69
RHYTHM ROUND-UP (aka HONEST JOHN)	1945	COL	66-68
SONG OF THE PRAIRIE (aka SENTIMENT AND SONG)	1945	COL	69
THROW A SADDLE ON A STAR	1946	COL	65
THAT TEXAS JAMBOREE (aka MEDICINE MAN)	1946	COL	67
COWBOY BLUES (aka BENEATH THE STARRY SKIES)	1946	COL	65
SINGING ON THE TRAIL (aka LOOKIN' FOR SOMEONE)	1946	COL	69
LONE STAR MOONLIGHT (aka AMONGST THE THIEVES)	1946	COL	67
OVER THE SANTA FE TRAIL (aka NO ESCAPE)	1947	COL	63
RIDERS OF THE PONY EXPRESS (C)	1949	KSC	60
STALLION CANYON (C)	1949	KSC	72
CALL OF THE FOREST	1949	LIP	74
EVERYBODY'S DANCIN'! (s)	1950	LIP	65
RIO GRANDE (s)	1950	REP	105
DON DAREDEVIL RIDES AGAIN (SER)	1951	REP	12CH
THE SEARCHERS (s) (C)	1956	WB	119
THE MISSOURI TRAVELER (s) (C)	1958	BV	103
ESCORT WEST (s)	1959	UA	75
THE YOUNG LAND (s) (C)	1959	COL	89
THE HORSE SOLDIERS (s) (C)	1959	UA	119
THE ALAMO (s) (C)	1960	UA	190
FRECKLES (s) (C)	1960	20T	84
TWO RODE TOGETHER (s) (C)	1961	COL	91-109
HOW THE WEST WAS WON (s) (C)	1963	MGM	155-165
CHEYENNE AUTUMN (s) (C)	1964	WB	145-160
PONY EXPRESS RIDER (s) (C)	1976	DD	100
ONCE UPON A STARRY NIGHT (s) (C)	1978	TVM	78
LEGEND OF THE WILD (s) (C)	1981	JFP	93
CALIFORNIA GOLD RUSH (s) (C)	1981	NBC-TV	100
ONCE UPON A TEXAS TRAIN (aka TEXAS GUNS) (s) (C)	1988	CBS-TV	100
CONAGHER (s) (C)	1991	TNT-TV	116

BOB CUSTER (1898 - 1974)

He starred in a series of independent westerns through the mid-1930s following success as an FBO silent movie cowboy 10 years earlier. Retired in 1938 to work for the city of Los Angeles.

Title	Year	Studio	Page
RIDERS OF THE RIO GRANDE	1929	SYN	54-59
CODE OF THE WEST	1929	SYN	57
COVERED WAGON TRAILS	1930	SYN	51
PARTING OF THE TRAILS	1930	SYN	60
UNDER TEXAS SKIES	1930	SYN	57
O'MALLEY RIDES ALONE	1930	SYN	57

BOB CUSTER, continued / 61

RIDERS OF THE NORTH	1931	SYN	59 ____
SON OF THE PLAINS (aka VULTURES OF THE LAW)	1931	SYN	60 ____
LAW OF THE RIO GRANDE	1931	SYN	58 ____
HEADIN' FOR TROUBLE	1931	B4	60 ____
QUICK TRIGGER LEE	1931	B4	60 ____
MARK OF THE SPUR	1932	B4	58 ____
SCARLET BRAND	1932	B4	58 ____
THE LAW OF THE WILD (SER)	1934	MAS	12CH ____
AMBUSH VALLEY	1936	REL	56 ____
VENGEANCE OF RANNAH	1936	REL	59 ____
SANTA FE RIDES	1937	REL	58 ____

JIM DAVIS (1915 - 1981)

A tall, tough guy who began in western films as an outlaw type—a marvelous meany with HELLFIRE and SILVER CANYON—but who developed into a leading man during the 1950s. Late in his career, Jim achieved his greatest fame on television as the elder Ewing on the CBS series "Dallas" before having an untimely death. Davis earlier starred in Republic's 30-minute 1954-55 TV series "Stories of the Century" (39 shows) and during 1974, had 13 half-hour episodes of "The Cowboys" for ABC-TV.

TENNESSEE JOHNSON (s)		1942	MGM	100-103 ____
(aka THE MAN ON AMERICA'S CONSCIENCE)				
THE ROMANCE OF ROSY RIDGE (s)		1947	MGM	105 ____
THE FABULOUS TEXAN (s)		1947	REP	98 ____
RED STALLION IN THE ROCKIES (s)	(C)	1949	EL	85 ____
HELLFIRE (s)	(C)	1949	REP	90 ____
BRIMSTONE (s)	(C)	1949	REP	90 ____
THE SAVAGE HORDE (s)		1950	REP	90 ____
THE CARIBOO TRAIL (s)	(C)	1950	20T	81 ____
THE SHOWDOWN (s)		1950	REP	86 ____
CALIFORNIA PASSAGE (s)		1950	REP	90 ____
3 DESPERATE MEN		1951	LIP	69 ____
OH! SUSANNA (s)	(C)	1951	REP	90 ____
CAVALRY SCOUT (cs)	(C)	1951	MON	78 ____
LITTLE BIG HORN		1951	LIP	85 ____
(aka THE FIGHTING SEVENTH) (s)				
SILVER CANYON (s)		1951	COL	70 ____
ROSE OF CIMARRON (s)	(C)	1952	20T	72 ____
THE BIG SKY (s)		1952	RKO	122 ____
WOMAN OF THE NORTH COUNTRY (s)	(C)	1952	REP	90 ____
THE BLAZING FOREST (s)	(C)	1952	PAR	90 ____
RIDE THE MAN DOWN (s)	(C)	1953	REP	90 ____
WOMAN THEY ALMOST LYNCHED (s)		1953	REP	90 ____
THE PRESIDENT'S LADY (s)		1953	20T	96 ____
JUBILEE TRAIL (s)	(C)	1954	REP	103 ____
THE OUTCAST (cs)	(C)	1954	REP	90 ____
HELL'S OUTPOST (s)		1954	REP	90 ____
THE OUTLAW'S DAUGHTER	(C)	1954	20T	75 ____
TIMBERJACK (s)	(C)	1955	REP	92-96 ____
THE LAST COMMAND (s)	(C)	1955	REP	110 ____
THE VANISHING AMERICAN (s)		1955	REP	90 ____
LAST OF THE DESPERADOS		1955	ASC	80 ____
THE BOTTOM OF THE BOTTLE (s)	(C)	1956	20T	88 ____
THE WILD DAKOTAS (cs)		1956	ASC	73 ____

62 / JIM DAVIS, continued

THE MAVERICK QUEEN (s)	(C)	1956...REP	90-92
FRONTIER GAMBLER (s)		1956...ASC	70
THE QUIET GUN (cs)		1957...20T	77-79
DUEL AT APACHE WELLS (s)		1957...REP	70
THE BADGE OF MARSHAL BRENNAN		1957...AA	74
THE RESTLESS BREED (s)	(C)	1957...20T	81-86
LAST STAGECOACH WEST		1957...REP	67-70
APACHE WARRIOR		1957...20T	73
GUNS DON'T ARGUE		1957...VIS	90
RAIDERS OF OLD CALIFORNIA		1957...REP	72
TOUGHEST GUN IN TOMBSTONE (s)		1958...UA	72
WOLF DOG		1958...20T	61-69
FLAMING FRONTIER (cs)		1958...20T	70
ALIAS JESSE JAMES (s)	(C)	1959...UA	92
NOOSE FOR A GUNMAN		1960...UA	69
LUST TO KILL		1960...BIE	69
FRONTIER UPRISING		1961...UA	60
THE GAMBLER WORE A GUN		1961...UA	66
JESSE JAMES VS. FRANKENSTEIN'S DAUGHTER (s)	(C)	1966...EMB	82
EL DORADO (s)	(C)	1967...PAR	126
FORT UTAH (s)	(C)	1967...PAR	83
HONDO AND THE APACHES (s)	(C)	1967...MGM	85
THEY RAN FOR THEIR LIVES (s)	(C)	1969...CV	92
GUN RIDERS (aka FIVE BLOODY GRAVES; LONELY MAN; FIVE BLOODY GRAVES TO TOMBSTONE) (s)	(C)	1970...II	98
MONTE WALSH (s)	(C)	1970...NG	95-98
RIO LOBO (s)	(C)	1970...NG	110
BIG JAKE (s)	(C)	1971...NG	110
THE TRACKERS (s)	(C)	1971...ASP-TV	90
THE HONKERS (s)	(C)	1972...UA	102-110
BAD COMPANY (cs)	(C)	1972...PAR	93
DELIVER US FROM EVIL (s)	(C)	1973...ABC-TV	78
ONE LITTLE INDIAN (s)	(C)	1973...BV	90
LAW OF THE LAND (aka THE DEPUTIES)	(C)	1976...QMP-TV	120
COMES A HORSEMAN (s)	(C)	1978...UA	118

EDDIE DEAN (1907 -)

In "B" western support parts for seven years until PRC signed him in 1945 for a starring oatuner series, Dean made five of them in Cinecolor—the best being WILD WEST—before filming ended in late 1947. Eddie was a Top Money-Making Western Star (1946-47) and is still the No. 1 singing cowboy today with his magnificent voice that never waivers. Has guested at several film conventions.

WESTERN JAMBOREE (s)		1938...REP	56
THE LONE RANGER RIDES AGAIN (s)	(SER)	1939...REP	15CH
THE RENEGADE TRAIL (s)		1939...PAR	58
RANGE WAR (s)		1939...PAR	66
LAW OF THE PAMPAS (s)		1939...PAR	74
THE LLANO KID (s)		1939...PAR	70
SANTA FE MARSHAL (s)		1940...PAR	68
KNIGHTS OF THE RANGE (s)		1940...PAR	70
THE SHOWDOWN (s)		1940...PAR	63
THE LIGHT OF WESTERN STARS (s)		1940...PAR	67

EDDIE DEAN, continued

HIDDEN GOLD (s)	1940	PAR	67
THE GOLDEN TRAIL (aka GOLD TRAIL) (s)	1940	MON	52
STAGECOACH WAR (s)	1940	PAR	63
OKLAHOMA RENEGADES (s)	1940	REP	57
ROLLING HOME TO TEXAS (aka RIDIN' HOME TO TEXAS) (s)	1940	MON	62
THE TRAIL OF THE SILVER SPURS (s)	1940	MON	58
PALS OF THE PECOS (s)	1941	REP	56
KANSAS CYCLONE (s)	1941	REP	58
SUNSET IN WYOMING (s)	1941	REP	65
OUTLAWS OF CHEROKEE TRAIL (s)	1941	REP	56
DOWN MEXICO WAY (s)	1941	REP	78
GAUCHOS OF ELDORADO (s)	1941	REP	56
SIERRA SUE (s)	1941	REP	64
WEST OF CIMARRON (s)	1941	REP	56
THE LONE RIDER AND THE BANDIT (s)	1942	PRC	54
RAIDERS OF THE WEST (s)	1942	PRC	64
STAGECOACH EXPRESS (s)	1942	REP	57
FIGHTING BILL FARGO (s)	1942	UNI	57
ARIZONA STAGECOACH (s)	1942	MON	58
KING OF THE COWBOYS (s)	1943	REP	67
HARMONY TRAIL (aka THE WHITE STALLION)	1944	MAT	58
WILDFIRE (C) (aka WILDFIRE: THE STORY OF A HORSE) (s)	1945	SG	60
SONG OF OLD WYOMING (C)	1945	PRC	65
ROMANCE OF THE WEST (C)	1946	PRC	57
THE CARAVAN TRAIL (C)	1946	PRC	58
COLORADO SERENADE (C)	1946	PRC	68
DRIFTIN' RIVER	1946	PRC	59
DOWN MISSOURI WAY (cs)	1946	PRC	75
TUMBLEWEED TRAIL	1946	PRC	58
STARS OVER TEXAS	1946	PRC	57-59
WILD WEST (C)	1946	PRC	73
WILD COUNTRY	1947	PRC	55-57
RANGE BEYOND THE BLUE	1947	PRC	53
WEST TO GLORY	1947	PRC	61
SHADOW VALLEY	1947	EL	58
BLACK HILLS	1947	EL	60
CHECK YOUR GUNS	1948	EL	55
TORNADO RANGE	1948	EL	56
THE WESTWARD TRAIL	1948	EL	58
THE HAWK OF POWDER RIVER	1948	EL	54
PRAIRIE OUTLAWS	1948	EL	58
THE TIOGA KID	1948	EL	54

YVONNE DE CARLO (1922 -   )

A Canadian-born actress who played fiery-tempered saloon girls, female outlaws, and glamorous women in films like SALOME, WHERE SHE DANCED, BLACK BART, and CALAMITY JANE AND SAM BASS.

DEERSLAYER (s)	1943	REP	67
SALOME, WHERE SHE DANCED (C)	1945	UNI	90
FRONTIER GAL (C) (aka THE BRIDE WASN'T WILLING)	1945	UNI	84-85

64 / YVONNE DE CARLO, continued

BLACK BART	(C)	1948...UI	80-88
(aka BLACK BART HIGHWAYMAN)			
RIVER LADY	(C)	1948...UI	78
CALAMITY JANE AND SAM BASS	(C)	1949...UI	85
THE GAL WHO TOOK THE WEST	(C)	1949...UI	84
TOMAHAWK (aka BATTLE OF POWDER RIVER)	(C)	1951...UI	82
SILVER CITY (aka HIGH VERMILION)	(C)	1951...PAR	90
THE SAN FRANCISCO STORY		1952...WB	80
SCARLET ANGEL	(C)	1952...UI	81
SOMBRERO (s)	(C)	1953...MGM	103
PASSION	(C)	1954...RKO	84
BORDER RIVER	(C)	1954...UI	81
SHOTGUN	(C)	1955...AA	80
RAW EDGE	(C)	1956...UI	76
McLINTOCK! (cs)	(C)	1963...UA	122
LAW OF THE LAWLESS	(C)	1964...PAR	87
(aka INVITATION TO A HANGING)			
HOSTILE GUNS	(C)	1967...PAR	91
ARIZONA BUSHWHACKERS	(C)	1968...PAR	86
THE MARK OF ZORRO (s)	(C)	1974...20T-TV	90
BLAZING STEWARDESSES	(C)	1975...II	85
(aka TEXAS LAYOVER)			

RICHARD DENNING (1914 -)

He appeared in numerous "B" dramas of the 1940s-1950s, along with several moderate-budgeted "A" westerns. Denning's greatest role was that of the governor on the superior "Hawaii Five-O" CBS-TV series (1968-80).

THE TEXANS (s)		1938...PAR	90
UNION PACIFIC (s)		1939...PAR	125
GERONIMO (s)		1940...PAR	90
NORTH WEST MOUNTED POLICE (s)	(C)	1940...PAR	125
DOUBLE DEAL		1950...RKO	65
SCARLET ANGEL (s)	(C)	1952...UI	81
HANGMAN'S KNOT (s)	(C)	1952...COL	84
BATTLE OF ROGUE RIVER	(C)	1954...COL	71
THE GUN THAT WON THE WEST (cs)	(C)	1955...COL	71
THE MAGNIFICENT MATADOR	(C)	1955...20T	94
(aka THE BRAVE AND THE BEAUTIFUL) (s)			
THE OKLAHOMA WOMAN		1956...ARC	72-80
THE BUCKSKIN LADY		1957...UA	66

JOHN DEREK (1926 -)

He starred in a number of tough "A" westerns for major studios during the 1950s, among them being Columbia's AMBUSH AT TOMAHAWK GAP and Republic's THE OUTCAST. Derek then participated in 39 hour-long episodes of "Frontier Circus" for CBS-TV (1961-62).

AMBUSH AT TOMAHAWK GAP	(C)	1953...COL	73
THE LAST POSSE		1953...COL	73
THE OUTCAST	(C)	1954...REP	90
RUN FOR COVER (cs)	(C)	1955...PAR	92

JOHN DEREK, continued / 65

MASSACRE AT SAND CREEK	1956	COL-TV	80
FURY AT SHOWDOWN	1957	UA	75
HIGH HELL	1958	PAR	87

EDDIE DEW (1909 - 1972)

He had brief stardom with Republic's *John Paul Revere* series (1943), but Dew's better success came as co-star with Rod Cameron in "B" westerns at Universal (1944-45). Eddie directed a number of the late 1950s "Sergeant Preston of the Yukon" 30-minute CBS-TV shows and WINGS OF CHANCE in 1961 with James Brown.

ARMY GIRL	1938	REP	80
(aka THE LAST OF THE CAVALRY) (s)			
CYCLONE ON HORSEBACK (s)	1941	RKO	60
SUNSET IN WYOMING (s)	1941	REP	65
BADLANDS OF DAKOTA (s)	1941	UNI	74
KING OF THE TEXAS RANGERS (s) (SER)	1941	REP	12CH
DUDE COWBOY (s)	1941	RKO	59
RIDING THE WIND (s)	1942	RKO	60
SHADOWS ON THE SAGE (s)	1942	REP	57
PIRATES OF THE PRAIRIE (s)	1942	RKO	57
FIGHTING FRONTIER (s)	1943	RKO	57
KING OF THE COWBOYS (s)	1943	REP	67
RED RIVER ROBIN HOOD (s)	1943	RKO	59
SIX-GUN GOSPEL (s)	1943	MON	55
BEYOND THE LAST FRONTIER	1943	REP	55
(starts *John Paul Revere* series)			
RAIDERS OF SUNSET PASS	1943	REP	56
(ends *John Paul Revere* series)			
TRIGGER TRAIL (cs)	1944	UNI	58
TRAIL TO GUNSIGHT	1944	UNI	57
RIDERS OF THE SANTA FE	1944	UNI	63
(aka MILE A MINUTE) (cs)			
THE OLD TEXAS TRAIL	1944	UNI	59
(aka STAGECOACH LINE) (cs)			
BEYOND THE PECOS (cs)	1945	UNI	59
RENEGADES OF THE RIO GRANDE	1945	UNI	56
(aka BANK ROBBERY) (cs)			
SCARLET ANGEL (s) (C)	1952	UI	81

RICHARD DIX (1894 - 1949)

A silent star who continued into sound films was the leading man of the only western film to this date to win an Oscar for best picture, CIMARRON. He made numerous westerns into the early 1940s, among them being MAN OF CONQUEST, Republic's first prestige "A" picture.

REDSKIN	1929	PAR	81
CIMARRON	1931	RKO	124
THE CONQUERORS (aka PIONEER BUILDERS)	1932	RKO	80-88
WEST OF THE PECOS	1935	RKO	68-69
THE ARIZONIAN	1935	RKO	75
YELLOW DUST	1936	RKO	68
MAN OF CONQUEST	1939	REP	97-105

66 / RICHARD DIX, continued

RENO	1939	RKO	70-73
CHEROKEE STRIP	1940	PAR	84-86
THE ROUND-UP	1941	PAR	90
BADLANDS OF DAKOTA	1941	UNI	74
TOMBSTONE, THE TOWN TOO TOUGH TO DIE	1942	PAR	79-80
AMERICAN EMPIRE (aka MY SON ALONE)	1942	UA	81-82
BUCKSKIN FRONTIER (aka THE IRON ROAD)	1943	UA	76
THE KANSAN	1943	UA	79

BRIAN DONLEVY (1901 - 1972)

A colorful character, he was better known for his villainous roles rather than as a western lead. Donlevy appeared in such banner year 1939 "A" westerns as JESSE JAMES, UNION PACIFIC, and DESTRY RIDES AGAIN.

BARBARY COAST (s)	1935	UA	90
IN OLD CHICAGO (s)	1938	20T	110
JESSE JAMES (s) (C)	1939	20T	105
UNION PACIFIC (s)	1939	PAR	125-135
ALLEGHENY UPRISING	1939	RKO	81
(aka THE FIRST REBEL; ALLEGHENY FRONTIER) (cs)			
DESTRY RIDES AGAIN (s)	1939	UNI	94
WHEN THE DALTONS RODE (cs)	1940	UNI	80
BRIGHAM YOUNG—FRONTIERSMAN	1940	20T	114
(aka BRIGHAM YOUNG) (s)			
BILLY THE KID (C)	1941	MGM	95
THE GREAT MAN'S LADY (cs)	1942	PAR	90
THE VIRGINIAN (C)	1946	PAR	86
CANYON PASSAGE (C)	1946	UNI	90
HEAVEN ONLY KNOWS (aka MONTANA MIKE)	1947	UA	95
A SOUTHERN YANKEE (aka MY HERO!)	1948	MGM	90
KANSAS RAIDERS (C)	1950	UI	80
SLAUGHTER TRAIL (C)	1951	RKO	78
RIDE THE MAN DOWN (C)	1953	REP	90
WOMAN THEY ALMOST LYNCHED (s)	1953	REP	90
ESCAPE FROM RED ROCK	1958	20T	75-79
COWBOY (s) (C)	1958	COL	92
WACO (cs) (C)	1966	PAR	85
HOSTILE GUNS (s) (C)	1967	PAR	91
ARIZONA BUSHWHACKERS (s) (C)	1968	PAR	86

KIRK DOUGLAS (1916 -   )

A major star who made numerous western films and co-starred in many others. Best remembered for his portrayal of the modern cowboy who comes afoul of the law in LONELY ARE THE BRAVE. Douglas is great as John Wayne's semi-crooked pal in THE WAR WAGON where he blends toughness and comedy with perfection.

OUT OF THE PAST (cs)	1947	RKO	97
ALONG THE GREAT DIVIDE	1951	WB	88
THE BIG TREES (C)	1952	WB	89
THE BIG SKY	1952	RKO	122-140
MAN WITHOUT A STAR (C)	1955	UI	88-89
THE INDIAN FIGHTER (C)	1955	UA	88

KIRK DOUGLAS, continued / 67

GUNFIGHT AT THE O.K. CORRAL	(C)..1957	...PAR	...122 ___
LAST TRAIN FROM GUN HILL	(C)..1959	...PAR	...94 ___
THE LAST SUNSET	(C)..1961	...UI	...112 ___
LONELY ARE THE BRAVE (aka LAST HERO)	1962	...UI	...107 ___
THE WAY WEST	(C)..1967	...UA	...122 ___
THE WAR WAGON	(C)..1967	...UNI	...101 ___
THERE WAS A CROOKED MAN	(C)..1970	...WB	..125-126 ___
A GUNFIGHT	(C)..1971	...PAR	...90 ___
SCALAWAG	(C)..1973	...PAR	...93 ___
POSSE	(C)..1975	...PAR	...94 ___
THE VILLAIN (aka CACTUS JACK)	(C)..1979	...COL	...83-89 ___
THE MAN FROM SNOWY RIVER	(C)..1982	...20T	...115 ___
DRAW!	(C)..1984	...HBO-TV	98-100 ___

HOWARD DUFF (1914 - 1990)
Good-looking stage actor who played shifty types often. He made only a few westerns. Duff's distinctive voice added to the genre.

RED CANYON	(C)..1949	...UI	...82 ___
CALAMITY JANE AND SAM BASS	(C)..1949	...UI	...85 ___
THE LADY FROM TEXAS	(C)..1951	...UI	...77-78 ___
THE YELLOW MOUNTAIN (s)	(C)..1954	...UI	...78 ___
BLACKJACK KETCHUM, DESPERADO	1956	...COL	...76 ___
THE BROKEN STAR	1956	...UA	...82 ___
SIERRA STRANGER	1957	...COL	...74-78 ___
THE WILD WOMEN OF CHASTITY GULCH (s) (C)..1982		...ABC-TV	..100 ___

THE DURANGO KID series (1940; 1945 - 1952)
Charles Starrett, Columbia Pictures' long-time action ace, helmed this "B" western series involving a fast-shooting masked Robin Hood dressed in black who routed every type of outlaw preying on innocent citizens. Best entry was the very first one— THE DURANGO KID. Stock footage used extensively.

(CHARLES STARRETT, SONS OF THE PIONEERS)
THE DURANGO KID (aka MASKED STRANGER) .... 1940...COL ....61 ___

(CHARLES STARRETT, TEX HARDING, BRITT WOOD)
THE RETURN OF THE DURANGO KID .... 1945...COL ....58 ___
   (aka STOLEN TIME)

(CHARLES STARRETT, TEX HARDING, DUB TAYLOR)
BOTH BARRELS BLAZING .... 1945...COL ....58 ___
   (aka THE YELLOW STREAK)
RUSTLERS OF THE BADLANDS .... 1945...COL .....55-58 ___
   (aka BY WHOSE HAND?)
OUTLAWS OF THE ROCKIES (aka ROVING ROGUE) 1945...COL ....55 ___
BLAZING THE WESTERN TRAIL .... 1945...COL ....60 ___
   (aka WHO KILLED WARING?)
LAWLESS EMPIRE (aka POWER OF POSSESSION) 1945...COL ....59 ___
TEXAS PANHANDLE .... 1945...COL .....55-57 ___
FRONTIER GUN LAW (aka MENACING SHADOWS)1946 ..COL ....60 ___

THE DURANGO KID series, continued
(CHARLES STARRETT, SMILEY BURNETTE)

Title	Year	Studio	Pages
ROARING RANGERS (aka FALSE HERO)	1946	COL	56
GUNNING FOR VENGEANCE (aka JAIL BREAK)	1946	COL	53-56
GALLOPING THUNDER (aka ON BOOT HILL)	1946	COL	54
TWO-FISTED STRANGER (aka HIGH STAKES)	1946	COL	50
THE DESERT HORSEMAN (aka CHECKMATE)	1946	COL	57
HEADING WEST (aka THE CHEAT'S LAST THROW)	1946	COL	54-56
LANDRUSH (aka THE CLAW STRIKES)	1946	COL	54
TERROR TRAIL (aka HANDS OF MENACE)	1946	COL	55
THE FIGHTING FRONTIERSMAN (aka GOLDEN LADY)	1946	COL	61
SOUTH OF THE CHISHOLM TRAIL	1947	COL	58
THE LONE HAND TEXAN (aka THE CHEAT)	1947	COL	54
WEST OF DODGE CITY (aka THE SEA WALL)	1947	COL	57
LAW OF THE CANYON (aka THE PRICE OF CRIME)	1947	COL	55
PRAIRIE RAIDERS (aka THE FORGER)	1947	COL	54
THE STRANGER FROM PONCA CITY	1947	COL	56
RIDERS OF THE LONE STAR	1947	COL	55
BUCKAROO FROM POWDER RIVER	1947	COL	55
LAST DAYS OF BOOT HILL	1947	COL	56
SIX-GUN LAW	1948	COL	54
PHANTOM VALLEY	1948	COL	53
WEST OF SONORA	1948	COL	52-55
WHIRLWIND RAIDERS (aka STATE POLICE)	1948	COL	54
BLAZING ACROSS THE PECOS	1948	COL	55
TRAIL TO LAREDO (aka SIGN OF THE DAGGER)	1948	COL	54
EL DORADO PASS (aka DESPERATE MEN)	1948	COL	56
QUICK ON THE TRIGGER (aka CONDEMNED IN ERROR)	1948	COL	55
CHALLENGE OF THE RANGE (aka MOONLIGHT RAID)	1949	COL	56
DESERT VIGILANTE	1949	COL	56
LARAMIE	1949	COL	55
THE BLAZING TRAIL (aka THE FORGED WILL)	1949	COL	56
SOUTH OF DEATH VALLEY (aka RIVER OF POISON)	1949	COL	54
HORSEMEN OF THE SIERRAS (aka REMEMBER ME)	1949	COL	56
BANDITS OF EL DORADO (aka TRICKED)	1949	COL	56
RENEGADES OF THE SAGE (aka THE FORT)	1949	COL	56
TRAIL OF THE RUSTLERS (aka LOST RIVER)	1950	COL	55
OUTCAST OF BLACK MESA (aka THE CLUE)	1950	COL	54
TEXAS DYNAMO (aka SUSPECTED)	1950	COL	54
STREETS OF GHOST TOWN	1950	COL	54
ACROSS THE BADLANDS (aka THE CHALLENGE)	1950	COL	54
RAIDERS OF TOMAHAWK CREEK (aka CIRCLE OF FEAR)	1950	COL	55
LIGHTNING GUNS (aka TAKING SIDES)	1950	COL	55
FRONTIER OUTPOST	1950	COL	55
PRAIRIE ROUNDUP	1951	COL	53-55
RIDIN' THE OUTLAW TRAIL	1951	COL	54
FORT SAVAGE RAIDERS	1951	COL	55
SNAKE RIVER DESPERADOES	1951	COL	55
BONANZA TOWN (aka TWO-FISTED AGENT)	1951	COL	50-56
CYCLONE FURY	1951	COL	54
THE KID FROM AMARILLO (aka SILVER CHAINS)	1951	COL	56

THE DURANGO KID series, continued / 69

(CHARLES STARRETT, SMILEY BURNETTE, JACK MAHONEY)

PECOS RIVER (aka WITHOUT RISK)	1951	COL	55
SMOKY CANYON	1952	COL	55
THE HAWK OF WILD RIVER	1952	COL	54
LARAMIE MOUNTAINS	1952	COL	53
(aka MOUNTAIN DESPERADOES)			
THE ROUGH, TOUGH WEST	1952	COL	54
JUNCTION CITY	1952	COL	54
THE KID FROM BROKEN GUN	1952	COL	56

DAN DURYEA (1907 - 1968)

He was the epitome of the smooth-talking, underhanded villain who tested the mettle of many an "A" western hero, but Duryea sided with the law occasionally in several big-budgeters of the 1950s-1960s. In both movie and TV versions of the classic film, WINCHESTER '73.

ALONG CAME JONES (s)	1945	RKO	90
BLACK BART	(C) 1948	UI	80
(aka BLACK BART HIGHWAYMAN)			
RIVER LADY	(C) 1948	UI	78
WINCHESTER '73 (cs)	1950	UI	92
AL JENNINGS OF OKLAHOMA	(C) 1951	COL	79
RIDE CLEAR OF DIABLO	(C) 1954	UI	80
RAILS INTO LARAMIE (cs)	(C) 1954	UI	81
SILVER LODE (cs)	(C) 1954	RKO	80
THE MARAUDERS	(C) 1955	MGM	80
FOXFIRE (cs)	(C) 1955	UI	91
NIGHT PASSAGE (cs)	(C) 1957	UI	90
SIX BLACK HORSES	(C) 1962	UNI	80
GUNFIGHT AT SANDOVAL	1963	BV	74
HE RIDES TALL (aka THE GUN HAND)	1964	UNI	84
TAGGART	(C) 1964	UNI	85
THE BOUNTY KILLER	(C) 1965	EMB	92
INCIDENT AT PHANTOM HILL	(C) 1966	UNI	88
WINCHESTER '73 (cs)	(C) 1967	UNI-TV	97
THE HILLS RUN RED	(C) 1967	UA	89
(aka A RIVER OF DOLLARS) (s)			
STRANGER ON THE RUN	(C) 1967	UNI-TV	97
(aka DEATH DANCE AT BANNER) (s)			

CLINT EASTWOOD (1930 -   )

Eastwood's first gathering of fame came as Rowdy Yates on CBS-TV's "Rawhide" in 1959. From the 1960s, the only western star to challenge John Wayne's supremacy in the genre. He rose to head European westerns and continued as a superstar in American films, both galloper and otherwise. A standout with COOGAN'S BLUFF, TWO MULES FOR SISTER SARA, THE BEGUILED, and HIGH PLAINS DRIFTER. Clint's latest one, UNFORGIVEN, received rave reviews.

TARANTULA (s)	1955	UI	80
STAR IN THE DUST (s)	(C) 1956	UI	80
THE FIRST TRAVELING SALESLADY (s)	(C) 1956	RKO	92
AMBUSH AT CIMARRON PASS (s)	1958	20T	73
A FISTFUL OF DOLLARS	(C) 1967	UA	96

CLINT EASTWOOD, continued

FOR A FEW DOLLARS MORE	(C) .. 1967 ... UA ...	125-130	____
THE GOOD, THE BAD, AND THE UGLY	(C) .. 1967 ... UA ...	155-180	____
HANG 'EM HIGH	(C) .. 1968 ... UA	114	____
COOGAN'S BLUFF	(C) .. 1968 ... UNI	100	____
PAINT YOUR WAGON	(C) .. 1969 ... PAR.	151-166	____
TWO MULES FOR SISTER SARA	(C) .. 1970 ... UNI	105	____
THE BEGUILED	(C) .. 1971 ... UNI	109	____
JOE KIDD	(C) .. 1972 ... UNI	88	____
HIGH PLAINS DRIFTER	(C) .. 1973 ... UNI	105	____
THUNDERBOLT AND LIGHTFOOT	(C) .. 1974 ... UA	114	____
THE EIGER SANCTION	(C) .. 1975 ... UNI	128	____
THE OUTLAW—JOSEY WALES	(C) .. 1976 ... WB ..	136-137	____
THE GAUNTLET	(C) .. 1977 ... WB	110	____
BRONCO BILLY	(C) .. 1980 ... WB	119	____
PALE RIDER	(C) .. 1985 ... WB ..	113-115	____
UNFORGIVEN	(C) .. 1992 ... WB	131	____

NELSON EDDY (1901 - 1967)

He was Jeanette MacDonald's fine singing partner in a number of expensive MGM operettas during the 1930s-1940s, some of which were outdoors-oriented western adventures. Republic used Eddy's talents for NORTHWEST OUTPOST.

NAUGHTY MARIETTA	1935 ... MGM	105-106	____
ROSE MARIE (aka INDIAN LOVE CALL)	1936 ... MGM	110-116	____
THE GIRL OF THE GOLDEN WEST	1938 ... MGM	120	____
LET FREEDOM RING	1939 ... MGM	85	____
NEW MOON	1940 ... MGM	105	____
NORTHWEST OUTPOST	1947 ... REP	91	____
(aka END OF THE RAINBOW)			

RICHARD EGAN (1921 - 1987)

A virile leading man whose specialty was mainly in action dramas of all times. Egan starred in the brief "Redigo" NBC-TV 30-minute shows of 15 episodes (1963), and 32 hour-long episodes of "Empire" for NBC (1962-63).

RETURN OF THE FRONTIERSMAN (s)	(C) .. 1950 ... WB	74	____
KANSAS RAIDERS (s)	(C) .. 1950 ... UI	80	____
WYOMING MAIL (s)	(C) .. 1950 ... UI	87	____
THE BATTLE AT APACHE PASS (s)	(C) .. 1952 ... UI	85	____
CRIPPLE CREEK (s)	(C) .. 1952 ... COL	78	____
SPLIT SECOND (s)	1953 ... RKO	85	____
VIOLENT SATURDAY	(C) .. 1955 ... 20T	90-91	____
SEVEN CITIES OF GOLD	(C) .. 1955 ... 20T	103	____
TENSION AT TABLE ROCK	(C) .. 1956 ... RKO	93	____
LOVE ME TENDER	1956 ... 20T	89	____
THESE THOUSAND HILLS	(C) .. 1959 ... 20T	96	____
THE RUGGED LAND	(C) .. 1970 ... UNI	60	____
DAY OF THE WOLVES	(C) .. 1973 ... TVM	95	____
SHOOTOUT IN A ONE-DOG TOWN	(C) .. 1974 ... HBP-TV	78	____
KINO, THE PADRE ON HORSEBACK	(C) .. 1977 ... KI	116	____
(aka MISSION TO GLORY)			
THE SWEET CREEK COUNTY WAR	(C) .. 1979 ... KI	99	____

BILL ELLIOTT (1903 - 1965)
(aka WILD BILL ELLIOTT, WILLIAM ELLIOTT)
A popular 1940s "B" western film star, best known as either "Wild Bill" or "Red Ryder," who rose to lead big and medium budget "A" westerns in the late 1940s and 1950s with Republic and Monogram/Allied Artists. Elliott was a Top Money-Making Western Star from 1940 through 1954. Self-proclaimed as "I'm a peaceable man" with his distinguished voice, Bill was never shy when forced into knockdown-dragout slugfests. Good gallopers this cowboy made were BEYOND THE SACRAMENTO, ROARING FRONTIERS, HELLFIRE, and THE SAVAGE HORDE.

Title	Year	Studio	Page
THE GREAT DIVIDE (s)	1930	FN	72
MOONLIGHT ON THE PRAIRIE (s)	1935	WB	63-67
TRAILIN' WEST (aka ON SECRET SERVICE) (s)	1936	WB	56
GUNS OF THE PECOS (s)	1937	WB	65
BOOTS AND SADDLES (s)	1937	REP	60
ROLL ALONG COWBOY (s)	1937	20T	55
THE GREAT ADVENTURES OF WILD BILL (SER) HICKOK	1938	COL	15CH
IN EARLY ARIZONA	1938	COL	53
FRONTIERS OF '49	1939	COL	54
LONE STAR PIONEERS (aka UNWELCOME VISITORS)	1939	COL	56
THE LAW COMES TO TEXAS	1939	COL	58
OVERLAND WITH KIT CARSON (SER)	1939	COL	15CH
THE TAMING OF THE WEST (starts *Wild Bill Saunders* series)	1939	COL	55
PIONEERS OF THE FRONTIER (aka THE ANCHOR)	1940	COL	58
THE MAN FROM TUMBLEWEEDS	1940	COL	59
THE RETURN OF WILD BILL (aka FALSE EVIDENCE) (ends *Wild Bill Saunders* series)	1940	COL	60
PRAIRIE SCHOONERS (aka THROUGH THE STORM) (starts *Wild Bill Hickok* series)	1940	COL	58
BEYOND THE SACRAMENTO (aka POWER OF JUSTICE)	1940	COL	58
THE WILDCAT OF TUCSON (aka PROMISE FULFILLED)	1940	COL	58-60
ACROSS THE SIERRAS (aka WELCOME STRANGER)	1941	COL	58
NORTH FROM THE LONE STAR	1941	COL	58
THE RETURN OF DANIEL BOONE (aka THE MAYOR'S NEST) (non-series)	1941	COL	60
HANDS ACROSS THE ROCKIES	1941	COL	58
THE SON OF DAVY CROCKETT (aka BLUE CLAY) (non-series)	1941	COL	59
KING OF DODGE CITY	1941	COL	63
ROARING FRONTIERS (aka FRONTIER)	1941	COL	62
THE LONE STAR VIGILANTES (aka THE DEVIL'S PRICE)	1942	COL	58
BULLETS FOR BANDITS	1942	COL	55
NORTH OF THE ROCKIES (aka FALSE CLUES) (non-series)	1942	COL	60
THE DEVIL'S TRAIL (aka ROGUE'S GALLERY; DEVIL'S CANYON)	1942	COL	61
PRAIRIE GUNSMOKE (ends *Wild Bill Hickok* series)	1942	COL	56
VENGEANCE OF THE WEST (aka THE BLACK SHADOW)	1942	COL	60
THE VALLEY OF VANISHING MEN (SER)	1942	COL	15CH

BILL ELLIOTT, continued

Title	Year	Studio	Page
CALLING WILD BILL ELLIOTT	1943	REP	54
THE MAN FROM THUNDER RIVER	1943	REP	59
BORDERTOWN GUN FIGHTERS	1943	REP	55
WAGON TRACKS WEST	1943	REP	55
DEATH VALLEY MANHUNT	1943	REP	55
OVERLAND MAIL ROBBERY	1943	REP	55
MOJAVE FIREBRAND	1944	REP	55
HIDDEN VALLEY OUTLAWS	1944	REP	55
TUCSON RAIDERS (starts *Red Ryder* series)	1944	REP	55
MARSHAL OF RENO	1944	REP	54
THE SAN ANTONIO KID	1944	REP	59
CHEYENNE WILDCAT	1944	REP	56
VIGILANTES OF DODGE CITY	1944	REP	54
SHERIFF OF LAS VEGAS	1944	REP	55
GREAT STAGECOACH ROBBERY	1945	REP	56
LONE TEXAS RANGER	1945	REP	56
BELLS OF ROSARITA (non-series) (gs)	1945	REP	68
PHANTOM OF THE PLAINS	1945	REP	56
MARSHAL OF LAREDO	1945	REP	56
COLORADO PIONEERS	1945	REP	55
WAGON WHEELS WESTWARD	1945	REP	55
CALIFORNIA GOLD RUSH	1946	REP	56
SHERIFF OF REDWOOD VALLEY	1946	REP	54
SUN VALLEY CYCLONE	1946	REP	56
IN OLD SACRAMENTO	1946	REP	89
(aka FLAME OF SACRAMENTO) (non-series)			
CONQUEST OF CHEYENNE (ends *Red Ryder* series)	1946	REP	55
PLAINSMAN AND THE LADY	1946	REP	87
WYOMING	1947	REP	84
THE FABULOUS TEXAN	1947	REP	95
OLD LOS ANGELES (aka CALIFORNIA OUTPOST)	1948	REP	88
THE GALLANT LEGION	1948	REP	88
THE LAST BANDIT (C)	1949	REP	80
HELLFIRE (C)	1949	REP	90
THE SAVAGE HORDE	1950	REP	90
THE SHOWDOWN	1950	REP	86
THE LONGHORN	1951	MON	70
WACO (aka THE OUTLAW AND THE LADY)	1952	MON	68
KANSAS TERRITORY	1952	MON	73
FARGO	1952	MON	69
THE MAVERICK	1952	AA	71
THE HOMESTEADERS	1953	AA	62
REBEL CITY	1953	AA	63
TOPEKA	1953	AA	60-69
VIGILANTE TERROR	1953	AA	70
BITTER CREEK	1954	AA	74
THE FORTY-NINERS	1954	AA	71

SAM ELLIOTT (1944 -   )

Leading man of the 1970s-1980s, whose portrayals of Louis L'Amour's western character, Tell Sackett, in films have been his best-known roles. Elliott continued this prolific author's stories during 1991 with TNT-TV's CONAGHER.

Title	Year	Studio	Page
BUTCH CASSIDY AND THE SUNDANCE KID (s)(C)	1969	20T	110-112
MOLLY AND LAWLESS JOHN (C)	1972	PDC	100

SAM ELLIOTT, continued / 73

I WILL FIGHT NO MORE FOREVER (s)	(C).. 1975	...DWP-TV	97-98 ___
THE SACKETTS (aka THE DAYBREAKERS)	...(C).. 1979	...NBC-TV	..200 ___
WILD TIMES	(C).. 1980	...GC-TV	....200 ___
THE SHADOW RIDERS	(C).. 1982	...CBS-TV	..100 ___
(aka LOUIS L'AMOUR'S THE SHADOW RIDERS)			
HOUSTON: THE LEGEND OF TEXAS	(C).. 1986	...TEG-TV	..150 ___
(aka GONE TO TEXAS)			
THE QUICK AND THE DEAD	(C).. 1987	...HBO-TV	....93 ___
CONAGHER	(C).. 1991	...TNT-TV	...116 ___

JIMMY ELLISON (1910 -   )
(aka JAMES ELLISON, JIMMIE "SHAMROCK" ELLISON)

After finishing eight features as Johnny Nelson in the *Hopalong Cassidy* series (1935-37), he stayed out of westerns for the most part until *The Irish Cowboys* sagas in 1950. Then Ellison joined Johnny Mack Brown for six Monogram oaters (1951-52).

HOP-A-LONG CASSIDY	1935	...PAR	.....59-62 ___
(aka HOPALONG CASSIDY ENTERS) (starts *Hopalong Cassidy* series)			
THE EAGLE'S BROOD	1935	...PAR	..........60 ___
BAR 20 RIDES AGAIN	1935	...PAR	..........63 ___
CALL OF THE PRAIRIE	1936	...PAR	..........67 ___
THREE ON THE TRAIL	1936	...PAR	..........67 ___
HEART OF THE WEST	1936	...PAR	.....65-78 ___
TRAIL DUST	1936	...PAR	..........77 ___
THE PLAINSMAN (non-series) (cs)	1937	...PAR.	113-115 ___
BORDERLAND (ends *Hopalong Cassidy* series)	1937	...PAR	..........82 ___
THE BARRIER (cs)	1937	...PAR	..........90 ___
THEY MET IN ARGENTINA	1941	...RKO	..........77 ___
LAST OF THE WILD HORSES	1948	...SG	...........85 ___
HOSTILE COUNTRY	1950	...LIP	...........60 ___
(aka GUNS OF JUSTICE) (starts *The Irish Cowboys* series)			
EVERYBODY'S DANCIN'! (non-series) (s)	1950	...LIP	...........65 ___
MARSHAL OF HELDORADO (aka BLAZING GUNS)	1950	...LIP	...........53 ___
CROOKED RIVER (aka THE LAST BULLET)	1950	...LIP	...........55 ___
COLORADO RANGER (aka OUTLAW FURY)	1950	...LIP	...........54 ___
WEST OF THE BRAZOS (aka RANGELAND EMPIRE)	1950	...LIP	...........58 ___
FAST ON THE DRAW (aka SUDDEN DEATH)	1950	...LIP	...........55 ___
(ends *The Irish Cowboys* series)			
I KILLED GERONIMO	1950	...EL	............62 ___
THE TEXAN MEETS CALAMITY JANE	(C).. 1950	...COL	........71 ___
OKLAHOMA JUSTICE	1951	...MON	.........56 ___
WHISTLING HILLS	1951	...MON	.........58 ___
TEXAS LAWMEN (aka LONE STAR LAWMAN)	1951	...MON	.........54 ___
TEXAS CITY	1952	...MON	.........54 ___
MAN FROM THE BLACK HILLS	1952	...MON	.........56 ___
DEAD MAN'S TRAIL	1952	...MON	.........59 ___

JOHN ERICSON (1926 -   )
A German-born leading man who played outdoor action roles often.

BAD DAY AT BLACK ROCK (s)	(C).. 1955	...MGM	.........81 ___
THE RETURN OF JACK SLADE (aka TEXAS ROSE)	1955	..AA	.............79 ___
FORTY GUNS (aka WOMAN WITH A WHIP) (s)	1957	...20T	..........80 ___
OREGON PASSAGE	(C).. 1958	..AA	.............82 ___

74 / JOHN ERICSON, continued

DAY OF THE BAD MAN (cs) ....(C).. 1958... UI .... 81 ____
THE VENGEANCE OF PANCHO VILLA .... (C).. 1966... LAC .... 83 ____
THE BOUNTY MAN (cs) ....(C).. 1972... ABCCF-TV 73 ____

FAMOUS WESTERNS series (1947 - 1953)
Allan "Rocky" Lane led the charge for Republic Pictures in this highly acclaimed, hard-riding series of 38 oatburners portraying various lawmen of the "B" West after numerous baddies—but mainly Roy Barcroft who paired off with him in a bunch of tough fight scenes. Outstanding in the group were THE WILD FRONTIER, OKLAHOMA BADLANDS, THE BOLD FRONTIERSMAN, SUNDOWN IN SANTA FE, and FRONTIER INVESTIGATOR. Vast amounts of stock footage used.

(ALLAN "ROCKY" LANE, EDDY WALLER)
THE WILD FRONTIER .... 1947... REP .... 59 ____
BANDITS OF DARK CANYON .... 1947... REP .... 59 ____
OKLAHOMA BADLANDS .... 1948... REP .... 59 ____
THE BOLD FRONTIERSMAN .... 1948... REP .... 60 ____
CARSON CITY RAIDERS .... 1948... REP .... 60 ____
MARSHAL OF AMARILLO .... 1948... REP .... 60 ____
DESPERADOES OF DODGE CITY .... 1948... REP .... 60 ____
THE DENVER KID .... 1948... REP .... 60 ____
SUNDOWN IN SANTA FE .... 1948... REP .... 60 ____
RENEGADES OF SONORA .... 1948... REP .... 60 ____
SHERIFF OF WICHITA .... 1949... REP .... 60 ____
DEATH VALLEY GUNFIGHTER .... 1949... REP .... 60 ____
FRONTIER INVESTIGATOR .... 1949... REP .... 60 ____
THE WYOMING BANDIT .... 1949... REP .... 60 ____
BANDIT KING OF TEXAS .... 1949... REP .... 60 ____
NAVAJO TRAIL RAIDERS .... 1949... REP .... 60 ____
POWDER RIVER RUSTLERS .... 1949... REP .... 60 ____
GUNMEN OF ABILENE .... 1950... REP .... 60 ____
CODE OF THE SILVER SAGE .... 1950... REP .... 60 ____
SALT LAKE RAIDERS .... 1950... REP .... 60 ____
COVERED WAGON RAID .... 1950... REP .... 60 ____
VIGILANTE HIDEOUT .... 1950... REP .... 60 ____
FRISCO TORNADO .... 1950... REP .... 60 ____
RUSTLERS ON HORSEBACK .... 1950... REP .... 60 ____

(ALLAN "ROCKY" LANE, WALTER BALDWIN)
ROUGH RIDERS OF DURANGO .... 1951... REP .... 60 ____

(ALLAN "ROCKY" LANE, CHUBBY JOHNSON)
NIGHT RIDERS OF MONTANA .... 1951... REP .... 60 ____
WELLS FARGO GUNMASTER .... 1951... REP .... 60 ____
FORT DODGE STAMPEDE .... 1951... REP .... 60 ____

(ALLAN "ROCKY" LANE, IRVING BACON)
DESERT OF LOST MEN .... 1951... REP .... 54 ____

(ALLAN "ROCKY" LANE, CLEM BEVANS)
CAPTIVE OF BILLY THE KID .... 1952... REP .... 54 ____

(ALLAN "ROCKY" LANE, EDDY WALLER)
LEADVILLE GUNSLINGER .... 1952... REP .... 54 ____
BLACK HILLS AMBUSH .... 1952... REP .... 54 ____

FAMOUS WESTERNS series, continued / 75

THUNDERING CARAVANS	1952	REP	54
DESPERADOES' OUTPOST	1952	REP	54
MARSHAL OF CEDAR ROCK	1953	REP	54
SAVAGE FRONTIER	1953	REP	54
BANDITS OF THE WEST	1953	REP	54
EL PASO STAMPEDE	1953	REP	54

TEX FLETCHER (1909 - 1986)
His chance as a new singing movie cowboy was quickly dashed after one film in 1939 when Grand National collapsed financially. Left-handed guitar player.

SIX-GUN RHYTHM	1939	GN	55

ERROL FLYNN (1909 - 1959)
A Tasmanian-born actor, best known for his swashbuckling roles, but who made a number of fine western films also. Remembered in westerns for his dashing portrayal of the ill-fated Custer in THEY DIED WITH THEIR BOOTS ON, Flynn was first-rate, as well, with DODGE CITY and SAN ANTONIO.

DODGE CITY	(C) .. 1939	WB	104
VIRGINIA CITY	1940	WB	121
SANTA FE TRAIL	1940	WB	110
THEY DIED WITH THEIR BOOTS ON	1942	WB	140
NORTHERN PURSUIT	1943	WB	94-95
SAN ANTONIO	(C) .. 1945	WB	111-112
SILVER RIVER	1948	WB	110
MONTANA	(C) .. 1950	WB	76
ROCKY MOUNTAIN	1950	WB	83

HENRY FONDA (1905 - 1982)
Excellent Broadway stage actor whose American characters have always been imbued with honesty and integrity. He played heroes mostly, but towards the latter part of his career, also played villains. Best known in westerns for his portrayal of the arrogant cavalry Colonel in John Ford's FORT APACHE, Fonda mainlined "The Deputy" 30-minute TV show on NBC (1959-61) for 76 episodes.

TRAIL OF THE LONESOME PINE	(C) .. 1936	PAR	102-106
JEZEBEL	1938	WB	104
SPAWN OF THE NORTH	1938	PAR	110
JESSE JAMES	(C) .. 1939	20T	105-106
YOUNG MR. LINCOLN	1939	20T	101
DRUMS ALONG THE MOHAWK	(C) .. 1939	20T	103
THE GRAPES OF WRATH	1940	20T	129
THE RETURN OF FRANK JAMES	(C) .. 1940	20T	92
WILD GEESE CALLING	1941	20T	72-78
THE OX-BOW INCIDENT (aka STRANGE INCIDENT)	1943	20T	75
MY DARLING CLEMENTINE	1946	20T	91-97
THE FUGITIVE	1947	RKO	104
FORT APACHE	1948	RKO	127
THE TIN STAR	1957	PAR	93

HENRY FONDA, continued

WARLOCK	(C) .. 1959	20T ..	121-122
SPENCER'S MOUNTAIN	(C) .. 1963	WB ..	118-119
HOW THE WEST WAS WON (s)	(C) .. 1963	MGM	155-165
THE ROUNDERS	(C) .. 1965	MGM	85
A BIG HAND FOR THE LITTLE LADY	(C) .. 1966	WB	95
(aka BIG DEAL AT DODGE CITY)			
WELCOME TO HARD TIMES	(C) .. 1967	MGM	103-105
(aka KILLER ON A HORSE)			
STRANGER ON THE RUN	(C) .. 1967	UNI-TV	97
(aka DEATH DANCE AT BANNER)			
FIRECREEK	(C) .. 1968	WB	104
BORN TO BUCK (nr)	(C) .. 1968	CTI	94
ONCE UPON A TIME IN THE WEST	(C) .. 1969	PAR	165
THE CHEYENNE SOCIAL CLUB	(C) .. 1970	NG	103
THERE WAS A CROOKED MAN	(C) .. 1970	WB ..	125-126
SOMETIMES A GREAT NOTION	(C) .. 1971	UNI	114
(aka NEVER GIVE AN INCH)			
THE RED PONY	(C) .. 1973	UNI-TV	100
MY NAME IS NOBODY	(C) .. 1974	UNI ..	115-130
THE SWARM (s)	(C) .. 1978	PAR	116
WANDA NEVADA (s)	(C) .. 1979	UA	105

DICK FORAN (1910 - 1979)

A movie cowboy with tremendous singing talents, he enjoyed success as star for Warner Brothers "B" westerns (1935-37), then was relegated to mostly support parts for another 30 years. Foran was a Top Money-Making Western Star (1936-38). Good in LAND BEYOND THE LAW and EMPTY HOLSTERS.

MOONLIGHT ON THE PRAIRIE		1935 ... WB	63-67
SONG OF THE SADDLE		1936 ... WB	56-58
THE PETRIFIED FOREST (s)		1936 ... WB	83
TREACHERY RIDES THE RANGE		1936 ... WB	56
TRAILIN' WEST (aka ON SECRET SERVICE)		1936 ... WB	56
CALIFORNIA MAIL		1936 ... WB	56-60
GUNS OF THE PECOS		1937 ... WB	65
LAND BEYOND THE LAW		1937 ... WB	54
THE CHEROKEE STRIP (aka STRANGE LAWS)		1937 ... WB	56
BLAZING SIXES		1937 ... WB	55
EMPTY HOLSTERS		1937 ... WB	58-62
THE DEVIL'S SADDLE LEGION		1937 ... WB	52-57
PRAIRIE THUNDER		1937 ... WB	54
COWBOY FROM BROOKLYN		1937 ... WB	80
(aka ROMANCE AND RHYTHM) (s)			
HEART OF THE NORTH	(C) .. 1938	WB	80
MY LITTLE CHICKADEE (s)		1940 ... UNI	85
WINNERS OF THE WEST	(SER)	1940 ... UNI	13CH
RANGERS OF FORTUNE		1940 ... PAR	80
RIDERS OF DEATH VALLEY	(SER)	1941 ... UNI	15CH
ROAD AGENT (aka TEXAS ROAD AGENT)		1941 ... UNI	60
RIDE 'EM COWBOY (s)		1942 ... UNI	86
FORT APACHE (s)		1948 ... RKO	127
EL PASO (s)	(C) .. 1949	PAR	92
DEPUTY MARSHAL (s)		1949 ... LIP	60
AL JENNINGS OF OKLAHOMA (cs)	(C) .. 1951	COL	79
TREASURE OF RUBY HILLS (s)		1955 ... AA	71

DICK FORAN, continued / 77

SIERRA STRANGER (cs)	1957	COL	74	____
TAGGART (cs)	(C).. 1964	UNI	85	____
BRIGHTY OF THE GRAND CANYON (s)	(C).. 1967	FFC	89-92	____

GLENN FORD (1916 -)

Easygoing, laid-back leading man whose authentic look has made him an excellent western star. He has played heroes and villains equally well in numerous western features throughout his career. Some of Ford's more highly-praised films in the genre are THE FASTEST GUN ALIVE, 3:10 TO YUMA, THE SHEEPMAN, and COWBOY. He completed 24 hour-long episodes for CBS-TV'S "Cade's County" (1971-72).

HEAVEN WITH A BARBED WIRE FENCE	1939	20T	63	____
TEXAS	1941	COL	93-94	____
GO WEST, YOUNG LADY	1941	COL	70	____
THE DESPERADOES	(C).. 1943	COL	85	____
THE LOVES OF CARMEN	(C).. 1948	COL	98	____
THE MAN FROM COLORADO	(C).. 1948	COL	99	____
LUST FOR GOLD	1949	COL	90	____
THE REDHEAD AND THE COWBOY	1951	PAR	82	____
THE SECRET OF CONVICT LAKE	1951	20T	83	____
THE MAN FROM THE ALAMO	(C).. 1953	UI	79	____
PLUNDER OF THE SUN	1953	WB	81	____
THE VIOLENT MEN (aka ROUGH COMPANY)	(C).. 1955	COL	96	____
THE AMERICANO	(C).. 1955	RKO	85	____
JUBAL	(C).. 1956	COL	101	____
THE FASTEST GUN ALIVE	1956	MGM	89-92	____
3:10 TO YUMA	1957	COL	92	____
COWBOY	(C).. 1958	COL	92	____
THE SHEEPMAN	(C).. 1958	MGM	85	____
CIMARRON	(C).. 1960	MGM	140-147	____
ADVANCE TO THE REAR (aka COMPANY OF COWARDS)	1964	MGM	97	____
THE ROUNDERS	(C).. 1965	MGM	85	____
RAGE	(C).. 1966	WB	100	____
THE LAST CHALLENGE (aka THE PISTOLERO OF RED RIVER)	(C).. 1967	MGM	105	____
A TIME FOR KILLING (aka THE LONG RIDE HOME)	(C).. 1967	COL	88	____
DAY OF THE EVIL GUN (aka EVIL GUN)	(C).. 1968	MGM	93-95	____
HEAVEN WITH A GUN	(C).. 1969	MGM	101	____
SMITH!	(C).. 1969	BV	102-112	____
MARSHAL OF MADRID	(C).. 1972	CBS-TV	100	____
SANTEE	(C).. 1973	CRP	93	____
THE SACKETTS (aka THE DAY BREAKERS) (s)	(C).. 1979	NBC-TV	240	____
BORDER SHOOTOUT (cs)	(C).. 1990	PPP-TV	110	____

STEVE FORREST (1924 -)

The brother of Dana Andrews who became a leading man in a few westerns. Best known in western films for his portrayal of Hawkeye, the woodsman hero in the stories of James Fenimore Cooper. Forrest possessed a rich, deep voice.

| LAST OF THE COMANCHES (aka THE SABRE AND THE ARROW) (s) | (C).. 1953 | COL | 85 | ____ |
| HELLER IN PINK TIGHTS (s) | (C).. 1960 | PAR | 100 | ____ |

78 / STEVE FORREST, continued

FLAMING STAR (cs)	(C)	1960	20T	101
THE SECOND TIME AROUND	(C)	1961	20T	99
(aka STAR IN THE WEST)				
THE WILD COUNTRY (aka THE NEWCOMERS)	(C)	1971	BV	100
THE SAGITTARIUS MINE	(C)	1972	GK	91
THE HANGED MAN	(C)	1974	ABC-TV	74-78
THE HATFIELDS AND THE McCOYS	(C)	1975	CFP-TV	74
WANTED: THE SUNDANCE WOMAN	(C)	1976	20T-TV	100
(aka MRS. SUNDANCE RIDES AGAIN)				
LAST OF THE MOHICANS	(C)	1977	NBC-TV	100
THE DEERSLAYER	(C)	1978	NBC-TV	100
ROUGHNECKS	(C)	1980	MPC-TV	200
GUNSMOKE: RETURN TO DODGE (s)	(C)	1987	CBS-TV	100

PRESTON FOSTER (1902 - 1970)
A burly leading man who played both leads and supporting roles in western films. Best remembered in the genre for his portrayal of the father in the Mary O'Hara western horse stories. Foster starred in 12 hour-long CBS-TV shows of "Gunslinger" (1961).

THE ARIZONIAN (cs)		1935	RKO	75
ANNIE OAKLEY		1935	RKO	90
THE OUTCASTS OF POKER FLAT		1937	RKO	68
ARMY GIRL (aka THE LAST OF THE CAVALRY)		1938	REP	80
GERONIMO		1940	PAR	89-90
NORTH WEST MOUNTED POLICE	(C)	1940	PAR	125
THE ROUND-UP (cs)		1941	PAR	90
THUNDER BIRDS	(C)	1942	20T	78
AMERICAN EMPIRE (aka MY SON ALONE) (cs)		1942	UA	81-82
MY FRIEND FLICKA	(C)	1943	20T	90
THUNDERHEAD—SON OF FLICKA	(C)	1945	20T	78
THE HARVEY GIRLS	(C)	1946	MGM	101
KING OF THE WILD HORSES		1947	COL	73-79
RAMROD (s)		1947	UA	94
THUNDERHOOF (aka FURY)		1948	COL	77
I SHOT JESSE JAMES		1949	SG	81
THE BIG CAT	(C)	1949	EL	75
THE TOUGHER THEY COME (s)		1950	COL	69
3 DESPERATE MEN		1951	LIP	71
TOMAHAWK	(C)	1951	UI	82
(aka BATTLE OF POWDER RIVER) (cs)				
MONTANA TERRITORY (cs)	(C)	1952	COL	64
LAW AND ORDER (cs)	(C)	1953	UI	80
THE MARSHAL'S DAUGHTER (gs)		1953	UA	71
THE MAN FROM GALVESTON		1964	WB	57
ADVANCE TO THE REAR		1964	MGM	97
(aka COMPANY OF COWARDS) (s)				

THE FRONTIER MARSHALS series (1942)
A short-lived PRC series of "B" oaters about three U.S. marshals tracking down outlaws in the old West. Bill Boyd, Art Davis, and Lee Powell led the action sequences.

(LEE POWELL, BILL BOYD, ART DAVIS)

TEXAS MANHUNT		1942 PRC	60
RAIDERS OF THE WEST		1942 PRC	64

THE FRONTIER MARSHALS series, continued / 79

ROLLING DOWN THE GREAT DIVIDE	1942	PRC	60	____
TUMBLEWEED TRAIL	1942	PRC	57	____
PRAIRIE PALS	1942	PRC	60	____
ALONG THE SUNDOWN TRAIL	1942	PRC	59	____

ROBERT FULLER (1937 -   )

A rugged action cowboy who mainlined 128 hour-long color "Laramie" NBC-TV series shows (1959-63) as Jess Harper. Fuller teamed with the immensely popular "Wagon Train" episodes for its last couple of seasons on television. He starred in adult movie oaters sporadically over the next two decades.

INCIDENT AT PHANTOM HILL	(C)	1966	UNI	88	____
RETURN OF THE SEVEN	(C)	1966	UA	96	____
(aka RETURN OF THE MAGNIFICENT SEVEN)					
THE GATLING GUN (aka KING GUN) (s)	(C)	1972	EE	93	____
MUSTANG COUNTRY	(C)	1976	UNI	79	____
DONNER PASS: THE ROAD TO SURVIVAL	(C)	1978	SCP-TV	100	____
BONANZA: THE NEXT GENERATION	(C)	1988	COL-TV	100	____

CLARK GABLE (1901 - 1960)

The most famous film leading man of the sound era whose "A" oaters roles were few. He died shortly after completing THE MISFITS, a modern western film from 1961.

THE PAINTED DESERT (s)		1931	RKO	75	____
THE CALL OF THE WILD		1935	UA	81-95	____
SAN FRANCISCO		1936	MGM	115	____
GONE WITH THE WIND	(C)	1939	SEL/MGM	222	____
BOOM TOWN		1940	MGM	115-116	____
HONKY TONK		1941	MGM	.79-105	____
ACROSS THE WIDE MISSOURI	(C)	1951	MGM	78	____
CALLAWAY WENT THATAWAY		1951	MGM	81	____
(aka THE STAR SAID NO) (gs)					
LONE STAR		1952	MGM	90-94	____
THE TALL MEN	(C)	1955	20T	122	____
THE KING AND FOUR QUEENS	(C)	1956	UA	86	____
BAND OF ANGELS	(C)	1957	WB	127	____
THE MISFITS		1961	UA	124-125	____

JAMES GARNER (1928 -   )

He rose from supporting roles in western films to become a leading man. Best-known for his laid-back character "Maverick" from the ABC television series (1957-62) with 124 hour-long episodes followed by "Bret Maverick" (1981-82) on NBC-TV consisting of 18 new 60-minute shows. In between, Garner became "Nichols" (1971-72) for 29 episodes of that hour-long NBC-TV program. James was a comedic genius for the SUPPORT YOUR . . .features.

SHOOT-OUT AT MEDICINE BEND (s)	(C)	1957	WB	87	____
ALIAS JESSE JAMES (gs)	(C)	1959	UA	92	____
THE WHEELER DEALERS	(C)	1963	MGM	106	____
(aka SEPARATE BEDS)					

JAMES GARNER, continued

DUEL AT DIABLO	(C)	1966...UA	103-105
HOUR OF THE GUN	(C)	1967...UA	100-101
SUPPORT YOUR LOCAL SHERIFF!	(C)	1969...UA	92-93
SUPPORT YOUR LOCAL GUNFIGHTER	(C)	1971...UA	92
SKIN GAME	(C)	1971...WB	102
A MAN CALLED SLEDGE (aka SLEDGE)	(C)	1971...COL	92-93
ONE LITTLE INDIAN	(C)	1973...BV	90
THE CASTAWAY COWBOY	(C)	1974...BV	91
THE NEW MAVERICK	(C)	1978...WB-TV	100
SUNSET	(C)	1988...TS	107

HOOT GIBSON (1892 - 1962)

A proficient saddler whose comic touches enlivened westerns beginning in the 1910s. Gibson remained active with sound oaters into 1937, having been paid for a period during the 1920s $14,000 weekly by Universal. He was a Top Money-Making Western Star (1936). Hoot returned (1943-44) for Monogram's thrill-a-minute *The Trail Blazers* series, and was editorially praised by *The New York Times* after passing away in 1962.

THE LONG, LONG TRAIL	1929...UNI	59
COURTIN' WILDCATS	1929...UNI	57
BURNING THE WIND	1930...UNI	57
THE MOUNTED STRANGER	1930...UNI	65
TRAILIN' TROUBLE	1930...UNI	57
ROARING RANCH	1930...UNI	68
TRIGGER TRICKS	1930...UNI	60
SPURS	1930...UNI	59
THE CONCENTRATIN' KID	1930...UNI	57
CLEARING THE RANGE	1931...ALL	61
WILD HORSE (aka SILVER DEVIL)	1931...ALL	77
HARD HOMBRE	1931...ALL	65
THE LOCAL BAD MAN	1932...ALL	59
THE GAY BUCKAROO	1932...ALL	61
SPIRIT OF THE WEST	1932...ALL	60
A MAN'S LAND	1932...ALL	65
THE COWBOY COUNSELOR	1932...ALL	63
THE BOILING POINT	1932...ALL	70
THE DUDE BANDIT	1933...ALL	62-67
THE FIGHTING PARSON	1933...ALL	61-70
SUNSET RANGE	1935...FD	54-60
RAINBOW'S END	1935...FD	60
POWDERSMOKE RANGE	1935...RKO	71
SWIFTY	1935...GN	60
FRONTIER JUSTICE	1936...GN	58
LUCKY TERROR	1936...GN	61
FEUD OF THE WEST	1936...GN	62
THE LAST OUTLAW	1936...RKO	62
THE RIDING AVENGER	1936...GN	58
CAVALCADE OF THE WEST	1936...GN	59
THE PAINTED STALLION (SER)	1937...REP	12CH
WILD HORSE STAMPEDE	1943...MON	59
(starts *The Trail Blazers* series)		
THE LAW RIDES AGAIN	1943...MON	58
BLAZING GUNS	1943...MON	55
DEATH VALLEY RANGERS	1943...MON	55-59

HOOT GIBSON, continued / 81

WESTWARD BOUND	1944...MON	54-59
ARIZONA WHIRLWIND	1944...MON	59
OUTLAW TRAIL	1944...MON	53-55
SONORA STAGECOACH	1944...MON	60
(ends *The Trail Blazers* series)		
MARKED TRAILS	1944...MON	59
THE UTAH KID	1944...MON	55-57
TRIGGER LAW	1944...MON	56
FLIGHT TO NOWHERE (s)	1946...SG	74
THE MARSHAL'S DAUGHTER	1953...UA	71
THE HORSE SOLDIERS (s)	(C)..1959...UA	119

STEWART GRANGER (1913 -   )

A British actor whose mainstays were the swashbuckling 1940s-1950s costumed dramas, he lent additional talents to adult westerns both in the United States and overseas. Granger was a standout with NORTH TO ALASKA.

THE WILD NORTH (aka THE BIG NORTH)	(C)..1952...MGM	97
THE LAST HUNT	(C)..1956...MGM	108
GUN GLORY	(C)..1957...MGM	89
NORTH TO ALASKA	(C)..1960...20T	122
FRONTIER HELLCAT (aka AMONG VULTURES)	(C)..1966...COL	98-102
RAMPAGE AT APACHE WELLS	(C)..1966...COL	90
FLAMING FRONTIER	(C)..1968...WB	93

KIRBY GRANT (1911 - 1985)
(aka ROBERT STANTON)

Completing early 1940s Universal "B" musicals, Grant soon was lassoed into low-budget oaters (1945-46) as the studio's last movie cowboy, then did Monogram's *Northwest Mountie* series (1949-54). His greatest popularity came as rancher "Sky King" in the 1951-57 series of numerous 30-minute TV segments.

RED RIVER RANGE (s)	1938...REP	56
BULLET CODE (s)	1940...RKO	58
HELLO, FRISCO, HELLO (s)	(C)..1943...20T	98
THE STRANGER FROM PECOS (s)	1943...MON	56
LAW MEN (s)	1944...MON	58
BAD MEN OF THE BORDER	1945...UNI	56-60
CODE OF THE LAWLESS	1945...UNI	56-60
(aka THE MYSTERIOUS STRANGER)		
TRAIL TO VENGEANCE (aka VENGEANCE)	1945...UNI	54-58
GUN TOWN	1946...UNI	53-57
RUSTLER'S ROUNDUP (aka RUSTLER'S HIDEOUT)	1946...UNI	56
LAWLESS BREED (aka LAWLESS CLAN)	1946...UNI	58
GUNMAN'S CODE	1946...UNI	54-57
SONG OF IDAHO	1948...COL	66-69
SINGIN' SPURS	1948...COL	62
TRAIL OF THE YUKON	1949...MON	67-69
(starts *Northwest Mountie* series for Monogram/Allied Artists)		
THE WOLF HUNTERS	1949...MON	70
FEUDIN' RHYTHM (aka ACE LUCKY)	1949...COL	66
SNOW DOG	1950...MON	64

KIRBY GRANT, continued

INDIAN TERRITORY (s)	1950...COL	70
CALL OF THE KLONDIKE	1950...MON	65-67
COMIN' ROUND THE MOUNTAIN (s)	1951...UI	77
YUKON MANHUNT	1951...MON	63
NORTHWEST TERRITORY	1951...MON	61
YUKON GOLD	1952...MON	62
FANGS OF THE ARCTIC	1953...AA	63
NORTHERN PATROL	1953...AA	63
YUKON VENGEANCE	1954...AA	68

(ends *Northwest Mountie* series)

PETER GRAVES (1926 -   )

A former radio announcer, his distinguished voice was a major asset in 1950s "A" westerns. Graves found television fame with the "Fury" series on NBC (1955-58), and continues to star in contemporary films as well as hosting Arts and Entertainment Network's "Biography." Brother of James Arness.

ROGUE RIVER	(C)..1950...EL	81
FORT DEFIANCE (cs)	(C)..1951...UA	81
WAR PAINT (s)	(C)..1953...UA	89
THE YELLOW TOMAHAWK (s)	(C)..1954...UA	82
THE RAID (s)	(C)..1954...20T	83
ROBBERS' ROOST (s)	(C)..1955...UA	82
WICHITA (s)	(C)..1955...AA	81
FORT YUMA	(C)..1955...UA	78-79
CANYON RIVER (cs)	(C)..1956...AA	80
TEXAS ACROSS THE RIVER (s)	(C)..1966...UNI	101
THE BALLAD OF JOSIE	(C)..1968...UNI	102
THE FIVE MAN ARMY	(C)..1970...MGM	105
THE REBELS (s)	(C)..1978...UNI-TV	200

MONTE HALE (1921 -   )

His most pleasant warbling abilities compelled Republic Pictures to star Hale in its first 1940s Magnacolor—later named Trucolor—"B" western HOME ON THE RANGE. Monte completed another 18 actioners through 1950 for the studio, and won the Bale Clinch role in GIANT when director George Stevens was impressed with his ability to toss a cowboy hat onto an adjacent rack.

THE BIG BONANZA (s)	1944...REP	68
THE TOPEKA TERROR (s)	1945...REP	55
OREGON TRAIL (s)	1945...REP	55
BANDITS OF THE BADLANDS (s)	1945...REP	55
ROUGH RIDERS OF CHEYENNE (s)	1945...REP	56
COLORADO PIONEERS (s)	1945...REP	55
THE PHANTOM RIDER (s)	(SER)..1946...REP	12CH
CALIFORNIA GOLD RUSH (s)	1946...REP	56
HOME ON THE RANGE	(C)..1946...REP	55
SUN VALLEY CYCLONE (s)	1946...REP	56
MAN FROM RAINBOW VALLEY	(C)..1946...REP	56
OUT CALIFORNIA WAY	(C)..1946...REP	67
LAST FRONTIER UPRISING	(C)..1947...REP	67
ALONG THE OREGON TRAIL	(C)..1947...REP	64
UNDER COLORADO SKIES	(C)..1947...REP	65
CALIFORNIA FIREBRAND	(C)..1948...REP	63

THE TIMBER TRAIL .... (C) .. 1948 ... REP .... 67 ____
SON OF GOD'S COUNTRY .... 1948 ... REP .... 60 ____
PRINCE OF THE PLAINS .... 1949 ... REP .... 60 ____
LAW OF THE GOLDEN WEST .... 1949 ... REP .... 60 ____
OUTCASTS OF THE TRAIL .... 1949 ... REP .... 60 ____
SOUTH OF RIO .... 1949 ... REP .... 60 ____
SAN ANTONE AMBUSH .... 1949 ... REP .... 60 ____
RANGER OF CHEROKEE STRIP .... 1949 ... REP .... 60 ____
PIONEER MARSHAL .... 1949 ... REP .... 60 ____
THE VANISHING WESTERNER .... 1950 ... REP .... 60 ____
THE OLD FRONTIER .... 1950 ... REP .... 60 ____
THE MISSOURIANS .... 1950 ... REP .... 60 ____
TRAIL OF ROBIN HOOD (gs) .... (C) .. 1950 ... REP .... 67 ____
YUKON VENGEANCE .... 1954 ... AA .... 68 ____
GIANT (s) .... (C) .. 1956 ... WB .... 201 ____
THE CHASE (s) .... (C) .. 1966 ... COL .... 135 ____

JON HALL (1913 - 1979)
(aka CHARLES LOCHER)
A virile leading man who made a few western films. Best known in the genre for his portrayal of the frontier scout KIT CARSON.

THE MYSTERIOUS AVENGER (s) .... 1936 ... COL .... 55 ____
WINDS OF THE WASTELAND (s) .... 1936 ... REP .... 58 ____
KIT CARSON .... 1940 ... UA ...... 96-97 ____
MICHIGAN KID .... (C) .. 1947 ... UNI ..... 69-70 ____
THE VIGILANTES RETURN .... (C) .. 1947 ... UNI .... 67 ____
 (aka RETURN OF THE VIGILANTES)
LAST OF THE REDMEN .... (C) .. 1947 ... COL .... 77 ____
 (aka LAST OF THE REDSKINS)
DEPUTY MARSHAL .... 1949 ... LIP ...... 72-75 ____
WHEN THE REDSKINS RODE .... (C) .. 1951 ... COL ... 77-78 ____
BRAVE WARRIOR .... (C) .. 1952 ... COL .... 73 ____

RICHARD HARRIS (1930 -)
British actor whose *Man Called Horse* film series has been his main contribution to the genre. Harris exerted agonizing, tortuous agility.

MAJOR DUNDEE .... (C) .. 1965 ... COL . 124-134 ____
A MAN CALLED HORSE .... (C) .. 1970 ... NG .... 114 ____
MAN IN THE WILDERNESS .... (C) .. 1971 ... WB .. 103-105 ____
THE DEADLY TRACKERS .... (C) .. 1973 ... WB .... 110 ____
THE RETURN OF A MAN CALLED HORSE .... (C) .. 1976 ... UA ... 120-129 ____
TRIUMPHS OF A MAN CALLED HORSE .... (C) .. 1983 ... JFP ...... 86-90 ____
UNFORGIVEN (s) .... (C) .. 1992 ... WB .... 131 ____

RICHARD HARRISON (1936 -)
An American strongman who became a lead in European western films. Lives in Los Angeles, still active with features.

GRINGO (aka GUNFIGHT AT RED SANDS) ...... (C) .. 1965 ... SGE-TV .... 97 ____
$100,000 FOR RINGO .... (C) .. 1965 ... BAL .... 106 ____
SONS OF VENGEANCE .... (C) .. 1965 ... PEA-CF .... 98 ____

84 / RICHARD HARRISON, continued

VENGEANCE	(C)	1971	MGM	100
BETWEEN GOD, THE DEVIL, AND A WINCHESTER	(C)	1972	UV	98
JESSE AND LESTER, TWO BROTHERS IN A PLACE CALLED TRINITY	(C)	1972	HPI	97
TRINITY	(C)	1975	FP	92

RUSSELL HAYDEN (1910 - 1981)
(aka RUSS "LUCKY" HAYDEN)

As abrasive sidekick Lucky Jenkins in the *Hopalong Cassidy* series (1937-41), he went on to make more early 1940s "B" westerns at Columbia Pictures, and teamed up with Jimmy Ellison for *The Irish Cowboys* sagas at Lippert during 1950. Hayden helmed two TV series "Cowboy G-Men" (1952) for 26 half-hour episodes and "Judge Roy Bean" (1956) during 39 half-hour shows.

HILLS OF OLD WYOMING	1937	PAR	79
(starts *Hopalong Cassidy* series)			
NORTH OF THE RIO GRANDE	1937	PAR	70
RUSTLERS' VALLEY	1937	PAR	60
HOPALONG RIDES AGAIN	1937	PAR	65
TEXAS TRAIL	1937	PAR	63
PARTNERS OF THE PLAINS	1938	PAR	68
CASSIDY OF BAR 20	1938	PAR	56
HEART OF ARIZONA	1938	PAR	68
BAR 20 JUSTICE	1938	PAR	70
PRIDE OF THE WEST	1938	PAR	55
IN OLD MEXICO	1938	PAR	62
THE MYSTERIOUS RIDER	1938	PAR	73
(aka MARK OF THE AVENGER) (non-series) (cs)			
SUNSET TRAIL	1938	PAR	60
THE FRONTIERSMEN	1938	PAR	74
SILVER ON THE SAGE	1939	PAR	68
HERITAGE OF THE DESERT (non-series) (cs)	1939	PAR	75
THE RENEGADE TRAIL	1939	PAR	58
RANGE WAR	1939	PAR	66
LAW OF THE PAMPAS	1939	PAR	74
SANTA FE MARSHAL	1940	PAR	68
KNIGHTS OF THE RANGE (non-series)	1940	PAR	70
THE SHOWDOWN	1940	PAR	63
THE LIGHT OF WESTERN STARS (non-series)	1940	PAR	67
HIDDEN GOLD	1940	PAR	61
STAGECOACH WAR	1940	PAR	63
THREE MEN FROM TEXAS	1940	PAR	76
DOOMED CARAVAN	1941	PAR	61
IN OLD COLORADO	1941	PAR	67
BORDER VIGILANTES	1941	PAR	62
PIRATES ON HORSEBACK	1941	PAR	69
WIDE OPEN TOWN (ends *Hopalong Cassidy* series)	1941	PAR	78
THE ROYAL MOUNTED PATROL	1941	COL	59
(aka GIANTS A'FIRE)			
RIDERS OF THE BADLANDS	1941	COL	57
WEST OF TOMBSTONE	1942	COL	59
LAWLESS PLAINSMEN (aka ROLL ON)	1942	COL	59
DOWN RIO GRANDE WAY	1942	COL	57
(aka THE DOUBLE PUNCH)			

RIDERS OF THE NORTHLAND (aka NEXT IN LINE) 1942...COL.........58 ____
BAD MEN OF THE HILLS (aka WRONGLY ACCUSED) 1942...COL.........58 ____
OVERLAND TO DEADWOOD (aka FALLING STONES) 1942...COL.........58 ____
THE LONE PRAIRIE (aka INSIDE INFORMATION) ..1942...COL.........58 ____
A TORNADO IN THE SADDLE (aka AMBUSHED) ....1942...COL.........59 ____
RIDERS OF THE NORTHWEST MOUNTED ....1943...COL.........57 ____
SADDLES AND SAGEBRUSH (aka THE PAY-OFF).1943...COL.........57 ____
SILVER CITY RAIDERS (aka LEGAL LARCENY) .....1943...COL.........55 ____
FRONTIER LAW..1943...UNI.........55 ____
MARSHAL OF GUNSMOKE ....1944...UNI.........58 ____
  (aka SHERIFF OF GUNSMOKE)
THE VIGILANTES RIDE (aka HUNTED) ....1944...COL.........55 ____
WYOMING HURRICANE (aka PROVED GUILTY) ....1944...COL.........58 ____
THE LAST HORSEMAN..1944...COL.........55 ____
'NEATH CANADIAN SKIES ....1946...SG............41 ____
NORTH OF THE BORDER ....1946...SG............42 ____
WHERE THE NORTH BEGINS ....1947...SG............42 ____
TRAIL OF THE MOUNTIES ....1947...SG............42 ____
ALBUQUERQUE (aka SILVER CITY) (s) ....(C)..1948...PAR.........90 ____
SONS OF ADVENTURE ....1948...REP.........60 ____
DEPUTY MARSHAL (cs) ....1949...LIP........72-75 ____
APACHE CHIEF (s)..1949...LIP...........60 ____
HOSTILE COUNTRY (aka GUNS OF JUSTICE) ....1950...LIP...........60 ____
  (starts *The Irish Cowboys* series)
EVERYBODY'S DANCIN'! (non-series) (s) ....1950...LIP...........65 ____
MARSHAL OF HELDORADO (aka BLAZING GUNS) 1950...LIP...........53 ____
CROOKED RIVER (aka THE LAST BULLET) ....1950...LIP...........55 ____
COLORADO RANGER (aka OUTLAW FURY) ....1950...LIP...........54 ____
WEST OF THE BRAZOS (aka RANGELAND EMPIRE).1950...LIP...........58 ____
FAST ON THE DRAW (aka SUDDEN DEATH) ....1950...LIP...........55 ____
  (ends *The Irish Cowboys* series)
TEXANS NEVER CRY (s) ....1951...COL.........70 ____
VALLEY OF FIRE (s) ....1951...COL.........63 ____

STERLING HAYDEN (1916 - 1986)

A tall, rugged, taciturn actor whose forceful presence in drama and western roles made him an absolute standout. Was superb in both Republic's JOHNNY GUITAR and THE LAST COMMAND.

EL PASO..(C)..1949...PAR.........89 ____
FLAMING FEATHER......................................(C)..1952...PAR.....77-78 ____
THE DENVER AND THE RIO GRANDE ....(C)..1952...PAR.........89 ____
HELLGATE ....1952...LIP...........87 ____
KANSAS PACIFIC ....(C)..1953...AA............73 ____
TAKE ME TO TOWN ....(C)..1953...UI.............81 ____
ARROW IN THE DUST ....(C)..1954...AA............80 ____
JOHNNY GUITAR ....(C)..1954...REP........110 ____
SUDDENLY...1954...UA............77 ____
NAKED ALIBI ....1954...UI.............86 ____
TIMBERJACK ....(C)..1955...REP.....92-94 ____
SHOTGUN ....(C)..1955...AA............80 ____
THE LAST COMMAND ....(C)..1955...REP........110 ____
TOP GUN ....1955...UA............73 ____
THE IRON SHERIFF ....1957...UA............73 ____

86 / STERLING HAYDEN, continued

VALERIE	1957	UA	84
GUN BATTLE AT MONTEREY	1957	AA	67-84
TERROR IN A TEXAS TOWN	1958	UA	80-81
TEN DAYS TO TULARA	1958	UA	77
THE BLUE AND THE GRAY (s)	(C).. 1982	CBS-TV	295

VAN HEFLIN (1910 - 1971)

An outstanding character actor who became a leading man. His best-known western film role was that of the nester whom Alan Ladd aided in the classic SHANE.

THE OUTCASTS OF POKER FLAT (cs)	1937	RKO	68
SANTA FE TRAIL (s)	1940	WB	110
TENNESSEE JOHNSON	1942	MGM	100-103
(aka THE MAN ON AMERICA'S CONSCIENCE)			
TAP ROOTS	(C).. 1948	UI	109
TOMAHAWK (aka BATTLE OF POWDER RIVER)	(C).. 1951	UI	82
SHANE (cs)	(C).. 1953	PAR	117
WINGS OF THE HAWK	(C).. 1953	UI	77-81
THE RAID	(C).. 1954	20T	83
COUNT THREE AND PRAY	(C).. 1955	COL	102
3:10 TO YUMA	1957	COL	92
GUNMAN'S WALK	(C).. 1958	COL	97
THEY CAME TO CORDURA (cs)	(C).. 1959	COL	123
STAGECOACH (s)	(C).. 1966	20T	115
THE RUTHLESS FOUR	(C).. 1968	GFE	96-97
(aka EVERY MAN FOR HIMSELF; EACH ONE FOR HIMSELF; EACH MAN FOR HIMSELF; SAM COOPER'S GOLD)			

CHARLTON HESTON (1924 -)

A tall, brooding actor who is remembered mainly for his epic roles. But he has made several fine western films, including WILL PENNY.

THE SAVAGE	(C).. 1952	PAR	95
THE PRESIDENT'S LADY	1953	20T	96
PONY EXPRESS	(C).. 1953	PAR	101
ARROWHEAD	(C).. 1953	PAR	105
THE FAR HORIZONS (aka THE UNTAMED WEST)	(C).. 1955	PAR	108
LUCY GALLANT (aka OIL TOWN)	(C).. 1955	PAR	104
THREE VIOLENT PEOPLE	(C).. 1957	PAR	100
TOUCH OF EVIL	1958	UI	95-105
THE BIG COUNTRY (s)	(C).. 1958	UA	156-166
MAJOR DUNDEE	(C).. 1965	COL	124-134
WILL PENNY	(C).. 1968	PAR	106-109
CALL OF THE WILD	(C).. 1973	IRC	102
THE LAST HARD MEN	(C).. 1976	20T	98-103
THE MOUNTAIN MEN	(C).. 1980	COL	102
MOTHER LODE	(C).. 1982	AGM	101
(aka SEARCH FOR THE MOTHER LODE: THE LAST GREAT TREASURE)			
PROUD MEN	(C).. 1987	AFP-TV	100

WILD BILL HICKOK series (1940 - 1942; 1951 - 1955)
The famous prairie lawman's adventures were brought to the screen twice—first with Bill Elliott at Columbia Pictures (1940-42), and then from 1951-55 through Guy Madison's starrers at Monogram/Allied Artists which were "pasteups" of his half-hour TV shows.

(BILL ELLIOTT, DUB "CANNONBALL" TAYLOR)

PRAIRIE SCHOONERS (aka THROUGH THE STORM)	1940	COL	58
BEYOND THE SACRAMENTO	1940	COL	58
(aka POWER OF JUSTICE)			
THE WILDCAT OF TUCSON	1941	COL	58-60
(aka PROMISE FULFILLED)			
ACROSS THE SIERRAS	1941	COL	58
(aka WELCOME STRANGER)			
NORTH FROM THE LONE STAR	1941	COL	58
HANDS ACROSS THE ROCKIES	1941	COL	58

(BILL ELLIOTT, TEX RITTER, DUB "CANNONBALL" TAYLOR)

KING OF DODGE CITY	1941	COL	63

(BILL ELLIOTT, TEX RITTER, FRANK "CANNONBALL" MITCHELL)

ROARING FRONTIERS (aka FRONTIER)	1941	COL	62
THE LONE STAR VIGILANTES	1942	COL	58
(aka THE DEVIL'S PRICE)			
BULLETS FOR BANDITS	1942	COL	55
THE DEVIL'S TRAIL	1942	COL	61
(aka ROGUE'S GALLERY; DEVIL'S CANYON)			
PRAIRIE GUNSMOKE	1942	COL	56

(GUY MADISON, ANDY DEVINE)

BEHIND SOUTHERN LINES	1952	MON	51
THE GHOST OF CROSSBONES CANYON	1952	MON	56
TRAIL OF THE ARROW	1952	MON	54
THE YELLOW HAIRED KID	1952	MON	56
BORDER CITY RUSTLERS	1953	AA	54
SECRET OF OUTLAW FLATS	1953	AA	54
SIX-GUN DECISION	1953	AA	54
TWO-GUN MARSHAL	1953	AA	52
MARSHALS IN DISGUISE	1954	AA	53
OUTLAW'S SON	1954	AA	53
TROUBLE ON THE TRAIL	1954	AA	54
THE TWO-GUN TEACHER	1954	AA	50
TIMBER COUNTRY TROUBLE	1955	AA	55
THE MATCH-MAKING MARSHAL	1955	AA	55
THE TITLED TENDERFOOT	1955	AA	55
PHANTOM TRAILS	1955	AA	55

TERENCE HILL (1931 -   )
Italian leading man of European westerns. Best known for his character, "Trinity."

GOD FORGIVES, I DON'T	(C)	1969	AI	101
ACE HIGH	(C)	1969	PAR	120-123
REVENGE IN EL PASO	(C)	1969	PAR	103
THEY CALL ME TRINITY	(C)	1971	AE	109-117
BOOT HILL	(C)	1972	FVI	87

88 / TERENCE HILL, continued

TRINITY IS STILL MY NAME	(C)	1972	AE	117-121
MAN OF THE EAST	(C)	1972	AE	122
MY NAME IS NOBODY	(C)	1974	UNI	115-130
THE GENIUS	(C)	1976	TIT	126

JOHN HODIAK (1914 - 1955)

An MGM drama star of the 1940s, his appearances in moderate-budget "A" westerns would have lasted longer had Hodiak not suffered a premature 1955 death. Hodiak was tough in DESERT FURY and AMBUSH AT TOMAHAWK GAP.

MAISIE GOES TO RENO		1944	MGM	90
(aka YOU CAN'T DO THAT TO ME)				
THE HARVEY GIRLS (cs)	(C)	1946	MGM	101
DESERT FURY	(C)	1947	PAR	95
AMBUSH		1950	MGM	89
ACROSS THE WIDE MISSOURI (cs)	(C)	1951	MGM	78
AMBUSH AT TOMAHAWK GAP	(C)	1953	COL	73
CONQUEST OF COCHISE	(C)	1953	COL	70

WILLIAM HOLDEN (1918 - 1981)

Sincere, likeable leading man whose range allowed him to play both heroes and villains equally well. Holden co-starred with good friend Glenn Ford during the 1940s in TEXAS and THE MAN FROM COLORADO. Best known in "A" oaters for his portrayal of the leader of THE WILD BUNCH.

ARIZONA		1940	COL	127
TEXAS		1941	COL	93-94
THE MAN FROM COLORADO	(C)	1948	COL	99
RACHEL AND THE STRANGER		1948	RKO	79-93
STREETS OF LAREDO	(C)	1949	PAR	92
ESCAPE FROM FORT BRAVO	(C)	1953	MGM	98
THE HORSE SOLDIERS	(C)	1959	UA	119
ALVAREZ KELLY	(C)	1966	COL	116
THE WILD BUNCH	(C)	1969	WB	134-144
WILD ROVERS	(C)	1971	MGM	106-136
THE REVENGERS	(C)	1972	NG	107-112

JACK HOLT (1888 - 1951)

Rugged silent star who successfully made the move to sound films and continued as a character actor late in his career. The father of "B" western star Tim Holt, Jack's hard-edge dramatics greatly enhanced such highly-praised oaters as MY PAL TRIGGER, THE ARIZONA RANGER, and THE STRAWBERRY ROAN.

THE BORDER LEGION		1930	PAR	68
THE LITTLEST REBEL (cs)		1935	20T	70-73
SAN FRANCISCO (s)		1936	MGM	115
END OF THE TRAIL (aka REVENGE)		1936	COL	70
NORTH OF NOME		1936	COL	63
ROARING TIMBER		1937	COL	65
THUNDER BIRDS (s)	(C)	1942	20T	78

JACK HOLT, continued

Title	Year	Studio	Min
NORTHWEST RANGERS (s)	1942	MGM	64
MY PAL TRIGGER (s)	1946	REP	79
FLIGHT TO NOWHERE (s)	1946	SG	74
RENEGADE GIRL (s)	1946	SG	65
THE WILD FRONTIER (cs)	1947	REP	59
THE TREASURE OF THE SIERRA MADRE (s)	1948	WB	126
THE ARIZONA RANGER	1948	RKO	63
THE GALLANT LEGION (s)	1948	REP	88
THE STRAWBERRY ROAN (C) (aka FOOLS AWAKE) (s)	1948	COL	76
LOADED PISTOLS (s)	1949	COL	79
THE LAST BANDIT (s) (C)	1949	REP	80
BRIMSTONE (s) (C)	1949	REP	90
RED DESERT (s)	1949	LIP	60
RETURN OF THE FRONTIERSMAN (s) (C)	1950	WB	74
TRAIL OF ROBIN HOOD (s) (C)	1950	REP	67
THE DALTONS' WOMEN (cs)	1951	WA	80
KING OF THE BULLWHIP (s)	1951	WA	59
ACROSS THE WIDE MISSOURI (s) (C)	1951	MGM	78

TIM HOLT (1918 - 1973)

He was a top-flight "B" star in quality oaters for RKO Radio Pictures (1940-43; 1947-52), but his dramatic abilities also enabled Holt to do classic "A" westerns like MY DARLING CLEMENTINE and THE TREASURE OF THE SIERRA MADRE. The cowboy was a Top Money-Making Western Star (1941-43, 1948-52) who diversified in later years doing work on Oklahoma radio and TV.

Title	Year	Studio	Min
GOLD IS WHERE YOU FIND IT (s) (C)	1938	WB	90
THE RENEGADE RANGER (cs)	1938	RKO	59
THE LAW WEST OF TOMBSTONE	1938	RKO	73
STAGECOACH (s)	1939	UA	96
THE GIRL AND THE GAMBLER	1939	RKO	63
WAGON TRAIN	1940	RKO	59
THE FARGO KID	1940	RKO	63
ALONG THE RIO GRANDE	1941	RKO	61-64
ROBBERS OF THE RANGE	1941	RKO	61
CYCLONE ON HORSEBACK	1941	RKO	60
SIX-GUN GOLD	1941	RKO	57
THE BANDIT TRAIL	1941	RKO	60
DUDE COWBOY	1941	RKO	59
THUNDERING HOOFS	1941	RKO	61
RIDING THE WIND	1942	RKO	60
LAND OF THE OPEN RANGE	1942	RKO	60
COME ON DANGER	1942	RKO	58
BANDIT RANGER	1942	RKO	61
PIRATES OF THE PRAIRIE	1942	RKO	57
FIGHTING FRONTIER	1943	RKO	57
THE AVENGING RIDER	1943	RKO	55
SAGEBRUSH LAW	1943	RKO	56
RED RIVER ROBIN HOOD	1943	RKO	59
MY DARLING CLEMENTINE (s)	1946	20T	91-97
THUNDER MOUNTAIN	1947	RKO	60
UNDER THE TONTO RIM	1947	RKO	61
WILD HORSE MESA	1947	RKO	60-65

TIM HOLT, continued

THE TREASURE OF THE SIERRA MADRE (cs)	1948...WB	126
WESTERN HERITAGE	1948...RKO	61
THE ARIZONA RANGER	1948...RKO	63
GUNS OF HATE (aka GUNS OF WRATH)	1948...RKO	62
INDIAN AGENT	1948...RKO	63-65
GUN SMUGGLERS	1948...RKO	62
BROTHERS IN THE SADDLE	1949...RKO	60
RUSTLERS	1949...RKO	61
STAGECOACH KID	1949...RKO	60
THE MYSTERIOUS DESPERADO	1949...RKO	61
MASKED RAIDERS	1949...RKO	60
RIDERS OF THE RANGE	1950...RKO	60
STORM OVER WYOMING	1950...RKO	60
RIDER FROM TUCSON	1950...RKO	60
DYNAMITE PASS	1950...RKO	61
BORDER TREASURE	1950...RKO	60
RIO GRANDE PATROL	1950...RKO	60
LAW OF THE BADLANDS	1950...RKO	60
SADDLE LEGION	1951...RKO	60
GUNPLAY	1951...RKO	60
PISTOL HARVEST	1951...RKO	60
HOT LEAD (aka A TASTE OF HOT LEAD)	1951...RKO	60
OVERLAND TELEGRAPH	1951...RKO	60
TRAIL GUIDE	1952...RKO	60
ROAD AGENT	1952...RKO	60
TARGET	1952...RKO	60
DESERT PASSAGE	1952...RKO	60
THE MONSTER THAT CHALLENGED THE WORLD	1957...UA	83

BOB HOPE (1903 -)

Famous radio, screen, and television comedian who has made several western comedies. Best-known for his "Paleface" roles at Paramount Pictures.

NEVER SAY DIE	1939...PAR	82
ROAD TO UTOPIA	1945...PAR	90
THE PALEFACE	(C)..1948...PAR	91
FANCY PANTS	(C)..1950...PAR	92
SON OF PALEFACE	(C)..1952...PAR	95
ALIAS JESSE JAMES	(C)..1959...UA	92
CANCEL MY RESERVATION	(C)..1972...WB	99

GEORGE HOUSTON (1898 - 1944)

Despite a strong singing voice from sporadic film roles in the late 1930s, Houston lasted only one-and-a-half years starring in *The Lone Rider* series at PRC (1941-42) with 11 low-budgeters. He was organizing an opera division of the New York Theatre Guild at the time of his sudden passing.

FRONTIER SCOUT	1938...GN	61
THE HOWARDS OF VIRGINIA	1940...COL	122
(aka TREE OF LIBERTY) (s)		
THE LONE RIDER RIDES ON	1941...PRC	61-64
(starts *The Lone Rider* series)		
THE LONE RIDER CROSSES THE RIO	1941...PRC	63
THE LONE RIDER IN GHOST TOWN	1941...PRC	64

GEORGE HOUSTON, continued / 91

THE LONE RIDER IN FRONTIER FURY	1941	PRC	62
THE LONE RIDER AMBUSHED	1941	PRC	63
THE LONE RIDER FIGHTS BACK	1941	PRC	64
THE LONE RIDER AND THE BANDIT	1942	PRC	54
THE LONE RIDER IN CHEYENNE	1942	PRC	59
THE LONE RIDER IN TEXAS JUSTICE	1942	PRC	59
BORDER ROUNDUP	1942	PRC	57
OUTLAWS OF BOULDER PASS	1942	PRC	64

(ends *The Lone Rider* series)

JACK HOXIE (1888 - 1965)

An early silent western veteran in the 1910s-1920s, he was to find only brief stardom in sound features (1932-33).

GOLD	1932	MAJ	53-58
OUTLAW JUSTICE	1932	MAJ	61
LAW AND LAWLESS	1932	MAJ	59-62
VIA PONY EXPRESS	1933	MAJ	60-62
GUN LAW	1933	MAJ	59-62
TROUBLE BUSTERS	1933	MAJ	55

ROCK HUDSON (1925 - 1985)

Tall, handsome leading man whose western roles were mainly during the early years of his film career. Rescued wife Donna Reed from abductors with GUN FURY. Best remembered in the genre for his portrayal of the modern Texan in GIANT.

WINCHESTER '73 (s)		1950	UI	92
TOMAHAWK	(C)	1951	UI	82
(aka BATTLE OF POWDER RIVER) (s)				
BEND OF THE RIVER	(C)	1952	UI	91
(aka WHERE THE RIVER BENDS) (s)				
SCARLET ANGEL	(C)	1952	UI	80
HORIZONS WEST (cs)	(C)	1952	UI	81
THE LAWLESS BREED	(C)	1953	UI	83
SEMINOLE	(C)	1953	UI	86-87
GUN FURY	(C)	1953	COL	83
BACK TO GOD'S COUNTRY	(C)	1953	UI	78
TAZA, SON OF COCHISE	(C)	1954	UI	79
ONE DESIRE	(C)	1955	UI	94
GIANT	(C)	1956	WB	201
THE LAST SUNSET	(C)	1961	UI	112
THE UNDEFEATED	(C)	1969	20T	119
SHOWDOWN	(C)	1973	UNI	99

JEFFREY HUNTER (1927 - 1969)

Handsome leading man whose best western roles were in John Ford films. Hunter starred in NBC-TV's "Temple Houston" (1963-64) with 26 hour-long shows.

RED SKIES OF MONTANA	(C)	1952	20T	89
THREE YOUNG TEXANS (cs)	(C)	1954	20T	78
WHITE FEATHER	(C)	1955	20T	102
SEVEN ANGRY MEN (cs)		1955	AA	90
SEVEN CITIES OF GOLD (cs)	(C)	1955	20T	103

JEFFREY HUNTER, continued

THE SEARCHERS (cs)	(C) .. 1956 ... WB	119	
THE PROUD ONES (cs)	(C) .. 1956 ... 20T	92-94	
THE GREAT LOCOMOTIVE CHASE	(C) .. 1956 ... BV	85	
(aka ANDREWS' RAIDERS)			
THE TRUE STORY OF JESSE JAMES	(C) .. 1957 ... 20T	92	
(aka THE JAMES BROTHERS)			
GUN FOR A COWARD	(C) .. 1957 ... UI	73-88	
THE WAY TO THE GOLD	1957 ... 20T	94	
SERGEANT RUTLEDGE	(C) .. 1960 ... WB	111-118	
THE MAN FROM GALVESTON	1964 ... WB	57	
MURIETTA	(C) .. 1965 ... WB	108	
(aka JOAQUIN MURIETTA; VENDETTA)			
THE CHRISTMAS KID	(C) .. 1967 ... PRO	87-89	
CUSTER OF THE WEST	(C) .. 1967 ... CRO	140-143	
(aka GOOD DAY FOR FIGHTING)			
FIND A PLACE TO DIE	(C) .. 1971 ... GGP	100	

TAB HUNTER (1931 -   )

His all-American athletic ability, plus good looks, in the 1950s made Hunter a natural for big-budget "A" westerns such as Columbia Pictues' popular GUNMAN'S WALK and THEY CAME TO CORDURA.

THE LAWLESS (aka THE DIVIDING LINE) (s)	1950 ... PAR	83	
GUN BELT	(C) .. 1953 ... UA	77	
TRACK OF THE CAT (cs)	(C) .. 1954 ... WB	102	
THE BURNING HILLS	(C) .. 1956 ... WB	94	
GUNMAN'S WALK	(C) .. 1958 ... COL	97	
THEY CAME TO CORDURA (s)	(C) .. 1959 ... COL	123	
HOSTILE GUNS (cs)	(C) .. 1967 ... PAR	91	
THE LIFE AND TIMES OF JUDGE ROY BEAN (s)	(C) .. 1972 ... NG	120	
LUST IN THE DUST	(C) .. 1984 ... FR	85	

WALTER HUSTON (1884 - 1950)

His careful selection of film roles over a distinguished career added to Huston's stature, even when it came to those rough-hewn appearances in "A" western classics like THE VIRGINIAN, LAW AND ORDER, and THE TREASURE OF THE SIERRA MADRE. Was director John Huston's father.

THE VIRGINIAN (cs)	1929 ... PAR	90	
THE BAD MAN	1930 ... FN	80	
ABRAHAM LINCOLN	1930 ... UA	97	
LAW AND ORDER (aka GUNS A'BLAZING)	1932 ... UNI	70	
OF HUMAN HEARTS	1938 ... MGM	100	
THE OUTLAW (cs)	1943 ... UA	115	
DUEL IN THE SUN (s)	(C) .. 1947 ... SEL	130-138	
THE TREASURE OF THE SIERRA MADRE	1948 ... WB	126	
THE FURIES	1950 ... PAR	109	

JOHN IRELAND (1914 - 1992)

Canadian stage actor whose early character roles in westerns have been superior to his later leading parts. Best known as the gunfighting drover in the epic John Wayne film, RED RIVER. Ireland was good with the off-beat GUNSLINGER.

Title	Year	Studio	Page
MY DARLING CLEMENTINE (s)	1946	20T	91-97
RED RIVER (s)	1948	UA	125-133
A SOUTHERN YANKEE (aka MY HERO!) (s)	1948	MGM	90
I SHOT JESSE JAMES	1949	SG	81-83
THE WALKING HILLS (s)	1949	COL	78
ROUGHSHOD (s)	1949	RKO	88
THE DOOLINS OF OKLAHOMA (s) (aka THE GREAT MANHUNT)	1949	COL	90
THE RETURN OF JESSE JAMES	1950	LIP	73-77
VENGEANCE VALLEY (s) (C)	1951	MGM	82
RED MOUNTAIN (cs) (C)	1951	PAR	84
LITTLE BIG HORN (aka THE FIGHTING SEVENTH)	1951	LIP	85
THE BUSHWHACKERS (aka THE REBEL)	1951	REA	70
HANNAH LEE (aka OUTLAW TERRITORY) (cs)(C)	1953	REA	79
SOUTHWEST PASSAGE (aka CAMELS WEST) (C)	1954	UA	82
GUNSLINGER (C)	1956	ARC	78-83
GUNFIGHT AT THE O.K. CORRAL (s) (C)	1957	PAR	122
FORT UTAH (C)	1967	PAR	83
ARIZONA BUSHWHACKERS (C)	1968	PAR	86
VILLA RIDES (s) (C)	1968	PAR	125
THE CHALLENGE OF THE MacKENNAS (C)	1969	PIC	101
GO FOR BROKE (C)	1972	STE	
CHINO (C)	1976	IRC	98
TASTE OF DEATH (C)	1977	WES	90
KINO, THE PADRE ON HORSEBACK (cs) (C) (aka MISSION TO GLORY)	1977	KI	116
THE COURAGE OF KAVIK, THE WOLF DOG (C) (aka KAVIK, THE WOLF DOG)	1980	NBC-TV	100
DEAD FOR A DOLLAR (C)	1985	ZIV	92
BONANZA, THE NEXT GENERATION (C)	1988	COL-TV	100

THE IRISH COWBOYS series (1950)

These low-budget oaters were to be followed by 24 more—six each year—through 1954 under a deal Jimmy Ellison and Russell Hayden made with Lippert Pictures. Evidently, low box-office receipts were a factor in the short life of this series.

(JIMMIE "SHAMROCK" ELLISON, RUSS "LUCKY" HAYDEN)

Title	Year	Studio	Page
HOSTILE COUNTRY (aka GUNS OF JUSTICE)	1950	LIP	60
MARSHAL OF HELDORADO (aka BLAZING GUNS)	1950	LIP	53
CROOKED RIVER (aka THE LAST BULLET)	1950	LIP	55
COLORADO RANGER (aka OUTLAW FURY)	1950	LIP	54
WEST OF THE BRAZOS (aka RANGELAND EMPIRE)	1950	LIP	58
FAST ON THE DRAW (aka SUDDEN DEATH)	1950	LIP	55

ART JARRETT (1906 - 1987)

He was another actor who lost out to cowboy stardom in 1939 when Grand National shut down. TRIGGER PALS was to have initiated a new studio "B" western series.

Title	Year	Studio	Page
TRIGGER PALS	1939	GN	55-60

BEN JOHNSON (1918 -)

From horse wrangler to stuntman, Ben Johnson rose to stardom and later became a fine character actor whose distinctive voice and realistic western appearance marked him as a real westerner. A former rodeo star, he also acquired a 1972 Oscar for his performance in THE LAST PICTURE SHOW. Johnson participated in ABC-TV's "The Monroes" (1966-67). Still active with features.

Title	Year	Studio	Page
LAWLESS PLAINSMEN (s)	1942	COL	59
NORTH OF THE ROCKIES (aka FALSE CLUES) (s)	1942	COL	60
PRAIRIE GUNSMOKE (s)	1942	COL	56
RIDERS OF THE RIO GRANDE (s)	1943	REP	55
BORDERTOWN GUN FIGHTERS (s)	1943	REP	55
THE OUTLAW (s)	1943	UA	121
NEVADA (s)	1944	RKO	62
TALL IN THE SADDLE (s)	1944	RKO	87
SANTA FE SADDLEMATES (s)	1945	REP	56
THE NAUGHTY NINETIES (s)	1945	UNI	76
COLORADO PIONEERS (s)	1945	REP	55
CALIFORNIA GOLD RUSH (s)	1946	REP	56
BADMAN'S TERRITORY (s)	1946	RKO	98
SMOKY (s)	(C) 1946	20T	87
OUT CALIFORNIA WAY (s)	(C) 1946	REP	67
ANGEL AND THE BADMAN (s)	1947	REP	100
WYOMING (s)	1947	REP	84
THE FABULOUS TEXAN (s)	1947	REP	98
THE GALLANT LEGION (s)	1948	REP	88
FORT APACHE (s)	1948	RKO	127
3 GODFATHERS (s)	(C) 1949	MGM	106
MIGHTY JOE YOUNG	1949	RKO	94
SHE WORE A YELLOW RIBBON (s)	(C) 1949	RKO	104
WAGON MASTER	1950	RKO	86
RIO GRANDE (s)	1950	REP	105
FORT DEFIANCE	(C) 1951	UA	81
WILD STALLION	(C) 1952	MON	70-72
SHANE (s)	(C) 1953	PAR	118
OKLAHOMA! (s)	(C) 1955	20T	145
REBEL IN TOWN (s)	1956	UA	78
WAR DRUMS (cs)	(C) 1957	UA	75
SLIM CARTER (s)	(C) 1957	UI	82
FORT BOWIE	1958	UA	80
TEN WHO DARED (s)	(C) 1960	BV	92
TOMBOY AND THE CHAMP	(C) 1961	UI	92
ONE-EYED JACKS (s)	(C) 1961	PAR	141
CHEYENNE AUTUMN (s)	(C) 1964	WB	145-160
MAJOR DUNDEE (s)	(C) 1965	COL	124-134
THE RARE BREED (s)	(C) 1966	UNI	97-108
WILL PENNY (s)	(C) 1968	PAR	108
HANG 'EM HIGH (s)	(C) 1968	UA	115
RIDE A NORTHBOUND HORSE (cs)	(C) 1969	BV	79
THE WILD BUNCH (s)	(C) 1969	WB	134-144
THE UNDEFEATED (s)	(C) 1969	20T	119
CHISUM (s)	(C) 1970	WB	111
SOMETHING BIG (s)	(C) 1971	NG	108
THE LAST PICTURE SHOW (cs)	1971	COL	118
JUNIOR BONNER (s)	(C) 1972	CRC	100-103
THE GETAWAY (cs)	(C) 1972	NG	122

BEN JOHNSON, continued / 95

THE RED PONY (cs)	(C)	1973	UNI-TV	100 ____
THE TRAIN ROBBERS (s)	(C)	1973	WB	92 ____
KID BLUE (cs)	(C)	1973	20T	100 ____
LOCUSTS	(C)	1974	TVM	78 ____
THE SUGARLAND EXPRESS	(C)	1974	UNI	109 ____
BITE THE BULLET (s)	(C)	1975	COL	131 ____
THE BULL OF THE WEST (s)	(C)	1975	UNI	150 ____
BREAKHEART PASS	(C)	1976	UA	95 ____
THE TOWN THAT DREADED SUNDOWN	(C)	1977	AI	90 ____
GREYEAGLE	(C)	1977	AI	104 ____
THE SWARM (s)	(C)	1978	PAR	116 ____
THE SACKETTS (aka THE DAYBREAKERS) (s)	(C)	1979	NBC-TV	200 ____
WILD TIMES	(C)	1980	GC-TV	200 ____
THE SHADOW RIDERS	(C)	1982	CBS-TV	100 ____
(aka LOUIS L'AMOUR'S THE SHADOW RIDERS) (cs)				
TEX (cs)	(C)	1982	BV	103 ____
WILD HORSES (cs)	(C)	1985	CBS-TV	100 ____
DREAM WEST (s)	(C)	1986	CBS-TV	420 ____
TRESPASSES (s)	(C)	1987	SE	100 ____
DARK BEFORE DAWN (s)	(C)	1988	PSM	95 ____
CHERRY 2000	(C)	1988	ORI	93 ____
OKLAHOMA PASSAGE (ho)	(C)	1989	OETA-TV	300 ____
MY HEROES HAVE ALWAYS BEEN COWBOYS (cs)	(C)	1991	SGC	106 ____
THE CHASE	(C)	1991	SPF-TV	100 ____

BUCK JONES (1891 - 1942)
(aka CHARLES "BUCK" JONES)

Following almost a decade of stardom as a silent lead in Fox westerns, Jones joined Columbia Pictures in 1930 and made four years of this studio's finest "B" galloper releases like THE FIGHTING SHERIFF and THE FIGHTING CODE. Buck continued with Universal westerns and serials plus another year at Columbia (1934-38). 1941 saw Monogram corral him for *The Rough Riders* series (1941-42) which surely would have lasted a few more movie seasons had it not been for that fateful 1942 Boston nightclub fire. Buck was a Top Money-Making Western Star (1936-39).

THE BIG HOP	1928	BJP	67 ____
THE LONE RIDER	1930	COL	65 ____
SHADOW RANCH	1930	COL	63 ____
MEN WITHOUT LAW	1930	COL	61-65 ____
THE DAWN TRAIL	1930	COL	66 ____
DESERT VENGEANCE	1931	COL	59-64 ____
THE AVENGER	1931	COL	62-65 ____
THE TEXAS RANGER	1931	COL	61 ____
THE FIGHTING SHERIFF	1931	COL	61-67 ____
BRANDED	1931	COL	61 ____
THE RANGE FEUD	1931	COL	56-64 ____
DEADLINE	1931	COL	59 ____
BORDER LAW	1931	COL	61-63 ____
ONE MAN LAW	1931	COL	63 ____
RIDIN' FOR JUSTICE	1932	COL	64 ____
SOUTH OF THE RIO GRANDE	1932	COL	60 ____
HELLO TROUBLE	1932	COL	67 ____
McKENNA OF THE MOUNTED	1932	COL	66 ____

96 / BUCK JONES, continued

Title	Year	Studio	Page
WHITE EAGLE	1932	COL	67
FORBIDDEN TRAIL	1932	COL	71
TREASON	1933	COL	61-63
UNKNOWN VALLEY	1933	COL	69
THE CALIFORNIA TRAIL	1933	COL	67
GORDON OF GHOST CITY (SER)	1933	UNI	15CH
THE THRILL HUNTER	1933	COL	58-60
THE FIGHTING CODE	1933	COL	65
SUNDOWN RIDER	1933	COL	65-69
THE MAN TRAILER	1934	COL	58
THE FIGHTING RANGER	1934	COL	60-62
THE RED RIDER (SER)	1934	UNI	15CH
ROCKY RHODES	1934	UNI	60-64
WHEN A MAN SEES RED	1934	UNI	60
THE CRIMSON TRAIL	1935	UNI	58-60
STONE OF SILVER CREEK	1935	UNI	60-63
BORDER BRIGANDS	1935	UNI	56
OUTLAWED GUNS	1935	UNI	62
THE ROARING WEST (SER)	1935	UNI	15CH
THE THROWBACK	1935	UNI	58-60
THE IVORY HANDLED GUN	1935	UNI	59
SUNSET OF POWER	1935	UNI	57-66
SILVERSPURS	1936	UNI	61
FOR THE SERVICE	1936	UNI	65
THE COWBOY AND THE KID	1936	UNI	58
THE PHANTOM RIDER (SER)	1936	UNI	15CH
RIDE 'EM COWBOY (aka COWBOY ROUNDUP)	1936	UNI	60
THE BOSS RIDER OF GUN GREEK	1936	UNI	60-65
EMPTY SADDLES	1936	UNI	62-67
SANDFLOW	1937	UNI	58
LEFT-HANDED LAW	1937	UNI	63
SMOKE TREE RANGE	1937	UNI	59
BLACK ACES	1937	UNI	59
LAW FOR TOMBSTONE	1937	UNI	59
BOSS OF LONELY VALLEY	1937	UNI	60
HOLLYWOOD ROUND-UP	1937	COL	64
HEADIN' EAST	1937	COL	67
SUDDEN BILL DORN	1937	UNI	60
THE OVERLAND EXPRESS	1938	COL	55
THE STRANGER FROM ARIZONA	1938	COL	54
LAW OF THE TEXAN	1938	COL	54
CALIFORNIA FRONTIER	1938	COL	54
WAGONS WESTWARD (cs)	1940	REP	70
WHITE EAGLE (SER)	1941	COL	15CH
RIDERS OF DEATH VALLEY (SER)	1941	UNI	15CH
ARIZONA BOUND (starts *The Rough Riders* series)	1941	MON	57
THE GUNMAN FROM BODIE	1941	MON	62
FORBIDDEN TRAILS	1941	MON	59
BELOW THE BORDER	1942	MON	57
GHOST TOWN LAW	1942	MON	62
DOWN TEXAS WAY	1942	MON	57
RIDERS OF THE WEST	1942	MON	58-60
WEST OF THE LAW	1942	MON	55-60
DAWN ON THE GREAT DIVIDE	1942	MON	63-66

(ends *The Rough Riders* series)

HOWARD KEEL (1917 -   )

A leading actor with an excellent singing voice whose large stature made him a natural for western roles. But he has been mainly known for his musical parts, most notably in the genre as the marksman, Frank Butler, in support of Betty Hutton in ANNIE GET YOUR GUN. Keel also appeared in a number of the last seasons' episodes of CBS-TV's "Dallas." Hilarious as the funny Indian for THE WAR WAGON.

ANNIE GET YOUR GUN	(C)	1950	MGM	107
SHOW BOAT (cs)	(C)	1951	MGM	103
TEXAS CARNIVAL	(C)	1951	MGM	77
ACROSS THE WIDE MISSOURI (nr)	(C)	1951	MGM	78
CALLAWAY WENT THATAWAY		1951	MGM	81
(aka THE STAR SAID NO)				
DESPERATE SEARCH		1952	MGM	73
RIDE, VAQUERO! (cs)	(C)	1953	MGM	90
CALAMITY JANE	(C)	1953	WB	101
ROSE MARIE	(C)	1954	MGM	104-115
SEVEN BRIDES FOR SEVEN BROTHERS	(C)	1954	MGM	103
THE MAN FROM BUTTON WILLOW (vo)	(C)	1964	USA	84
WACO	(C)	1966	PAR	85
RED TOMAHAWK	(C)	1967	PAR	82
THE WAR WAGON (cs)	(C)	1967	UNI	101
ARIZONA BUSHWHACKERS	(C)	1968	PAR	86

TOM KEENE (1896 - 1963)
(aka GEORGE DURYEA, RICHARD POWERS)

He had one- and two-season spurts of oater stardom for RKO Radio, Crescent, and Monogram portraying aggressive heroes. Keene settled into strong support roles by the mid-1940s and mainlined Republic's 12-chapter serial DESPERADOES OF THE WEST in 1950. One of many guests for TRAIL OF ROBIN HOOD. Tom portrayed the sheriff on the "Fury" NBC-TV 30-minute shows (1955-58).

TIDE OF EMPIRE	1929	MGM	72-73
IN OLD CALIFORNIA (cs)	1929	AUD	60
BEAU BANDIT (cs)	1930	RKO	69
THE DUDE WRANGLER	1930	WW	69
PARDON MY GUN	1930	RKO	63
SUNDOWN TRAIL	1931	RKO	51-55
FREIGHTERS OF DESTINY	1931	RKO	60
PARTNERS	1932	RKO	58
THE SADDLE BUSTER	1932	RKO	60
GHOST VALLEY	1932	RKO	54
BEYOND THE ROCKIES	1932	RKO	60
COME ON DANGER	1932	RKO	60
RENEGADES OF THE WEST	1932	RKO	55
THE CHEYENNE KID	1933	RKO	54-61
SCARLET RIVER	1933	RKO	57
SON OF THE BORDER	1933	RKO	55-60
SUNSET PASS	1933	PAR	65
CROSS FIRE	1933	RKO	55-60
DRIFT FENCE (aka TEXAS DESPERADOES) (cs)	1936	PAR	58
DESERT GOLD (s)	1936	PAR	58
THE GLORY TRAIL (aka GLORIOUS SACRIFICE)	1936	CRE	65
REBELLION	1936	CRE	60

TOM KEENE, continued

Title	Year	Studio	#
BATTLE OF GREED	1937	CRE	65
OLD LOUISIANA (aka TREASON; LOUISIANA GAL)	1937	CRE	64
UNDER STRANGE FLAGS	1937	CRE	64
THE LAW COMMANDS	1937	CRE	60
DRUMS OF DESTINY	1937	CRE	60
RAW TIMBER	1937	CRE	63
GOD'S COUNTRY AND THE MAN	1937	MON	56
WHERE TRAILS DIVIDE	1937	MON	59
ROMANCE OF THE ROCKIES	1937	MON	53
THE PAINTED TRAIL	1938	MON	50
WANDERERS OF THE WEST	1941	MON	58
DYNAMITE CANYON	1941	MON	58
RIDING THE SUNSET TRAIL	1941	MON	56
THE DRIFTIN' KID	1941	MON	55-57
LONE STAR LAW MEN	1941	MON	58-61
WESTERN MAIL	1942	MON	55
ARIZONA ROUND-UP	1942	MON	56
WHERE TRAILS END	1942	MON	55
LIGHTS OF OLD SANTA FE (s)	1944	REP	78
THUNDER MOUNTAIN (s)	1947	RKO	60
UNDER THE TONTO RIM (s)	1947	RKO	61
WILD HORSE MESA (s)	1947	RKO	60-65
WESTERN HERITAGE (s)	1948	RKO	61
RETURN OF THE BAD MEN (s)	1948	RKO	96
BLOOD ON THE MOON (s)	1948	RKO	88
INDIAN AGENT (s)	1948	RKO	63-65
BROTHERS IN THE SADDLE (s)	1949	RKO	60
STORM OVER WYOMING (s)	1950	RKO	60
DESPERADOES OF THE WEST (SER)	1950	REP	12CH
TRAIL OF ROBIN HOOD (gs) (C)	1950	REP	67
TEXANS NEVER CRY (s)	1951	COL	70
THE ADVENTURES OF THE TUCSON KID	1953	TKP	50
THE OUTLAW'S DAUGHTER (s) (C)	1954	20T	75
DIG THAT URANIUM (s)	1956	AA	61
WETBACKS (s) (C)	1956	BAN	89
ONCE UPON A HORSE (aka HOT HORSE) (gs)	1958	UI	85

BRIAN KEITH (1921 -)

An Eastern actor who looks as though he was born in the saddle. His best roles have been those in support, rather than as a star, in westerns. Best known in such films as THE HALLELUJAH TRAIL as the whiskey baron taking a load of booze out west in the comedy western. Keith ramroded 13 half-hour shows of NBC-TV's "The Westerner" (1960). Brian's parts highlight authoritative toughness.

Title	Year	Studio	#
ARROWHEAD (s) (C)	1953	PAR	105
ALASKA SEAS (s)	1954	PAR	78
THE VIOLENT MEN (aka ROUGH COMPANY) (s) (C)	1955	COL	96
RUN OF THE ARROW (aka HOT LEAD) (cs) (C)	1957	RKO	85
HELL CANYON OUTLAWS	1957	REP	72
SIERRA BARON (C)	1958	20T	72-80
FORT DOBBS (cs)	1958	WB	80
VILLA! (C)	1958	20T	72
TEN WHO DARED (C)	1960	BV	92

BRIAN KEITH, continued / 99

THE DEADLY COMPANIONS	(C)	1961	PAT	90	___
(aka TRIGGER HAPPY) (cs)					
JOHNNY SHILOH	(C)	1963	BV	90	___
SAVAGE SAM	(C)	1963	BV	103	___
A TIGER WALKS	(C)	1964	BV	91	___
THE RAIDERS (aka THE PLAINSMAN)	(C)	1964	UNI	75-78	___
THE HALLELUJAH TRAIL (s)	(C)	1965	UA	156-165	___
THE RARE BREED (cs)	(C)	1966	UNI	97-108	___
NEVADA SMITH (cs)	(C)	1966	PAR	128-135	___
SCANDALOUS JOHN	(C)	1971	BV	113-117	___
SOMETHING BIG	(C)	1971	NG	108	___
SECOND CHANCE	(C)	1972	ABC-TV	74	___
JOE PANTHER	(C)	1976	ARN	110	___
THE QUEST (aka THE LONGEST DRIVE) (cs)	(C)	1976	COL-TV	100	___
THE COURT MARTIAL OF GENERAL GEORGE ARMSTRONG CUSTER	(C)	1977	WB-TV	100	___
HOOPER (s)	(C)	1978	WB	100	___
THE CHISHOLMS (s)	(C)	1979	ALP-TV	300	___
THE SEEKERS (s)	(C)	1979	UNI-TV	200	___
THE MOUNTAIN MEN	(C)	1980	COL	102	___
THE ALAMO: 13 DAYS TO GLORY	(C)	1987	NBC-TV	145	___
YOUNG GUNS (s)	(C)	1988	20T	102-107	___
THE GAMBLER, PART IV— THE LUCK OF THE DRAW (gs)	(C)	1991	NBC-TV	200	___

PAUL KELLY (1899 - 1956)

His forte was in character parts for different film genres including westerns for 25 years. Paul had a glorious time confusing Roy Rogers in MAN FROM MUSIC MOUNTAIN when portraying the chief villain. Such underhandedness was put to good use once Kelly was discovered as the ringleader craftily playing both sides while selling illegal guns in SPRINGFIELD RIFLE.

THE GIRL FROM CALGARY		1932	MON	64	___
WHEN A MAN'S A MAN		1935	FOX	66	___
(aka SAGA OF THE WEST) (cs)					
THE COUNTRY BEYOND		1936	20T	73	___
IT HAPPENED OUT WEST		1937	20T	56	___
WYOMING		1940	MGM	89	___
(aka MAN FROM WYOMING; BAD MAN OF WYOMING) (s)					
THE HOWARDS OF VIRGINIA		1940	COL	122	___
(aka TREE OF LIBERTY) (s)					
MAN FROM MUSIC MOUNTAIN		1943	REP	71	___
(aka TEXAS LEGIONNAIRES) (s)					
SAN ANTONIO (s)	(C)	1945	WB	111	___
SPOILERS OF THE NORTH		1947	REP	66	___
FRENCHIE (cs)	(C)	1951	UI	81	___
THE PAINTED HILLS	(C)	1951	MGM	69	___
SPRINGFIELD RIFLE (s)	(C)	1952	WB	93	___
GUNSMOKE (cs)	(C)	1953	UI	93	___
SPLIT SECOND (s)		1953	RKO	85	___

GEORGE KENNEDY (1926 -   )

A hefty character actor whose early heavy roles such as THE SONS OF KATIE ELDER have led to later more sympathetic parts in westerns like DIRTY DINGUS MAGEE.

LITTLE SHEPHERD OF KINGDOM COME (s) .. (C) ..	1961 ...	20T	108
GUNFIGHT AT BLACK HORSE CANYON	1962 ...	REV	100
LONELY ARE THE BRAVE (aka THE LAST HERO) (s) .	1962 ...	UI	107
THE SONS OF KATIE ELDER (s) .... (C) ..	1965 ...	PAR	122
SHENANDOAH (s) .... (C) ..	1965 ...	UNI ..	103-105
THE BALLAD OF JOSIE (cs) .... (C) ..	1968 ...	UNI	102
BANDOLERO! (s) .... (C) ..	1968 ...	20T	106
GUNS OF THE MAGNIFICENT SEVEN .... (C) ..	1969 ...	UA	106
THE GOOD GUYS AND THE BAD GUYS .... (C) ..	1969 ...	WB	91
DIRTY DINGUS MAGEE .... (C) ..	1970 ...	MGM ...	79-90
FOOLS' PARADE .... (C) ..	1971 ...	COL	97
(aka DYNAMITE MAN FROM GLORY JAIL) (s)			
CAHILL UNITED STATES MARSHAL .... (C) ..	1973 ...	WB	103
(aka CAHILL)			
DELIVER US FROM EVIL .... (C) ..	1973 ...	ABC-TV	74-78
THUNDERBOLT AND LIGHTFOOT (s) .... (C) ..	1974 ...	UA	114
A CRY IN THE WILDERNESS .... (C) ..	1974 ...	ABC-TV	74-78
THE EIGER SANCTION .... (C) ..	1975 ...	UNI	128
LAST OF THE KNUCKLEMEN .... (C) ..	1981 ...	HEX	93
THE GUNFIGHTERS (s) .... (C) ..	1987 ...	SYT-TV ...	100
THE GAMBLER, PART III— .... (C) ..	1987 ...	CBS-TV ..	200
THE LEGEND CONTINUES (gs)			

JOHN KIMBROUGH (1918 -   )

An ex-football star who had brief stardom with two 20th Century-Fox oaters in 1942. John's distinguished gridiron career started at Texas A&M University—in the Sugar Bowl, 1940; Cotton Bowl, 1941. World War II Air Corps pilot, he played each year for an Army team. Pro ball then, four years. Now president of The Sports Parade Award Co. in Haskell, Texas.

LONE STAR RANGER	1942 ...	20T	57
SUNDOWN JIM	1942 ...	20T	58-63

FRED KOHLER, JR. (1911 -   )

Even though galloper stardom lasted with him for only two mid-1930s Commodore "B" releases, Kohler followed in the screen footsteps of Fred, Sr. to carve out an equally successful movie villain career. Both Kohlers plagued George O'Brien in the classic LAWLESS VALLEY. Arrogant for TWILIGHT IN THE SIERRAS.

TOLL OF THE DESERT	1935 ...	COM	60
STEAMBOAT ROUND THE BEND (s)	1935 ...	FOX	96
THE PECOS KID	1936 ...	COM	56
THE PRISONER OF SHARK ISLAND (s)	1936 ...	20T	95
ROARING TIMBER (s)	1937 ...	COL	65
LAWLESS VALLEY (s)	1938 ...	RKO	59
TEXAS STAMPEDE (s)	1939 ...	COL	57

FRED KOHLER, JR., continued / 101

MAN OF CONQUEST (s)	1939	REP	97-105
YOUNG MR. LINCOLN (s)	1939	20T	101
TWO-GUN SHERIFF (s)	1941	REP	56
NEVADA CITY (s)	1941	REP	58
RAIDERS OF THE RANGE (s)	1942	REP	55
LONE STAR RANGER (s)	1942	20T	57
BOSS OF HANGTOWN MESA (s)	1942	UNI	58
CALLING WILD BILL ELLIOTT (s)	1943	REP	54
COLT COMRADES (s)	1943	UA	67
THE BIG BONANZA (s)	1944	REP	68
UNCONQUERED (s) (C)	1948	PAR	146-147
FEUDIN', FUSSIN', AND A-FIGHTIN' (s)	1948	UI	78
THE GALLANT LEGION (s)	1948	REP	88
LOADED PISTOLS (s)	1949	COL	79
THE GAY AMIGO (s)	1949	UA	90-97
RANGE JUSTICE (s)	1949	MON	57
TOUGH ASSIGNMENT (s)	1949	LIP	64
THE BARON OF ARIZONA (s)	1950	LIP	90-97
TWILIGHT IN THE SIERRAS (s) (C)	1950	REP	67
DESPERADOES OF THE WEST (s) (SER)	1950	REP	12CH
TALES OF THE WEST #3 (s)	1950	UI	50-55
SPOILERS OF THE PLAINS (s)	1951	REP	68
THE RED BADGE OF COURAGE (s)	1951	MGM	69
SKY FULL OF MOON (s)	1952	MGM	75
BORN TO THE SADDLE (s) (C)	1953	AST	73
SIX-GUN DECISION (s)	1953	AA	54
RACING BLOOD (s) (C)	1954	20T	76
DANIEL BOONE, TRAIL BLAZER (s) (C)	1956	REP	76
TERROR IN A TEXAS TOWN (s)	1958	UA	80
ALIAS JESSE JAMES (s) (C)	1959	UA	92
13 FIGHTING MEN (s)	1960	20T	69
CUSTER OF THE WEST)(s) (C)	1967	CRO	143

(aka GOOD DAY FOR FIGHTING)

KRIS KRISTOFFERSON (1936 -   )
A contemporary actor who made his own niche also with rock-oriented recordings, Kristofferson has starred in several adult gun-toting hayburners. He appeared in TNT-TV's 1991 MIRACLE IN THE WILDERNESS.

PAT GARRETT AND BILLY THE KID (C)	1973	MGM	106-122
BRING ME THE HEAD OF ALFREDO GARCIA(s) (C)	1974	UA	112
VIGILANTE FORCE (C)	1976	UA	89
HEAVEN'S GATE (C)	1980	UA	149-219
FLASHPOINT (C)	1984	TS	94
SONGWRITER (C)	1984	TS	94
THE LAST DAYS OF FRANK AND JESSE JAMES (C)	1986	JCP-TV	100
STAGECOACH (C)	1986	HE-TV	100
THE TRACKER(aka DEAD OR ALIVE) (C)	1988	HBO-TV	115
PAIR OF ACES (C)	1990	TVM	100
MIRACLE IN THE WILDERNESS (C)	1991	TNT-TV	100
ANOTHER PAIR OF ACES: THREE OF A KIND(C)	1991	PF-TV	100

ALAN LADD (1913 - 1964)

A 1940s superstar whose western leads included one of the most famous films of the genre, that of SHANE. He made numerous other westerns, but none as good as the classic SHANE.

BORN TO THE WEST (aka HELL TOWN) (s)	1937	PAR	66
THE LIGHT OF WESTERN STARS (s)	1940	PAR	67
THE HOWARDS OF VIRGINIA (aka TREE OF LIBERTY) (s)	1940	COL	122
GREAT GUNS (s)	1941	20T	73
WILD HARVEST	1947	PAR	92
WHISPERING SMITH (C)	1949	PAR	88
BRANDED (C)	1951	PAR	95
RED MOUNTAIN (C)	1951	PAR	84
THE IRON MISTRESS (C)	1952	WB	110
SHANE (C)	1953	PAR	118
SASKATCHEWAN (C) (aka O'ROARKE OF THE ROYAL MOUNTED)	1954	UI	87
DRUM BEAT (C)	1954	WB	111
THE BIG LAND (aka STAMPEDED) (C)	1957	WB	93-98
THE PROUD REBEL (C)	1958	BV	103
THE BADLANDERS (C)	1958	MGM	83-85
GUNS OF THE TIMBERLAND (C) (aka STAMPEDE)	1960	WB	91
ONE FOOT IN HELL (C)	1960	20T	90

BURT LANCASTER (1913 -   )

A versatile, athletic leading man who made numerous western films, although he was better known as a swashbuckler than cowboy. Included in his westerns are several outstanding examples of the genre: THE UNFORGIVEN; THE PROFESSIONALS; and VALDEZ IS COMING.

DESERT FURY (C)	1947	PAR	75-95
VENGEANCE VALLEY (C)	1951	MGM	83
JIM THORPE—ALL AMERICAN (aka MAN OF BRONZE)	1951	WB	107
APACHE (C)	1954	UA	91-93
VERA CRUZ (C)	1954	UA	94
THE KENTUCKIAN (C)	1955	UA	104
THE RAINMAKER (C)	1957	PAR	121
GUNFIGHT AT THE O.K. CORRAL (C)	1957	PAR	122
THE UNFORGIVEN (C)	1960	UA	120-125
THE HALLELUJAH TRAIL (C)	1965	UA	156-165
THE PROFESSIONALS (C)	1966	COL	117
THE SCALPHUNTERS (C)	1968	UA	102
VALDEZ IS COMING (C)	1971	UA	90
LAWMAN (C)	1971	UA	98-99
ULZANA'S RAID (C)	1972	UNI	103
BUFFALO BILL AND THE INDIANS, (C) OR SITTING BULL'S HISTORY LESSON (s)	1976	UA	120-123
CATTLE ANNIE AND LITTLE BRITCHES (C)	1981	UNI	95
LITTLE TREASURE (C)	1985	TS	95

MICHAEL LANDON (1936 - 1991)
He became a big-name superstar in two popular western television series with "Bonanza" (1959-73) and "Little House on the Prairie" (1974-83), both hour-long hits for NBC-TV. Landon was continually praised by peers in the entertainment industry for striving to orient his productions for family viewing.

THE LEGEND OF TOM DOOLEY	1959	COL	79
RIDE THE WIND	(C).. 1966	NBC-TV	120
LITTLE HOUSE ON THE PRAIRIE	(C).. 1974	NBC-TV	100
LITTLE HOUSE: LOOK BACK TO YESTERDAY	(C).. 1983	NBC-TV	100
LITTLE HOUSE: THE LAST FAREWELL	(C).. 1984	NBC-TV	100

ALLAN "ROCKY" LANE (1904 - 1973)
(aka ALLAN LANE)
"Action" was the key component for this ace boots-and-saddles star's popularity in 51 thundering "B" gallopers at Republic Pictures (1944-53) that included the *Red Ryder* and *Famous Westerns* series. Lane became a Top Money-Making Western Star (1951, 1953), but his career stalled after low-budgeters until accepting the TV voice of the talking horse "Mr. Ed" (1961-66).

THE TENDERFOOT (s)	1932	FN	70
THE LAW WEST OF TOMBSTONE (s)	1938	RKO	73
KING OF THE ROYAL MOUNTED	(SER).. 1940	REP	12CH
YUKON PATROL	1942	REP	66
(feature version of KING OF THE ROYAL MOUNTED serial)			
KING OF THE MOUNTIES	(SER). 1942	REP	12CH
DAREDEVILS OF THE WEST	(SER).. 1943	REP	12CH
THE TIGER WOMAN	(SER).. 1944	REP	12CH
(aka JUNGLE GOLD; PERILS OF THE DARKEST JUNGLE)			
SILVER CITY KID (starts *Action Westerns* series)	1944	REP	55
STAGECOACH TO MONTEREY	1944	REP	55
SHERIFF OF SUNDOWN	1944	REP	57
THE TOPEKA TERROR	1945	REP	55
CORPUS CHRISTI BANDITS	1945	REP	55-57
BELLS OF ROSARITA (non-series) (gs)	1945	REP	68
TRAIL OF KIT CARSON (ends *Action Westerns* series)	1945	REP	55
SANTA FE UPRISING (starts *Red Ryder* series)	1946	REP	55
OUT CALIFORNIA WAY (non-series) (gs)	(C).. 1946	REP	67
STAGECOACH TO DENVER	1946	REP	56
VIGILANTES OF BOOMTOWN	1947	REP	56
HOMESTEADERS OF PARADISE VALLEY	1947	REP	59
OREGON TRAIL SCOUTS	1947	REP	58
RUSTLERS OF DEVIL'S CANYON	1947	REP	58
MARSHAL OF CRIPPLE CREEK	1947	REP	58
(ends *Red Ryder* series)			
THE WILD FRONTIER (starts *Famous Westerns* series)	1947	REP	59
BANDITS OF DARK CANYON	1947	REP	59
OKLAHOMA BADLANDS	1948	REP	59
THE BOLD FRONTIERSMAN	1948	REP	60
CARSON CITY RAIDERS	1948	REP	60
MARSHAL OF AMARILLO	1948	REP	60
DESPERADOES OF DODGE CITY	1948	REP	60
THE DENVER KID	1948	REP	60
SUNDOWN IN SANTA FE	1948	REP	60
RENEGADES OF SONORA	1948	REP	60

ALLAN "ROCKY" LANE, continued

SHERIFF OF WICHITA	1949	REP	60
DEATH VALLEY GUNFIGHTER	1949	REP	60
FRONTIER INVESTIGATOR	1949	REP	60
THE WYOMING BANDIT	1949	REP	60
BANDIT KING OF TEXAS	1949	REP	60
NAVAJO TRAIL RAIDERS	1949	REP	60
POWDER RIVER RUSTLERS	1949	REP	60
GUNMEN OF ABILENE	1950	REP	60
CODE OF THE SILVER SAGE	1950	REP	60
SALT LAKE RAIDERS	1950	REP	60
COVERED WAGON RAID	1950	REP	60
VIGILANTE HIDEOUT	1950	REP	60
FRISCO TORNADO	1950	REP	60
RUSTLERS ON HORSEBACK	1950	REP	60
TRAIL OF ROBIN HOOD (non-series) (gs) (C)	1950	REP	67
ROUGH RIDERS OF DURANGO	1951	REP	60
NIGHT RIDERS OF MONTANA	1951	REP	60
WELLS FARGO GUNMASTER	1951	REP	60
FORT DODGE STAMPEDE	1951	REP	60
DESERT OF LOST MEN	1951	REP	54
CAPTIVE OF BILLY THE KID	1952	REP	54
LEADVILLE GUNSLINGER	1952	REP	54
BLACK HILLS AMBUSH	1952	REP	54
THUNDERING CARAVANS	1952	REP	54
DESPERADOES' OUTPOST	1952	REP	54
MARSHAL OF CEDAR ROCK	1953	REP	54
SAVAGE FRONTIER	1953	REP	54
BANDITS OF THE WEST	1953	REP	54
EL PASO STAMPEDE (ends *Famous Westerns* series)	1953	REP	54
THE SAGA OF HEMP BROWN (s) (C)	1958	UI	80
HELL BENT FOR LEATHER (s) (C)	1960	UI	82
POSSE FROM HELL (s) (C)	1961	UI	89
GERONIMO'S REVENGE (s)	1965	BV	61

KEITH LARSEN (1925 -   )
American leading man mainly of programmers. He starred in 19 "Brave Eagle" (1955-56) half-hour TV shows and then headed MGM-TV's prestigious "Northwest Passage" 30-minute episodes during the mid-1950s.

HIAWATHA (C)	1952	UA	80
FORT VENGEANCE (cs) (C)	1953	AA	75
SON OF BELLE STARR (C)	1953	AA	70
WAR PAINT (s) (C)	1953	UA	89
ARROW IN THE DUST (cs) (C)	1954	AA	80
CHIEF CRAZY HORSE (C)	1955	UI	86
(aka VALLEY OF FURY) (s)			
WICHITA (s) (C)	1955	AA	81
LAST OF THE BAD MEN (s) (C)	1957	AA	80
BADLANDS OF MONTANA (cs)	1957	20T	75
APACHE WARRIOR	1957	20T	72-74
FURY RIVER (C)	1962	MGM	74
TRAP ON COUGAR MOUNTAIN (C)	1972	SI	94
RUN TO THE HIGH COUNTRY (C)	1972	SI	97
YOUNG AND FREE (C)	1978	MHV	87
WHITE WATER SAM (C)	1979	MHV	90

Sound-era saddlers featured throughout *MORE COWBOY SHOOTING STARS* have been galloping into the hearts of motion picture goers and television viewers with their well-produced, six-shootin' westerns spanning over 65 years which range the gamut from Buck Jones' THE BIG HOP way back in 1928 to Clint Eastwood's UNFORGIVEN, released during 1992. The following nine pages of photographs are just a brief representation of those individuals whom we honor.

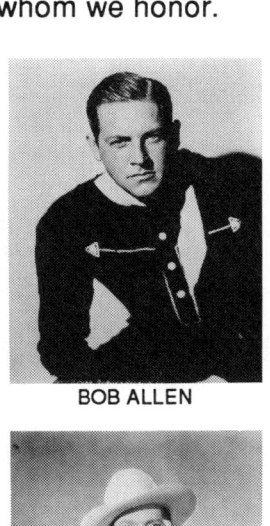

BOB ALLEN	REX ALLEN	JAMES ARNESS
GENE AUTRY	BOB BAKER	SMITH BALLEW
DON "RED" BARRY	RICHARD BOONE	JAMES BROWN

LLOYD BRIDGES	 JOHNNY "MACK" BROWN	 RORY CALHOUN
 ROD CAMERON	 JUDY CANOVA	 HARRY CAREY, SR.
 HARRY CAREY, JR.	 LEO CARRILLO	 SUNSET CARSON
 JAMES COBURN	 BILL CODY	 CHUCK CONNORS

RAY CORRIGAN	 BUSTER CRABBE	 KEN CURTIS
 JIM DAVIS	 EDDIE DEAN	 YVONNE DeCARLO
 RICHARD DIX	 CLINT EASTWOOD	 NELSON EDDY w/ JEANNETTE MacDONALD
 BILL ELLIOTT	 SAM ELLIOTT	 JIMMY ELLISON

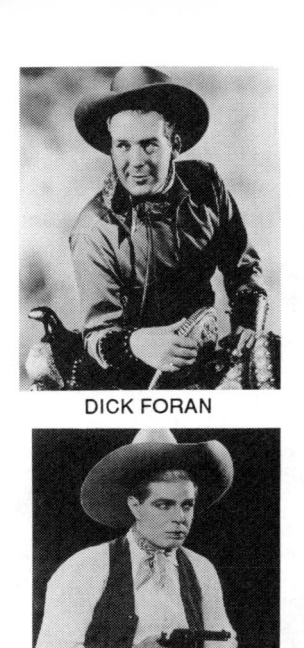

DICK FORAN	 CLARK GABLE	 JAMES GARNER
HOOT GIBSON	 KIRBY GRANT	 MONTE HALE
 RUSSELL HAYDEN	 STERLING HAYDEN	 VAN HEFLIN
 JACK HOLT	 TIM HOLT	 GEORGE HOUSTON

JACK HOXIE	 BEN JOHNSON	 BUCK JONES
 TOM KEENE	 GEORGE KENNEDY	 ALAN LADD
 MICHAEL LANDON	 ALLAN "ROCKY" LANE	 LASH LaRUE
 REX LEASE	 ROBERT LIVINGSTON	 GUY MADISON

JOCK MAHONEY	 LEE MARVIN	 KEN MAYNARD
 KERMIT MAYNARD	 TIM McCOY	 JOEL McCREA
 STEVE McQUEEN	 RAY MILLAND	 ROBERT MITCHUM
 TOM MIX	 GEORGE MONTGOMERY	 CLAYTON MOORE

AUDIE MURPHY	WILLIE NELSON	PAUL NEWMAN
HUGH O'BRIAN	DAVE O'BRIEN	GEORGE O'BRIEN
FESS PARKER	VERA RALSTON	JACK RANDALL
RONALD REAGAN	ROBERT REDFORD	DUNCAN RENALDO

BURT REYNOLDS	 RIN TIN TIN w/ LEE AAKER	 TEX RITTER
 DALE ROBERTSON	 KENNY ROGERS	 ROY ROGERS
 JANE RUSSELL	 REB RUSSELL	 FRED SCOTT
 RANDOLPH SCOTT	 ROBERT STACK	 BARBARA STANWYCK

CHARLES STARRETT	BOB STEELE	JAMES STEWART
BARRY SULLIVAN	TOM TYLER	JIMMY WAKELY
WALLY WALES	CLINT WALKER	JOHN WAYNE
BILL WILLIAMS	WHIP WILSON	LORETTA YOUNG

LASH LaRUE (1917 -   )
(aka AL LaRUE, AL "LASH" LaRUE)

Cracking a whip and dressing in black paved the path to "B" western stardom (1947-52) for this tough-talking cowboy at PRC and Western Adventure Productions with action-packed features like PIONEER JUSTICE and KING OF THE BULLWHIP. LaRue appeared in the 1950s TV shows "Lash of the West," "Judge Roy Bean," "26 Men," and was sheriff Johnny Behan during the 1959 season of ABC-TV's "The Life and Legend of Wyatt Earp." Nowadays, Lash makes occasional support roles in TV western features, and is a perennial guest at numerous film conventions.

Title		Year	Studio	Pages
SONG OF OLD WYOMING (s)	(C)	1945	PRC	65
THE CARAVAN TRAIL (s)	(C)	1946	PRC	57
WILD WEST (s)	(C)	1946	PRC	73
LAW OF THE LASH		1947	PRC	53
BORDER FEUD		1947	PRC	55
PIONEER JUSTICE		1947	PRC	56
GHOST TOWN RENEGADES		1947	PRC	57
STAGE TO MESA CITY		1947	EL	52-56
RETURN OF THE LASH		1947	EL	53-55
THE FIGHTING VIGILANTES		1947	EL	51-61
CHEYENNE TAKES OVER		1947	EL	58
PRAIRIE OUTLAWS (s)		1948	EL	57
DEAD MAN'S GOLD		1948	WAS	60
MARK OF THE LASH		1948	WAS	60
FRONTIER REVENGE		1948	WAS	55
OUTLAW COUNTRY		1949	WAS	76
SON OF BILLY THE KID		1949	WAS	65
SON OF A BAD MAN		1949	WAS	64
THE DALTONS' WOMEN		1951	WA	80
KING OF THE BULLWHIP		1951	WA	59
THE THUNDERING TRAIL (aka THUNDER ON THE TRAIL)		1951	WA	55
THE VANISHING OUTPOST		1951	WA	56
THE BLACK LASH		1952	WA	55
THE FRONTIER PHANTOM		1952	WA	56
GUNS DON'T ARGUE (s)		1957	VIS	90
HARD ON THE TRAIL (aka HARD TRAIL)	(C)	1971	BI	92
DARK POWER	(C)	1985	TMP	87
STAGECOACH (s)	(C)	1986	HE-TV	100
ALIEN OUTLAW	(C)	1987	TMP	91
PAIR OF ACES (s)	(C)	1990	TVM	100

REX LEASE (1901 - 1966)

He was unsuccessful as star of early 1930s low-budget cactusers, but Lease achieved status as character support to other horse opera saddlers. Rex did most of his latter "A" and "B" acting at Republic and Universal into the 1950s.

Title		Year	Studio	Pages
TROOPERS THREE		1930	TIF	80
WINGS OF ADVENTURE		1930	TIF	53
THE UTAH KID		1930	TIF	57
IN OLD CHEYENNE		1931	WW	59-62
THE SIGN OF THE WOLF	(SER)	1931	MET	10CH
THE LONE TRAIL		1932	SYN	55
(feature version of THE SIGN OF THE WOLF serial)				

REX LEASE, continued

Title	Year	Studio	Pages
THE COWBOY AND THE BANDIT	1935	SYN	55
CYCLONE OF THE SADDLE	1935	SPR	57
PALS OF THE RANGE	1935	SPR	53
FIGHTING CABALLERO	1935	SPR	57
THE GHOST RIDER	1935	SPR	59
ROUGH RIDING RANGER (aka THE SECRET STRANGER)	1935	SPR	56
ROARIN' GUNS (s)	1936	SPR	57
FAST BULLETS (aka LAW AND ORDER) (s)	1936	COM	57
RIDIN' ON (s)	1936	COM	56
LIGHTNING BILL CARSON (s)	1936	PUR	57-75
ACES AND EIGHTS (s)	1936	PUR	62
CAVALCADE OF THE WEST (s)	1936	GN	59
CUSTER'S LAST STAND (SER)	1936	S&S	15CH
THE SILVER TRAIL	1937	REL	56-58
HEROES OF THE ALAMO	1938	COL	75
LAND OF FIGHTING MEN (s)	1938	MON	53
CODE OF THE RANGERS (s)	1938	MON	56
DESERT PATROL (s)	1938	REP	56
THE LONE RANGER RIDES AGAIN (s) (SER)	1939	REP	15CH
IN OLD MONTEREY (s)	1939	REP	73
SOUTH OF THE BORDER (aka SOUTH OF TEXAS) (s)	1939	REP	71
THE GRAPES OF WRATH (s)	1940	20T	129
RANCHO GRANDE (s)	1940	REP	68
ONE MAN'S LAW (s)	1940	REP	57
UNDER TEXAS SKIES (s)	1940	REP	57
RIDERS OF BLACK MOUNTAIN (s)	1940	PDC	59
THE TRAIL BLAZERS (s)	1940	REP	58
LONE STAR RAIDERS (s)	1940	REP	57
BILLY THE KID'S GUN JUSTICE (s)	1940	PRC	63
BILLY THE KID'S RANGE WAR (s)	1941	PRC	60
THE PHANTOM COWBOY (s)	1941	REP	56
OUTLAWS OF THE RIO GRANDE (s)	1941	PRC	63
SADDLEMATES (s)	1941	REP	56
NEVADA CITY (s)	1941	REP	58
BILLY THE KID IN SANTA FE (s)	1941	PRC	66
BAD MAN OF DEADWOOD (s)	1941	REP	61
OUTLAWS OF CHEROKEE TRAIL (s)	1941	REP	56
DEATH VALLEY OUTLAWS (s)	1941	REP	56
TONTO BASIN OUTLAWS (s)	1941	MON	60
JESSE JAMES AT BAY (s)	1941	REP	56
SIERRA SUE (s)	1941	REP	64
ARIZONA TERRORS (s)	1942	REP	56
RAIDERS OF THE WEST (s)	1942	PRC	64
SABOTEUR (s)	1942	UNI	108
HOME IN WYOMIN' (s)	1942	REP	67
STARDUST ON THE SAGE (s)	1942	REP	65
IN OLD CALIFORNIA (s)	1942	REP	88
THE CYCLONE KID (s)	1942	REP	56
THE SILVER BULLET (s)	1942	UNI	56
BOSS OF HANGTOWN MESA (s)	1942	UNI	58
SHADOWS ON THE SAGE (s)	1942	REP	57
SUNSET SERENADE (s)	1942	REP	58
TENTING TONIGHT ON THE OLD CAMP GROUND (aka TENTING TONIGHT) (s)	1943	UNI	61
HAUNTED RANCH (aka DEAD MEN DON'T RIDE) (s)	1943	MON	57

116 / REX LEASE, continued

DEAD MAN'S GULCH (s)		1943...REP	56
IDAHO (s)		1943...REP	70
KING OF THE COWBOYS (s)		1943...REP	67
SANTA FE SCOUTS (s)		1943...REP	55
DAREDEVILS OF THE WEST (s)	(SER)	1943...REP	12CH
RIDERS OF THE RIO GRANDE (s)		1943...REP	55
COWBOY AND THE SENORITA (s)		1944...REP	78
THE TIGER WOMAN	(SER)	1944...REP	12CH
(aka JUNGLE GOLD; PERILS OF THE DARKEST JUNGLE) (s)			
THE YELLOW ROSE OF TEXAS (s)		1944...REP	69
CALL OF THE ROCKIES (s)		1944...REP	54
RAIDERS OF GHOST CITY (s)	(SER)	1944...UNI	13CH
BORDERTOWN TRAIL (s)		1944...REP	55
CHEYENNE WILDCAT (s)		1944...REP	56
CODE OF THE PRAIRIE (s)		1944...REP	56
SHERIFF OF SUNDOWN (s)		1944...REP	57
FIREBRANDS OF ARIZONA (s)		1944...REP	55
LONE TEXAS RANGER (s)		1945...REP	56
FLAME OF BARBARY COAST (s)		1945...REP	91
SANTA FE SADDLEMATES (s)		1945...REP	56
SPRINGTIME IN TEXAS (s)		1945...MON	55
BELLS OF ROSARITA (s)		1945...REP	68
THE NAUGHTY NINETIES (s)		1945...UNI	76
OREGON TRAIL (s)		1945...REP	55
CODE OF THE LAWLESS (s)		1945...UNI	56-60
ROUGH RIDERS OF CHEYENNE (s)		1945...REP	56
FRONTIER GAL	(C)	1945...UNI	85
(aka THE BRIDE WASN'T WILLING) (s)			
DAKOTA (s)		1945...REP	82
THE SCARLET HORSEMAN (s)	(SER)	1946...UNI	13CH
THE PHANTOM RIDER (s)	(SER)	1946...REP	12CH
DAYS OF BUFFALO BILL (s)		1946...REP	56
KING OF THE FOREST RANGERS (s)	(SER)	1946...REP	12CH
SUN VALLEY CYCLONE (s)		1946...REP	56
CANYON PASSAGE (s)	(C)	1946...UNI	90
RUSTLER'S ROUNDUP		1946...UNI	57
(aka RUSTLER'S HIDEOUT) (s)			
PLAINSMAN AND THE LADY (s)		1946...REP	87
HELDORADO (s)		1946...REP	70
CALIFORNIA (s)	(C)	1947...PAR	98
ANGEL AND THE BADMAN (s)		1947...REP	100
THE VIGILANTES RETURN	(C)	1947...UNI	67
(aka RETURN OF THE VIGILANTES) (s)			
THE PERILS OF PAULINE (s)	(C)	1947...PAR	96
WYOMING (s)		1947...REP	84
THE WISTFUL WIDOW OF WAGON GAP		1947...UNI	78
(aka THE WISTFUL WIDOW) (s)			
THE GALLANT LEGION (s)		1948...REP	88
NIGHT TIME IN NEVADA (s)	(C)	1948...REP	67
THE PLUNDERERS (s)	(C)	1948...REP	87
ROSE OF THE YUKON (s)		1949...REP	59
MA AND PA KETTLE (s)		1949...UI	75
THE LADY GAMBLES (s)		1949...UI	99
THE LAST BANDIT (s)	(C)	1949...REP	80
BELLS OF CORONADO (s)	(C)	1950...REP	67
SINGING GUNS (s)	(C)	1950...REP	91

REX LEASE, continued /117

Title	Year	Studio	Length
CODE OF THE SILVER SAGE (s)	1950	REP	60
HILLS OF OKLAHOMA (s)	1950	REP	67
CURTAIN CALL AT CACTUS CREEK (C)	1950	UI	86
(aka TAKE THE STAGE) (s)			
COVERED WAGON RAID (s)	1950	REP	60
FRISCO TORNADO (s)	1950	REP	60
COPPER CANYON (s) (C)	1950	PAR	83
OUTLAWS OF TEXAS (s)	1950	MON	56
SPOILERS OF THE PLAINS (s)	1951	REP	68
PALS OF THE GOLDEN WEST (s)	1951	REP	68
LONE STAR (s)	1952	MGM	90-94
COLORADO SUNDOWN (s)	1952	REP	67
THE WILD NORTH (aka THE BIG NORTH) (s) (C)	1952	MGM	97
LOST IN ALASKA	1952	UI	76
(aka ABBOTT AND COSTELLO LOST IN ALASKA) (s)			
TOUGHEST MAN IN ARIZONA (s) (C)	1952	REP	90
MONTANA BELLE (s) (C)	1952	RKO	81
THE MAN BEHIND THE GUN (s) (C)	1953	WB	82
RIDE, VAQUERO! (s) (C)	1953	MGM	90
GUN BELT (s) (C)	1953	UA	77
SHADOWS OF TOMBSTONE (s)	1953	REP	54
CALAMITY JANE (s) (C)	1953	WB	101
RAILS INTO LARAMIE (s) (C)	1954	UI	81
DESTRY (s) (C)	1955	UI	95
OKLAHOMA! (s) (C)	1955	20T	145
PERILS OF THE WILDERNESS (s) (SER)	1956	COL	15CH
BACKLASH (s) (C)	1956	UI	84
THE RAWHIDE YEARS (s) (C)	1956	UI	85
TENSION AT TABLE ROCK (s) (C)	1956	RKO	93

ROBERT LIVINGSTON (1904 - 1988)
(aka BOB LIVINGSTON)

He joined Republic Pictures in 1936 to portray the polished, yet outspoken, Stony Brooke in *The Three Mesquiteers* series "B" westerns for 29 entries through 1941, except for the 1938-39 season that included starring in the studio's 15-chapter serial THE LONE RANGER RIDES AGAIN. After *The Lone Rider* stint at PRC (1942-43), Livingston headed three more 1944 low-budget oaters for Republic, then mixed dramas and support parts in other westerns into the early 1950s. His splendid talents were uplifting for Rogers' GRAND CANYON TRAIL and Autry's WINNING OF THE WEST. Robert had a brief return to stardom during the 1970s.

Title	Year	Studio	Length
THREE GODFATHERS	1936	MGM	82
(aka MIRACLE IN THE SAND) (s)			
THE VIGILANTES ARE COMING (SER)	1936	REP	12CH
THE THREE MESQUITEERS	1936	REP	56-61
(starts *The Three Mesquiteers* series)			
GHOST-TOWN GOLD	1936	REP	55
ROARIN' LEAD	1936	REP	53
THE RIDERS OF THE WHISTLING SKULL	1937	REP	55
(aka THE GOLDEN TRAIL)			
THE BOLD CABALLERO (C)	1937	REP	71
(aka THE BOLD CAVALIER) (non-series)			
HIT THE SADDLE	1937	REP	57
GUNSMOKE RANCH	1937	REP	56

ROBERT LIVINGSTON, continued

COME ON, COWBOYS!	1937	REP	57
RANGE DEFENDERS	1937	REP	56
HEART OF THE ROCKIES	1937	REP	56
WILD HORSE RODEO	1937	REP	56
THE PURPLE VIGILANTES	1938	REP	58
(aka THE PURPLE RIDERS)			
CALL THE MESQUITEERS	1938	REP	55
(aka OUTLAWS OF THE WEST)			
OUTLAWS OF SONORA	1938	REP	55
RIDERS OF THE BLACK HILLS	1938	REP	55
(aka RIDERS OF BLACK HILLS)			
HEROES OF THE HILLS	1938	REP	56
(halts *The Three Mesquiteers* series)			
THE LONE RANGER RIDES AGAIN (SER)	1939	REP	15CH
THE KANSAS TERRORS	1939	REP	57
(resumes *The Three Mesquiteers* series)			
COWBOYS FROM TEXAS	1939	REP	57
HEROES OF THE SADDLE	1940	REP	56
PIONEERS OF THE WEST	1940	REP	56
COVERED WAGON DAYS	1940	REP	56
ROCKY MOUNTAIN RANGERS	1940	REP	58
OKLAHOMA RENEGADES	1940	REP	57
UNDER TEXAS SKIES	1940	REP	57
THE TRAIL BLAZERS	1940	REP	58
LONE STAR RAIDERS	1940	REP	57
PRAIRIE PIONEERS	1941	REP	58
PALS OF THE PECOS	1941	REP	56
SADDLEMATES	1941	REP	56
GANGS OF SONORA	1941	REP	56
(ends *The Three Mesquiteers* series)			
OVERLAND STAGECOACH	1942	PRC	58
(starts *The Lone Rider* series)			
WILD HORSE RUSTLERS	1943	PRC	55
DEATH RIDES THE PLAINS	1943	PRC	57
WOLVES OF THE RANGE	1943	PRC	60
LAW OF THE SADDLE	1943	PRC	57
RAIDERS OF RED GAP (ends *The Lone Rider* series)	1943	PRC	54
PISTOL PACKIN' MAMA	1943	REP	64
PRIDE OF THE PLAINS	1944	REP	58
(starts *John Paul Revere* series)			
BENEATH WESTERN SKIES	1944	REP	56
(ends *John Paul Revere* series)			
THE LARAMIE TRAIL	1944	REP	55
THE BIG BONANZA	1944	REP	68
BELLS OF ROSARITA (gs)	1945	REP	68
DON'T FENCE ME IN (s)	1945	REP	71
DAKOTA (s)	1945	REP	82
DAREDEVILS OF THE CLOUDS	1948	REP	60
GRAND CANYON TRAIL (s) (C)	1948	REP	67
THE FEATHERED SERPENT (s)	1948	MON	68
THE MYSTERIOUS DESPERADO (s)	1949	RKO	61
RIDERS IN THE SKY (s)	1949	COL	70
MULE TRAIN (s)	1950	COL	70
LAW OF THE BADLANDS (cs)	1950	RKO	60
SADDLE LEGION (cs)	1951	RKO	61
NIGHT STAGE TO GALVESTON (s)	1952	COL	60

ROBERT LIVINGSTON, continued / 119

WINNING OF THE WEST (s)	1953	COL	57
ONCE UPON A HORSE (aka HOT HORSE) (gs)	1958	UI	85
BLAZING STEWARDESSES (C) (aka TEXAS LAYOVER)	1975	II	89

ROBERT LOGAN (1941 -   )
Brawny hero of American family outdoor adventure films of the 1970s.

THE ADVENTURES OF THE WILDERNESS FAMILY	(C)	1975	PI	100
ACROSS THE GREAT DIVIDE	(C)	1976	PI	101
THE FURTHER ADVENTURES OF THE WILDERNESS FAMILY	(C)	1978	PI	105
SHIPWRECK!	(C)	1979	PI	102
KELLY	(C)	1981	PAR	93

THE LONE RIDER series (1941 - 1943)
A cheaply-financed bunch of oaters—17 in all—from PRC which starred singing cowboy George Houston (1941-42) for one-and-a-half seasons and ex-Mesquiteer Bob Livingston during the 1942-43 wrap-up year.

(GEORGE HOUSTON, AL "FUZZY" ST. JOHN)
THE LONE RIDER RIDES ON	1941	PRC	61-64
THE LONE RIDER CROSSES THE RIO	1941	PRC	63
THE LONE RIDER IN GHOST TOWN	1941	PRC	64
THE LONE RIDER IN FRONTIER FURY	1941	PRC	62
THE LONE RIDER AMBUSHED	1941	PRC	63
THE LONE RIDER FIGHTS BACK	1941	PRC	64

(GEORGE HOUSTON, AL "FUZZY" ST. JOHN, DENNIS "SMOKY" MOORE)
THE LONE RIDER AND THE BANDIT	1942	PRC	54
THE LONE RIDER IN CHEYENNE	1942	PRC	59
THE LONE RIDER IN TEXAS JUSTICE	1942	PRC	59
BORDER ROUNDUP	1942	PRC	57
OUTLAWS OF BOULDER PASS	1942	PRC	64

(BOB LIVINGSTON, AL "FUZZY" ST. JOHN, DENNIS "SMOKY" MOORE)
| OVERLAND STAGECOACH | 1942 | PRC | 58 |

(BOB LIVINGSTON, AL "FUZZY" ST. JOHN)
WILD HORSE RUSTLERS	1943	PRC	55
DEATH RIDES THE PLAINS	1943	PRC	57
WOLVES OF THE RANGE	1943	PRC	60
LAW OF THE SADDLE	1943	PRC	57
RAIDERS OF RED GAP	1943	PRC	54

JACK LUDEN (1902 - 1951)
He racked up only four routine starring "B" oaters with Columbia Pictures in 1938. Luden's voice was completely dubbed for the role of Sunset Carson's brother in BORDERTOWN TRAIL. Jack left films after the mid-1940s.

| KING OF THE ROYAL MOUNTED (cs) | 1936 | 20T | 61 |
| ROLLING CARAVANS | 1938 | COL | 55 |

120 / JACK LUDEN, continued

STAGECOACH DAYS	1938	COL	58
PIONEER TRAIL	1938	COL	55-59
PHANTOM GOLD	1938	COL	56
SUSANNAH OF THE MOUNTIES (s)	1939	20T	78
NORTH WEST MOUNTED POLICE (s) (C)	1940	PAR	125
BORDERTOWN TRAIL (s)	1944	REP	55
INCENDIARY BLONDE (s) (C)	1945	PAR	113
ROUGH RIDERS OF CHEYENNE (s)	1945	REP	56

JOHN LUND (1911 - 1992)
Leading man with Broadway experience. Best known for his second leads in non-western films. John was good in Republic's DAKOTA INCIDENT.

THE PERILS OF PAULINE (C)	1947	PAR	96
MY FRIEND IRMA GOES WEST (s)	1950	PAR	90
THE BATTLE AT APACHE PASS (C)	1952	UI	85
BRONCO BUSTER (C)	1952	UI	80
WOMAN THEY ALMOST LYNCHED	1953	REP	90
WHITE FEATHER (s) (C)	1955	20T	102
CHIEF CRAZY HORSE (C)	1955	UI	86
(aka VALLEY OF FURY) (cs)			
FIVE GUNS WEST (C)	1955	ARC	78-79
DAKOTA INCIDENT (cs) (C)	1956	REP	88
AFFAIR IN RENO	1957	REP	75
THE DEVIL'S BEDROOM	1963	AA	72

JEANETTE MacDONALD (1901 - 1965)
Fine operatic singer whose MGM western leads were all musical films with Nelson Eddy as her singing partner.

NAUGHTY MARIETTA	1935	MGM	105-106
ROSE MARIE (aka INDIAN LOVE CALL)	1936	MGM	110-116
SAN FRANCISCO	1936	MGM	115
THE GIRL OF THE GOLDEN WEST	1938	MGM	120
NEW MOON	1940	MGM	105

FRED MacMURRAY (1908 - 1991)
Versatile leading man who made numerous westerns, but who is better known for his comedy films. Included in MacMurray's genre of films is the excellent feature, THE TEXAS RANGERS. Great in NEVER A DULL MOMENT.

TRAIL OF THE LONESOME PINE (cs) (C)	1936	PAR	102
THE TEXAS RANGERS	1936	PAR	80
RANGERS OF FORTUNE	1940	PAR	80
THE FOREST RANGERS (C)	1942	PAR	87
WHERE DO WE GO FROM HERE? (C)	1945	20T	77
SMOKY (C)	1946	20T	87
FAMILY HONEYMOON	1948	UI	80
BORDERLINE	1950	UI	88-89
NEVER A DULL MOMENT	1950	RKO	89

FRED MacMURRAY, continued / 121

CALLAWAY WENT THATAWAY	1951	MGM	81
(aka THE STAR SAID NO)			
THE MOONLIGHTER	1953	WB	75-77
THE FAR HORIZONS	(C).. 1955	PAR	108
(aka THE UNTAMED WEST)			
AT GUNPOINT (aka GUNPOINT)	(C).. 1955	AA	81
GUN FOR A COWARD	(C).. 1957	UI	73-88
QUANTEZ	(C).. 1957	UI	80
DAY OF THE BAD MAN	(C).. 1958	UI	81-82
GOOD DAY FOR A HANGING	(C).. 1959	COL	85
FACE OF A FUGITIVE	(C).. 1959	COL	81
THE OREGON TRAIL	(C).. 1959	20T	82-86
THE SWARM (s)	(C).. 1978	PAR	116

GUY MADISON (1922 -   )

Best known in westerns as television's "Wild Bill Hickok" in the syndicated 30-minute show (1951-57) for 113 episodes, Madison's excellent physical agility for the rugged action scenes enabled him to ease into feature "A" westerns simultaneously for Warner Brothers, Columbia, and Allied Artists, many of which were European productions through the early 1970s.

TEXAS, BROOKLYN AND HEAVEN	1948	UA	76-89
(aka THE GIRL FROM TEXAS)			
MASSACRE RIVER	1949	AA	75
DRUMS IN THE DEEP SOUTH	(C).. 1951	RKO	78-87
BEHIND SOUTHERN LINES	1952	MON	51
(starts *Wild Bill Hickok* series for Monogram/Allied Artists)			
THE GHOST OF CROSSBONES CANYON	1952	MON	56
TRAIL OF THE ARROW	1952	MON	54
THE YELLOW-HAIRED KID	1952	MON	56
THE CHARGE AT FEATHER RIVER	(C).. 1953	WB	96
BORDER CITY RUSTLERS	1953	AA	54
SECRET OF OUTLAW FLATS	1953	AA	54
SIX-GUN DECISION	1953	AA	54
TWO-GUN MARSHAL	1953	AA	52
THE COMMAND	(C).. 1954	WB	88
MARSHALS IN DISGUISE	1954	AA	53
OUTLAW'S SON	1954	AA	53
TROUBLE ON THE TRAIL	1954	AA	54
THE TWO-GUN TEACHER	1954	AA	50
TIMBER COUNTRY TROUBLE	1955	AA	55
THE MATCH-MAKING MARSHAL	1955	AA	55
THE TITLED TENDERFOOT	1955	AA	55
PHANTOM TRAILS (ends *Wild Bill Hickok* series)	1955	AA	55
THE LAST FRONTIER	(C).. 1956	COL	98
(aka SAVAGE WILDERNESS)			
THE BEAST OF HOLLOW MOUNTAIN	(C).. 1956	UA	79-80
REPRISAL!	(C).. 1956	COL	74
THE HARD MAN	(C).. 1957	COL	80
BULLWHIP	(C).. 1958	AA	80
GUNMEN OF THE RIO GRANDE	(C).. 1964	AA	86
THE ADVENTURES OF TORTUGA	(C).. 1965	LIB	101
FIVE GIANTS FROM TEXAS	(C).. 1966	MCB	90
THE LEGACY OF THE INCAS	(C).. 1966	ORB	100

122 / GUY MADISON, continued

OLD SHATTERHAND	(C)..1967	GFE	89
(aka SHATTERHAND; APACHES LAST BATTLE)			
THE BANG BANG KID (aka BANG BANG)	(C)..1968	AJA	90
PAYMENT IN BLOOD	(C)..1968	COL	90
THIS MAN CAN'T DIE	(C)..1970	CP	90
THE REVEREND COLT	(C)..1971	RMF	90
RED RIVER (s)	(C)..1988	MGM/ UA-TV	100

JOCK MAHONEY (1919 - 1989)
(aka JACK MAHONEY, JACQUES O'MAHONEY)

Rising from superb stunt double for Charles Starrett in *The Durango Kid* "B" western films, he became a television star in "The Range Rider" (1952-54) for 76 half-hour shows and "Yancy Derringer" (1958-59) during 34 episodes—30 minutes each—for CBS. Mahoney did several Universal "A" westerns in the 1950s, and was the muscular Tarzan for two 1960s MGM features.

THE FIGHTING FRONTIERSMAN		1946...COL	61
(aka GOLDEN LADY) (s)			
SOUTH OF THE CHISHOLM TRAIL (s)		1947...COL	58
THE STRANGER FROM PONCA CITY (s)		1947...COL	56
RIDERS OF THE LONE STAR (s)		1947...COL	55
BUCKAROO FROM POWDER RIVER (s)		1947...COL	55
LAST DAYS OF BOOT HILL (s)		1947...COL	56
SIX-GUN LAW (s)		1948...COL	54
PHANTOM VALLEY (s)		1948...COL	53
WEST OF SONORA (s)		1948...COL	52-55
WHIRLWIND RAIDERS (aka STATE POLICE) (s)		1948...COL	54
BLAZING ACROSS THE PECOS (s)		1948...COL	55
TRAIL TO LAREDO (aka SIGN OF THE DAGGER) (s)		1948...COL	54
EL DORADO PASS (aka DESPERATE MEN) (s)		1948...COL	56
QUICK ON THE TRIGGER		1948...COL	55
(aka CONDEMNED IN ERROR) (s)			
SMOKY MOUNTAIN MELODY (s)		1948...COL	61
CHALLENGE OF THE RANGE		1949...COL	56
(aka MOONLIGHT RAID) (s)			
DESERT VIGILANTE (s)		1949...COL	56
LARAMIE (s)		1949...COL	56
THE BLAZING TRAIL (aka THE FORGED WILL) (s)		1949...COL	56
THE DOOLINS OF OKLAHOMA		1949...COL	90
(aka THE GREAT MANHUNT) (s)			
RIM OF THE CANYON (s)		1949...COL	70
SOUTH OF DEATH VALLEY		1949...COL	54
(aka RIVER OF POISON) (s)			
HORSEMEN OF THE SIERRAS		1949...COL	56
(aka REMEMBER ME) (s)			
BANDITS OF EL DORADO (aka TRICKED) (s)		1949...COL	56
RENEGADES OF THE SAGE (aka THE FORT) (s)		1949...COL	56
THE NEVADAN	(C)..1950	COL	81
(aka THE MAN FROM NEVADA) (s)			
CODY OF THE PONY EXPRESS	(SER)..1950	COL	15CH
COW TOWN (s)		1950...COL	70
TEXAS DYNAMO (aka SUSPECTED) (s)		1950...COL	54
HOEDOWN (s)		1950...COL	64
THE KANGAROO KID		1950...UA	73

Title	Year	Studio	Page
LIGHTNING GUNS (aka TAKING SIDES) (s)	1950	COL	55
FRONTIER OUTPOST (s)	1950	COL	55
SANTA FE (s) (C)	1951	COL	89
ROAR OF THE IRON HORSE (SER)	1951	COL	15CH
THE TEXAS RANGERS (s) (C)	1951	COL	74
PECOS RIVER (aka WITHOUT RISK) (cs)	1951	COL	55
SMOKY CANYON (cs)	1951	COL	55
THE HAWK OF WILD RIVER (cs)	1952	COL	54
LARAMIE MOUNTAINS (aka MOUNTAIN DESPERADOES) (cs)	1952	COL	54
THE ROUGH, TOUGH WEST (cs)	1952	COL	54
JUNCTION CITY (cs)	1952	COL	54
THE KID FROM BROKEN GUN (cs)	1952	COL	56
GUNFIGHTERS OF THE NORTHWEST (SER)	1953	COL	15CH
OVERLAND PACIFIC (C)	1954	UA	72
A DAY OF FURY (cs) (C)	1956	UI	78
SHOWDOWN AT ABILENE (C)	1956	UI	80
JOE DAKOTA (C)	1957	UI	79
SLIM CARTER (C)	1957	UI	82
THE LAST OF THE FAST GUNS (C)	1958	UI	82
MONEY, WOMEN AND GUNS (C)	1959	UI	80
CALIFORNIA	1963	AI	86
BANDOLERO! (s) (C)	1968	20T	106
THEIR ONLY CHANCE (C)	1978	SEN	84

DEAN MARTIN (1917 -)

Best known as a singer and straight man of the "Martin and Lewis" comedy team early in his career, he went on to become a fine screen actor, making several westerns, mostly spoofs in nature. Good in PARDNERS and 4 FOR TEXAS.

Title	Year	Studio	Page
MY FRIEND IRMA GOES WEST (s)	1950	PAR	90
LIVING IT UP (C)	1954	PAR	95
PARDNERS (C)	1956	PAR	88-90
RIO BRAVO (C)	1959	WB	141
PEPE (gs) (C)	1960	COL	95
SERGEANTS 3 (C)	1962	UA	112
4 FOR TEXAS (C)	1963	WB	124
THE SONS OF KATIE ELDER (C)	1965	PAR	122
TEXAS ACROSS THE RIVER (C)	1966	UNI	101
ROUGH NIGHT IN JERICHO (C)	1967	UNI	97-104
BANDOLERO! (C)	1968	20T	106
5 CARD STUD (C)	1968	PAR	102-103
SOMETHING BIG (C)	1971	NG	108
SHOWDOWN (C)	1973	UNI	99

LEE MARVIN (1924 - 1987)

Rising from heavy to hero in "A" westerns, Marvin's Oscar was won for his portrayal of the woebegone, drunken gunfighter in the comedy musical western CAT BALLOU. Very good, as well, with THE PROFESSIONALS.

Title	Year	Studio	Page
THE DUEL AT SILVER CREEK (s) (C)	1952	UI	77
HANGMAN'S KNOT (s) (C)	1952	COL	81

124 / LEE MARVIN, continued

SEMINOLE (s)	(C) .. 1953 ... UI	87	___
THE STRANGER WORE A GUN (s)	(C) .. 1953 ... COL	83	___
GUN FURY (s)	(C) .. 1953 ... COL	83	___
THE RAID (s)	(C) .. 1954 ... 20T	83	___
BAD DAY AT BLACK ROCK (s)	(C) .. 1955 ... MGM	81	___
VIOLENT SATURDAY (s)	(C) .. 1955 ... 20T	91	___
SEVEN MEN FROM NOW (cs)	(C) .. 1956 ... WB	78	___
PILLARS OF THE SKY	(C) .. 1956 ... UI	95	___
(aka THE TOMAHAWK AND THE CROSS) (s)			
RAINTREE COUNTY (s)	(C) .. 1957 ... MGM	168	___
THE MISSOURI TRAVELER	(C) .. 1958 ... BV	103	___
THE COMANCHEROS (cs)	(C) .. 1961 ... 20T	107	___
THE MAN WHO SHOT LIBERTY VALANCE (s)	1962 ... PAR	119	___
THE MEANEST MEN IN THE WEST	(C) .. 1962 ... NBC-TV	92	___
CAT BALLOU	(C) .. 1965 ... COL	96	___
THE PROFESSIONALS	(C) .. 1966 ... COL	117	___
PAINT YOUR WAGON	(C) .. 1969 ... PAR	151-166	___
MONTE WALSH	(C) .. 1970 ... NG	95-106	___
POCKET MONEY	(C) .. 1972 ... NG	102	___
EMPEROR OF THE NORTH POLE	(C) .. 1973 ... 20T	118	___
(aka EMPEROR OF THE NORTH)			
THE SPIKES GANG	(C) .. 1974 ... UA	96	___
GREAT SCOUT AND CATHOUSE THURSDAY	(C) .. 1976 ... AI	102	___
(aka WILD CAT)			
DEATH HUNT	(C) .. 1980 ... 20T	96	___

VICTOR MATURE (1916 -   )

Husky leading man far better known for his he-man roles in epics rather than for "A" westerns. Mature was outstanding as the drunken Doc Holliday in the John Ford classic MY DARLING CLEMENTINE.

MY DARLING CLEMENTINE (cs)	1946 ... 20T	91-97	___
FURY AT FURNACE CREEK	1948 ... 20T	83-88	___
THE LAS VEGAS STORY	1952 ... RKO	88	___
DANGEROUS MISSION	(C) .. 1954 ... RKO	75	___
CHIEF CRAZY HORSE (aka VALLEY OF FURY)	(C) . 1955 ... UI	86	___
THE LAST FRONTIER	(C) .. 1956 ... COL	98	___
(aka SAVAGE WILDERNESS)			
ESCORT WEST	1959 ... UA	75	___

KEN MAYNARD (1895 - 1973)

Riding like he was born to the saddle, Maynard added zest, and began such thrills in 1920s silents. He did a bunch of "B" gallopers in the sound era (1930-40) for such studios as Universal, Tiffany, and Columbia. Two of his best oaters were HELL-FIRE AUSTIN and WESTERN FRONTIER. Ken returned briefly for *The Trail Blazers* series at Monogram (1943-44). He was a Top Money-Making Western Star (1936-37).

THE ROYAL RIDER	1929 ... FN	67	___
THE WAGON MASTER	1929 ... UNI	70	___
SENOR AMERICANO	1929 ... UNI	71	___
PARADE OF THE WEST	1930 ... UNI	65	___
LUCKY LARKIN	1930 ... UNI	65	___

KEN MAYNARD, continued / 125

Title	Year	Studio	Pages
THE FIGHTING LEGION	1930	UNI	75
MOUNTAIN JUSTICE (aka KETTLE CREEK)	1930	UNI	75
SONG OF THE CABALLERO	1930	UNI	70
SONS OF THE SADDLE	1930	UNI	70
FIGHTING THRU (aka CALIFORNIA IN 1878)	1930	TIF	71
THE TWO-GUN MAN	1931	TIF	60
ALIAS THE BAD MAN	1931	TIF	66
THE ARIZONA TERROR	1931	TIF	64
RANGE LAW	1931	TIF	63
BRANDED MEN	1931	TIF	70
THE POCATELLO KID	1931	TIF	61
THE SUNSET TRAIL	1932	TIF	62
TEXAS GUN FIGHTER	1932	TIF	63
WHISTLIN' DAN	1932	TIF	64
HELL-FIRE AUSTIN	1932	TIF	70
DYNAMITE RANCH	1932	WW	59
COME ON TARZAN	1932	WW	64
BETWEEN FIGHTING MEN	1932	WW	62
FARGO EXPRESS	1932	WW	62
TOMBSTONE CANYON	1932	WW	62
DRUM TAPS	1933	WW	61
PHANTOM THUNDERBOLT	1933	WW	62
THE LONE AVENGER	1933	WW	61
KING OF THE ARENA	1933	UNI	59-66
THE FIDDLIN' BUCKAROO	1933	UNI	65
THE TRAIL DRIVE	1933	UNI	60
STRAWBERRY ROAN	1933	UNI	59
GUN JUSTICE	1933	UNI	59
WHEELS OF DESTINY	1934	UNI	64
HONOR OF THE RANGE	1934	UNI	62
SMOKING GUNS	1934	UNI	62-65
IN OLD SANTA FE	1934	MAS	64
MYSTERY MOUNTAIN (SER)	1934	MAS	12CH
WESTERN FRONTIER	1935	COL	57-59
WESTERN COURAGE	1935	COL	58-61
HEIR TO TROUBLE	1935	COL	59
LAWLESS RIDERS	1935	COL	57
THE CATTLE THIEF	1936	COL	57
HEROES OF THE RANGE	1936	COL	57
AVENGING WATERS	1936	COL	57
THE FUGITIVE SHERIFF (aka LAW AND ORDER)	1936	COL	58
TRAILIN' TROUBLE	1937	GN	57
BOOTS OF DESTINY	1937	GN	56
WHIRLWIND HORSEMAN	1938	GN	58
SIX-SHOOTIN' SHERIFF	1938	GN	58
FLAMING LEAD	1939	CLY	57
DEATH RIDES THE RANGE	1940	CLY	58
PHANTOM RANCHER	1940	CLY	61
LIGHTNING STRIKES WEST	1940	CLY	56
WILD HORSE STAMPEDE	1943	MON	59
(starts *The Trail Blazers* series)			
THE LAW RIDES AGAIN	1943	MON	58
BLAZING GUNS	1943	MON	55
DEATH VALLEY RANGERS	1943	MON	55-59
WESTWARD BOUND	1944	MON	54-59
ARIZONA WHIRLWIND (ends *The Trail Blazers* series)	1944	MON	59

126 / KEN MAYNARD, continued

HARMONY TRAIL (aka THE WHITE STALLION)	1944	MAT	57
BIG FOOT (s)	(C) 1971	EE	94

KERMIT MAYNARD (1897 - 1971)

He could ride just like brother Ken, but Kermit had limited stardom in 18 Ambassador "B" features (1934-37) that included 10 outdoors sagas for the *Northwest Mountie* series. Maynard corraled good support roles afterwards for about one decade, then by the late 1940s, he was reduced to walk-ons and background bits.

THE PHANTOM OF THE WEST (s)	(SER) 1931	MAS	10CH
WEST OF BROADWAY (s)	1931	MGM	66
LIGHTNING WARRIOR (s)	(SER) 1931	MAS	12CH
DYNAMITE RANCH (s)	1932	WW	59
OUTLAW JUSTICE (s)	1932	MAJ	61
DRUM TAPS (s)	1933	WW	61
THE FIGHTING TROOPER	1934	AMB	58
(starts *Northwest Mountie* series)			
NORTHERN FRONTIER	1935	AMB	57-60
WILDERNESS MAIL	1935	AMB	58-65
RED BLOOD OF COURAGE	1935	AMB	55
CODE OF THE MOUNTED	1935	AMB	60
TRAILS OF THE WILD	1935	AMB	60
HIS FIGHTING BLOOD	1935	AMB	60
TIMBER WAR	1935	AMB	60
SONG OF THE TRAIL (non-series)	1936	AMB	59
WILDCAT TROOPER	1936	AMB	60
PHANTOM PATROL (ends *Northwest Mountie* series)	1936	AMB	60
WILD HORSE ROUND-UP	1936	AMB	55
VALLEY OF TERROR	1937	AMB	58
WHISTLING BULLETS	1937	AMB	57
THE FIGHTING TEXAN	1937	AMB	59
GALLOPING DYNAMITE	1937	AMB	58
ROUGH RIDING RHYTHM	1937	AMB	57-66
ROARING SIX GUNS	1937	AMB	57
WILD HORSE RODEO (s)	1937	REP	55
THE GREAT ADVENTURES OF WILD BILL HICKOK (s)	(SER) 1938	COL	15CH
THE LAW WEST OF TOMBSTONE (s)	1938	RKO	73
WESTERN JAMBOREE (s)	1938	REP	56
CODE OF THE CACTUS (s)	1939	VIC	56
THE NIGHT RIDERS (s)	1939	REP	58
WYOMING OUTLAW (s)	1939	REP	56
ROVIN' TUMBLEWEEDS (s)	1939	REP	56
COLORADO SUNSET (s)	1939	REP	64
CHIP OF THE FLYING U (s)	1939	UNI	55
DESTRY RIDES AGAIN (s)	1939	UNI	94
HEROES OF THE SADDLE (s)	1940	REP	56-59
WEST OF CARSON CITY (s)	1940	UNI	57
THE SHOWDOWN (s)	1940	PAR	63
RIDERS OF PASCO BASIN (s)	1940	UNI	56
THE RANGE BUSTERS (s)	1940	MON	56
THE RETURN OF FRANK JAMES (s)	(C) 1940	20T	92
RAGTIME COWBOY JOE (s)	1940	UNI	58
LAW AND ORDER (s)	1940	UNI	57

KERMIT MAYNARD, continued

Title	Year	Studio	Length
PONY POST (s)	1940	UNI	59
NORTH WEST MOUNTED POLICE (s) (C)	1940	PAR	125
THE TRAIL OF THE SILVER SPURS (s)	1941	MON	58
WYOMING WILDCAT (s)	1941	REP	56
BOSS OF BULLION CITY (s)	1941	UNI	61
BURY ME NOT ON THE LONE PRAIRIE (s)	1941	UNI	57
BILLY THE KID (s) (C)	1941	MGM	95
BADLANDS OF DAKOTA (s)	1941	UNI	74
MAN FROM MONTANA (aka MONTANA JUSTICE) (s)	1941	UNI	56
BELLE STARR (s) (C)	1941	20T	87
STICK TO YOUR GUNS (s)	1941	PAR	63
KING OF THE TEXAS RANGERS (s) (SER)	1941	REP	12CH
SIERRA SUE (s)	1941	REP	64
THE ROYAL MOUNTED PATROL (aka GIANTS A'FIRE) (s)	1941	COL	59
ARIZONA CYCLONE (s)	1941	UNI	57
A MISSOURI OUTLAW (s)	1941	REP	58
GO WEST, YOUNG LADY (s)	1941	COL	70
ARIZONA TERRORS (s)	1942	REP	56
BELOW THE BORDER (s)	1942	MON	57
STAGECOACH BUCKAROO (s)	1942	UNI	59
ROCK RIVER RENEGADES (s)	1942	MON	56
JESSE JAMES, JR. (aka SUNDOWN FURY) (s)	1942	REP	56
FIGHTING BILL FARGO (s)	1942	UNI	57
DOWN RIO GRANDE WAY (aka THE DOUBLE PUNCH) (s)	1942	COL	57
SABOTEUR (s)	1942	UNI	108
HOME IN WYOMIN' (s)	1942	REP	67
PERILS OF THE ROYAL MOUNTED (s) (SER)	1942	COL	15CH
TEXAS TROUBLE SHOOTERS (s)	1942	MON	55
LAW AND ORDER (s)	1942	PRC	58
RIDERS OF THE WEST (s)	1942	MON	60
THE OMAHA TRAIL (s)	1942	MGM	61
ARIZONA STAGE COACH (s)	1942	MON	58
PRAIRIE PALS (s)	1942	PRC	60
ALONG THE SUNDOWN TRAIL (s)	1942	PRC	59
RIDING THROUGH NEVADA (s)	1942	COL	61
SHERIFF OF SAGE VALLEY (aka BILLY THE KID, SHERIFF OF SAGE VALLEY) (s)	1942	PRC	60
THE LONE PRAIRIE (aka INSIDE INFORMATION) (s)	1942	COL	58
VALLEY OF HUNTED MEN (s)	1942	REP	60
THE MYSTERIOUS RIDER (s)	1942	PRC	55
TRAIL RIDERS (s)	1942	MON	55
TWO-FISTED JUSTICE (s)	1943	MON	61
BAD MEN OF THUNDER GAP (s)	1943	PRC	57
THE BLOCKED TRAIL (s)	1943	REP	55
FUGITIVE OF THE PLAINS (s)	1943	PRC	56
SANTA FE SCOUTS (s)	1943	REP	55
CHEYENNE ROUNDUP (s)	1943	UNI	59
DEATH RIDES THE PLAINS (s)	1943	PRC	57
WESTERN CYCLONE (s)	1943	PRC	56
BORDER BUCKAROOS (s)	1943	PRC	59
THE STRANGER FROM PECOS (s)	1943	MON	56
FRONTIER BADMEN (s)	1943	UNI	77
SILVER SPURS (s)	1943	REP	68
BLAZING FRONTIER (s)	1943	PRC	59

128 / KERMIT MAYNARD, continued

BEYOND THE LAST FRONTIER (s)	1943	REP	55
RAIDERS OF RED GAP (s)	1943	PRC	54
THE DEVIL RIDERS (s)	1943	PRC	58
THE TEXAS KID (s)	1943	MON	57
GUNSMOKE MESA (s)	1944	PRC	59
RAIDERS OF THE BORDER (s)	1944	MON	58
FRONTIER OUTLAWS (s)	1944	PRC	58
THUNDERING GUN SLINGERS (s)	1944	PRC	60
BUFFALO BILL (s) (C)	1944	20T	90
THE PINTO BANDIT (s)	1944	PRC	56
THE DRIFTER (s)	1944	PRC	62
BRAND OF THE DEVIL (s)	1944	PRC	57
WILD HORSE PHANTOM (s)	1944	PRC	56
OATH OF VENGEANCE (s)	1944	PRC	57
MARKED FOR MURDER (s)	1945	PRC	56
SING ME A SONG OF TEXAS (s)	1945	COL	66
ROUGH RIDIN' JUSTICE (s)	1945	COL	58
FLAME OF THE WEST (aka FLAMING FRONTIER) (s)	1945	MON	60
ENEMY OF THE LAW (s)	1945	PRC	59
GANGSTER'S DEN (s)	1945	PRC	55
STAGECOACH OUTLAWS (s)	1945	PRC	59
FLAMING BULLETS (s)	1945	PRC	59
OUTLAWS OF THE ROCKIES (s)	1945	COL	55
FIGHTING BILL CARSON (s)	1945	PRC	51
PRAIRIE RUSTLERS (s)	1945	PRC	56
ROARING RANGERS (aka FALSE HERO) (s)	1946	COL	56
AMBUSH TRAIL (s)	1946	PRC	60
BADMAN'S TERRITORY (s)	1946	RKO	98
GALLOPING THUNDER (aka ON BOOT HILL) (s)	1946	COL	54
UNDER ARIZONA SKIES (s)	1946	MON	59
PRAIRIE BADMEN (s)	1946	PRC	55
RUSTLER'S ROUNDUP (aka RUSTLER'S HIDEOUT) (s)	1946	UNI	56
TERRORS ON HORSEBACK (s)	1946	PRC	55
'NEATH CANADIAN SKIES (s)	1946	SG	41
TUMBLEWEED TRAIL (s)	1946	PRC	57
STARS OVER TEXAS (s)	1946	PRC	57
MY DARLING CLEMENTINE (s)	1946	20T	91-97
RENEGADE GIRL (s)	1946	SG	66
SOUTH OF THE CHISHOLM TRAIL (s)	1947	COL	58
DUEL IN THE SUN (s) (C)	1947	SEL	130-138
THE VIGILANTE (s) (SER)	1947	COL	15CH
THE LAW COMES TO GUNSIGHT (s)	1947	MON	56
ALONG THE OREGON TRAIL (s) (C)	1947	REP	64
RIDIN' DOWN THE TRAIL (s)	1947	MON	53
RETURN OF THE LASH (s)	1947	PRC	55
BUCKAROO FROM POWDER RIVER (s)	1947	COL	55
THE ARIZONA RANGER (s)	1948	RKO	63
THE GALLANT LEGION (s)	1948	REP	88
FURY AT FURNACE CREEK (s)	1948	20T	88
NORTHWEST STAMPEDE (s) (C)	1948	EL	76
A SOUTHERN YANKEE (aka MY HERO!) (s)	1948	MGM	90
FRONTIER REVENGE (s)	1948	SG	55
THE PALEFACE (s) (C)	1948	PAR	91
CHALLENGE OF THE RANGE (aka MOONLIGHT RAID) (s)	1949	COL	56

Title		Year	Studio	Min
MASSACRE RIVER (s)		1949	AA	78
LARAMIE (s)		1949	COL	55
THE YOUNGER BROTHERS (s)	(C)	1949	WB	77
MIGHTY JOE YOUNG (s)		1949	RKO	94
LUST FOR GOLD (s)		1949	COL	90
THE MYSTERIOUS DESPERADO .(s)		1949	RKO	61
RIDERS IN THE SKY (s)		1949	COL	70
RANGE LAND (s)		1949	MON	56
FIGHTING MAN OF THE PLAINS (s)	(C)	1949	20T	94
THE TRAVELING SALESWOMAN (s)		1950	COL	75
THE SAVAGE HORDE (s)		1950	REP	90
THE CARIBOO TRAIL (s)	(C)	1950	20T	81
SILVER RAIDERS (s)		1950	MON	55
DEVIL'S DOORWAY (s)		1950	MGM	84
LAW OF THE PANHANDLE (s)		1950	MON	55
TRAIL OF ROBIN HOOD (gs)	(C)	1950	REP	67
SHORT GRASS (s)		1950	AA	82
3 DESPERATE MEN (s)		1951	LIP	69
IN OLD AMARILLO (s)		1951	REP	67
FORT WORTH (s)	(C)	1951	WB	80
FORT DODGE STAMPEDE (s)		1951	REP	60
GOLDEN GIRL (s)	(C)	1951	20T	108
THE BLACK LASH (s)		1952	WA	55
RANCHO NOTORIOUS (s)	(C)	1952	RKO	89
OUTLAW WOMEN (s)	(C)	1952	LIP	75
HELLGATE (s)		1952	LIP	87
GUNFIGHTERS OF THE NORTHWEST (s)	(SER)	1953	COL	15CH
LAW AND ORDER (s)	(C)	1953	UI	80
THE GREAT SIOUX UPRISING (s)	(C)	1953	UI	80
PACK TRAIN (s)		1953	COL	57
CALAMITY JANE (s)	(C)	1953	WB	101
LAST OF THE PONY RIDERS (s)		1953	COL	59
THE COMMAND (s)	(C)	1954	WB	88
THE YELLOW MOUNTAIN (s)	(C)	1954	UI	78
WICHITA (s)	(C)	1955	AA	81
THE LAST COMMAND (s)	(C)	1955	REP	110
APACHE AMBUSH (s)		1955	COL	68
A LAWLESS STREET (s)	(C)	1955	COL	78
THE OX-BOW INCIDENT (s)		1955	20T-TV	45
PERILS OF THE WILDERNESS (s)	(SER)	1956	COL	15CH
THE LONE RANGER (s)	(C)	1956	WB	86
RED SUNDOWN (s)	(C)	1956	UI	82
BLACKJACK KETCHUM, DESPERADO (s)	(C)	1956	COL	76
BACKLASH (s)	(C)	1956	UI	84
GREAT DAY IN THE MORNING (s)	(C)	1956	RKO	92
STAR IN THE DUST (s)	(C)	1956	UI	80
GUNSLINGER (s)	(C)	1956	AI	83
THE RAWHIDE YEARS (s)	(C)	1956	UI	85
THE FASTEST GUN ALIVE (s)		1956	MGM	92
REBEL IN TOWN (s)		1956	UA	78
BLAZING THE OVERLAND TRAIL (s)	(SER)	1956	COL	15CH
THE FIRST TRAVELING SALESLADY (s)	(C)	1956	RKO	92
FLESH AND THE SPUR (s)	(C)	1956	AI	80
TWO-GUN LADY (s)		1956	AFR	70
REPRISAL! (s)	(C)	1956	COL	80
FRIENDLY PERSUASION (s)	(C)	1956	AA	140

130 / KERMIT MAYNARD, continued

Title	Color	Year	Studio	Min
GIANT (s)	(C)	1956	WB	201
DRANGO (s)		1957	UA	92
FURY AT SHOWDOWN (s)		1957	UA	75
THE PHANTOM STAGECOACH (s)		1957	COL	69
THE OKLAHOMAN (s)	(C)	1957	AA	81
RUN OF THE ARROW (aka HOT LEAD) (s)	(C)	1957	RKO	85
GUN BATTLE AT MONTEREY (s)		1957	UA	76
THE DOMINO KID (s)		1957	COL	73
THE HARD MAN (s)	(C)	1957	COL	80
MAN FROM GOD'S COUNTRY (s)	(C)	1958	AA	70
COLE YOUNGER, GUNFIGHTER (s)	(C)	1958	AA	79
THE SHEEPMAN (s)	(C)	1958	MGM	85
ONCE UPON A HORSE (aka HOT HORSE) (gs)		1958	UI	85
GUNMEN FROM LAREDO (s)	(C)	1959	COL	67
WESTBOUND (s)	(C)	1959	WB	96
CAST A LONG SHADOW (s)		1959	UA	82
THE OREGON TRAIL (s)	(C)	1959	20T	86
HELL BENT FOR LEATHER (s)	(C)	1960	UI	82
TOBY TYLER (s)	(C)	1960	BV	96
NOOSE FOR A GUNMAN (s)		1960	UA	69
ONE FOOT IN HELL (s)	(C)	1960	20T	90
THE SIGN OF ZORRO (s)		1960	BV	91
NORTH TO ALASKA (s)	(C)	1960	20T	122
CIMARRON (s)	(C)	1960	MGM	147

TIM McCOY (1891 - 1978)

McCoy did quality "B" horse operas for Columbia Pictures (1931-35) such as THE PRESCOTT KID. Being named a Top Money-Making Western Star in 1936, Tim starred in cheaper oaters at Puritan, Monogram, Victory, and PRC from 1935-41, then joined ex-Columbia stablemate Buck Jones for the action-packed *The Rough Riders* series for Monogram (1941-42). McCoy maintained a youthful appearance even in 1965 for a character support in REQUIEM FOR A GUNFIGHTER.

Title	Type	Year	Studio	Min
THE INDIANS ARE COMING	(SER)	1930	UNI	12CH
THE ONE WAY TRAIL		1931	COL	55-60
SHOTGUN PASS		1931	COL	59
THE FIGHTING MARSHAL		1931	COL	59
THE FIGHTING FOOL		1932	COL	58
TEXAS CYCLONE		1932	COL	58
DARING DANGER		1932	COL	57
THE RIDING TORNADO		1932	COL	64
TWO-FISTED LAW		1932	COL	57-64
CORNERED		1932	COL	58
THE WESTERN CODE		1932	COL	61
FIGHTING FOR JUSTICE		1932	COL	61-64
END OF THE TRAIL		1932	COL	59
MAN OF ACTION		1933	COL	57
SILENT MEN		1933	COL	68
WHIRLWIND		1933	COL	62-68
RUSTY RIDES ALONE		1933	COL	58
BEYOND THE LAW		1934	COL	58-60
THE PRESCOTT KID		1934	COL	58-60
THE WESTERNER (aka THE FIGHTING WESTERNER)		1934	COL	58
SQUARE SHOOTER		1935	COL	57

TIM McCOY, continued / 131

Title	Year	Studio	Pages
LAW BEYOND THE RANGE	1935	COL	58-60
THE REVENGE RIDER	1935	COL	57-60
FIGHTING SHADOWS	1935	COL	58
JUSTICE OF THE RANGE	1935	COL	58
RIDING WILD	1935	COL	57
THE OUTLAW DEPUTY	1935	PUR	56-59
THE MAN FROM GUNTOWN	1935	PUR	61
BULLDOG COURAGE	1935	PUR	60
ROARIN' GUNS	1936	PUR	59
BORDER CABALLERO	1936	PUR	59
LIGHTNIN' BILL CARSON	1936	PUR	57-75
ACES AND EIGHTS	1936	PUR	62
THE LION'S DEN	1936	PUR	58
GHOST PATROL	1936	PUR	60
THE TRAITOR	1936	PUR	56
WEST OF RAINBOW'S END	1938	MON	57
CODE OF THE RANGERS	1938	MON	56
TWO GUN JUSTICE	1938	MON	57
PHANTOM RANGER	1938	MON	53
LIGHTNING CARSON RIDES AGAIN	1938	VIC	59
(starts *Lightnin' Bill Carson* series)			
SIX-GUN TRAIL	1938	VIC	59
CODE OF THE CACTUS	1939	VIC	56
TEXAS WILDCATS	1939	VIC	57
OUTLAW'S PARADISE	1939	VIC	62
TRIGGER FINGERS	1939	VIC	60
THE FIGHTING RENEGADE	1939	VIC	58
STRAIGHT SHOOTER	1939	VIC	54
(ends *Lightnin' Bill Carson* series)			
TEXAS RENEGADES	1940	PDC	59
FRONTIER CRUSADER	1940	PRC	62
GUN CODE	1940	PRC	54-57
ARIZONA GANG BUSTERS	1940	PRC	60
RIDERS OF BLACK MOUNTAIN	1940	PRC	57-59
OUTLAWS OF THE RIO GRANDE	1941	PRC	63
THE TEXAS MARSHAL	1941	PRC	58-62
ARIZONA BOUND (starts *The Rough Riders* series)	1941	MON	57
THE GUNMAN FROM BODIE	1941	MON	62
FORBIDDEN TRAILS	1941	MON	59
BELOW THE BORDER	1942	MON	57
GHOST TOWN LAW	1942	MON	62
DOWN TEXAS WAY	1942	MON	57
RIDERS OF THE WEST	1942	MON	58-60
WEST OF THE LAW (ends *The Rough Riders* series)	1942	MON	55-60
RUN OF THE ARROW (aka HOT LEAD) (s) ..... (C)	1957	RKO	85
REQUIEM FOR A GUNFIGHTER (s) .... (C)	1965	EMB	91

JOEL McCREA (1905 - 1990)

One of the truly great western stars who made many excellent films in the genre. Outstanding as the strong, silent type in UNION PACIFIC, RAMROD, and RIDE THE HIGH COUNTRY, the latter with Randolph Scott. McCrea did 26 half-hour episodes of "Wichita Town" for NBC-TV (1959-60).

Title	Year	Studio	Pages
LIGHTNIN' (s)	1930	FOX	94
THE SILVER HORDE	1930	RKO	67-75

JOEL McCREA, continued

Title	Year	Studio	Pages
SCARLET RIVER (gs)	1933	RKO	57
BARBARY COAST (s)	1935	UA	90
COME AND GET IT (aka ROARING TIMBERS)	1936	UA	99
BANJO ON MY KNEE (s)	1936	20T	96
WELLS FARGO	1937	PAR	94-115
UNION PACIFIC	1939	PAR	125-135
THE GREAT MAN'S LADY	1942	PAR	90
BUFFALO BILL (C)	1944	20T	90
THE VIRGINIAN (C)	1946	PAR	87
RAMROD	1947	UA	94
FOUR FACES WEST (aka THEY PASSED THIS WAY)	1948	UA	90
SOUTH OF ST. LOUIS (C)	1949	WB	88
COLORADO TERRITORY	1949	WB	94
THE OUTRIDERS (C)	1950	MGM	93
STARS IN MY CROWN	1950	MGM	89
SADDLE TRAMP (C)	1950	UI	76-77
FRENCHIE (C)	1951	UI	80-81
CATTLE DRIVE (C)	1951	UI	77
THE SAN FRANCISCO STORY	1952	WB	80
LONE HAND (C)	1953	UI	79-80
BORDER RIVER (C)	1954	UI	81
BLACK HORSE CANYON (C)	1954	UI	81
STRANGER ON HORSEBACK (C)	1955	UA	66
WICHITA (C)	1955	AA	81
THE FIRST TEXAN (C)	1956	AA	82
THE OKLAHOMAN (C)	1957	AA	73-81
TROOPER HOOK	1957	UA	81-82
GUNSIGHT RIDGE	1957	UA	85
THE TALL STRANGER (C)	1957	AA	81-83
CATTLE EMPIRE (C)	1958	20T	82-83
FORT MASSACRE (C)	1958	UA	80
THE GUNFIGHT AT DODGE CITY (C)	1959	UA	81
RIDE THE HIGH COUNTRY (C) (aka GUNS IN THE AFTERNOON)	1962	MGM	94
CRY BLOOD, APACHE (gs) (C)	1970	GEA	82
THE GREAT AMERICAN COWBOY (nr) (C)	1974	ANE	90
MUSTANG COUNTRY (C)	1976	UNI	79

NEVADA JACK McKENZIE series (1943 - 1946)

The immediate successor to and in the same mold as *The Rough Riders* series at Monogram. It starred Johnny Mack Brown and Raymond Hatton which allowed the latter player to continue as U.S. Marshal Sandy Hopkins in 19 more action "B" oaters. Standouts are THE TEXAS KID and STRANGER FROM SANTA FE.

(JOHNNY MACK BROWN, RAYMOND HATTON)

Title	Year	Studio	Pages
THE GHOST RIDER	1943	MON	52-58
THE STRANGER FROM PECOS	1943	MON	56
SIX-GUN GOSPEL	1943	MON	55
OUTLAWS OF STAMPEDE PASS	1943	MON	55
THE TEXAS KID	1943	MON	57
RAIDERS OF THE BORDER	1944	MON	53-59
PARTNERS OF THE TRAIL	1944	MON	54

NEVADA JACK McKENZIE series, continued / 133

LAW MEN	1944	MON	57 ____
RANGE LAW	1944	MON	57 ____
WEST OF THE RIO GRANDE	1944	MON	57 ____
LAND OF THE OUTLAWS	1944	MON	55 ____
LAW OF THE VALLEY	1944	MON	52 ____
GHOST GUNS	1944	MON	60 ____
THE NAVAJO TRAIL	1945	MON	60 ____
GUN SMOKE	1945	MON	57 ____
STRANGER FROM SANTA FE	1945	MON	56 ____
THE LOST TRAIL	1945	MON	53 ____
FRONTIER FEUD	1945	MON	54 ____
BORDER BANDITS	1946	MON	58 ____

STEPHEN McNALLY (1912 -)

Excellent character actor who usually has played villains such as the evil brother of James Stewart in WINCHESTER '73. Cunning, forceful, and tough.

THE HARVEY GIRLS (s)	(C)	1946	MGM	101 ____
THE LADY GAMBLES (cs)		1949	UI	99 ____
WINCHESTER '73 (s)		1950	UI	92 ____
WYOMING MAIL	(C)	1950	UI	87 ____
APACHE DRUMS	(C)	1951	UI	75 ____
THE DUEL AT SILVER CREEK	(C)	1952	UI	77 ____
SPLIT SECOND		1953	RKO	85 ____
DEVIL'S CANYON (cs)	(C)	1953	RKO	93 ____
THE STAND AT APACHE RIVER	(C)	1953	UI	77 ____
MAKE HASTE TO LIVE		1954	REP	90 ____
A BULLET IS WAITING (cs)	(C)	1954	COL	82 ____
VIOLENT SATURDAY (cs)		1955	20T	91 ____
THE MAN FROM BITTER RIDGE	(C)	1955	UI	80 ____
TRIBUTE TO A BADMAN (cs)	(C)	1956	MGM	95 ____
HELL'S CROSSROADS		1957	REP	73-77 ____
THE FIEND WHO WALKED THE WEST (s)		1958	20T	100-101 ____
HELL BENT FOR LEATHER (cs)	(C)	1960	UI	82 ____
REQUIEM FOR A GUNFIGHTER	(C)	1965	EMB	91 ____
NAKIA (s)	(C)	1974	COL-TV	78 ____
KINO, THE PADRE ON HORSEBACK	(C)	1977	KI	116 ____

(aka MISSION TO GLORY) (s)

STEVE McQUEEN (1930 - 1980)

He became bounty hunter Josh Randall in the popular "Wanted—Dead or Alive" CBS-TV series (1958-61) for 94 half-hour episodes. Then McQueen filmed several well-received "A" mustangers over a 20-year period such as NEVADA SMITH.

THE MAGNIFICENT SEVEN	(C)	1960	UA	126 ____
NEVADA SMITH	(C)	1966	PAR	135 ____
THE REIVERS	(C)	1969	NG	107 ____
(aka THE YELLOW WINTON FLYER)				
JUNIOR BONNER	(C)	1972	CRC	103 ____
THE GETAWAY	(C)	1972	NG	122 ____
TOM HORN	(C)	1980	WB	98 ____

RAY MILLAND (1905 - 1986)
Excellent British leading man whose riding and gun-handling skills have made him look good in westerns. Highly praised for Republic's A MAN ALONE.

UNTAMED	(C).. 1940... PAR	83
CALIFORNIA	(C).. 1947... PAR	98
COPPER CANYON	(C).. 1950... PAR	83
BUGLES IN THE AFTERNOON	(C).. 1952... WB	85
A MAN ALONE	(C).. 1955... REP	96
THE RIVER'S EDGE	(C).. 1957... 20T	87
BLACK NOON (s)	(C).. 1971... COL-TV	73

ROBERT MITCHUM (1917 -   )
(aka BOB MITCHUM)
Laid-back actor who began his film career with bit parts in "B" westerns, most notably the *Hopalong Cassidy* series. He rose rapidly to leading man status by the late 1940s, making numerous western films both as a star and supporting actor. Good features Mitchum made in the genre were Republic's THE RED PONY and RKO's THE LUSTY MEN. Great as the drunken sheriff in EL DORADO.

HOPPY SERVES A WRIT (s)	1943... UA	67
BORDER PATROL (s)	1943... UA	67
LEATHER BURNERS (s)	1943... UA	58
COLT COMRADES (s)	1943... UA	67
THE LONE STAR TRAIL (s)	1943... UNI	58
BEYOND THE LAST FRONTIER (s)	1943... REP	55
BAR 20 (s)	1943... UA	54
FALSE COLORS (s)	1943... UA	65
RIDERS OF THE DEADLINE (s)	1943... UA	70
GIRL RUSH (s)	1944... RKO	65
NEVADA	1944... RKO	62
WEST OF THE PECOS	1945... RKO	66-68
PURSUED	1947... WB	101
OUT OF THE PAST	1947... RKO	97
RACHEL AND THE STRANGER (cs)	1948... RKO	93
BLOOD ON THE MOON	1948... RKO	88
THE RED PONY	(C).. 1949... REP	89
THE BIG STEAL	1949... RKO	71
THE LUSTY MEN	1952... RKO	113
SECOND CHANCE	(C).. 1953... RKO	81
RIVER OF NO RETURN	(C).. 1954... 20T	91
TRACK OF THE CAT	(C).. 1954... WB	102
MAN WITH THE GUN	1955... UA	83
(aka THE TROUBLE SHOOTER; MAN WITHOUT A GUN)		
BANDIDO	(C).. 1956... UA	92
THE WONDERFUL COUNTRY	(C).. 1959... UA	96
HOME FROM THE HILL	(C).. 1960... MGM	150
THE SUNDOWNERS	(C).. 1960... WB	113
THE WAY WEST	(C).. 1967... UA	122
EL DORADO	(C).. 1967... PAR	126
VILLA RIDES	(C).. 1968... PAR	122
5 CARD STUD	(C).. 1968... PAR	103
YOUNG BILLY YOUNG	(C).. 1969... UA	88-89
(aka WHO RIDES WITH KANE)		

ROBERT MITCHUM, continued / 135

THE GOOD GUYS AND THE BAD GUYS	(C)	1969	WB	91	____
THE WRATH OF GOD	(C)	1972	MGM	111	____

TOM MIX (1871 - 1940)

He was the American hero-showman to millions in silents with Selig shorts and Fox oater features through the late 1920s. Mix, once having earned $17,000 a week from Fox, mainlined nine Universal westerns (1932-33) that included the superior and highly praised THE RIDER OF DEATH VALLEY. Tom closed out his film career with Mascot's 15-chapter serial THE MIRACLE RIDER in 1935, and continued with personal appearances until that fatal Arizona car accident.

DESTRY RIDES AGAIN (aka JUSTICE RIDES AGAIN)	1932	UNI	53-61	____
THE RIDER OF DEATH VALLEY	1932	UNI	63-78	____
(aka RIDERS OF THE DESERT)				
THE TEXAS BAD MAN	1932	UNI	60-63	____
MY PAL THE KING	1932	UNI	63-76	____
THE FOURTH HORSEMAN	1932	UNI	63	____
HIDDEN GOLD	1932	UNI	52-61	____
FLAMING GUNS (aka ROUGH RIDING ROMEO)	1932	UNI	57	____
TERROR TRAIL	1933	UNI	57	____
THE RUSTLERS' ROUNDUP	1933	UNI	56-60	____
THE MIRACLE RIDER (SER)	1935	MAS	15CH	____

DOCTOR MONROE series (1941)

By early May 1941, Charles Starrett had not filmed a Columbia "B" western in almost nine months when the studio thrust him at that time into this new series of oaters as a frontier medico. But such films before the cameras stopped after the third entry finished lensing the following July when Columbia had legal problems over author James L. Rubel's stories.

(CHARLES STARRETT)

THE MEDICO OF PAINTED SPRINGS	1941	COL	59	____
(aka DOCTOR'S ALIBI)				

(CHARLES STARRETT, CLIFF "UKELELE IKE" EDWARDS)

THUNDER OVER THE PRAIRIE	1941	COL	60	____
PRAIRIE STRANGER (aka MARKED BULLET)	1941	COL	58	____

MONTIE MONTANA (1910 -   )

A professional rodeo cowboy, he is best known for tossing a loop over President Eisenhower during the ex-Army general's January 1953 inaugural parade in Washington, DC. Good as the sheriff in DOWN DAKOTA WAY.

CIRCLE OF DEATH	1935	KEN	60	____
COURAGE OF THE NORTH (s)	1935	S&S	55	____
SMOKY TRAILS (s)	1939	MET	57	____
LAW OF THE PAMPAS (s)	1939	PAR	74	____
DOWN DAKOTA WAY (s)	(C) 1949	REP	67	____
THE MAN WHO SHOT LIBERTY VALANCE (s)	1962	PAR	123	____
HUD (s)	1963	PAR	112	____
ARIZONA BUSHWHACKERS (s)	(C) 1968	PAR	86	____

GEORGE MONTGOMERY (1916 -   )
(aka GEORGE LETZ)

A prolific western star who began as a stuntman in "B" oaters. Gave fine performances in westerns such as THE TEXAS RANGERS, then steered NBC-TV's "Cimarron City" (1958-59) for 26 shows that were one hour each. In latter years, Montgomery has devoted his outstanding talents to painting and sculpture.

Title	Year	Studio	Page
THE SINGING VAGABOND (s)	1936	REP	52
SPRINGTIME IN THE ROCKIES (s)	1937	REP	60
THE OLD BARN DANCE (s)	1938	REP	60
THE LONE RANGER (cs) (SER)	1938	REP	15CH
UNDER WESTERN STARS (s)	1938	REP	65
GOLD MINE IN THE SKY (s)	1938	REP	60
ARMY GIRL (aka THE LAST OF THE CAVALRY) (s)	1938	REP	80
PALS OF THE SADDLE	1938	REP	60
BILLY THE KID RETURNS (s)	1938	REP	56
SANTA FE STAMPEDE (s)	1938	REP	56
COME ON, RANGERS (s)	1938	REP	58
HAWK OF THE WILDERNESS (SER)	1938	REP	12CH
(aka LOST ISLAND OF KIOGA) (s)			
SHINE ON HARVEST MOON (s)	1938	REP	57
ROUGH RIDERS' ROUND-UP (s)	1939	REP	58
THE NIGHT RIDERS (s)	1939	REP	58
FRONTIER PONY EXPRESS (s)	1939	REP	58
MAN OF CONQUEST (s)	1939	REP	97
SOUTHWARD, HO! (s)	1939	REP	58
IN OLD CALIENTE (s)	1939	REP	58
WYOMING OUTLAW (s)	1939	REP	56
NEW FRONTIER (aka FRONTIER HORIZON) (s)	1939	REP	57
IN OLD MONTEREY (s)	1939	REP	73
WALL STREET COWBOY (s)	1939	REP	66
THE ARIZONA KID (s)	1939	REP	61
SAGA OF DEATH VALLEY (s)	1939	REP	58
SOUTH OF THE BORDER (aka SOUTH OF TEXAS) (s)	1939	REP	71
THE CISCO KID AND THE LADY (s)	1939	20T	73
HI-YO-SILVER	1940	REP	69
(feature version of THE LONE RANGER serial) (cs)			
THE COWBOY AND THE BLONDE	1941	20T	68
THE LAST OF THE DUANES	1941	20T	55-57
RIDERS OF THE PURPLE SAGE	1941	20T	56
TEN GENTLEMEN FROM WEST POINT	1942	20T	102
BELLE STARR'S DAUGHTER	1948	20T	85-86
DAVY CROCKETT INDIAN SCOUT	1950	UA	71
(aka INDIAN SCOUT)			
DAKOTA LIL (C)	1950	20T	88
THE IROQUOIS TRAIL (aka THE TOMAHAWK TRAIL)	1950	UA	85-86
THE TEXAS RANGERS (C)	1951	COL	74
INDIAN UPRISING (C)	1952	COL	74-75
CRIPPLE CREEK (C)	1952	COL	78
THE PATHFINDER (C)	1953	COL	78
JACK McCALL, DESPERADO (C)	1953	COL	76
FORT TI (C)	1953	COL	73
GUN BELT (C)	1953	UA	77
BATTLE OF ROGUE RIVER (C)	1954	COL	71
THE LONE GUN (C)	1954	UA	73-78
MASTERSON OF KANSAS (C)	1955	COL	73

GEORGE MONTGOMERY, continued /137

SEMINOLE UPRISING	(C)	1955	COL	74
ROBBERS' ROOST	(C)	1955	UA	82
CANYON RIVER	(C)	1956	AA	80
LAST OF THE BAD MEN	(C)	1957	AA	79-80
GUN DUEL IN DURANGO (aka DUEL IN DURANGO)		1957	UA	73
PAWNEE (aka PALE ARROW)	(C)	1957	REP	80
BLACK PATCH		1957	WB	83
MAN FROM GOD'S COUNTRY	(C)	1958	AA	70
TOUGHEST GUN IN TOMBSTONE		1958	UA	72
BADMAN'S COUNTRY		1958	WB	68
KING OF THE WILD STALLIONS	(C)	1959	AA	75-78
HOSTILE GUNS	(C)	1967	PAR	91
OUTLAWS OF RED RIVER	(C)	1967	FHG	76
STRANGERS AT SUNRISE	(C)	1969	CU	99

CLAYTON MOORE (1914 -)
A stalwart Republic hero by 1949 that included cliffhangers like JESSE JAMES RIDES AGAIN and GHOST OF ZORRO, Moore achieved greater prominence that year by becoming "The Lone Ranger," the 30-minute TV series masked rider for justice. Clayton would always be identified with the popular character that included two feature-length color movies, THE LONE RANGER and THE LONE RANGER AND THE LOST CITY OF GOLD.

KIT CARSON (s)		1940	UA	96-97
OUTLAWS OF PINE RIDGE (s)		1942	REP	57
HELDORADO (s)		1946	REP	70
JESSE JAMES RIDES AGAIN	(SER)	1947	REP	13CH
ALONG THE OREGON TRAIL (s)	(C)	1947	REP	64
MARSHAL OF AMARILLO (s)		1948	REP	60
ADVENTURES OF FRANK AND JESSE JAMES	(SER)	1948	REP	13CH
THE PLUNDERERS (s)	(C)	1948	REP	87
THE FAR FRONTIER (s)	(C)	1948	REP	67
SHERIFF OF WICHITA (s)		1949	REP	60
GHOST OF ZORRO	(SER)	1949	REP	12CH
FRONTIER INVESTIGATOR (s)		1949	REP	60
THE GAY AMIGO (s)		1949	UA	60
RIDERS OF THE WHISTLING PINES (s)		1949	COL	70
SOUTH OF DEATH VALLEY (aka RIVER OF POISON) (s)		1949	COL	54
THE COWBOY AND THE INDIANS (s)		1949	COL	70
MASKED RAIDERS (s)		1949	RKO	60
BANDITS OF EL DORADO (aka TRICKED) (s)		1949	COL	56
THE LEGEND OF THE LONE RANGER		1949	APE	75
SONS OF NEW MEXICO (aka THE BRAT) (s)		1950	COL	70
CYCLONE FURY (s)		1951	COL	54
CAPTIVE OF BILLY THE KID (s)		1952	REP	54
BUFFALO BILL IN TOMAHAWK TERRITORY		1952	UA	66
THE HAWK OF WILD RIVER (s)		1952	COL	54
NIGHT STAGE TO GALVESTON (s)		1952	COL	61
DESERT PASSAGE (s)		1952	RKO	60
MONTANA TERRITORY (s)	(C)	1952	COL	64
BARBED WIRE (aka FALSE NEWS) (s)		1952	COL	61
SON OF GERONIMO	(SER)	1952	COL	15CH
KANSAS PACIFIC (s)	(C)	1953	AA	73
GUNFIGHTERS OF THE NORTHWEST	(SER)	1953	COL	15CH

138 / CLAYTON MOORE, continued

Title	Year	Studio	Pages
DOWN LAREDO WAY (s)	1953	REP	54
THE BLACK DAKOTAS (s) (C)	1954	COL	65
THE TITLED TENDERFOOT (s)	1955	AA	55
APACHE AMBUSH (s)	1955	COL	68
THE LONE RANGER (C)	1956	WB	86
CHAMPIONS OF JUSTICE (C)	1956	WRA-TV	75
COUNT THE CLUES (C)	1956	WRA-TV	75
JUSTICE OF THE WEST (C)	1956	WRA-TV	75
THE LAWLESS (C)	1956	WRA-TV	75
MASQUERADE (C)	1956	WRA-TV	75
MORE THAN MAGIC (C)	1956	WRA-TV	75
NOT ABOVE SUSPICION (C)	1956	WRA-TV	75
ONE MASK TOO MANY (C)	1956	WRA-TV	75
THE SEARCH (C)	1956	WRA-TV	75
TALE OF GOLD (C)	1956	WRA-TV	75
TRACKERS (C)	1956	WRA-TV	75
THE TRUTH (C)	1956	WRA-TV	75
VENGEANCE VOW (C)	1956	WRA-TV	75
THE LONE RANGER AND THE LOST CITY OF GOLD (C)	1958	UA	80
GHOST OF ZORRO	1959	REP	69

(feature version of GHOST OF ZORRO serial)

DENNIS MOORE (1908 - 1964)
(aka DENNY MEADOWS; DENNIS "SMOKY" MOORE)

Despite being mainly limited to support roles in "B" westerns, Moore starred briefly in a few early 1940s series including Jimmy Wakely's at Monogram. Dennis mainlined the last two Columbia western serials PERILS OF THE WILDERNESS and BLAZING THE OVERLAND TRAIL. He also did numerous character parts in 1950s TV oater shows which included Gene Autry and Roy Rogers.

Title	Year	Studio	Pages
THE RED RIDER (s) (SER)	1934	UNI	15CH
WEST ON PARADE	1934	REL	20
THE DAWN RIDER (s)	1935	LMO	57
THE SAGEBRUSH TROUBADOUR (s)	1935	REP	54
VALLEY OF THE LAWLESS (s)	1936	SUP	56
SILVERSPURS (s)	1936	UNI	64
TOO MUCH BEEF (s)	1936	CLY	60
THE LONELY TRAIL (s)	1936	REP	55-58
HAIR-TRIGGER CASEY (s)	1936	ATL	59
DESERT JUSTICE (s)	1936	ATL	58
WILDCAT SAUNDERS (s)	1936	ATL	60
WILD HORSE CANYON (s)	1938	MON	50
TRIGGER SMITH (s)	1939	MON	60
ACROSS THE PLAINS (s)	1939	MON	59
OVERLAND MAIL (s)	1939	MON	57
FANGS OF THE WILD	1939	MET	55
ROCKY MOUNTAIN RANGERS (s)	1940	REP	58
RAINBOW OVER THE RANGE (s)	1940	MON	60
PALS OF THE PECOS (s)	1941	REP	56
LAW OF THE WOLF	1941	ZIE	55
PIRATES ON HORSEBACK (s)	1941	PAR	69
CYCLONE ON HORSEBACK (s)	1941	RKO	60
BILLY THE KID IN SANTA FE (s)	1941	PRC	66
ARIZONA BOUND (s)	1941	MON	57

DENNIS MOORE, continued

Title	Year	Studio	Min
THE LONE RIDER FIGHTS BACK (s)	1941	PRC	64
BILLY THE KID'S ROUNDUP (s)	1941	PRC	58
DUDE COWBOY (s)	1941	RKO	59
TEXAS MAN HUNT (s)	1942	PRC	60
THE LONE RIDER AND THE BANDIT	1942	PRC	54

(starts *The Lone Rider* series for PRC)

Title	Year	Studio	Min
BELOW THE BORDER (s)	1942	MON	57
RAIDERS OF THE RANGE (s)	1942	REP	55
THE LONE RIDER IN CHEYENNE	1942	PRC	59
ROLLING DOWN THE GREAT DIVIDE (s)	1942	PRC	60
TEXAS JUSTICE	1942	PRC	60
RIDERS OF THE WEST (s)	1942	MON	60
BANDIT RANGER (s)	1942	RKO	61
BORDER ROUNDUP	1942	PRC	57
OUTLAWS OF BOULDER PASS	1942	PRC	64
OVERLAND STAGECOACH	1942	PRC	58

(ends *The Lone Rider* series)

Title	Year	Studio	Min
DAWN ON THE GREAT DIVIDE (s)	1942	MON	63-66
TENTING TONIGHT ON THE OLD CAMP GROUND (s)	1943	UNI	61
LAND OF HUNTED MEN	1943	MON	58

(starts *The Range Busters* series for Monogram)

Title	Year	Studio	Min
COWBOY COMMANDOS	1943	MON	55
BLACK MARKET RUSTLERS	1943	MON	58
ARIZONA TRAIL (aka SUNDOWN TRAIL) (cs)	1943	UNI	57
BULLETS AND SADDLES	1943	MON	54

(ends *The Range Busters* series)

Title	Year	Studio	Min
FRONTIER LAW (s)	1943	UNI	55
OKLAHOMA RAIDERS	1944	UNI	58

(aka MIDNIGHT RAIDERS; RIDERS OF OKLAHOMA) (s)

Title	Year	Studio	Min
TWILIGHT ON THE PRAIRIE (s)	1944	UNI	62
RAIDERS OF GHOST CITY (SER)	1944	UNI	13CH
WEST OF THE RIO GRANDE (cs)	1944	MON	57
SONG OF THE RANGE	1944	MON	55
SPRINGTIME IN TEXAS	1945	MON	55
FRONTIER FEUD (s)	1945	MON	54
COLORADO SERENADE (s) (C)	1946	PRC	68
DRIFTIN' RIVER (s)	1946	PRC	59
RAINBOW OVER THE ROCKIES (cs)	1947	MON	54
THE GAY RANCHERO (s) (C)	1948	REP	72
FRONTIER AGENT (s)	1948	MON	56
RANGE RENEGADES (s)	1948	MON	54
THE TIOGA KID (s)	1948	EL	54
ACROSS THE RIO GRANDE (s)	1949	MON	56
HAUNTED TRAILS (s)	1949	MON	60
ROARING WESTWARD	1949	MON	58

(aka BOOM TOWN BADMEN) (s)

Title	Year	Studio	Min
NAVAJO TRAIL RAIDERS (s)	1949	REP	60
RIDERS IN THE SKY (s)	1949	COL	70
WEST OF WYOMING (s)	1950	MON	57
SINGING GUNS (s) (C)	1950	REP	91
HOSTILE COUNTRY (aka GUNS OF JUSTICE) (s)	1950	LIP	60
GUNSLINGERS (s)	1950	MON	55
MARSHAL OF HELDORADO (aka BLAZING GUNS) (s)	1950	LIP	53
CROOKED RIVER (aka THE LAST BULLET) (s)	1950	LIP	55
COLORADO RANGER (aka OUTLAW FURY) (s)	1950	LIP	59
WEST OF THE BRAZOS	1950	LIP	58

(aka RANGELAND EMPIRE) (s)

DENNIS MOORE, continued

FAST ON THE DRAW (aka SUDDEN DEATH) (s)	1950	LIP	55
ARIZONA TERRITORY (s)	1950	MON	56
SNOW DOG (s)	1950	MON	64
DESPERADOES OF THE WEST (s) (SER)	1950	REP	12CH
I KILLED GERONIMO (s)	1950	EL	62
SILVER RAIDERS (s)	1950	MON	55
KING OF THE BULLWHIP (s)	1951	WA	59
ABILENE TRAIL (s)	1951	MON	64
MAN FROM SONORA (s)	1951	MON	54
BLAZING BULLETS (s)	1951	MON	54
FORT DEFIANCE (s) (C)	1951	UA	81
THE LUSTY MEN (s)	1952	RKO	113
CANYON AMBUSH (s)	1952	MON	53
MONTANA BELLE (s) (C)	1952	RKO	81
RAGE AT DAWN (s) (C)	1955	RKO	87
ONE DESIRE (s) (C)	1955	UI	94
THE GUN THAT WON THE WEST (s) (C)	1955	COL	71
PERILS OF THE WILDERNESS (SER)	1956	COL	15CH
TRIBUTE TO A BAD MAN (s) (C)	1956	MGM	95
GREAT DAY IN THE MORNING (s) (C)	1956	RKO	92
BLAZING THE OVERLAND TRAIL (SER)	1956	COL	15CH
THE WHITE SQUAW (s)	1956	COL	73
CHAMPIONS OF JUSTICE (s) (C)	1956	WRA-TV	75
NOT ABOVE SUSPICION (s) (C)	1956	WRA-TV	75
THE TRUTH (s) (C)	1956	WRA-TV	75
UTAH BLAINE (s)	1957	COL	75
THE PHANTOM STAGECOACH (s)	1957	COL	69
GUNFIGHT AT THE O.K. CORRAL (s) (C)	1957	PAR	122
THE DOMINO KID (s)	1957	COL	73

DENNIS MORGAN (1910 -   )

Irish tenor leading man who curiously did not sing much in his western films. Best remembered in the genre as Cole Younger in BAD MEN OF MISSOURI.

RIVER'S END	1940	WB	69
BAD MEN OF MISSOURI	1941	WB	71-74
CHEYENNE (aka THE WYOMING KID)	1947	WB	100
TWO GUYS FROM TEXAS (C)	1948	WB	86
(aka TWO TEXAS KNIGHTS)			
RATON PASS (aka CANYON PASS)	1951	WB	84
CATTLE TOWN	1952	WB	71
THE GUN THAT WON THE WEST (C)	1955	COL	71
URANIUM BOOM	1956	COL	67

CHESTER MORRIS (1901 - 1970)

A fast, sharp-talking actor who mainlined "B" dramas and crime mysteries in the 1930s, Morris made several westerns with equal effectiveness. He was best-known for the *Boston Blackie* series at Columbia (1941-49).

THREE GODFATHERS (aka MIRACLE IN THE SAND)	1936	MGM	82
FRANKIE AND JOHNNIE	1936	REP	66
WAGONS WESTWARD	1940	REP	69-70
GIRL FROM GOD'S COUNTRY	1940	REP	75

WAYNE MORRIS (1914 - 1959)
World War II flying ace whose western roles were mainly programmers. High-spirited Morris is always credited with having starred in the last official "B" western, 1954's TWO GUNS AND A BADGE.

LAND BEYOND THE LAW (s)		1937...WB	54
THE KID COMES BACK		1938...WB	61
VALLEY OF THE GIANTS	(C)..	1938...WB	79
BAD MEN OF MISSOURI (cs)		1941...WB	71-74
DEEP VALLEY (cs)		1947...WB	104
THE YOUNGER BROTHERS	(C)..	1949...WB	77
THE TOUGHER THEY COME		1950...COL	69
STAGE TO TUCSON	(C)..	1951...COL	82
(aka LOST STAGE VALLEY)			
SIERRA PASSAGE		1951...MON	81
THE BUSHWHACKERS (aka THE REBEL)		1951...REA	70
DESERT PURSUIT		1952...MON	71
ARCTIC FLIGHT		1952...MON	78
STAR OF TEXAS		1953...AA	68
THE MARKSMAN		1953...AA	61-62
THE FIGHTING LAWMAN		1953...AA	71
TEXAS BAD MAN		1953...AA	62
RIDING SHOTGUN	(C)..	1954...WB	75
THE DESPERADO		1954...AA	81-82
TWO GUNS AND A BADGE		1954...AA	69
THE LONESOME TRAIL		1955...LIP	73

AUDIE MURPHY (1924 - 1971)
Texas-born, World War II's most decorated hero whose soft-spoken manner and youthful looks allowed him to play deadly gunfighters like Billy the Kid in numerous Universal Technicolor westerns during the 1950s through mid-1960s. Murphy became "Whispering Smith" in 1961 on NBC-TV for 26 half-hour episodes.

TEXAS, BROOKLYN, AND HEAVEN		1948...UA	76
(aka THE GIRL FROM TEXAS) (s)			
BAD BOY (cs)		1949...AA	86
THE KID FROM TEXAS	(C)..	1950...UI	78
(aka TEXAS KID, OUTLAW)			
SIERRA	(C)..	1950...UI	83
KANSAS RAIDERS	(C)..	1950...UI	80-90
THE RED BADGE OF COURAGE		1951...MGM	69
THE CIMARRON KID	(C)..	1952...UI	65-84
THE DUEL AT SILVER CREEK	(C)..	1952...UI	77
GUNSMOKE	(C)..	1953...UI	79
COLUMN SOUTH	(C)..	1953...UI	84-85
TUMBLEWEED	(C)..	1953...UI	79-80
RIDE CLEAR OF DIABLO	(C)..	1954...UI	80-81
DRUMS ACROSS THE RIVER	(C)..	1954...UI	78
DESTRY	(C)..	1955...UI	93-95
WALK THE PROUD LAND	(C)..	1956...UI	88
THE GUNS OF FORT PETTICOAT	(C)..	1957...COL	82
NIGHT PASSAGE	(C)..	1957...UI	90
RIDE A CROOKED TRAIL	(C)..	1958...UI	87
NO NAME ON THE BULLET	(C)..	1959...UI	77

142 / AUDIE MURPHY, continued

THE WILD AND THE INNOCENT	(C)	1959...UI	84
CAST A LONG SHADOW		1959...UA	82
HELL BENT FOR LEATHER	(C)	1960...UI	82
THE UNFORGIVEN (cs)	(C)	1960...UA	125
SEVEN WAYS FROM SUNDOWN	(C)	1960...UI	86-87
POSSE FROM HELL	(C)	1961...UI	89
SIX BLACK HORSES	(C)	1962...UI	80
SHOWDOWN		1963...UNI	79
GUNFIGHT AT COMANCHE CREEK	(C)	1963...AA	91
THE QUICK GUN	(C)	1964...COL	87-88
BULLET FOR A BADMAN	(C)	1964...UNI	80
APACHE RIFLES	(C)	1964...20T	92
ARIZONA RAIDERS	(C)	1965...COL	88
GUNPOINT	(C)	1966...UNI	86
THE TEXICAN (aka THE TEXAS KID)	(C)	1966...COL	86-91
40 GUNS TO APACHE PASS	(C)	1967...COL	95
A TIME FOR DYING (s)	(C)	1969...FIP	90

DON MURRAY (1929 -   )

Earnest-type actor who began his film career in westerns. Best remembered as the rodeo cowboy who attempted to carry off Marilyn Monroe in BUS STOP. Murray starred with 26 hour-long shows of ABC-TV's "The Outcasts" (1966-69).

BUS STOP (aka THE WRONG KIND OF GIRL)	(C)	1956...20T	96
FROM HELL TO TEXAS (aka MANHUNT)	(C)	1958...20T	100
THESE THOUSAND HILLS	(C)	1959...20T	96
ONE FOOT IN HELL	(C)	1960...20T	90
KID RODELO		1966...PAR	91
THE PLAINSMAN	(C)	1966...UNI	92
THE INTRUDERS	(C)	1970...UNI-TV	95
JUSTIN MORGAN HAD A HORSE	(C)	1972...BV	100
COTTER	(C)	1973...GK	94

WILLIE NELSON (1933 -   )

He has been a popular country-western music singer for over two decades whose talents have included "A" gallopers and western TV movies. Nelson is also a booster of American farmers with annual fund-raising benefits.

THE ELECTRIC HORSEMAN (s)	(C)	1979...COL/UNI	122
HONEYSUCKLE ROSE (aka ON THE ROAD AGAIN)	(C)	1980...WB	119
BARBAROSA	(C)	1982...UNI	90
SONGWRITER	(C)	1984...TS	94
RED-HEADED STRANGER	(C)	1986...AF	105
STAGECOACH	(C)	1986...HE-TV	100
THE LAST DAYS OF FRANK AND JESSE JAMES	(C)	1988...JCP-TV	97
WHERE THE HELL'S THAT GOLD?	(C)	1988...KS-TV	100
BAJA OKLAHOMA (s)	(C)	1988...HBO-TV	105
ONCE UPON A TEXAS TRAIN (aka TEXAS GUNS)	(C)	1988...CBS-TV	100
PAIR OF ACES	(C)	1990...TVM	100
ANOTHER PAIR OF ACES: THREE OF A KIND	(C)	1991...PF-TV	100

FRANCO NERO (1942 -   )
Italian leading man best known for his portrayal of Lancelot in the musical, CAMELOT, rather than his European western films.

DJANGO	(C) .. 1966 ... BRC	90	___
THE AVENGER	(C) .. 1966 ... BRC	92	___
THE TRAMPLERS (s)	(C) .. 1966 ... EMB	105	___
THE BRUTE AND THE BEAST	(C) .. 1968 ... AI	87-88	___
THE MERCENARY	(C) .. 1970 ... UA	105	___
COMPANEROS!	(C) .. 1972 ... CRC	105-118	___
DEAF SMITH AND JOHNNY EARS	(C) .. 1973 ... MGM	91	___
(aka LOS AMIGOS)			
DON'T TURN THE OTHER CHEEK	(C) .. 1974 ... IA	93	___
CHALLENGE TO WHITE FANG	(C) .. 1975 ... PIE	97	___
(aka WHITE FANG)			

JAMES NEWILL (1911 - 1975)
(aka JIM NEWILL)

A fine singer who starred in two "B" western series—*Renfrew of the Royal Mounted* (1937-40) at Grand National, then Monogram; and *The Texas Rangers* (1942-44) for PRC. Newill and Dave O'Brien were active goat ranchers during World War II while they lensed the latter series.

RENFREW OF THE ROYAL MOUNTED	1937 ... GN	57	___
(starts *Renfrew of the Royal Mounted* series)			
ON THE GREAT WHITE TRAIL	1938 ... GN	58	___
FIGHTING MAD	1939 ... MON	60	___
CRASHING THRU	1939 ... MON	60-65	___
YUKON FLIGHT	1939 ... MON	57	___
DANGER AHEAD	1940 ... MON	60	___
MURDER ON THE YUKON	1940 ... MON	58	___
SKY BANDITS	1940 ... MON	56-62	___
(ends *Renfrew of the Royal Mounted* series)			
THE RANGERS TAKE OVER	1942 ... PRC	60	___
(starts *The Texas Rangers* series)			
BAD MEN OF THUNDER GAP	1943 ... PRC	57	___
(aka THUNDERGAP OUTLAWS)			
WEST OF TEXAS (aka SHOOTIN' IRONS)	1943 ... PRC	54	___
BORDER BUCKAROOS	1943 ... PRC	59	___
FIGHTING VALLEY	1943 ... PRC	59	___
TRAIL OF TERROR	1943 ... PRC	63	___
RETURN OF THE RANGERS	1943 ... PRC	61	___
BOSS OF RAWHIDE	1943 ... PRC	57-59	___
GUNSMOKE MESA	1944 ... PRC	59	___
OUTLAW ROUNDUP	1944 ... PRC	55	___
GUNS OF THE LAW	1944 ... PRC	55-57	___
THE PINTO BANDIT	1944 ... PRC	56	___
SPOOK TOWN	1944 ... PRC	59	___
BRAND OF THE DEVIL	1944 ... PRC	59	___
(ends *The Texas Rangers* series)			

PAUL NEWMAN (1925 -   )
Excellent actor whose Billy the Kid portrayal in THE LEFT-HANDED GUN is considered the most realistic. Outstanding, as well, for BUTCH CASSIDY AND THE SUNDANCE KID, one of the most popular 1960s "A" westerns ever to reach the screen.

THE LEFT-HANDED GUN	1958 ... WB	102	___
HUD	1963 ... PAR	112	___

144 / PAUL NEWMAN, continued

THE OUTRAGE	1964	MGM	97
HOMBRE	(C) .. 1967	20T	110-111
BUTCH CASSIDY AND THE SUNDANCE KID	(C) .. 1969	20T	110-112
SOMETIMES A GREAT NOTION (aka NEVER GIVE AN INCH)	(C) .. 1971	UNI	113-114
POCKET MONEY	(C) .. 1972	NG	102
THE LIFE AND TIMES OF JUDGE ROY BEAN	(C) .. 1972	NG	120
BUFFALO BILL AND THE INDIANS, OR SITTING BULL'S HISTORY LESSON	(C) .. 1976	UA	120-123

JACK NICHOLSON (1937 -)

Versatile actor whose western roles have been mainly at the beginning of his career. Better known in films for his portrayal of the villainous Joker in BATMAN.

THE BROKEN LAND (s)	(C) .. 1962	20T	60
RIDE IN THE WHIRLWIND	(C) .. 1965	JHH	82-83
THE SHOOTING	(C) .. 1967	JHH	82
THE MISSOURI BREAKS	(C) .. 1976	UA	126
GOIN' SOUTH	(C) .. 1978	PAR	101-109
THE BORDER	(C) .. 1982	RKO/UNI	107

NORTHWEST MOUNTIE series (1934 - 1936; 1949 - 1954)

This was a group of north-woods sagas involving routine capture of criminals first done by Kermit Maynard for Ambassador (1934-36) and then Kirby Grant at Monogram/Allied Artists (1949-54).

(KERMIT MAYNARD)

THE FIGHTING TROOPER	1934	AMB	58
NORTHERN FRONTIER	1935	AMB	57-60
WILDERNESS MAIL	1935	AMB	58-65
RED BLOOD OF COURAGE	1935	AMB	55
CODE OF THE MOUNTED	1935	AMB	60
TRAILS OF THE WILD	1935	AMB	60
HIS FIGHTING BLOOD	1935	AMB	60
TIMBER WAR	1935	AMB	60
WILDCAT TROOPER	1936	AMB	60
PHANTOM PATROL	1936	AMB	60

(KIRBY GRANT)

TRAIL OF THE YUKON	1949	MON	67-69
THE WOLF HUNTERS	1949	MON	70
SNOW DOG	1950	MON	64
CALL OF THE KLONDIKE	1950	MON	65-67
YUKON MANHUNT	1951	MON	63
NORTHWEST TERRITORY	1951	MON	61
YUKON GOLD	1952	MON	62
FANGS OF THE ARCTIC	1953	AA	63
NORTHERN PATROL	1953	AA	63
YUKON VENGEANCE	1954	AA	68

HUGH O'BRIAN (1925 -   )
Tough guy, leading man whose best-known role in westerns has been that of television's "The Life and Legend of Wyatt Earp" (1955-61) with 266 half-hour shows on ABC. Today, O'Brian devotes a vast majority of time to his youth foundation.

BEYOND THE PURPLE HILLS (s)	1950	COL	70
THE RETURN OF JESSE JAMES (s)	1950	LIP	73-75
TOMAHAWK (C)	1951	UI	82
(aka BATTLE OF POWDER RIVER) (s)			
VENGEANCE VALLEY (s) (C)	1951	MGM	83
BUCKAROO SHERIFF OF TEXAS (s)	1951	REP	60
LITTLE BIG HORN (aka THE FIGHTING SEVENTH) (s)	1951	LIP	85-86
CAVE OF OUTLAWS (s) (C)	1951	UI	75-78
THE CIMARRON KID (s) (C)	1952	UI	84
THE BATTLE AT APACHE PASS (s) (C)	1952	UI	85
THE RAIDERS (C)	1952	UI	80
(aka RIDERS OF VENGEANCE) (s)			
MEET ME AT THE FAIR (s) (C)	1953	UI	87
THE LAWLESS BREED (cs) (C)	1953	UI	83
SEMINOLE (s) (C)	1953	UI	86-87
THE MAN FROM THE ALAMO (s) (C)	1953	UI	79
THE STAND AT APACHE RIVER (s) (C)	1953	UI	77
BACK TO GOD'S COUNTRY (s) (C)	1953	UI	78
SASKATCHEWAN (C)	1954	UI	87
(aka O'ROARKE OF THE ROYAL MOUNTED) (s)			
DRUMS ACROSS THE RIVER (s) (C)	1954	UI	78
BROKEN LANCE (s) (C)	1954	20T	96
WHITE FEATHER (s) (C)	1955	20T	102
THE TWINKLE IN GOD'S EYE (cs)	1955	REP	73
THE BRASS LEGEND	1956	UA	79
THE FIEND WHO WALKED THE WEST	1958	20T	100-101
ALIAS JESSE JAMES (gs) (C)	1959	UA	92
AFRICA—TEXAS STYLE! (C)	1967	PAR.	106-109
WILD WOMEN (C)	1970	ABC-TV	73
THE SHOOTIST (gs) (C)	1976	PAR	99-100
THE SEEKERS (s) (C)	1979	UNI-TV	200
GUNSMOKE: THE LAST APACHE (s) (C)	1990	CBS-TV	100
THE GAMBLER, PART IV— (C)	1991	NBC-TV	200
THE LUCK OF THE DRAW (gs)			

DAVE O'BRIEN (1912 - 1969)
(aka DAVID BARCLAY)
Work in "B" westerns saddled this talented thespian who could deftly handle rough slugfests, to mainly support roles until he was tapped by PRC to ramrod *The Texas Rangers* series (1942-45). O'Brien also did numerous "Pete Smith" MGM shorts, and later was an Emmy Award-winning writer for the "Red Skelton" TV show starting in the 1950s. Dave's sudden, fatal heart attack came during a sailboat cruise.

THE LITTLE COLONEL (s)	1935	FOX	80
OREGON TRAIL (s)	1936	REP	59
"LIGHTNIN'" CRANDALL (cs)	1937	REP	60
BROTHERS OF THE WEST (s)	1937	VIC	55
ROUGH RIDING RHYTHM (s)	1937	AMB	57
RENFREW OF THE ROYAL MOUNTED (s)	1937	GN	57
WHIRLWIND HORSEMAN (s)	1938	GN	58

DAVE O'BRIEN, continued

Title	Year	Studio	Page
MAN'S COUNTRY (s)	1938	MON	55
THE UTAH TRAIL (aka TRAIL TO UTAH) (s)	1938	GN	55
STARLIGHT OVER TEXAS (s)	1938	MON	56
(aka MOONLIGHT OVER TEXAS)			
WHERE THE BUFFALO ROAM (s)	1938	MON	62
FRONTIER SCOUT (s)	1938	GN	61
LAW OF THE TEXAN (s)	1938	COL	54
SONG OF THE BUCKAROO (s)	1938	MON	58
(aka THE SINGING BUCKAROO)			
WATER RUSTLERS	1939	GN	54
DRIFTING WESTWARD (s)	1939	MON	55
SUNDOWN ON THE PRAIRIE (s)	1939	MON	59
(aka PRAIRIE SUNDOWN)			
CODE OF THE CACTUS (s)	1939	VIC	56
ROLLIN' WESTWARD (aka ROLLIN' WEST) (s)	1939	MON	55
TRIGGER SMITH (s)	1939	MON	60
TEXAS WILDCATS (s)	1939	VIC	57
OUTLAW'S PARADISE (s)	1939	VIC	62
WYOMING OUTLAW (s)	1939	REP	56
THE SINGING COWGIRL	1939	GN	57
RIDERS OF THE SAGE (s)	1939	MET	57
NEW FRONTIER (aka FRONTIER HORIZON) (s)	1939	REP	57
THE FIGHTING RENEGADE (cs)	1939	VIC	58
THE ARIZONA KID (s)	1939	REP	61
FIGHTING MAD	1939	MON	60
(starts *Renfrew of the Royal Mounted* series for Monogram)			
FLAMING LEAD (cs)	1939	CLY	57
CRASHING THRU	1939	MON	60-65
YUKON FLIGHT	1939	MON	57
DANGER AHEAD	1940	MON	60
MURDER ON THE YUKON	1940	MON	58
PHANTOM RANCHER (s)	1940	CLY	61
SKY BANDITS	1940	MON	56
(ends *Renfrew of the Royal Mounted* series)			
COWBOY FROM SUNDOWN (s)	1940	MON	58
THE KID FROM SANTA FE (s)	1940	MON	50
GUN CODE (s)	1940	PRC	54
QUEEN OF THE YUKON (s)	1940	MON	70
BUZZY RIDES THE RANGE	1940	ZIE	60
BUZZY AND THE PHANTOM PINTO	1941	ZIE	55
BILLY THE KID IN SANTA FE (s)	1941	PRC	66
THE TEXAS MARSHAL (s)	1941	PRC	62
THE GUNMAN FROM BODIE (s)	1941	MON	62
BILLY THE KID WANTED	1941	PRC	64
(starts *Billy the Kid* series for PRC)			
FORBIDDEN TRAILS (s)	1941	MON	59
DOWN TEXAS WAY (s)	1942	MON	57
BILLY THE KID'S SMOKING GUNS	1942	PRC	58
LAW AND ORDER	1942	PRC	58
KING OF THE STALLIONS	1942	MON	63
SHERIFF OF SAGE VALLEY	1942	PRC	60
(aka BILLY THE KID, SHERIFF OF SAGE VALLEY) (ends *Billy the Kid* series)			
THE RANGERS TAKE OVER	1942	PRC	60
(starts *The Texas Rangers* series)			

DAVE O'BRIEN, continued / 147

BAD MEN OF THUNDER GAP	1943	PRC	57
(aka THUNDER GAP OUTLAWS)			
WEST OF TEXAS (aka SHOOTIN' IRONS)	1943	PRC	54
BORDER BUCKAROOS	1943	PRC	59
FIGHTING VALLEY	1943	PRC	59
TRAIL OF TERROR	1943	PRC	63
RETURN OF THE RANGERS	1943	PRC	61
BOSS OF RAWHIDE	1943	PRC	57-59
GUNSMOKE MESA	1944	PRC	59
OUTLAW ROUNDUP	1944	PRC	55
GUNS OF THE LAW	1944	PRC	55-57
THE PINTO BANDIT	1944	PRC	56
SPOOK TOWN	1944	PRC	59
BRAND OF THE DEVIL	1944	PRC	59
GANGSTERS OF THE FRONTIER	1944	PRC	56
(aka RAIDERS OF THE FRONTIER)			
DEAD OR ALIVE (aka WANTED BY THE LAW)	1944	PRC	56
THE WHISPERING SKULL	1944	PRC	55
MARKED FOR MURDER	1944	PRC	56
ENEMY OF THE LAW	1945	PRC	59
THREE IN THE SADDLE	1945	PRC	61
FRONTIER FUGITIVES	1945	PRC	58
(aka FUGITIVES OF THE FRONTIER)			
FLAMING BULLETS (ends *The Texas Rangers* series)	1945	PRC	59
THE KETTLES IN THE OZARKS (s)	1956	UI	81
THE DESPERADOS ARE IN TOWN (s)	1956	20T	73

EDMOND O'BRIEN (1915 - 1985)

Excellent character actor who starred in several western films early in his career. Better known in the genre for his drunken newspaper editor role in THE MAN WHO SHOT LIBERTY VALANCE. Always tough talking to make a point.

THE REDHEAD AND THE COWBOY (cs)	1951	PAR	82
WARPATH	(C) 1951	PAR	95
SILVER CITY (aka HIGH VERMILION)	(C) 1951	PAR	90
THE HITCH-HIKER	1953	RKO	71
COW COUNTRY	1953	AA	82
THE BIG LAND (aka STAMPEDE) (cs)	(C) 1957	WB	92
THE MAN WHO SHOT LIBERTY VALANCE (s)	1962	PAR	119
RIO CONCHOS (s)	(C) 1964	20T	107
THE WILD BUNCH (s)	(C) 1969	WB	134-144
THE INTRUDERS	(C) 1970	UNI-TV	95

GEORGE O'BRIEN (1900 - 1985)

This muscular cowboy star was a big success with Fox through 1936. O'Brien went on to RKO Radio for a series of top-quality oaters into 1940, the best of the group being LAWLESS VALLEY, a highly-prized favorite of fellow saddler Bill Elliott. George made the Top Money-Making Western Film Star ranks (1936-40). In between films, he was a naval officer who retired as rear admiral. O'Brien wowed fans at the 1980 Memphis Film Festival with a sparkling memory of his glory years in the western genre.

THE LONE STAR RANGER	1930	FOX	64
ROUGH ROMANCE	1930	FOX	53

GEORGE O'BRIEN, continued

Title	Year	Studio	Pages
THE LAST OF THE DUANES	1930	FOX	56-62
FAIR WARNING	1931	FOX	74
A HOLY TERROR	1931	FOX	53-63
RIDERS OF THE PURPLE SAGE	1931	FOX	57-59
THE RAINBOW TRAIL	1932	FOX	60
THE GAY CABALLERO	1932	FOX	60
MYSTERY RANCH (aka THE KILLER)	1932	FOX	65
THE GOLDEN WEST	1932	FOX	74
ROBBERS' ROOST	1933	FOX	64
SMOKE LIGHTNING	1933	FOX	63
LIFE IN THE RAW	1933	FOX	62
THE LAST TRAIL	1933	FOX	60
FRONTIER MARSHAL	1934	FOX	66
THE DUDE RANGER	1934	FOX	65
WHEN A MAN'S A MAN (aka SAGA OF THE WEST)	1935	FOX	66
THE COWBOY MILLIONAIRE	1935	FOX	67-74
HARD ROCK HARRIGAN	1935	FOX	60
THUNDER MOUNTAIN	1935	20T	58
WHISPERING SMITH SPEAKS	1935	20T	67
O'MALLEY OF THE MOUNTED	1936	20T	59
THE BORDER PATROLMAN	1936	20T	60
DANIEL BOONE	1936	RKO	77
PARK AVENUE LOGGER	1937	RKO	65-67
HOLLYWOOD COWBOY (aka WINGS OVER WYOMING)	1937	RKO	64
GUN LAW	1938	RKO	60
BORDER G-MAN	1938	RKO	60
PAINTED DESERT	1938	RKO	60
THE RENEGADE RANGER	1938	RKO	59
LAWLESS VALLEY	1938	RKO	59
ARIZONA LEGION	1939	RKO	58
TROUBLE IN SUNDOWN	1939	RKO	60
RACKETEERS OF THE RANGE	1939	RKO	62
TIMBER STAMPEDE	1939	RKO	59
THE FIGHTING GRINGO	1939	RKO	59
THE MARSHAL OF MESA CITY	1939	RKO	62
LEGION OF THE LAWLESS	1940	RKO	59
BULLET CODE	1940	RKO	58
PRAIRIE LAW	1940	RKO	58
STAGE TO CHINO	1940	RKO	58
TRIPLE JUSTICE	1940	RKO	66
FORT APACHE (s)	1948	RKO	127
SHE WORE A YELLOW RIBBON (s)	(C) 1949	RKO	104
GOLD RAIDERS (aka STOOGES GO WEST)	1951	UA	56
CHEYENNE AUTUMN (s)	(C) 1964	WB	145-160

MAUREEN O'HARA (1921 -   )

Beautiful red-haired, Irish actress whose portrayal of fiery women has often been teamed with John Wayne in such films as McLINTOCK!

Title	Year	Studio	Pages
THEY MET IN ARGENTINA	1941	RKO	77
BUFFALO BILL	(C) 1944	20T	90
COMANCHE TERRITORY	(C) 1950	UI	76

MAUREEN O'HARA, continued / 149

RIO GRANDE		1950...REP	105 ___
KANGAROO	(C)	1952...20T	84 ___
THE REDHEAD FROM WYOMING	(C)	1953...UI	80 ___
WAR ARROW	(C)	1954...UI	78 ___
THE MAGNIFICENT MATADOR	(C)	1955...20T	94 ___
(aka THE BRAVE AND THE BEAUTIFUL)			
THE DEADLY COMPANIONS	(C)	1961...PAT	90 ___
(aka TRIGGER HAPPY)			
SPENCER'S MOUNTAIN	(C)	1963...WB	119 ___
McLINTOCK!	(C)	1963...UA	122 ___
THE RARE BREED	(C)	1966...UNI	97-108 ___
BIG JAKE (cs)	(C)	1971...NG	110 ___
THE RED PONY	(C)	1973...UNI-TV	100 ___

DOROTHY PAGE (1912 -   )

She was the only starring cowgirl in several "B" westerns who had the advantage of filming in Arizona. A former radio songstress.

WATER RUSTLERS	1939...GN	54 ___
RIDE 'EM COWGIRL	1939...GN	52 ___
THE SINGING COWGIRL	1939...GN	57-59 ___

JACK PALANCE (1920 -   )

Menacing-looking actor who played mainly villains early in his film career. Best known for his sinister gunfighter role in SHANE, the classic "A" western where he was nominated for an Oscar. Palance waited 38 years to receive a coveted 1992 Academy Award trophy for CITY SLICKERS.

SECOND CHANCE (cs)	(C)	1953...RKO	81 ___
ARROWHEAD	(C)	1953...PAR	105 ___
SHANE (s)	(C)	1953...PAR	117 ___
KISS OF FIRE	(C)	1955...UI	87 ___
THE LONELY MAN		1957...PAR	87 ___
THE PROFESSIONALS (s)	(C)	1966...COL	117 ___
A PROFESSIONAL GUN (cs)	(C)	1968...PRO	105 ___
THE DESPERADOS	(C)	1969...COL	91 ___
THE McMASTERS (aka THE BLOOD CROWD)	(C)	1969...CHE	89-97 ___
THE MERCENARY (cs)	(C)	1970...UA	106 ___
MONTE WALSH (cs)	(C)	1970...NG	95-106 ___
COMPANEROS!	(C)	1971...CRC	105-118 ___
IT CAN BE DONE... AMIGO	(C)	1972...WW	95 ___
(aka THE BIG AND THE BAD)			
CHATO'S LAND	(C)	1972...UA	92 ___
OKLAHOMA CRUDE	(C)	1973...COL	108 ___
BROTHERS BLUE	(C)	1973...WB	81 ___
THE CON MEN	(C)	1973...TEC	91 ___
THE GODCHILD	(C)	1974...MGM-TV	78 ___
THE STING OF THE WEST	(C)	1975...FV	98 ___
THE HATFIELDS AND THE McCOYS	(C)	1975...CFP-TV	74 ___
THE GREAT ADVENTURE	(C)	1976...PI	87 ___
WELCOME TO BLOOD CITY	(C)	1977...FPL	96 ___
GOD'S GUN	(C)	1977...IYC	93 ___
COCAINE COWBOYS	(C)	1979...IH	87 ___

150 / JACK PALANCE, continued

THE LAST RIDE OF THE DALTON GANG (s)	(C)	1979	NBC-TV	150
YOUNG GUNS (s)	(C)	1988	20T	102-107
CITY SLICKERS (s)	(C)	1991	COL	114
KEEP THE CHANGE	(C)	1992	TNT-TV	100

FESS PARKER (1925 -   )

A tall, Texas actor who became a star as Walt Disney's "Davy Crockett" on television in 1954-55 for five 60-minute episodes. He went on to star in several western features. Fess garnered more TV fame as "Daniel Boone" on NBC (1964-70) with 165 hour-long segments. Now operates a California vineyard.

UNTAMED FRONTIER (s)	(C)	1952	UI	75
SPRINGFIELD RIFLE (s)	(C)	1952	WB	93
TAKE ME TO TOWN (s)	(C)	1953	UI	81-83
THUNDER OVER THE PLAINS (s)	(C)	1953	WB	82
DAVY CROCKETT, KING OF THE WILD FRONTIER	(C)	1955	BV	93-95
THE GREAT LOCOMOTIVE CHASE	(C)	1956	BV	85
(aka ANDREWS' RAIDERS)				
DAVY CROCKETT AND THE RIVER PIRATES	(C)	1956	BV	81
WESTWARD HO THE WAGONS!	(C)	1957	BV	90
OLD YELLER	(C)	1958	BV	83
THE LIGHT IN THE FOREST	(C)	1958	BV	93
ALIAS JESSE JAMES (gs)	(C)	1959	UA	92
THE HANGMAN (cs)		1959	PAR	86
THE JAYHAWKERS	(C)	1959	PAR	100
SMOKY	(C)	1966	20T	103
CLIMB AN ANGRY MOUNTAIN	(C)	1972	WB-TV	97-100

WILLARD PARKER (1912 -   )

Tall stage actor who made a few western films as a star. He was Jace Pearson on "Tales of the Texas Rangers" CBS-TV series for 52 half-hour episodes (1955-57).

RENEGADES	(C)	1946	COL	87
RELENTLESS (cs)	(C)	1948	COL	93
CALAMITY JANE AND SAM BASS (s)	(C)	1949	UI	85
BANDIT QUEEN		1950	LIP	70
APACHE DRUMS (cs)	(C)	1951	UI	75
THE VANQUISHED (s)	(C)	1953	PAR	84
THE GREAT JESSE JAMES RAID	(C)	1953	LIP	73-74
THE NAKED GUN		1956	AFRC	69-73
LONE TEXAN		1959	20T	70
YOUNG JESSE JAMES		1960	20T	73
WALK TALL	(C)	1960	20T	60
WACO (s)	(C)	1966	PAR	85

JOHN PAYNE (1912 - 1989)

Versatile leading man whose early career was in big-budget musicals, but who later moved in western leads. From 1957-60, Payne starred in "The Restless Gun" on NBC-TV and ABC-TV for 77 half-hour episodes. During 1969, the actor hosted 52 episodes of "Call of the West" 30-minute segments.

BAD LANDS (s)	1939	RKO	70
KING OF THE LUMBERJACKS	1940	WB	58

JOHN PAYNE, continued / 151

SPRINGTIME IN THE ROCKIES	(C).. 1942	...20T	 91
HELLO, FRISCO, HELLO	(C).. 1943	...20T	 98
EL PASO	(C).. 1949	...PAR	 101
THE EAGLE AND THE HAWK	(C).. 1950	...PAR	 104
(aka SPREAD EAGLE)			
PASSAGE WEST (aka HIGH VENTURE)	(C).. 1951	...PAR	..80-81
THE BLAZING FOREST	(C).. 1952	...PAR	 90
THE VANQUISHED	(C).. 1953	...PAR	 84
RAILS INTO LARAMIE	(C).. 1954	...UI	 81
SILVER LODE	(C).. 1954	...RKO	 80
SANTA FE PASSAGE	(C).. 1955	...REP	 90
THE ROAD TO DENVER	(C).. 1955	...REP	 90
TENNESSEE'S PARTNER	(C).. 1955	...RKO	..86-87
REBEL IN TOWN		1956	...UA 78
THEY RAN FOR THEIR LIVES	(C).. 1969	...CV	 92
GO WEST, YOUNG GIRL (s)	(C).. 1978	...COL-TV	 74

GREGORY PECK (1916 -)

Tall, outstanding actor who made numerous fine western films, including the classic, THE GUNFIGHTER. His latest one in the genre was OLD GRINGO in 1989 with Jane Fonda. Peck has personally chosen his starring features.

THE YEARLING	(C).. 1946	...MGM	128-131
DUEL IN THE SUN	(C).. 1947	...SEL	.130-138
YELLOW SKY		1948	...20T 98
THE GUNFIGHTER		1950	...20T 84
ONLY THE VALIANT		1951	...WB ..105-107
THE WORLD IN HIS ARMS	(C).. 1952	...UI	 104
THE BRAVADOS	(C).. 1958	...20T	 98
THE BIG COUNTRY	(C).. 1958	...UA	...156-166
HOW THE WEST WAS WON (s)	(C).. 1963	...MGM	155-165
THE STALKING MOON	(C).. 1969	...NG	 109
MacKENNA'S GOLD	(C).. 1969	...COL	 128
SHOOT OUT	(C).. 1971	...UNI	..94-95
BILLY TWO HATS	(C).. 1973	...UA	..97-99
(aka THE LADY AND THE OUTLAW)			
THE BLUE AND THE GRAY (s)	(C).. 1982	...CBS-TV	.. 295
OLD GRINGO	(C).. 1989	...COL	 119

GEORGE PEPPARD (1928 -)

He achieved "A" galloper stardom with MGM's blockbuster HOW THE WEST WAS WON, then did others in the oater genre between different film assignments.

HOME FROM THE HILL (cs)	(C).. 1960	...MGM	 150
HOW THE WEST WAS WON	(C).. 1963	...MGM	155-165
ROUGH NIGHT IN JERICHO (cs)	(C).. 1967	...UNI	 104
CANNON FOR CORDOBA	(C).. 1970	...UA	 104
ONE MORE TRAIN TO ROB	(C).. 1971	...UNI	 108
THE BRAVOS	(C).. 1972	...UNI-TV	... 100

JACK PERRIN (1895 - 1967)
(aka JACK GABLE, RICHARD TERRY)

He made the successful transition from silent cactusers into soundies which lasted through 1936. By 1937, Perrin mustered some "B" supports, and within a few years suffered the humiliation of being seen in only walk-ons.

ROMANCE OF THE WEST	1930	CFE	53
THE LONE STAR RANGER (s)	1930	FOX	64
OVERLAND BOUND	1930	SYN	58
BEYOND THE RIO GRANDE	1930	B4	60
RIDIN' LAW	1930	B4	62
TRAILS OF PERIL (aka TRAILS OF DANGER)	1930	B4	60
PHANTOM OF THE DESERT	1930	SYN	58
THE APACHE KID'S ESCAPE	1930	RJH	52
WILD WEST WHOOPEE	1931	ALL	57
RIDER OF THE PLAINS (s)	1931	SYN	61
THE KID FROM ARIZONA	1931	COS	55
THE SHERIFF'S SECRET	1931	COS	58
LARIATS AND SIXSHOOTERS	1931	COS	65
THE SIGN OF THE WOLF (s) (SER)	1931	MET	10CH
HELL-FIRE AUSTIN (s)	1932	TIF	70
SON OF OKLAHOMA (s)	1932	WW	55
DYNAMITE RANCH (cs)	1932	WW	59
BETWEEN FIGHTING MEN (s)	1932	WW	62
TEX TAKES A HOLIDAY (s) (C)	1932	FD	60
FORTY-FIVE CALIBRE ECHO	1932	HP	60
THE LONE TRAIL	1932	SYN	55
(feature version of THE SIGN OF THE WOLF serial) (s)			
JAWS OF JUSTICE	1933	PRN	58
GIRL TROUBLE	1933	REL	
THE MYSTERY SQUADRON (s) (SER)	1933	MAS	12CH
MYSTERY RANCH (cs)	1934	COM	56
ARIZONA NIGHTS	1934	REL	56
RAWHIDE MAIL	1934	REL	59
RAINBOW RIDERS	1934	REL	31
RIDIN' GENTS	1934	REL	32
THE CACTUS KID	1934	REL	56
LOSER'S END	1934	REL	60
NORTH OF ARIZONA (aka BORDER RAIDERS)	1935	REL	60
TEXAS JACK	1935	REL	52
WOLF RIDERS	1935	REL	56
GUN GRIT	1936	ATL	60
HAIR-TRIGGER CASEY	1936	ATL	59
DESERT JUSTICE	1936	ATL	58
WILDCAT SAUNDERS	1936	ATL	58
RECKLESS RANGER (cs)	1937	COL	56
THE PAINTED STALLION (s) (SER)	1937	REP	12CH
THE TRIGGER TRIO (s)	1937	REP	56-60
THE PURPLE VIGILANTES	1938	REP	58
(aka THE PURPLE RIDERS) (s)			
THE LONE RANGER (s) (SER)	1938	REP	15CH
THE GREAT ADVENTURES OF WILD (SER)	1938	COL	15CH
BILL HICKOK (s)			
THE TEXANS (s)	1938	PAR	90
WESTERN JAMBOREE (s)	1938	REP	56
TROUBLE IN SUNDOWN (s)	1939	RKO	60

JACK PERRIN, continued / 153

THE KID FROM TEXAS (s)	1939	MGM	71
THE ARIZONA KID (s)	1939	REP	61
THE PAL FROM TEXAS (s)	1939	MET	56
THE MAN FROM DAKOTA (s)	1940	MGM	74
LAND OF THE SIX GUNS (s)	1940	MON	54
NEW MOON (s)	1940	MGM	104
BILLY THE KID OUTLAWED (s)	1940	PRC	60
RIDE, TENDERFOOT, RIDE (s)	1940	REP	65
WEST OF PINTO BASIN (s)	1940	MON	56
TEXAS RANGERS RIDE AGAIN (s)	1940	PAR	67
RIDERS OF DEATH VALLEY (s) (SER)	1941	UNI	15CH
DYNAMITE CANYON (s)	1941	MON	58
DIXIE (s) (C)	1943	PAR	89
NORTHERN PURSUIT (s)	1943	WB	94
SONG OF NEVADA (s)	1944	REP	75
BELLE OF THE YUKON (s) (C)	1944	RKO	84
SAN ANTONIO (s) (C)	1945	WB	112
SHADOWS ON THE RANGE (s)	1946	MON	58
CHEYENNE (aka THE WYOMING KID) (s)	1947	WB	100
THE GALLANT LEGION (s)	1948	REP	88
BRIMSTONE (s) (C)	1949	REP	90
BEYOND THE FOREST (s)	1949	WB	96
MONTANA (s) (C)	1950	WB	76
DAKOTA LIL (s) (C)	1950	20T	88
RIDERS OF THE RANGE (s)	1950	RKO	60
TWILIGHT IN THE SIERRAS (s) (C)	1950	REP	67
I SHOT BILLY THE KID (s)	1950	LIP	57
TRAIN TO TOMBSTONE (s)	1950	LIP	60
SUNSET IN THE WEST (s) (C)	1950	REP	67
KANSAS RAIDERS (s) (C)	1950	UI	80
BANDIT QUEEN (s)	1950	LIP	70
WELLS FARGO GUNMASTER (s)	1951	REP	60
JIM THORPE—ALL AMERICAN (aka MAN OF BRONZE) (s)	1951	WB	107
TREASURE OF LOST CANYON (s) (C)	1952	UI	87
THE REDHEAD FROM WYOMING (s) (C)	1953	UI	80
THE SUN SHINES BRIGHT (s)	1953	REP	90
BANDITS OF THE WEST (s)	1953	REP	54
THE STRANGER WORE A GUN (s) (C)	1953	COL	83
RED RIVER SHORE (s)	1953	REP	54
UNTAMED HEIRESS (s)	1954	REP	70
DESTRY (s) (C)	1955	UI	95
TEN WANTED MEN (s) (C)	1955	COL	80
SEVEN ANGRY MEN (s)	1955	AA	90
LAST OF THE DESPERADOS (s)	1955	ASC	70
A LAWLESS STREET (s) (C)	1955	COL	78
THE SPOILERS (s) (C)	1956	UI	84
THE RAWHIDE YEARS (s) (C)	1956	UI	86
REBEL IN TOWN (s)	1956	UA	78
TENSION AT TABLE ROCK (s) (C)	1956	RKO	93
GIANT (s) (C)	1956	WB	201
OUTLAW QUEEN (s)	1957	GLB	70
HELL'S CROSSROADS (s)	1957	REP	73-77
WESTBOUND (s) (C)	1959	WB	96
CAST A LONG SHADOW (s)	1959	UA	82
NOOSE FOR A GUNMAN (s)	1960	UA	69

154 / JACK PERRIN, continued

SERGEANT RUTLEDGE (s)	(C)	1960	WB	111
ICE PALACE (s)	(C)	1960	WB	143

LEE POWELL (1908 - 1944)

He zoomed to stardom as the masked rider of THE LONE RANGER, Republic's famous 15-chapter serial, then was sued while on tour with Wallace Brothers Circus for cashing in on the George Trendle character. Powell resumed a cowboy-lead career briefly in 1942 with PRC's *The Frontier Marshals* series.

FORLORN RIVER (s)		1937	PAR	56
THE LONE RANGER	(SER)	1938	REP	15CH
COME ON, RANGERS (s)		1938	REP	58
TRIGGER PALS		1939	GN	55-60
HI-YO-SILVER		1940	REP	69
(feature version of THE LONE RANGER serial)				
THE LONE RIDER RIDES ON (s)		1941	PRC	64
THE RETURN OF DANIEL BOONE		1941	COL	60
(aka THE MAYOR'S NEST) (s)				
TEXAS MANHUNT (starts *The Frontier Marshals* series)		1942	PRC	60
RAIDERS OF THE WEST		1942	PRC	64
ROLLING DOWN THE GREAT DIVIDE		1942	PRC	60
TUMBLEWEED TRAIL		1942	PRC	57
PRAIRIE PALS		1942	PRC	60
ALONG THE SUNDOWN TRAIL		1942	PRC	59
(ends *The Frontier Marshals* series)				
THE ADVENTURES OF MARK TWAIN (s)		1944	WB	130

TYRONE POWER (1913 - 1958)

A versatile leading man better known for his swashbuckling roles than western leads. Best remembered in the genre for his sympathetic portrayal of JESSE JAMES.

NORTHERN PATROL (s)		1935	AMB	57-60
IN OLD CHICAGO		1938	20T	95-115
JESSE JAMES	(C)	1939	20T	105
BRIGHAM YOUNG—FRONTIERSMAN		1940	20T	113-114
(aka BRIGHAM YOUNG)				
THE MARK OF ZORRO		1940	20T	93
BLOOD AND SAND	(C)	1941	20T	123
RAWHIDE (aka DESPERATE SIEGE)		1951	20T	86
PONY SOLDIER	(C)	1952	20T	82
(aka MacDONALD OF THE CANADIAN MOUNTIES)				
THE MISSISSIPPI GAMBLER	(C)	1953	UI	98-99

ELVIS PRESLEY (1935 - 1977)

Famous singer who starred in a few western films, although he was best known in features for his musical work. Presley's greatest one was FLAMING STAR.

LOVE ME TENDER		1956	20T	89
FLAMING STAR	(C)	1960	20T	101
VIVA LAS VEGAS	(C)	1964	MGM	85

ELVIS PRESLEY, continued / 155

TICKLE ME	(C)	1965	AA	90
FRANKIE AND JOHNNY	(C)	1966	UA	87
STAY AWAY, JOE	(C)	1968	MGM	101-102
CHARRO!	(C)	1969	NG	98-99

ROBERT PRESTON (1919 - 1987)

Excellent character actor who became a star late in his film career. In westerns he often played the second lead, frequently villains or irresponsible types. Preston's distinguished dramatic abilities were an asset for "The Chisholms" CBS-TV show (1979-80). Great with WHISPERING SMITH and TULSA.

UNION PACIFIC (cs)		1939	PAR	125-135
NORTH WEST MOUNTED POLICE (s)	(C)	1940	PAR	125
THE LADY FROM CHEYENNE		1941	UNI	87
WILD HARVEST (cs)		1947	PAR	92
BLOOD ON THE MOON (cs)		1948	RKO	88
WHISPERING SMITH (cs)	(C)	1949	PAR	88
TULSA	(C)	1949	EL	90
THE LADY GAMBLES		1949	UI	99
THE SUNDOWNERS	(C)	1950	EL	83-89
(aka THUNDER IN THE DUST)				
MY OUTLAW BROTHER		1951	EL	82
(aka MY BROTHER, THE OUTLAW) (cs)				
BEST OF THE BADMEN (cs)	(C)	1951	RKO	84
THE BRIDE COMES TO YELLOW SKY		1952	RKO	45
(part of FACE TO FACE)				
THE LAST FRONTIER	(C)	1956	COL	97-98
(aka SAVAGE WILDERNESS) (cs)				
HOW THE WEST WAS WON (s)	(C)	1963	MGM	155-165
JUNIOR BONNER	(C)	1972	CRC	103
THE CHISHOLMS	(C)	1979	ALP-TV	300
SEPTEMBER GUN	(C)	1983	CBS-TV	94

ANTHONY QUINN (1915 -)

Excellent Irish-Mexican dramatic actor who has frequently been cast as an Indian or Hispanic type in westerns. Best remembered in the genre for his Oscar-winning role in VIVA ZAPATA! Quinn's roles contain vocal robustness.

THE PLAINSMAN (s)		1937	PAR	113-115
UNION PACIFIC (s)		1939	PAR	125-135
TEXAS RANGERS RIDE AGAIN (s)		1940	PAR	68
BLOOD AND SAND (s)	(C)	1941	20T	123
THEY DIED WITH THEIR BOOTS ON (s)		1942	WB	140
THE OX-BOW INCIDENT		1943	20T	75
(aka STRANGE INCIDENT) (s)				
BUFFALO BILL (s)	(C)	1944	20T	90
WHERE DO WE GO FROM HERE? (s)	(C)	1945	20T	77
CALIFORNIA (s)	(C)	1947	PAR	97
BLACK GOLD	(C)	1947	AA	92
THE BRAVE BULLS (cs)		1951	COL	108-114
VIVA ZAPATA! (cs)		1952	20T	113
THE WORLD IN HIS ARMS (s)	(C)	1952	UI	104

ANTHONY QUINN, continued

SEMINOLE (cs)	(C).. 1953... UI	86-87	
RIDE, VAQUERO! (cs)	(C).. 1953... MGM	90	
BLOWING WILD (s)	1953... WB	90	
THE MAGNIFICENT MATADOR	(C).. 1955... 20T	94	
(aka THE BRAVE AND THE BEAUTIFUL)			
SEVEN CITIES OF GOLD	(C).. 1955... 20T	103	
MAN FROM DEL RIO	1956... UA	82	
THE RIVER'S EDGE	(C).. 1957... 20T	87	
THE RIDE BACK	1957... UA	79	
WILD IS THE WIND	1958... PAR	114	
WARLOCK (cs)	(C).. 1959... 20T	121-122	
LAST TRAIN FROM GUN HILL	(C).. 1959... PAR	94	
HELLER IN PINK TIGHTS	(C).. 1960... PAR	100	
THE SAVAGE INNOCENTS	(C).. 1960... PAR	110	
GUNS FOR SAN SEBASTIAN	(C).. 1968... MGM	111	
FLAP	(C).. 1970... WB	105-106	
DEAF SMITH AND JOHNNY EARS	(C).. 1973... MGM	91	
(aka LOS AMIGOS)			
CHILDREN OF SANCHEZ	(C).. 1978... CE	103-126	
CARAVANS	(C).. 1978... UNI	123	

VERA RALSTON (1921 -   )

Czechoslavakian-born actress who was a former skating star. She became the wife of Herbert Yates, the boss of Republic Studios, where she starred in several western films including DAKOTA and THE FIGHTING KENTUCKIAN with John Wayne.

DAKOTA	1945... REP	82	
PLAINSMAN AND THE LADY	1946... REP	87	
WYOMING	1947... REP	84	
THE FIGHTING KENTUCKIAN	1949... REP	100	
SURRENDER	1950... REP	90	
BELLE LE GRAND	1951... REP	90	
A PERILOUS JOURNEY	1953... REP	90	
JUBILEE TRAIL	(C).. 1954... REP	103	
TIMBERJACK	(C).. 1955... REP	92	
SPOILERS OF THE FOREST	(C).. 1957... REP	68	
GUNFIRE AT INDIAN GAP	1958... REP	70	

JACK RANDALL (1906 - 1945)

He was Monogram Pictures' "B" singing cowboy in 1937 with oatuners like RIDERS OF THE DAWN, but the songs were later sacrificed for straight actioners through 1940. Just as highly emotional in tense dramatic scenes when compared with movie cowboy brother Robert Livingston, Randall was accidentally killed July 16, 1945 while on rapid horseback for a Universal serial. His hat blew off, and attempting to grab it, Jack lost balance and fell striking a tree.

RIDERS OF THE DAWN	1937... MON	55	
STARS OVER ARIZONA	1937... MON	62	
DANGER VALLEY	1937... MON	58	
WHERE THE WEST BEGINS	1938... MON	54	
MAN'S COUNTRY	1938... MON	53-55	
LAND OF FIGHTING MEN	1938... MON	53	

JACK RANDALL, continued / 157

Title	Year	Studio	Pages
GUNSMOKE TRAIL	1938	MON	57
THE MEXICALI KID	1938	MON	51
GUN PACKER	1938	MON	49-61
WILD HORSE CANYON	1938	MON	50-56
DRIFTING WESTWARD	1939	MON	58
TRIGGER SMITH	1939	MON	60
ACROSS THE PLAINS	1939	MON	58
OKLAHOMA TERROR	1939	MON	50
OVERLAND MAIL	1939	MON	51
PIONEER DAYS	1940	MON	51
THE CHEYENNE KID	1940	MON	50
COVERED WAGON TRAILS	1940	MON	52
LAND OF THE SIX GUNS	1940	MON	54
THE KID FROM SANTA FE	1940	MON	50-57
RIDERS FROM NOWHERE	1940	MON	45-55
WILD HORSE RANGE	1940	MON	58

THE RANGE BUSTERS series (1940 - 1943)
These "B" oaters were a supposed challenge to Republic's *The Three Mesquiteers* hayburners, but never quite made the grade. However, the action—especially running inserts—was great along with that eerily inviting Monogram background scoring. Good entries were THE TRAIL OF THE SILVER SPURS and SADDLE MOUNTAIN ROUNDUP. Corrigan, King, and Terhune were the main trio.

(RAY "CRASH" CORRIGAN, JOHN "DUSTY" KING, MAX "ALIBI" TERHUNE)

Title	Year	Studio	Pages
THE RANGE BUSTERS	1940	MON	56
TRAILING DOUBLE TROUBLE	1940	MON	56-58
WEST OF PINTO BASIN	1940	MON	56-60
THE TRAIL OF THE SILVER SPURS	1941	MON	58
THE KID'S LAST RIDE	1941	MON	55
TUMBLEDOWN RANCH IN ARIZONA	1941	MON	60
WRANGLER'S ROOST	1941	MON	57
FUGITIVE VALLEY	1941	MON	61
SADDLE MOUNTAIN ROUNDUP	1941	MON	55-60
TONTO BASIN OUTLAWS	1941	MON	60
UNDERGROUND RUSTLERS	1941	MON	56
THUNDER RIVER FEUD	1942	MON	51
ROCK RIVER RENEGADES	1942	MON	56
BOOT HILL BANDITS	1942	MON	58
TEXAS TROUBLE SHOOTERS	1942	MON	55
ARIZONA STAGE COACH	1942	MON	58

(JOHN "DUSTY" KING, DAVID "DAVY" SHARPE, MAX "ALIBI" TERHUNE)

Title	Year	Studio	Pages
TEXAS TO BATAAN (aka THE LONG, LONG TRAIL)	1942	MON	56
TRAIL RIDERS (aka OVERLAND TRAIL)	1942	MON	55
TWO-FISTED JUSTICE	1943	MON	61-62

(JOHN "DUSTY" KING, DAVID "DAVY" SHARPE, MAX "ALIBI" TERHUNE, REX LEASE)

Title	Year	Studio	Pages
HAUNTED RANCH (aka DEAD MEN DON'T RIDE)	1943	MON	57

(RAY "CRASH" CORRIGAN, DENNIS "DENNY" MOORE, MAX "ALIBI" TERHUNE)

Title	Year	Studio	Pages
LAND OF HUNTED MEN	1943	MON	58
COWBOY COMMANDOS	1943	MON	55

THE RANGE BUSTERS series, continued

BLACK MARKET RUSTLERS .... 1943 ... MON .... 58 ____
BULLETS AND SADDLES .... 1943 ... MON .... 55 ____

THE RANGE RIDER series (1936 - 1938)
These early Tex Ritter "B" gallopers for Grand National had the singular distinction in some entries of staging final shootouts with good guys and bad guys riding parallel to each other. THE UTAH TRAIL was best. This series was highly ballyhooed in the show-biz trades as part of the studio's initial features having extensive advertising.

(TEX RITTER, FUZZY KNIGHT)
SONG OF THE GRINGO (aka THE OLD CORRAL) .. 1936 ... GN .... 62 ____

(TEX RITTER, SYD SAYLOR)
HEADIN' FOR THE RIO GRANDE .... 1936 ... GN .... 61 ____
ARIZONA DAYS .... 1937 ... GN .... 52-57 ____

(TEX RITTER, HORACE MURPHY)
TROUBLE IN TEXAS .... 1937 ... GN .... 53-63 ____
   (aka TROUBLE ALONG THE RIO GRANDE)

(TEX RITTER, HEBER SNOW (aka HANK WORDEN))
HITTIN' THE TRAIL .... 1937 ... GN .... 58 ____

(TEX RITTER, AL ST. JOHN)
SING, COWBOY, SING .... 1937 ... GN .... 59 ____

(TEX RITTER, HORACE MURPHY, SNUB POLLARD)
RIDERS OF THE ROCKIES .... 1937 ... GN .... 56 ____
   (aka ROCKY MOUNTAIN RAIDERS)

(TEX RITTER, HORACE MURPHY)
THE MYSTERY OF THE HOODED HORSEMEN .... 1937 ... GN .... 60 ____
   (aka HOODED HORSEMEN)

(TEX RITTER, HORACE MURPHY, SNUB POLLARD)
TEX RIDES WITH THE BOY SCOUTS .... 1937 ... GN .... 57 ____
FRONTIER TOWN (aka THE RODEO KID) .... 1938 ... GN .... 58-60 ____
ROLLIN' PLAINS .... 1938 ... GN .... 57 ____
THE UTAH TRAIL (aka TRAIL TO UTAH) .... 1938 ... GN .... 55 ____

RONALD REAGAN (1911 -   )
The future 40th President of the United States starred in several "A" oaters through the mid-1950s before ever thinking seriously of state/national politics.

COWBOY FROM BROOKLYN .... 1938 ... WB .... 80 ____
   (aka ROMANCE AND RHYTHM) (s)
SANTA FE TRAIL (s) .... 1940 ... WB .... 110 ____
THE BAD MAN (aka TWO-GUN CUPID) (s) .... 1941 ... MGM .... 70 ____
STALLION ROAD .... 1947 ... WB ..... 91-97 ____
THE LAST OUTPOST .... (C) .. 1951 ... PAR .... 88 ____
LAW AND ORDER .... (C) .. 1953 ... UI .... 80 ____
CATTLE QUEEN OF MONTANA .... (C) .. 1954 ... RKO .... 88 ____
TENNESSEE'S PARTNER .... (C) .. 1955 ... RKO .... 87 ____

ROBERT REDFORD (1937 -   )

Handsome leading man whose western roles have been few but notable as his portrayals of the Sundance Kid in BUTCH CASSIDY AND THE SUNDANCE KID and JEREMIAH JOHNSON indicate. Redford has been an active environmentalist for many years.

THE CHASE (cs)	(C)	1966	COL	130-135
BUTCH CASSIDY AND THE SUNDANCE KID	(C)	1969	20T	110-112
TELL THEM WILLIE BOY IS HERE	(C)	1970	UNI	96-98
JEREMIAH JOHNSON	(C)	1972	WB	107-108
THE ELECTRIC HORSEMAN	(C)	1979	UNI/COL	120

DUNCAN RENALDO (1904 - 1980)

He began the climb to mustanger stardom with *The Three Mesquiteers* series (1939-40) at Republic, then became popular as "The Cisco Kid" in 1940s Monogram and United Artists "B" oaters. Renaldo stayed as Cisco (1950-56) in 156 half-hour episodes for ZIV Television.

PALS OF THE PRAIRIE (s)	1929	FBO	50
REBELLION (cs)	1936	CRE	60
THE PAINTED STALLION (s) (SER)	1937	REP	12CH
ZORRO RIDES AGAIN (s) (SER)	1937	REP	12CH
ROSE OF THE RIO GRANDE (s)	1938	MON	60
SPAWN OF THE NORTH (s)	1938	PAR	110
THE LONE RANGER RIDES AGAIN (cs) (SER)	1939	REP	15CH
ROUGH RIDERS' ROUND-UP (s)	1939	REP	58
THE KANSAS TERRORS	1939	REP	57
(starts *The Three Mesquiteers* series)			
COWBOYS FROM TEXAS	1939	REP	57
SOUTH OF THE BORDER	1939	REP	71
(aka SOUTH OF TEXAS) (non-series) (s)			
HEROES OF THE SADDLE	1940	REP	56
PIONEERS OF THE WEST	1940	REP	56
COVERED WAGON DAYS	1940	REP	56
GAUCHO SERENADE (non-series) (s)	1940	REP	66
ROCKY MOUNTAIN RANGERS	1940	REP	58
OKLAHOMA RENEGADES	1940	REP	57
(ends *The Three Mesquiteers* series)			
BAD MEN OF MISSOURI (s)	1941	WB	71-74
KING OF THE TEXAS RANGERS (s) (SER)	1941	REP	12CH
DOWN MEXICO WAY (s)	1941	REP	78
GAUCHOS OF ELDORADO (s)	1941	REP	56
OUTLAWS OF THE DESERT (s)	1941	PAR	66
KING OF THE MOUNTIES (s) (SER)	1942	REP	12CH
BORDER PATROL (s)	1943	UA	67
HANDS ACROSS THE BORDER (s)	1943	REP	73
THE TIGER WOMAN (SER)	1944	REP	12CH
(aka JUNGLE GOLD; PERILS OF THE DARKEST JUNGLE) (s)			
THE SAN ANTONIO KID (s)	1944	REP	59
SHERIFF OF SUNDOWN (s)	1944	REP	57
THE CISCO KID RETURNS	1945	MON	64
(starts *The Cisco Kid* series)			
IN OLD NEW MEXICO	1945	MON	62
SOUTH OF THE RIO GRANDE	1945	MON	62

DUNCAN RENALDO, continued

THE VALIANT HOMBRE	1949	UA	60
THE GAY AMIGO	1949	UA	62
THE DARING CABALLERO	1949	UA	60
SATAN'S CRADLE	1949	UA	60
THE GIRL FROM SAN LORENZO	1950	UA	59

(ends *The Cisco Kid* series)

THE CAPTURE (s)	1950	RKO	91
ZORRO RIDES AGAIN	1959	REP	68

(feature version of ZORRO RIDES AGAIN serial) (s)

RENFREW OF THE ROYAL MOUNTED series (1937 - 1940)

James Newill portrayed loyal mountie Renfrew in another north-woods group of outdoors adventures (1937-40) first at Grand National, then wrapped the series up at Monogram with co-star Dave O'Brien.

(JAMES NEWILL, WILLIAM AUSTIN)

RENFREW OF THE ROYAL MOUNTED	1937	GN	57

(JAMES NEWILL, BOB TERRY)

ON THE GREAT WHITE TRAIL	1938	GN	58

(JAMES NEWILL, DAVE O'BRIEN)

FIGHTING MAD	1939	MON	60
CRASHING THRU	1939	MON	60-65
YUKON FLIGHT	1939	MON	57
DANGER AHEAD	1940	MON	60
MURDER ON THE YUKON	1940	MON	58
SKY BANDITS	1940	MON	56-62

JOHN PAUL REVERE series (1943 - 1944)

A brief Republic "B" series where the principal character assumed different law officer roles to bring evildoers to justice. Eddie Dew helmed the first two oaters as lead player with Bob Livingston taking over the remaining entries. Smiley Burnette was continuing sidekick. Bob Mitchum acted in BEYOND THE LAST FRONTIER.

(EDDIE DEW, SMILEY BURNETTE)

BEYOND THE LAST FRONTIER	1943	REP	55
RAIDERS OF SUNSET PASS	1943	REP	56

(BOB LIVINGSTON, SMILEY BURNETTE)

PRIDE OF THE PLAINS	1944	REP	58
BENEATH WESTERN SKIES	1944	REP	56

BURT REYNOLDS (1936 -   )

He began as a supporting character actor in the classic television series "Gunsmoke" as the halfbreed blacksmith, Quint. Although he has made several westerns to date, Reynolds is better known in films for his *Smokey and the Bandit* series.

NAVAJO JOE	(C)	1967	UA	89
FADE-IN	(C)	1968	PAR-TV	93
100 RIFLES (cs)	(C)	1969	20T	110
SAM WHISKEY	(C)	1969	UA	95-96

RUN, SIMON, RUN (aka SAVAGE RUN) ....(C).. 1970 ... ABC-TV ....74 ____
THE MAN WHO LOVED CAT DANCING ....(C).. 1973 ... MGM 114-122 ____
SMOKEY AND THE BANDIT ....(C).. 1977 ... UNI ....96 ____
HOOPER ....(C).. 1978 ... WB ....100 ____
SMOKEY AND THE BANDIT 2 ....(C).. 1980 ... UNI ....104 ____
   (aka SMOKEY AND THE BANDIT RIDE AGAIN)
THE BEST LITTLE WHOREHOUSE IN TEXAS ..(C).. 1982 ... RKO/UNI 114 ____
SMOKEY AND THE BANDIT 3 (s) ....(C).. 1983 ... UNI ....88 ____
UPHILL ALL THE WAY (cs) ....(C).. 1986 ... NW ....86 ____

RIN-TIN-TIN (1918 - 1932) (NOT A COWBOY, BUT A WESTERN STAR)
A four-legged canine who sometimes created more excitement than his male rivals with action scenes.

LAND OF THE SILVER FOX .... 1928 ... WB ....60 ____
ON THE BORDER .... 1930 ... WB ....46 ____
THE LONE DEFENDER ....(SER).. 1930 ... MAS .....12CH ____
LIGHTNING WARRIOR ....(SER).. 1931 ... MAS .....12CH ____
HUMAN TARGETS .... 1932 ... B4 ....55 ____

TEX RITTER (1905 - 1974)
An early singing cowboy with Grand National's *The Range Rider* series in 1936, Ritter made his best oatuners for Monogram (1938-41) and the top entry was TAKE ME BACK TO OKLAHOMA. Tex wrapped up a "B" starring career in *The Texas Rangers* series (1944-45), and became a Top Money-Making Western Star (1937, 1941, 1944-45). His beautiful background warbling of "Do Not Forsake Me, Oh My Darlin'" helped elevate HIGH NOON into an immortal classic.

SONG OF THE GRINGO .... 1936 ... GN ....62 ____
   (aka THE OLD CORRAL) (starts *The Range Rider* series)
HEADIN' FOR THE RIO GRANDE .... 1936 ... GN ....61 ____
ARIZONA DAYS .... 1937 ... GN ....52-57 ____
TROUBLE IN TEXAS .... 1937 ... GN ....53-63 ____
   (aka TROUBLE ALONG THE RIO GRANDE)
HITTIN' THE TRAIL .... 1937 ... GN ....58 ____
SING, COWBOY, SING .... 1937 ... GN ....59 ____
RIDERS OF THE ROCKIES .... 1937 ... GN ....56 ____
   (aka ROCKY MOUNTAIN RAIDERS)
THE MYSTERY OF THE HOODED HORSEMEN .... 1937 ... GN ....60 ____
   (aka HOODED HORSEMEN)
TEX RIDES WITH THE BOY SCOUTS .... 1937 ... GN ....57 ____
FRONTIER TOWN (aka THE RODEO KID) .... 1938 ... GN ....58-60 ____
ROLLIN' PLAINS .... 1938 ... GN ....57 ____
THE UTAH TRAIL (aka TRAIL TO UTAH) .... 1938 ... GN ....55 ____
   (ends *The Range Rider* series)
STARLIGHT OVER TEXAS .... 1938 ... MON ....56-58 ____
   (aka MOONLIGHT OVER TEXAS)
WHERE THE BUFFALO ROAM .... 1938 ... MON ....62 ____
SONG OF THE BUCKAROO .... 1938 ... MON ....56-58 ____
   (akaTHE SINGING BUCKAROO)
SUNDOWN ON THE PRAIRIE .... 1939 ... MON ....59 ____
   (aka PRAIRIE SUNDOWN)
ROLLIN' WESTWARD (aka ROLLIN' WEST) .... 1939 ... MON ....55 ____

TEX RITTER, continued

DOWN THE WYOMING TRAIL .... 1939...MON....56-62 ____
   (aka TRAIL TO WYOMING)
RIDERS OF THE FRONTIER .... 1939...MON........58 ____
   (aka RIDIN' THE FRONTIER)
THE MAN FROM TEXAS (aka MEN FROM TEXAS) .1939...MON....56-60 ____
WESTBOUND STAGE .... 1939...MON........56 ____
RHYTHM OF THE RIO GRANDE .... 1940...MON........53 ____
   (aka TRAIL TO THE RIO GRANDE)
PALS OF THE SILVER SAGE (aka ROUNDUP TIME) 1940...MON........52 ____
COWBOY FROM SUNDOWN .... 1940...MON........58 ____
RAINBOW OVER THE RANGE .... 1940...MON....58-60 ____
THE GOLDEN TRAIL (aka GOLD TRAIL) .... 1940...MON........52 ____
ROLL WAGONS ROLL .... 1940...MON........52 ____
   (aka ROLL, COVERED WAGONS)
ARIZONA FRONTIER .... 1940...MON....55-60 ____
TAKE ME BACK TO OKLAHOMA .... 1940...MON....57-64 ____
   (aka OKLAHOMA BOUND)
ROLLIN' HOME TO TEXAS .... 1940...MON....60-62 ____
   (aka RIDIN' HOME TO TEXAS)
RIDIN' THE CHEROKEE TRAIL .... 1941...MON........62 ____
   (aka THE CHEROKEE TRAIL)
THE PIONEERS .... 1941...MON....58-61 ____
KING OF DODGE CITY (starts *Wild Bill Hickok* series) 1941...COL.....59-63 ____
ROARING FRONTIERS (aka FRONTIER) .... 1941...COL.....60-63 ____
THE LONE STAR VIGILANTES .... 1942...COL.........58 ____
   (aka THE DEVIL'S PRICE)
BULLETS FOR BANDITS .... 1942...COL.........55 ____
NORTH OF THE ROCKIES .... 1942...COL.........60 ____
   (aka FALSE CLUES) (non-series)
THE DEVIL'S TRAIL .... 1942...COL.........61 ____
   (aka ROGUE'S GALLERY; DEVIL'S CANYON)
PRAIRIE GUNSMOKE (ends *Wild Bill Hickok* series) 1942...COL.........56 ____
VENGEANCE OF THE WEST .... 1942...COL.........60 ____
   (aka THE BLACK SHADOW)
DEEP IN THE HEART OF TEXAS .... 1942...UNI..........62 ____
LITTLE JOE, THE WRANGLER .... 1942...UNI..........64 ____
THE OLD CHISHOLM TRAIL .... 1942...UNI..........61 ____
TENTING TONIGHT ON THE OLD CAMP GROUND . 1943...UNI.......58-62 ____
   (aka TENTING TONIGHT)
CHEYENNE ROUNDUP .... 1943...UNI..........59 ____
RAIDERS OF SAN JOAQUIN .... 1943...UNI..........59 ____
   (aka RIDERS OF SAN JOAQUIN)
THE LONE STAR TRAIL .... 1943...UNI..........58 ____
FRONTIER BADMEN (s) .... 1943...UNI..........77 ____
ARIZONA TRAIL (aka SUNDOWN TRAIL) .... 1943...UNI..........57 ____
MARSHAL OF GUNSMOKE .... 1944...UNI..........59 ____
   (aka SHERIFF OF GUNSMOKE)
COWBOY CANTEEN (aka CLOSE HARMONY) (s) .1944...COL.........72 ____
OKLAHOMA RAIDERS .... 1944...UNI..........57 ____
   (aka MIDNIGHT RAIDERS; RIDERS OF OKLAHOMA)
GANGSTERS OF THE FRONTIER .... 1944...PRC.........56 ____
   (aka RAIDERS OF THE FRONTIER) (starts *The Texas Rangers* series)
DEAD OR ALIVE (aka WANTED BY THE LAW) .... 1944...PRC.........56 ____
THE WHISPERING SKULL .... 1944...PRC.........55 ____
MARKED FOR MURDER .... 1944...PRC.........56 ____
ENEMY OF THE LAW .... 1945...PRC.........59 ____

TEX RITTER, continued /**163**

THREE IN THE SADDLE	1945	PRC	61
FRONTIER FUGITIVES	1945	PRC	58
(aka FUGITIVES OF THE FRONTIER)			
FLAMING BULLETS (ends *The Texas Rangers* series)	1945	PRC	59
HIGH NOON (so)	1952	UA	85
THE MARSHAL'S DAUGHTER (so)	1953	UA	71
THE COWBOY (nr)	(C).. 1954	LIP	69
WICHITA (so)	(C).. 1955	AA	81
APACHE AMBUSH (s)	1955	COL	68
DOWN LIBERTY ROAD (s)	(C).. 1956	WB	40
TROOPER HOOK (so)	1957	UA	81-82
NASHVILLE REBEL	(C).. 1966	AI	91
WHAT AM I BID? (s)	(C).. 1967	EFE	92

DALE ROBERTSON (1923 -   )
Western-type leading man who began in 20th Century-Fox films, but soon moved into television with the series, "Tales of Wells Fargo" (1957-63) for 167 episodes and "Iron Horse" (1966-68) on ABC-TV with 47 hour-long shows. Dale has appeared in numerous westerns throughout his career. Great with THE SILVER WHIP.

FIGHTING MAN OF THE PLAINS (s)	(C).. 1949	20T	94
THE CARIBOO TRAIL (s)	(C).. 1950	20T	81
TWO FLAGS WEST (s)	1950	20T	92
GOLDEN GIRL	(C).. 1951	20T	108
RETURN OF THE TEXAN	(C).. 1952	20T	87-88
THE OUTCASTS OF POKER FLAT (cs)	1952	20T	81
THE SILVER WHIP	1953	20T	73
DEVIL'S CANYON	(C).. 1953	RKO	92
CITY OF BAD MEN	(C).. 1953	20T	82
THE GAMBLER FROM NATCHEZ	(C).. 1954	20T	88
SITTING BULL	(C).. 1954	UA	105
A DAY OF FURY	(C).. 1956	UI	78
DAKOTA INCIDENT	(C).. 1956	REP	88
HELL CANYON OUTLAWS	1957	REP	72
GUNFIGHT AT BLACK HORSE CANYON	1962	REV	100
LAW OF THE LAWLESS	(C).. 1964	PAR	87
(aka INVITATION TO A HANGING)			
BLOOD ON THE ARROW	(C).. 1964	AA	91
THE MAN FROM BUTTON WILLOW	(C).. 1965	USA	84
(animated) (vo)			
SCALPLOCK	(C).. 1966	COL-TV	100
THE LAST RIDE OF THE DALTON GANG (s)	(C).. 1979	NBC-TV	150
OKLAHOMA PASSAGE (ho)	(C).. 1989	OETA-TV	300

KENNY ROGERS (1938 -   )
As an award-winning country music singer, he has gained ever more greater recognition by starring in "The Gambler" series of TV western feature movies he began in 1980. Kenny began his own restaurant chain during 1991.

THE GAMBLER	(C).. 1980	CBS-TV	94
THE GAMBLER, PART II—	(C).. 1983	CBS-TV	200
THE ADVENTURE CONTINUES			
WILD HORSES	(C).. 1985	CBS-TV	100

164 / KENNY ROGERS, continued

THE GAMBLER, PART III— THE LEGEND CONTINUES	(C)	1987...CBS-TV	..200
THE GAMBLER, PART IV— THE LUCK OF THE DRAW	(C)	1991...NBC-TV	..200

ROY ROGERS (1911 -   )
(aka LEONARD SLYE, DICK WESTON)

An outstanding singing movie cowboy debut with UNDER WESTERN STARS in 1938 at Republic Pictures propelled Rogers' ascension to "King of the Cowboys". By close of 1948, his top-quality Trucolor oatuners were consuming 65% of the studio budget for "B" westerns. Roy left Republic in 1951 after 81 starrers—the best were DON'T FENCE ME IN, MY PAL TRIGGER, and BELLS OF SAN ANGELO. He did 100 half-hour NBC-TV shows through 1957, and was a Top Money-Making Western Star (1939-54). In addition to numerous rodeos and other personal appearances, he has done lots of guest spots on TV variety shows, and hosted "Happy Trails Theater" on TNN in the late 1980s. Roy now oversees the Roy Rogers-Dale Evans Museum in Victorville, California, and has had his own family restaurant chain since the late 1960s. Signed new contract with Republic in 1992 to develop cartoon series and a personal film biography on his life.

THE OLD HOMESTEAD (s)	1935	LIB	72
GALLANT DEFENDER (s)	1935	COL	60
THE MYSTERIOUS AVENGER (s)	1936	COL	55-60
SONG OF THE SADDLE (s)	1936	WB	58
RHYTHM ON THE RANGE (s)	1936	PAR	85
CALIFORNIA MAIL (s)	1936	WB	60
THE BIG SHOW (aka HOME IN OKLAHOMA) (s)	1936	REP	70
THE OLD CORRAL (aka TEXAS SERENADE) (s)	1936	REP	56
THE OLD WYOMING TRAIL (s)	1937	COL	56
WILD HORSE RODEO (s)	1937	REP	56
THE OLD BARN DANCE (s)	1938	REP	60
UNDER WESTERN STARS	1938	REP	65
BILLY THE KID RETURNS	1938	REP	56-58
COME ON, RANGERS	1938	REP	58
SHINE ON HARVEST MOON	1938	REP	55-57
ROUGH RIDERS' ROUND-UP	1939	REP	58
FRONTIER PONY EXPRESS	1939	REP	58
MAN OF CONQUEST (s)	1939	REP	97-105
SOUTHWARD, HO!	1939	REP	58
IN OLD CALIENTE	1939	REP	57
WALL STREET COWBOY	1939	REP	66
THE ARIZONA KID	1939	REP	61
JEEPERS CREEPERS	1939	REP	69
SAGA OF DEATH VALLEY	1939	REP	58
DAYS OF JESSE JAMES	1939	REP	63
YOUNG BUFFALO BILL	1940	REP	59
DARK COMMAND (s)	1940	REP	94
THE CARSON CITY KID	1940	REP	57
THE RANGER AND THE LADY	1940	REP	59
COLORADO	1940	REP	57
YOUNG BILL HICKOK	1940	REP	59
THE BORDER LEGION (aka WEST OF THE BADLANDS)	1940	REP	57
ROBIN HOOD OF THE PECOS	1941	REP	59
ARKANSAS JUDGE	1941	REP	72

ROY ROGERS, continued / 165

IN OLD CHEYENNE	1941	REP	58
SHERIFF OF TOMBSTONE	1941	REP	56
NEVADA CITY	1941	REP	58
BAD MAN OF DEADWOOD	1941	REP	61
JESSE JAMES AT BAY	1941	REP	56
RED RIVER VALLEY	1941	REP	62
MAN FROM CHEYENNE	1942	REP	60
SOUTH OF SANTA FE	1942	REP	55
SUNSET ON THE DESERT	1942	REP	54
ROMANCE ON THE RANGE	1942	REP	63
SONS OF THE PIONEERS	1942	REP	61
SUNSET SERENADE	1942	REP	58
HEART OF THE GOLDEN WEST	1942	REP	65
RIDIN' DOWN THE CANYON	1942	REP	54
IDAHO	1943	REP	70
KING OF THE COWBOYS	1943	REP	67
SONG OF TEXAS	1943	REP	69
SILVER SPURS	1943	REP	65-68
MAN FROM MUSIC MOUNTAIN	1943	REP	71
(aka TEXAS LEGIONNAIRES)			
HANDS ACROSS THE BORDER	1943	REP	73
COWBOY AND THE SENORITA	1944	REP	78
THE YELLOW ROSE OF TEXAS	1944	REP	69
SONG OF NEVADA	1944	REP	75
SAN FERNANDO VALLEY	1944	REP	74
LIGHTS OF OLD SANTA FE	1944	REP	76-78
UTAH	1945	REP	78
BELLS OF ROSARITA	1945	REP	68
MAN FROM OKLAHOMA	1945	REP	68
SUNSET IN EL DORADO	1945	REP	65
DON'T FENCE ME IN	1945	REP	71
ALONG THE NAVAJO TRAIL	1945	REP	66
SONG OF ARIZONA	1946	REP	68
RAINBOW OVER TEXAS	1946	REP	65
MY PAL TRIGGER	1946	REP	79
UNDER NEVADA SKIES	1946	REP	69
ROLL ON TEXAS MOON	1946	REP	68
HOME IN OKLAHOMA	1946	REP	72
OUT CALIFORNIA WAY (gs)	(C) 1946	REP	67
HELDORADO	1946	REP	70
APACHE ROSE	(C) 1947	REP	75
HIT PARADE OF 1947 (gs)	1947	REP	90
BELLS OF SAN ANGELO	(C) 1947	REP	78
SPRINGTIME IN THE SIERRAS	(C) 1947	REP	75
(aka SONG OF THE SIERRAS)			
ON THE OLD SPANISH TRAIL	(C) 1947	REP	75
THE GAY RANCHERO	(C) 1948	REP	72
UNDER CALIFORNIA STARS	(C) 1948	REP	70
(aka UNDER CALIFORNIA SKIES)			
EYES OF TEXAS	(C) 1948	REP	70
MELODY TIME (part animation)	(C) 1948	RKO	75
NIGHT TIME IN NEVADA	(C) 1948	REP	67
GRAND CANYON TRAIL	(C) 1948	REP	67
THE FAR FRONTIER	(C) 1948	REP	67
SUSANNA PASS	(C) 1949	REP	67
DOWN DAKOTA WAY	(C) 1949	REP	67

ROY ROGERS, continued

THE GOLDEN STALLION	(C)	1949	REP	67
BELLS OF CORONADO	(C)	1950	REP	67
TWILIGHT IN THE SIERRAS	(C)	1950	REP	67
TRIGGER, JR.	(C)	1950	REP	68
SUNSET IN THE WEST	(C)	1950	REP	67
NORTH OF THE GREAT DIVIDE	(C)	1950	REP	67
(aka WEST OF THE GREAT DIVIDE)				
TRAIL OF ROBIN HOOD	(C)	1950	REP	67
SPOILERS OF THE PLAINS		1951	REP	68
HEART OF THE ROCKIES		1951	REP	67
IN OLD AMARILLO		1951	REP	67
SOUTH OF CALIENTE		1951	REP	67
PALS OF THE GOLDEN WEST		1951	REP	68
SON OF PALEFACE (cs)	(C)	1952	PAR	104
ALIAS JESSE JAMES (gs)	(C)	1959	UA	92
MacKINTOSH AND T. J.	(C)	1976	PEN	96
SMOKEY AND THE BANDIT 2	(C)	1980	UNI	104
(aka SMOKEY AND THE BANDIT RIDE AGAIN) (so)				

GILBERT ROLAND (1905 -   )
The son of a torero, he carried such tempestuousness into a popular screen career yet exuded personal charm opposite many leading ladies. Roland starred in *The Cisco Kid* series for Monogram Studios (1946-47), and was highly acclaimed for his part in Republic's prestigious BULLFIGHTER AND THE LADY, a film which originally ran 124 minutes when released in 1951.

MEN OF THE NORTH		1930	MGM	63
THUNDER TRAIL		1937	PAR	56
(aka THUNDER PASS; ARIZONA AMES)				
JUAREZ (s)		1939	WB	132
RANGERS OF FORTUNE (s)		1940	PAR	80
THE GAY CAVALIER (starts *The Cisco Kid* series)		1946	MON	65
SOUTH OF MONTEREY		1946	MON	63
BEAUTY AND THE BANDIT		1946	MON	77
RIDING THE CALIFORNIA TRAIL		1947	MON	59
ROBIN HOOD OF MONTEREY		1947	MON	55
KING OF THE BANDITS (ends *The Cisco Kid* series)		1947	MON	66
PIRATES OF MONTEREY (s)	(C)	1947	UI	77
THE DUDE GOES WEST (s)		1948	AA	87
THE TORCH (cs)		1950	EL	83-90
THE FURIES (s)		1950	PAR	109
BULLFIGHTER AND THE LADY (cs)		1951	REP	87-124
MARK OF THE RENEGADE (s)	(C)	1951	UI	81
THE MIRACLE OF OUR LADY FATIMA	(C)	1952	WB	102
(aka MIRACLE OF FATIMA)				
APACHE WAR SMOKE		1952	MGM	67
THE FRENCH LINE	(C)	1954	RKO	102
THE TREASURE OF PANCHO VILLA (cs)	(C)	1955	RKO	96
BANDIDO (s)	(C)	1956	UA	92
THREE VIOLENT PEOPLE (cs)	(C)	1957	PAR	100
THE LAST OF THE FAST GUNS	(C)	1958	UI	82
THE WILD AND THE INNOCENT (cs)	(C)	1959	UI	84
GUNS OF THE TIMBERLAND	(C)	1960	WB	91
(aka STAMPEDED) (cs)				
CHEYENNE AUTUMN (s)	(C)	1964	WB	145-160

THE REWARD (s)	(C).. 1965	...20T	92
ANY GUN CAN PLAY	(C).. 1968	...RAF	103
(aka FOR A FEW BULLETS MORE)			
THE RUTHLESS FOUR	(C).. 1969	...GFE	96
(aka EVERY MAN FOR HIMSELF; EACH ONE FOR HIMSELF; EACH MAN FOR HIMSELF; SAM COOPER'S GOLD)			
THE NEW LION OF SONORA	(C).. 1970	...NBC-TV	..100
JOHNNY HAMLET	(C).. 1972	...TP	91
BETWEEN GOD, THE DEVIL AND A WINCHESTER	(C).. 1972	...UV	98
RUNNING WILD (aka DELIVER US FROM EVIL)	(C).. 1973	...GC	103
TREASURE OF TAYOPA	(C).. 1974	...REI	90
THE MARK OF ZORRO (s)	(C).. 1974	...20T-TV	78
THE SACKETTS (aka THE DAYBREAKERS) (s)	(C).. 1979	...NBC-TV	..200
BARBAROSA (s)	(C).. 1982	...UNI	90

CESAR ROMERO (1907 -   )

He has been a dashing actor since the 1930s with comedies, dramas, and westerns. Romero helmed *The Cisco Kid* series at 20th Century-Fox (1939-41), was the comical Joker on the "Batman" TV series (1966-68), and currently hosts "Romance Classics" on AMC-TV cable network. During holiday seasons, Cesar joins other Hollywood stars in helping distribute meals to the homeless.

DIAMOND JIM (s)		1935 ...UNI	93
THE RETURN OF THE CISCO KID (s)		1939 ...20T	70
FRONTIER MARSHAL (cs)		1939 ...20T	71
THE CISCO KID AND THE LADY		1939 ...20T	73
(starts *The Cisco Kid* series)			
VIVA CISCO KID		1940 ...20T	70
LUCKY CISCO KID		1940 ...20T	68
THE GAY CABALLERO		1940 ...20T	57
ROMANCE OF THE RIO GRANDE		1941 ...20T	73
RIDE ON VAQUERO (ends *The Cisco Kid* series)		1941 ...20T	64
SPRINGTIME IN THE ROCKIES (s)	(C)..	1942 ...20T	91
THE BEAUTIFUL BLONDE FROM BASHFUL BEND	(C)..	1949 ...20T	77
VERA CRUZ (s)	(C)..	1954 ...UA	94
THE AMERICANO	(C)..	1955 ...RKO	85
VILLA!	(C)..	1958 ...20T	72
PEPE (gs)	(C)..	1960 ...COL	195
THE RED, WHITE AND BLACK	(C)..	1970 ...HN	97
(aka SOUL SOLDIER(S); MEN OF THE TENTH)			
THE PROUD AND THE DAMNED	(C)..	1972 ...COL	94
(aka PROUD, DAMNED AND DEAD) (cs)			
KINO, THE PADRE ON HORSEBACK	(C)..	1977 ...KI	116
(aka MISSION TO GLORY) (s)			
LUST IN THE DUST (s)	(C)..	1984 ...FR	85

BUDDY ROOSEVELT (1898 - 1973)

He was an authentic Colorado cowboy who, after starring in silent westerns, lost out to John Wayne for the Lone Star/Monogram flicks. After several sound mellers for Superior in 1934, Roosevelt spent the next 25 years doing character parts.

WAY OUT WEST (s)	1930 ...MGM	71
WESTWARD BOUND	1931 ...SYN	60

BUDDY ROOSEVELT, continued

Title	Year	Studio	Page/Ch
LIGHTNIN' SMITH RETURNS	1931	SYN	59
WEST OF BROADWAY (s)	1931	MGM	71
THE FOURTH HORSEMAN (s)	1932	UNI	63
WILD HORSE MESA (s)	1932	PAR	65
TEXAS TORNADO	1932	KEN	60
THE THRILL HUNTER (s)	1933	COL	58-60
BOSS COWBOY	1934	SPR	51
CIRCLE CANYON	1934	SPR	48
LIGHTNING RANGE	1934	SPR	53
RANGE RIDERS	1934	SPR	46
RAINBOW'S END (cs)	1935	FD	60
POWDERSMOKE RANGE (s)	1935	RKO	71
THE OLD CORRAL (aka TEXAS SERENADE) (s)	1936	REP	56-60
THE LONE RANGER RIDES AGAIN (s) (SER)	1939	REP	15CH
STAGECOACH (s)	1939	UA	96
MAN OF CONQUEST (s)	1939	REP	97-105
UNION PACIFIC (s)	1939	PAR	125-135
THE MAN FROM DAKOTA (aka AROUSE AND BEWARE) (s)	1940	MGM	74-75
WYOMING WILDCAT (s)	1941	REP	56
THE LONE RIDER RIDES ON (s)	1941	PRC	64
BILLY THE KID'S RANGE WAR (s)	1941	PRC	60
IN OLD CHEYENNE (s)	1941	REP	58
KANSAS CYCLONE (s)	1941	REP	58
GANGS OF SONORA (s)	1941	REP	58
THUNDER OVER THE PRAIRIE (s)	1941	COL	60
THE APACHE KID (s)	1941	REP	56
KING OF THE TEXAS RANGERS (s) (SER)	1941	REP	12CH
ABILENE TOWN (s)	1946	UA	89
SONG OF ARIZONA (s)	1946	REP	68
BADMAN'S TERRITORY (s)	1946	RKO	98
KING OF THE FOREST RANGERS (s) (SER)	1946	REP	12CH
THE SEA OF GRASS (s)	1947	MGM	131
UNCONQUERED (s) (C)	1948	PAR	146-147
COLT .45 (aka THUNDERCLOUD) (s) (C)	1950	WB	74
COPPER CANYON (s) (C)	1950	PAR	83
KANSAS RAIDERS (s) (C)	1950	UI	80
DALLAS (s) (C)	1950	WB	94
APACHE DRUMS (s) (C)	1951	UI	75
THE RED BADGE OF COURAGE (s)	1951	MGM	69
THE OLD WEST (s) (C)	1952	COL	61
WAGONS WEST (s) (C)	1952	MON	70
HORIZONS WEST (s) (C)	1952	UI	81
THE REDHEAD FROM WYOMING (s) (C)	1953	UI	80
THE LAWLESS BREED (s) (C)	1953	UI	83
THE MISSISSIPPI GAMBLER (s) (C)	1953	UI	98
LAW AND ORDER (s) (C)	1953	UI	80
RIDING SHOTGUN (s) (C)	1954	WB	75
THREE HOURS TO KILL (s) (C)	1954	COL	77
TALL MAN RIDING (s) (C)	1955	WB	83
THE LAST COMMAND (s) (C)	1955	REP	110
TRIBUTE TO A BAD MAN (s) (C)	1956	MGM	95
FLESH AND THE SPUR (s) (C)	1956	AI	80
SHOOT-OUT AT MEDICINE BEND (s) (C)	1957	WB	87
WESTBOUND (s) (C)	1959	WB	96
THE MAN WHO SHOT LIBERTY VALANCE (s)	1962	PAR	123

THE ROUGH RIDERS series (1941 - 1942)
Monogram Pictures in 1941 saw potential profit when it brought together former 1930s Columbia "B" western box-office saddle heroes Buck Jones and Tim McCoy for this exciting, action-packed series. Completing the trio of U.S. marshals, who captured desperadoes with cunning and directness, was veteran sidekick Raymond Hatton, back in the saddle again after finishing up a one-season stint (1939-40) with *The Three Mesquiteers* at Republic. Lensing commenced during June 1941 when Monogram had the first entry ARIZONA BOUND kick off exteriors near Prescott, Arizona. These features, with rapid background scoring, became unique at each one's concluding scenes when the trio galloped away separately to their respective states—Jones for Arizona, McCoy for Wyoming, and Hatton for Texas.

(BUCK JONES, TIM McCOY, RAYMOND HATTON)
ARIZONA BOUND	1941	MON	57
THE GUNMAN FROM BODIE	1941	MON	62
FORBIDDEN TRAILS	1941	MON	59
BELOW THE BORDER	1942	MON	57
GHOST TOWN LAW	1942	MON	62
DOWN TEXAS WAY	1942	MON	57
RIDERS OF THE WEST	1942	MON	58-60
WEST OF THE LAW	1942	MON	55-60

(BUCK JONES, REX BELL, RAYMOND HATTON)
DAWN ON THE GREAT DIVIDE	1942	MON	63-66

ROUGH-RIDIN' KIDS series (1951 - 1952)
Republic's short-lived group of juvenile-oriented horse operas having youngsters Michael Chapin and Eilene Janssen assist with corraling studio villains like Roy Barcroft under guidance of law officers. Originally intended as the "Buckeroo Sheriff" series, Chapin's character required him to dye his hair bright red for frequent public appearance tours.

(MICHAEL CHAPIN, EILENE JANSSEN, JAMES BELL)
BUCKAROO SHERIFF OF TEXAS	1951	REP	60
THE DAKOTA KID	1951	REP	60
ARIZONA MANHUNT	1951	REP	60
WILD HORSE AMBUSH	1952	REP	54

JANE RUSSELL (1921 -   )
This beautiful brunette was just as proficient with six-shooters and horseback riding as were many of her male counterparts. She shined in THE PALEFACE and its sequel SON OF PALEFACE. Tough and feminine for MONTANA BELLE.

THE OUTLAW	1943	UA	121
THE PALEFACE	(C) 1948	PAR	91
THE LAS VEGAS STORY	1952	RKO	88
SON OF PALEFACE	(C) 1952	PAR	104
MONTANA BELLE	(C) 1952	RKO	81
THE FRENCH LINE	(C) 1954	RKO	102
FOXFIRE	(C) 1955	UI	91
THE TALL MEN	(C) 1955	20T	121
JOHNNY RENO	(C) 1966	PAR	83
WACO	(C) 1966	PAR	85

REB RUSSELL (1905 - 1978)
He made two years of Kent oaters (1934-35), then voluntarily left Hollywood and did circus riding/whip acts for several years before retiring to the life of a prominent Kansas-Oklahoma rancher.

FIGHTING TO LIVE (cs)	1934	PRN	60
THE MAN FROM HELL	1934	KEN	58
FIGHTING THROUGH	1934	KEN	55
OUTLAW RULE	1935	KEN	61
RANGE WARFARE	1935	KEN	55
ARIZONA BAD MAN	1935	KEN	58
BLAZING GUNS	1935	KEN	54
BORDER VENGEANCE (aka TROUBLE BORDER)	1935	KEN	57
CHEYENNE TORNADO	1935	KEN	61
LIGHTNING TRIGGERS	1935	KEN	50

ROBERT RYAN (1909 - 1973)
An excellent actor whose "A" western roles ranged from villains to heroes. Ryan is best remembered in the genre for his supporting roles in THE PROFESSIONALS and THE WILD BUNCH.

TEXAS RANGERS RIDE AGAIN (s)	1940	PAR	68
NORTH WEST MOUNTED POLICE (s) (C)	1940	PAR	125
TRAIL STREET	1947	RKO	84
RETURN OF THE BAD MEN	1948	RKO	90
BEST OF THE BADMEN (C)	1951	RKO	81-84
HORIZONS WEST (C)	1952	UI	81-87
THE NAKED SPUR (cs) (C)	1953	MGM	91
INFERNO (C)	1953	20T	83
ALASKA SEAS	1954	PAR	78
BAD DAY AT BLACK ROCK (C)	1955	MGM	81
THE TALL MEN (cs) (C)	1955	20T	122
THE PROUD ONES (C)	1956	20T	92-94
DAY OF THE OUTLAW	1959	UA	91
ICE PALACE (C)	1960	WB	143
THE CANADIANS (C)	1961	20T	85
THE PROFESSIONALS (cs) (C)	1966	COL	117
HOUR OF THE GUN (cs) (C)	1967	UA	100
CUSTER OF THE WEST (s) (C) (aka GOOD DAY FOR FIGHTING)	1967	CRC	120-140
A MINUTE TO PRAY, A MINUTE TO DIE (C) (aka DEAD OR ALIVE) (cs)	1968	CRC	97-103
THE WILD BUNCH (cs) (C)	1969	WB	134-144
LAWMAN (C)	1971	UA	98
MAN WITHOUT A COUNTRY (C)	1973	ABC-TV	78

RED RYDER series (1944 - 1947; 1949)
Fred Harman's fighting redhead took a big leap from the comic pages to blaze a Republic Pictures trail of 23 "B" hour-long, exciting horse operas first starring Wild Bill Elliott (1944-46), then Allan Lane (1946-47). Jim Bannon was the more authentic in his portrayal with four 1949 features in Cinecolor from Eagle-Lion which had uncontrollable hysteria when Republic started re-releasing some of its black-and-white Ryder oaters at the same time as the tinters.

(WILD BILL ELLIOTT, BOBBY BLAKE, GEORGE "GABBY" HAYES)

TUCSON RAIDERS	1944	REP	55
MARSHAL OF RENO	1944	REP	54

RED RYDER series, continued / 171

(WILD BILL ELLIOTT, BOBBY BLAKE, EARLE HODGINS)
THE SAN ANTONIO KID .... 1944 ... REP .... 59 ____

(WILD BILL ELLIOTT, BOBBY BLAKE)
CHEYENNE WILDCAT .... 1944 ... REP .... 56 ____
VIGILANTES OF DODGE CITY .... 1944 ... REP .... 54 ____
SHERIFF OF LAS VEGAS .... 1944 ... REP .... 55 ____
GREAT STAGECOACH ROBBERY .... 1945 ... REP .... 56 ____
LONE TEXAS RANGER .... 1945 ... REP .... 56 ____
PHANTOM OF THE PLAINS .... 1945 ... REP .... 56 ____
MARSHAL OF LAREDO .... 1945 ... REP .... 56 ____
COLORADO PIONEERS .... 1945 ... REP .... 55 ____
WAGON WHEELS WESTWARD .... 1945 ... REP .... 55 ____
CALIFORNIA GOLD RUSH .... 1946 ... REP .... 56 ____

(WILD BILL ELLIOTT, BOBBY BLAKE, BOB STEELE)
SHERIFF OF REDWOOD VALLEY .... 1946 ... REP .... 54 ____

(WILD BILL ELLIOTT, BOBBY BLAKE)
SUN VALLEY CYCLONE .... 1946 ... REP .... 56 ____
CONQUEST OF CHEYENNE .... 1946 ... REP .... 55 ____

(ALLAN LANE, BOBBY BLAKE, EMMETT LYNN)
SANTA FE UPRISING .... 1946 ... REP .... 55 ____
STAGECOACH TO DENVER .... 1946 ... REP .... 56 ____

(ALLAN LANE, BOBBY BLAKE)
VIGILANTES OF BOOMTOWN .... 1947 ... REP .... 56 ____
HOMESTEADERS OF PARADISE VALLEY .... 1947 ... REP .... 59 ____

(ALLAN LANE, BOBBY BLAKE, EMMETT LYNN)
OREGON TRAIL SCOUTS .... 1947 ... REP .... 58 ____
RUSTLERS OF DEVIL'S CANYON .... 1947 ... REP .... 58 ____

(ALLAN LANE, BOBBY BLAKE)
MARSHAL OF CRIPPLE CREEK .... 1947 ... REP .... 58 ____

(JIM BANNON, DON KAY REYNOLDS, EMMETT LYNN)
RIDE, RYDER, RIDE! .... (C) .. 1949 ... EL .... 59 ____
ROLL, THUNDER, ROLL! .... (C) .. 1949 ... EL .... 58 ____
THE FIGHTING REDHEAD .... (C) .. 1949 ... EL .... 55 ____
COWBOY AND THE PRIZEFIGHTER .... (C) .. 1949 ... EL .... 59 ____

WILD BILL SAUNDERS series (1939 - 1940)
A short-lived law-and-order part done by Bill Elliott at Columbia (1939-40) which would be in the same, later vein of his other "Wild Bill" type "B" westerns.

(BILL ELLIOTT, DUB "CANNONBALL" TAYLOR)
THE TAMING OF THE WEST .... 1939 ... COL .... 55 ____
PIONEERS OF THE FRONTIER (aka THE ANCHOR) 1940 ... COL .... 58 ____
THE MAN FROM TUMBLEWEEDS .... 1940 ... COL .... 59 ____
THE RETURN OF WILD BILL (aka FALSE EVIDENCE) 1940 ... COL .... 60 ____

FRED SCOTT (1902 - 1991)

He was the beautifully strong-voiced singing troubadour with a series of low-budget "B" Spectrum oatuners for three years (1936-39), some of which were produced by Stan Laurel. During later years, Scott succeeded with a successful real estate career in California.

RIO RITA (s)	1929	RKO	135
THE LAST OUTLAW (s)	1936	RKO	62
ROMANCE RIDES THE RANGE	1936	SPE	59
THE SINGING BUCKAROO	1937	SPE	50
MELODY OF THE PLAINS	1937	SPE	55
THE FIGHTING DEPUTY	1937	SPE	55
MOONLIGHT ON THE RANGE	1937	SPE	52
THE ROAMING COWBOY	1937	SPE	56
THE RANGER'S ROUND-UP	1938	SPE	55
KNIGHT OF THE PLAINS	1938	SPE	57
SONGS AND BULLETS	1938	SPE	58
CODE OF THE FEARLESS	1939	SPE	56
IN OLD MONTANA	1939	SPE	61
TWO-GUN TROUBADOUR	1939	SPE	58
(aka THE LONE TROUBADOUR)			
RIDIN' THE TRAIL	1940	ZIE	57
THUNDERING HOOFS (s)	1941	RKO	61
RODEO RHYTHM	1942	PRC	72

RANDOLPH SCOTT (1898 - 1987)

One of the most famous of all western stars. Along with Cooper, Wayne and McCrea, he made some of the best and memorable "A" oaters. From his early Zane Grey roles at Paramount to his outstanding westerns at Columbia, Scott remained a favorite with film fans for many years. His last role as the slightly larcenous sidekick to lawman McCrea in RIDE THE HIGH COUNTRY is a fitting finale to a fine career. Randolph possessed an aristocratic gait, immaculate appearance, and rich intonation which made him one of the greatest and most gracious gentlemen of the silver screen.

THE VIRGINIAN (s)	1929	PAR	87
HERITAGE OF THE DESERT	1932	PAR	59-63
(aka WHEN THE WEST WAS YOUNG)			
WILD HORSE MESA	1932	PAR	65
SUNSET PASS	1933	PAR	61-65
MAN OF THE FOREST	1933	PAR	62
TO THE LAST MAN (aka LAW OF VENGEANCE)	1933	PAR	70
THE THUNDERING HERD	1933	PAR	59
(aka BUFFALO STAMPEDE; IN THE DAYS OF THE THUNDERING HERD)			
LONE COWBOY	1933	PAR	68
THE LAST ROUND-UP	1934	PAR	65
WAGON WHEELS (aka CARAVANS WEST)	1934	PAR	57
HOME ON THE RANGE	1934	PAR	55-65
ROCKY MOUNTAIN MYSTERY	1935	PAR	63-68
(aka THE FIGHTING WESTERNER)			
THE LAST OF THE MOHICANS	1936	UA	91
HIGH, WIDE, AND HANDSOME	1937	PAR	110
THE ROAD TO RENO	1938	UNI	69
THE TEXANS	1938	PAR	90-92

JESSE JAMES (s)	(C) .. 1939	... 20T	 106
SUSANNAH OF THE MOUNTIES	1939	... 20T	 78
FRONTIER MARSHAL	1939	... 20T	 71
VIRGINIA CITY (cs)	1940	... WB	 121
WHEN THE DALTONS RODE	1940	... UNI	 80
WESTERN UNION	(C) .. 1941	... 20T	 94
BELLE STARR	(C) .. 1941	... 20T	 87
THE SPOILERS	1942	... UNI	... 84-87
THE DESPERADOES	(C) .. 1943	... COL	 85
BELLE OF THE YUKON	(C) .. 1944	... RKO	 84
ABILENE TOWN	1946	... UA	 89
BADMAN'S TERRITORY	1946	... RKO	 98
TRAIL STREET	1947	... RKO	 84
GUNFIGHTERS (aka THE ASSASSIN)	(C) .. 1947	... COL	 87
ALBUQUERQUE (aka SILVER CITY)	(C) .. 1948	... PAR	 90
RETURN OF THE BAD MEN	1948	... RKO	 96
CORONER CREEK	(C) .. 1948	... COL	 90
THE WALKING HILLS	1949	... COL	 78
CANADIAN PACIFIC	(C) .. 1949	... 20T	 94
THE DOOLINS OF OKLAHOMA (aka THE GREAT MANHUNT)	1949	... COL	 90
FIGHTING MAN OF THE PLAINS	(C) .. 1949	... 20T	 95
THE NEVADAN (aka THE MAN FROM NEVADA)	(C) .. 1950	... COL	 81
COLT .45 (aka THUNDERCLOUD)	(C) .. 1950	... WB	 74
THE CARIBOO TRAIL	(C) .. 1950	... 20T	 81
SUGARFOOT (aka SWIRL OF GLORY)	(C) .. 1951	... WB	 80
SANTA FE	(C) .. 1951	... COL	 89
FORT WORTH	(C) .. 1951	... WB	... 87-88
MAN IN THE SADDLE (aka THE OUTCAST)	(C) .. 1951	... COL	 87
CARSON CITY	(C) .. 1952	... WB	 87
HANGMAN'S KNOT	(C) .. 1952	... COL	 84
THE MAN BEHIND THE GUN	(C) .. 1953	... WB	 83
THE STRANGER WORE A GUN	(C) .. 1953	... COL	 83
THUNDER OVER THE PLAINS	(C) .. 1953	... WB	 82
RIDING SHOTGUN	(C) .. 1954	... WB	 75
THE BOUNTY HUNTER	(C) .. 1954	... WB	 79
TEN WANTED MEN	(C) .. 1955	... COL	 80
RAGE AT DAWN (aka SEVEN BAD MEN)	(C) .. 1955	... RKO	 87
TALL MAN RIDING	(C) .. 1955	... WB	 83
A LAWLESS STREET	(C) .. 1955	... COL	 78
SEVEN MEN FROM NOW	(C) .. 1956	... WB	 78
7TH CAVALRY	(C) .. 1956	... COL	 75
THE TALL T	(C) .. 1957	... COL	 78
SHOOT-OUT AT MEDICINE BEND	(C) .. 1957	... WB	 87
DECISION AT SUNDOWN	(C) .. 1957	... COL	 77
BUCHANAN RIDES ALONE	(C) .. 1958	... COL	 78
RIDE LONESOME	(C) .. 1959	... COL	... 73-75
WESTBOUND	(C) .. 1959	... WB	 72
COMANCHE STATION	(C) .. 1960	... COL	 74
RIDE THE HIGH COUNTRY (aka GUNS IN THE AFTERNOON)	(C) .. 1962	... MGM	 94

FRANK SINATRA (1915 -   )
Famous singer and dramatic actor whose western films have mostly been spoofs.
Good in 4 FOR TEXAS and DIRTY DINGUS MAGEE.

THE KISSING BANDIT	(C).. 1948 ... MGM	102	
SUDDENLY	1954 ... UA	77	
MEET ME IN LAS VEGAS	(C).. 1956 ... MGM	112	
(aka VIVA LAS VEGAS) (gs)			
JOHNNY CONCHO	1956 ... UA	84-85	
PEPE (gs)	(C).. 1960 ... COL	195	
SERGEANTS 3	(C).. 1962 ... UA	112	
4 FOR TEXAS	(C).. 1963 ... WB	124	
DIRTY DINGUS MAGEE	(C).. 1970 ... MGM	79-90	

ROBERT STACK (1919 -   )
Versatile leading man who is best known for his "The Untouchables" television series on ABC (1959-63) as Elliott Ness in the 60-minute episodes. Stack reprised the Ness role in a 1991 two-hour TV movie.

BADLANDS OF DAKOTA	1941 ... UNI	74	
MEN OF TEXAS (aka MEN OF DESTINY)	1941 ... UNI	71-78	
MY OUTLAW BROTHER	1951 ... EL	82	
(aka MY BROTHER, THE OUTLAW) (s)			
BULLFIGHTER AND THE LADY	1951 ... REP	87-124	
WAR PAINT	(C).. 1953 ... UA	89-90	
CONQUEST OF COCHISE	(C).. 1953 ... COL	70	
GREAT DAY IN THE MORNING	(C).. 1956 ... RKO	92	

BARBARA STANWYCK (1907 - 1990)
Excellent actress whose versatility in films was truly amazing throughout a long career. Usually played a tough gal in westerns. Best remembered in the genre for RKO's ANNIE OAKLEY and her superb role with Republic's THE MAVERICK QUEEN. Stanwyck gained equal distinction on TV as the stubborn matriarch in "The Big Valley" on ABC (1965-69) during 112 hour-long segments.

MEXICALI ROSE (aka THE GIRL FROM MEXICO)	1929 ... COL	63	
ANNIE OAKLEY	1935 ... RKO	90	
A MESSAGE TO GARCIA	1936 ... 20T	77-85	
BANJO ON MY KNEE	1936 ... 20T	96	
UNION PACIFIC	1939 ... PAR	125-135	
THE GREAT MAN'S LADY	1942 ... PAR	90	
CALIFORNIA	(C).. 1947 ... PAR	98	
THE LADY GAMBLES	1949 ... UI	99	
THE FURIES	1950 ... PAR	109	
THE MOONLIGHTER	1953 ... WB	75-77	
BLOWING WILD	1953 ... WB	90	
CATTLE QUEEN OF MONTANA	(C).. 1954 ... RKO	88	
THE VIOLENT MEN (aka ROUGH COMPANY)	(C).. 1955 ... COL	96	
THE MAVERICK QUEEN	(C).. 1956 ... REP	90-92	
TROOPER HOOK	1957 ... UA	81	
FORTY GUNS (aka WOMAN WITH A WHIP)	1957 ... 20T	79-80	

CHARLES STARRETT (1903 - 1986)
He mainlined 131 "B" westerns for Columbia Pictures (1935-52), more than any other sound-era saddle star. Great with TWO-FISTED SHERIFF and THE OLD WYOMING TRAIL. Toughed it out during rugged slugfests when pummeling villainous Columbia hulk Dick Curtis. Starrett devoted the last seven years of his studio contract to filming 64 gun-blazing oaters in *The Durango Kid* series. Charles was a Top Money-Making Western Star (1937-42, 1944-52).

GALLANT DEFENDER	1935	COL	57-60
UNDERCOVER MEN	1935	BDP	60
THE MYSTERIOUS AVENGER	1936	COL	55
SECRET PATROL	1936	COL	55-60
STAMPEDE	1936	COL	56-58
CODE OF THE RANGE	1936	COL	55
THE COWBOY STAR	1936	COL	56
DODGE CITY TRAIL	1937	COL	64-72
WESTBOUND MAIL	1937	COL	54
TRAPPED	1937	COL	55
TWO-GUN LAW	1937	COL	56
TWO-FISTED SHERIFF	1937	COL	59
ONE MAN JUSTICE	1937	COL	59
THE OLD WYOMING TRAIL	1937	COL	56
OUTLAWS OF THE PRAIRIE	1937	COL	56-59
CATTLE RAIDERS	1938	COL	61
CALL OF THE ROCKIES	1938	COL	54
LAW OF THE PLAINS	1938	COL	56-58
WEST OF CHEYENNE	1938	COL	56-59
SOUTH OF ARIZONA	1938	COL	56
THE COLORADO TRAIL	1938	COL	55
WEST OF THE SANTA FE	1938	COL	57
RIO GRANDE (aka RIO GRANDE STAMPEDE)	1938	COL	59
THE THUNDERING WEST	1939	COL	57
TEXAS STAMPEDE	1939	COL	57
NORTH OF THE YUKON	1939	COL	64
SPOILERS OF THE RANGE	1939	COL	58
WESTERN CARAVANS	1939	COL	58
THE MAN FROM SUNDOWN (aka A WOMAN'S VENGEANCE)	1939	COL	59
RIDERS OF BLACK RIVER	1939	COL	59
OUTPOST OF THE MOUNTIES (aka ON GUARD)	1939	COL	63
THE STRANGER FROM TEXAS (aka THE STRANGER)	1939	COL	54
TWO-FISTED RANGERS	1940	COL	62
BULLETS FOR RUSTLERS (aka ON SPECIAL DUTY)	1940	COL	58
BLAZING SIX SHOOTERS (aka STOLEN WEALTH)	1940	COL	61-63
TEXAS STAGECOACH (aka TWO ROADS)	1940	COL	59
THE DURANGO KID (aka MASKED STRANGER)	1940	COL	61
WEST OF ABILENE (aka THE SHOWDOWN)	1940	COL	57
THUNDERING FRONTIER	1940	COL	57
THE PINTO KID (aka ALL SQUARE)	1941	COL	61
OUTLAWS OF THE PANHANDLE (aka FARO JACK)	1941	COL	59-63
THE MEDICO OF PAINTED SPRINGS (aka DOCTOR'S ALIBI) (starts *Doctor Monroe* series)	1941	COL	59
THUNDER OVER THE PRAIRIE	1941	COL	60
PRAIRIE STRANGER (aka MARKED BULLET) (ends *Doctor Monroe* series)	1941	COL	58

CHARLES STARRETT, continued

THE ROYAL MOUNTED PATROL	1941	COL	59
(aka GIANTS A'FIRE)			
RIDERS OF THE BADLANDS	1941	COL	57
WEST OF TOMBSTONE	1942	COL	59
LAWLESS PLAINSMEN (aka ROLL ON)	1942	COL	59
DOWN RIO GRANDE WAY	1942	COL	57
(aka THE DOUBLE PUNCH)			
RIDERS OF THE NORTHLAND (aka NEXT IN LINE)	1942	COL	58
BAD MEN OF THE HILLS	1942	COL	58
(aka WRONGLY ACCUSED)			
OVERLAND TO DEADWOOD	1942	COL	58
(aka FALLING STONES)			
RIDING THROUGH NEVADA	1942	COL	61
PARDON MY GUN	1942	COL	57
THE FIGHTING BUCKAROO	1943	COL	58
LAW OF THE NORTHWEST	1943	COL	57-59
FRONTIER FURY	1943	COL	55
ROBIN HOOD OF THE RANGE	1943	COL	57
HAIL TO THE RANGERS (aka ILLEGAL RIGHTS)	1943	COL	57
COWBOY IN THE CLOUDS	1943	COL	55
COWBOY CANTEEN (aka CLOSE HARMONY)	1944	COL	72
SUNDOWN VALLEY	1944	COL	55
RIDING WEST (aka FUGITIVE FROM TIME)	1944	COL	58
COWBOY FROM LONESOME RIVER	1944	COL	55
(aka SIGNED JUDGEMENT)			
CYCLONE PRAIRIE RANGERS	1944	COL	56
SADDLE LEATHER LAW (aka THE POISONER)	1944	COL	55
SAGEBRUSH HEROES	1945	COL	54
ROUGH RIDIN' JUSTICE (aka DECOY)	1945	COL	58
THE RETURN OF THE DURANGO KID	1945	COL	58
(aka STOLEN TIME) (starts *The Durango Kid* series)			
BOTH BARRELS BLAZING	1945	COL	58
(aka THE YELLOW STREAK)			
RUSTLERS OF THE BADLANDS	1945	COL	55-58
(aka BY WHOSE HAND?)			
OUTLAWS OF THE ROCKIES	1945	COL	55
(aka A ROVING ROGUE)			
BLAZING THE WESTERN TRAIL	1945	COL	60
(aka WHO KILLED WARING?)			
LAWLESS EMPIRE (aka POWER OF POSSESSION)	1945	COL	59
TEXAS PANHANDLE	1945	COL	55-57
FRONTIER GUN LAW (aka MENACING SHADOWS)	1946	COL	60
ROARING RANGERS (aka FALSE HERO)	1946	COL	56
GUNNING FOR VENGEANCE (aka JAIL BREAK)	1946	COL	53-56
GALLOPING THUNDER (aka ON BOOT HILL)	1946	COL	54
TWO-FISTED STRANGER (aka HIGH STAKES)	1946	COL	50
THE DESERT HORSEMAN (aka CHECKMATE)	1946	COL	57
HEADING WEST (aka THE CHEAT'S LAST THROW)	1946	COL	54-56
LANDRUSH (aka THE CLAW STRIKES)	1946	COL	54
TERROR TRAIL (aka HANDS OF MENACE)	1946	COL	55
THE FIGHTING FRONTIERSMAN	1946	COL	61
(aka GOLDEN LADY)			
SOUTH OF THE CHISHOLM TRAIL	1947	COL	58
THE LONE HAND TEXAN (aka THE CHEAT)	1947	COL	54
WEST OF DODGE CITY (aka THE SEA WALL)	1947	COL	57
LAW OF THE CANYON (aka THE PRICE OF CRIME)	1947	COL	55

CHARLES STARRETT, continued /177

PRAIRIE RAIDERS (aka THE FORGER) .... 1947 ... COL .... 54 ____
THE STRANGER FROM PONCA CITY .... 1947 ... COL .... 56 ____
RIDERS OF THE LONE STAR .... 1947 ... COL .... 55 ____
BUCKAROO FROM POWDER RIVER .... 1947 ... COL .... 55 ____
LAST DAYS OF BOOT HILL .... 1947 ... COL .... 56 ____
SIX-GUN LAW .... 1948 ... COL .... 54 ____
PHANTOM VALLEY .... 1948 ... COL .... 53 ____
WEST OF SONORA .... 1948 ... COL ..... 52-55 ____
WHIRLWIND RAIDERS (aka STATE POLICE) .... 1948 ... COL .... 54 ____
BLAZING ACROSS THE PECOS .... 1948 ... COL .... 55 ____
TRAIL TO LAREDO (aka SIGN OF THE DAGGER)... 1948 ... COL .... 54 ____
EL DORADO PASS (aka DESPERATE MEN) .... 1948 ... COL .... 56 ____
QUICK ON THE TRIGGER .... 1948 ... COL .... 55 ____
   (aka CONDEMNED IN ERROR)
CHALLENGE OF THE RANGE .... 1949 ... COL .... 56 ____
   (aka MOONLIGHT RAID)
DESERT VIGILANTE .... 1949 ... COL .... 56 ____
LARAMIE .... 1949 ... COL .... 55 ____
THE BLAZING TRAIL (aka THE FORGED WILL) .... 1949 ... COL .... 56 ____
SOUTH OF DEATH VALLEY (aka RIVER OF POISON) 1949 ... COL .... 54 ____
HORSEMEN OF THE SIERRAS .... 1949 ... COL .... 56 ____
   (aka REMEMBER ME)
BANDITS OF EL DORADO (aka TRICKED) .... 1949 ... COL .... 56 ____
RENEGADES OF THE SAGE (aka THE FORT) .... 1949 ... COL .... 56 ____
TRAIL OF THE RUSTLERS (aka LOST RIVER) .... 1950 ... COL .... 55 ____
OUTCAST OF BLACK MESA (aka THE CLUE) .... 1950 ... COL .... 54 ____
TEXAS DYNAMO (aka SUSPECTED) .... 1950 ... COL .... 54 ____
STREETS OF GHOST TOWN .... 1950 ... COL .... 54 ____
ACROSS THE BADLANDS (aka THE CHALLENGE) 1950 ... COL .... 54 ____
RAIDERS OF TOMAHAWK CREEK .... 1950 ... COL .... 55 ____
   (aka CIRCLE OF FEAR)
LIGHTNING GUNS (aka TAKING SIDES) .... 1950 ... COL .... 55 ____
FRONTIER OUTPOST .... 1950 ... COL .... 55 ____
PRAIRIE ROUNDUP .... 1951 ... COL ..... 53-55 ____
RIDIN' THE OUTLAW TRAIL .... 1951 ... COL .... 54 ____
FORT SAVAGE RAIDERS .... 1951 ... COL .... 55 ____
SNAKE RIVER DESPERADOES .... 1951 ... COL .... 55 ____
BONANZA TOWN (aka TWO-FISTED AGENT) .... 1951 ... COL ..... 50-56 ____
CYCLONE FURY .... 1951 ... COL .... 54 ____
THE KID FROM AMARILLO (aka SILVER CHAINS).. 1951 ... COL .... 56 ____
PECOS RIVER (aka WITHOUT RISK) .... 1951 ... COL .... 55 ____
SMOKY CANYON .... 1952 ... COL .... 55 ____
THE HAWK OF WILD RIVER .... 1952 ... COL .... 54 ____
LARAMIE MOUNTAINS .... 1952 ... COL .... 53 ____
   (aka MOUNTAIN DESPERADOES)
THE ROUGH, TOUGH WEST .... 1952 ... COL .... 54 ____
JUNCTION CITY .... 1952 ... COL .... 54 ____
THE KID FROM BROKEN GUN .... 1952 ... COL .... 56 ____
   (ends *The Durango Kid* series)

BOB STEELE (1907 - 1988)

The best fisticuffs star for 20 years' worth of "B" oaters (1926-46) at small studios with his lightning-swift punches, especially when it came to decking pudgy bad guys Charles King and Frank Ellis, Steele was also quick on the draw and a daredevil saddler. A Top Money-Making Western Star (1937-38), he elevated popularity of both *The Three Mesquiteers* (1940-43) and *The Trail Blazers* (1943-44) series. In later years, Bob did selective "A" support parts where he perfected the routine of a slow-dying gunfighter losing in a shootout such as THE SAVAGE HORDE. His last name was misspelled as "Steel" in THE PARSON AND THE OUTLAW. He was Duffy on the "F Troop" ABC-TV show (1965-67).

Title	Year	Studio	Pages
THE INVADERS	1929	SYN	62
THE COWBOY AND THE OUTLAW	1929	SYN	48
A TEXAS COWBOY	1929	SYN	50
BREEZY BILL	1930	SYN	46
HUNTED MEN	1930	SYN	48
MAN FROM NOWHERE	1930	SYN	49
NEAR THE RAINBOW'S END	1930	TIF	57
THE OKLAHOMA SHERIFF	1930	SYN	49
THE OKLAHOMA CYCLONE	1930	TIF	66
LAND OF MISSING MEN (aka AT THE RIDGE)	1930	TIF	58
HEADIN' NORTH	1930	TIF	59
THE SUNRISE TRAIL	1931	TIF	65-67
THE RIDIN' FOOL	1931	TIF	58-64
THE NEVADA BUCKAROO	1931	TIF	59-64
NEAR THE TRAIL'S END	1931	TIF	55
SOUTH OF SANTA FE	1932	WW	61
LAW OF THE WEST	1932	WW	58
RIDERS OF THE DESERT	1932	WW	59
SON OF OKLAHOMA (aka THE COWBOY)	1932	WW	55
THE MAN FROM HELL'S EDGES	1932	WW	61
TEXAS BUDDIES	1932	WW	59
HIDDEN VALLEY	1932	MON	60
YOUNG BLOOD	1932	MON	59
THE FIGHTING CHAMP	1932	MON	59
TRAILING NORTH	1933	MON	60
BREED OF THE BORDER (aka SPEED BRENT WINS)	1933	MON	58-60
THE GALLANT FOOL	1933	MON	60
GALLOPING ROMEO	1933	MON	60
RANGER'S CODE	1933	MON	56-59
THE MYSTERY SQUADRON (SER)	1933	MAS	12CH
A DEMON FOR TROUBLE	1935	COM	58
BRAND OF HATE	1935	COM	63
THE BIG CALIBRE	1935	COM	65
TOMBSTONE TERROR	1935	COM	58-63
WESTERN JUSTICE	1935	COM	65
KID COURAGEOUS	1935	COM	63
NO MAN'S RANGE (aka NO MAN'S LAND)	1935	COM	56
SMOKY SMITH	1935	COM	57-63
POWDERSMOKE RANGE (cs)	1935	RKO	71
THE RIDER OF THE LAW	1935	COM	66
ALIAS JOHN LAW	1935	SUP	59
TRAIL OF TERROR	1935	SUP	59
THE KID RANGER	1936	SUP	57
SUNDOWN SAUNDERS	1936	SUP	60
LAST OF THE WARRENS	1936	SUP	58-60

BOB STEELE, continued / 179

Title	Year	Studio	Pages
THE LAW RIDES	1936	SUP	57
BRAND OF THE OUTLAW	1936	SUP	60
CAVALRY	1936	REP	60-63
THE GUN RANGER	1936	REP	49-57
BORDER PHANTOM	1936	REP	58
THE TRUSTED OUTLAW	1937	REP	52-57
"LIGHTNIN'" CRANDALL	1937	REP	60
GUN LORDS OF STIRRUP BASIN	1937	REP	53
DOOMED AT SUNDOWN	1937	REP	53
THE RED ROPE	1937	REP	56
THE ARIZONA GUNFIGHTER	1937	REP	56-58
RIDIN' THE LONE TRAIL	1937	REP	56
THE COLORADO KID	1937	REP	55
PAROLED—TO DIE	1938	REP	55
THUNDER IN THE DESERT	1938	REP	56
THE FEUD MAKER	1938	REP	55
DESERT PATROL	1938	REP	56
DURANGO VALLEY RAIDERS	1938	REP	55
FEUD OF THE RANGE	1939	MET	56
SMOKY TRAILS	1939	MET	57
MESQUITE BUCKAROO	1939	MET	55
RIDERS OF THE SAGE	1939	MET	57
THE PAL FROM TEXAS	1939	MET	56
EL DIABLO RIDES	1939	MET	57
OF MICE AND MEN (s)	1940	UA	107
WILD HORSE VALLEY	1940	MET	57
PINTO CANYON	1940	MET	55
THE CARSON CITY KID (s)	1940	REP	57
BILLY THE KID OUTLAWED	1940	PRC	52-60

(starts *Billy the Kid* series for PRC and *The Three Mesquiteers* series for Republic; both sets of westerns were lensed simultaneously)

Title	Year	Studio	Pages
BILLY THE KID IN TEXAS	1940	PRC	52-63
UNDER TEXAS SKIES	1940	REP	57
THE TRAIL BLAZERS	1940	REP	58
LONE STAR RAIDERS	1940	REP	57
BILLY THE KID'S GUN JUSTICE	1940	PRC	57-63
BILLY THE KID'S RANGE WAR	1941	PRC	57-60
PRAIRIE PIONEERS	1941	REP	58
THE GREAT TRAIN ROBBERY (non-series)	1941	REP	61
PALS OF THE PECOS	1941	REP	56
BILLY THE KID'S FIGHTING PALS	1941	PRC	62
SADDLEMATES	1941	REP	56
GANGS OF SONORA	1941	REP	58
BILLY THE KID IN SANTA FE	1941	PRC	66
OUTLAWS OF CHEROKEE TRAIL	1941	REP	56

(resumes only *The Three Mesquiteers* series)

Title	Year	Studio	Pages
GAUCHOS OF ELDORADO	1941	REP	56
WEST OF CIMARRON	1941	REP	56
CODE OF THE OUTLAW	1942	REP	57
RAIDERS OF THE RANGE	1942	REP	55
WESTWARD HO	1942	REP	56
THE PHANTOM PLAINSMEN	1942	REP	56
SHADOWS ON THE SAGE	1942	REP	57
VALLEY OF HUNTED MEN	1942	REP	60
THUNDERING TRAILS	1943	REP	56
THE BLOCKED TRAIL	1943	REP	55-58

BOB STEELE, continued

Title	Year	Studio	Pages
SANTA FE SCOUTS	1943	REP	55-57
RIDERS OF THE RIO GRANDE	1943	REP	55
(ends *The Three Mesquiteers* series)			
DEATH VALLEY RANGERS	1943	MON	55-59
(starts *The Trail Blazers* series)			
WESTWARD BOUND	1944	MON	54-59
ARIZONA WHIRLWIND	1944	MON	59
OUTLAW TRAIL	1944	MON	53-55
SONORA STAGECOACH	1944	MON	60
(ends *The Trail Blazers* series)			
MARKED TRAILS	1944	MON	59
THE UTAH KID	1944	MON	55-57
TRIGGER LAW	1944	MON	56
WILDFIRE (C)	1945	SG	57-60
(aka WILDFIRE: THE STORY OF A HORSE)			
NORTHWEST TRAIL (C)	1945	SG	64
NAVAJO KID	1945	PRC	59
SIX-GUN MAN	1946	PRC	57-59
AMBUSH TRAIL	1946	PRC	60
THUNDER TOWN	1946	PRC	57
SHERIFF OF REDWOOD VALLEY (cs)	1946	REP	54
RIO GRANDE RAIDERS (cs)	1946	REP	57
TWILIGHT ON THE RIO GRANDE (s)	1947	REP	71
CHEYENNE (aka THE WYOMING KID) (s)	1947	WB	100
BANDITS OF DARK CANYON (cs)	1947	REP	59
SOUTH OF ST. LOUIS (s) (C)	1949	WB	88
THE SAVAGE HORDE (s)	1950	REP	90
SILVER CANYON (s)	1951	COL	70
FORT WORTH (s) (C)	1951	WB	80
CATTLE DRIVE (s) (C)	1951	UI	77
BUGLES IN THE AFTERNOON (s) (C)	1952	WB	85
ROSE OF CIMARRON (s) (C)	1952	20T	72
THE LION AND THE HORSE (cs) (C)	1952	WB	83
SAN ANTONE (s)	1953	REP	90
SAVAGE FRONTIER (cs)	1953	REP	54
COLUMN SOUTH (s) (C)	1953	UI	84
DRUMS ACROSS THE RIVER (s) (C)	1954	UI	78
THE OUTCAST (s) (C)	1954	REP	90
LAST OF THE DESPERADOS (s)	1955	ASC	71-78
THE SPOILERS (s) (C)	1956	UI	84
PARDNERS (s) (C)	1956	PAR	85-88
DUEL AT APACHE WELLS (s)	1957	REP	70
GUN FOR A COWARD (s) (C)	1957	UI	88
BAND OF ANGELS (s) (C)	1957	WB	127
THE PARSON AND THE OUTLAW (s) (C)	1957	COL	71
DECISION AT SUNDOWN (s) (C)	1957	COL	77
ONCE UPON A HORSE (aka HOT HORSE) (gs)	1958	UI	85
GIANT FROM THE UNKNOWN (s)	1958	AST	76
RIO BRAVO (s) (C)	1959	WB	141
HELL BENT FOR LEATHER (s) (C)	1960	UI	82
THE COMANCHEROS (s) (C)	1961	20T	107
THE WILD WESTERNERS (s) (C)	1962	COL	70
SIX BLACK HORSES (s) (C)	1962	UI	80
McLINTOCK! (s) (C)	1963	UA	127

BOB STEELE, continued / 181

Title		Year	Studio	Min
4 FOR TEXAS (s)	(C)	1963	WB	124
BULLET FOR A BADMAN (s)	(C)	1964	UNI	80
TAGGART (s)	(C)	1964	UNI	85
SHENANDOAH (s)	(C)	1965	UNI	105
THE BOUNTY KILLER (s)	(C)	1965	EMB	92
REQUIEM FOR A GUNFIGHTER (s)	(C)	1965	EMB	91
TOWN TAMER (s)	(C)	1965	PAR	89
HANG 'EM HIGH (s)	(C)	1968	UA	114
THE GREAT BANK ROBBERY (s)	(C)	1969	WB	98
RIO LOBO (s)	(C)	1970	NG	114
SKIN GAME (s)	(C)	1971	WB	102
SOMETHING BIG (s)	(C)	1971	NG	108
CHARLEY VARRICK (s)	(C)	1973	UNI	111

ANTHONY STEFFEN (1932 -   )

Leading man in European westerns. A Rome-based citizen and active as producer, scriptwriter.

Title		Year	Studio	Min
WHY KILL AGAIN? (aka STOP THE SLAYINGS)	(C)	1965	BAL	92
FEW DOLLARS FOR GYPSY (DJANGO)	(C)	1967	TLU	87
NO ROOM TO DIE	(C)	1969	JF	88
THE STRANGER'S GUNDOWN	(C)	1974	NLC	107

MARK STEVENS (1915 -   )

Leading man whose best-known role was as the killer, JACK SLADE.

Title		Year	Studio	Min
SAND (aka WILL JAMES' SAND)	(C)	1949	20T	77-78
JACK SLADE (aka SLADE)		1953	AA	90
GUNSIGHT RIDGE		1957	UA	85
GUN FEVER		1958	UA	81
GUNSMOKE IN TUCSON	(C)	1958	AA	79
SUNSCORCHED	(C)	1966	FFC	77

JAMES STEWART (1908 -   )

One of the great film actors of all time whose versatility in roles is unmatched. From early roles as a villain to comic and dramatic roles later, he began to make westerns in the 1950s. Among his many fine western films is the classic WINCHESTER '73, and the superb features THE NAKED SPUR, THE MAN FROM LARAMIE, and THE MAN WHO SHOT LIBERTY VALANCE.

Title		Year	Studio	Min
ROSE MARIE (aka INDIAN LOVE CALL) (s)		1936	MGM	110
OF HUMAN HEARTS		1938	MGM	100
DESTRY RIDES AGAIN		1939	UNI	94
YOU GOTTA STAY HAPPY		1948	UI	100
WINCHESTER '73		1950	UI	92
BROKEN ARROW	(C)	1950	20T	93
BEND OF THE RIVER (aka WHERE THE RIVER BENDS)	(C)	1952	UI	91
THE NAKED SPUR	(C)	1953	MGM	91

182 / JAMES STEWART, continued

THE FAR COUNTRY	(C)	1955	UI	97
THE MAN FROM LARAMIE	(C)	1955	COL	104
NIGHT PASSAGE	(C)	1957	UI	90
THE FBI STORY	(C)	1959	WB	149
TWO RODE TOGETHER	(C)	1961	COL	91-109
THE MAN WHO SHOT LIBERTY VALANCE		1962	PAR	119-123
HOW THE WEST WAS WON	(C)	1963	MGM	155-165
CHEYENNE AUTUMN	(C)	1964	WB	145-160
SHENANDOAH	(C)	1965	UNI	105
THE RARE BREED	(C)	1966	UNI	97-108
FIRECREEK	(C)	1968	WB	104
BANDOLERO!	(C)	1968	20T	106
THE CHEYENNE SOCIAL CLUB	(C)	1970	NG	103
FOOLS' PARADE	(C)	1971	COL	97
(aka DYNAMITE MAN FROM GLORY JAIL)				
THE SHOOTIST (gs)	(C)	1976	PAR	99-100
AN AMERICAN TAIL FIEVEL GOES WEST (vo)(C)		1991	UNI	75
(animated)				

BARRY SULLIVAN (1912 -   )

Reserved leading man who usually played cool, assured roles in westerns. Sullivan mainlined NBC-TV's "The Tall Men" for 75 half-hour shows (1960-62) and the same network's "The Road West" (1966-67). This hour-long show produced 26 episodes.

THE WOMAN OF THE TOWN (cs)		1943	UA	88-90
BAD MEN OF TOMBSTONE		1949	AA	74-75
THE OUTRIDERS (cs)	(C)	1950	MGM	93
INSIDE STRAIGHT (cs)		1951	MGM	89
TEXAS LADY	(C)	1955	RKO	86
THE MAVERICK QUEEN	(C)	1956	REP	90-92
DRAGOON WELLS MASSACRE	(C)	1957	AA	88
THE WAY TO THE GOLD (cs)		1957	20T	94
FORTY GUNS (aka WOMAN WITH A WHIP)		1957	20T	79-80
SEVEN WAYS FROM SUNDOWN	(C)	1960	UI	87
STAGE TO THUNDER ROCK	(C)	1964	PAR	82
(aka STAGECOACH TO HELL)				
BUCKSKIN (aka THE FRONTIERSMAN)	(C)	1968	PAR	97
THIS SAVAGE LAND (aka THE ROAD WEST)	(C)	1969	UNI	98
TELL THEM WILLIE BOY IS HERE (s)	(C)	1970	UNI	96
YUMA	(C)	1971	ABC-TV	73
PAT GARRETT AND BILLY THE KID (s)	(C)	1973	MGM	106-122
TAKE A HARD RIDE (s)	(C)	1975	20T	109
CARAVANS (s)	(C)	1978	UNI	123
THE IMMIGRANTS	(C)	1978	OPT-TV	200
THE BASTARD (s)	(C)	1978	UNI-TV	200

KENT TAYLOR (1907 - 1987)

Suave leading man of second features, better known for his non-western films. He starred in "The Rough Riders" ABC-TV series (1958-59) for 39 half-hour segments.

THE MYSTERIOUS RIDER		1933	PAR	61
(aka THE FIGHTING PHANTOM; BADMEN OF NEVADA)				
UNDER THE TONTO RIM (s)		1933	PAR	59
SUNSET PASS (s)		1933	PAR	65
RAMONA (cs)	(C)	1936	20T	90

KENT TAYLOR, continued / 183

FRISCO LIL	1942	UNI	60
TOMBSTONE, THE TOWN TOO TOUGH TO DIE	1942	PAR	79
ALASKA	1944	MON	76
THE DALTONS RIDE AGAIN	1945	UNI	71
WESTERN PACIFIC AGENT	1950	LIP	64-65
GHOST TOWN	1956	UA	75
FRONTIER GAMBLER (cs)	1956	ARC	70
THE IRON SHERIFF (s)	1957	UA	73
FORT BOWIE (cs)	1958	UA	80
WALK TALL (cs) (C)	1960	20T	60
THE PURPLE HILLS (cs) (C)	1961	20T	60
THE BROKEN LAND (C)	1962	20T	60
(aka VANISHING FRONTIER)			
THE FIREBRAND	1962	20T	63
LAW OF THE LAWLESS (s) (C)	1964	PAR	88
(aka INVITATION TO A HANGING)			
FORT COURAGEOUS (s)	1965	20T	72

ROBERT TAYLOR (1911 - 1969)

Handsome leading man who turned to "A" western roles late in his long film career. Best known in MGM westerns for his rather unusual portrayal of BILLY THE KID. Taylor was aggravated by Eleanor Parker's wiles for the frontier comedy MANY RIVERS TO CROSS. He was a 1960s host on TV's "Death Valley Days."

STAND UP AND FIGHT	1939	MGM	97
BILLY THE KID (C)	1941	MGM	95
AMBUSH	1950	MGM	89
DEVIL'S DOORWAY	1950	MGM	84
WESTWARD THE WOMEN	1952	MGM	112-118
RIDE, VAQUERO! (C)	1953	MGM	90
MANY RIVERS TO CROSS (C)	1955	MGM	92
THE LAST HUNT (C)	1956	MGM	108
SADDLE THE WIND (C)	1958	MGM	84
THE LAW AND JAKE WADE (C)	1958	MGM	86
THE HANGMAN	1959	PAR	86
CATTLE KING (aka GUNS OF WYOMING) (C)	1963	MGM	88
JOHNNY TIGER (C)	1966	UNI	100-102
RETURN OF THE GUNFIGHTER (aka WYATT) (C)	1967	MGM-TV	100
SAVAGE PAMPAS (C)	1967	COT	97
HONDO AND THE APACHES (s) (C)	1967	MGM	85

ROD TAYLOR (1930 -   )

An Australian native who has contributed to adventure-oriented sagas including a number of movie and television western features. Taylor mainlined "The Oregon Trail," a 60-minute NBC-TV show (1977-78) for six episodes.

TOP GUN (s)	1955	UA	73
GIANT (s) (C)	1956	WB	201
RAINTREE COUNTY (s) (C)	1957	MGM	168
CHUKA (C)	1967	PAR	105
POWDERKEG (C)	1971	FW-TV	100
THE TRAIN ROBBERS (cs) (C)	1973	WB	92
THE DEADLY TRACKERS (C)	1973	WB	110
THE OREGON TRAIL (C)	1977	UNI-TV	100
OUTLAWS (C)	1986	UNI-TV	100

THE TEXAS RANGERS series (1942 - 1945)

These low-budgeters involved three lawmen after the usual assortment of frontier crooks. Dave O'Brien, Jim Newill, and Guy Wilkerson headed the first two seasons (1942-44) which were just average storylines, but the last year (1944-45) with Tex Ritter replacing Newill, the oaters greatly increased in quality. Every cast frame of these PRC gallopers with Ritter's name misidentified him as a ranger when, actually, Tex was a lawyer in passing reference. Best "B" feature was THE WHISPERING SKULL.

(DAVE O'BRIEN, JIM NEWILL, GUY WILKERSON)
THE RANGERS TAKE OVER	1942	PRC	60
BAD MEN OF THUNDER GAP	1943	PRC	57
(aka THUNDERGAP OUTLAWS)			
WEST OF TEXAS (aka SHOOTIN' IRONS)	1943	PRC	54
BORDER BUCKAROOS	1943	PRC	59
FIGHTING VALLEY	1943	PRC	59
TRAIL OF TERROR	1943	PRC	63
RETURN OF THE RANGERS	1943	PRC	61
BOSS OF RAWHIDE	1943	PRC	57-59
GUNSMOKE MESA	1944	PRC	59
OUTLAW ROUNDUP	1944	PRC	55
GUNS OF THE LAW	1944	PRC	55-57
THE PINTO BANDIT	1944	PRC	56
SPOOK TOWN	1944	PRC	59
BRAND OF THE DEVIL	1944	PRC	59

(TEX RITTER, DAVE O'BRIEN, GUY WILKERSON)
GANGSTERS OF THE FRONTIER	1944	PRC	56
(aka RAIDERS OF THE FRONTIER)			
DEAD OR ALIVE (aka WANTED BY THE LAW)	1944	PRC	56
THE WHISPERING SKULL	1944	PRC	55
MARKED FOR MURDER	1944	PRC	56
ENEMY OF THE LAW	1945	PRC	59
THREE IN THE SADDLE	1945	PRC	61
FRONTIER FUGITIVES	1945	PRC	58
(aka FUGITIVES OF THE FRONTIER)			
FLAMING BULLETS	1945	PRC	59

THE THREE MESQUITEERS series (1936 - 1943)

After one 1935 outdoor special at RKO Radio, western author William Colt MacDonald's stories of three law-and-order saddlemates got rolling full-speed during 1936 with Republic Pictures and lasted into 1943. Despite infrequent player changes, it was the *only* trio series to make the list of Top Money-Making Western Stars (1937-43). THE RIDERS OF THE WHISTLING SKULL became the top "B" entry.

(HARRY CAREY, HOOT GIBSON, GUINN "BIG BOY" WILLIAMS)
POWDERSMOKE RANGE	1935	RKO	71

(ROBERT LIVINGSTON, RAY CORRIGAN, SYD SAYLOR)
THE THREE MESQUITEERS	1936	REP	56-61

(ROBERT LIVINGSTON, RAY CORRIGAN, MAX TERHUNE)
GHOST-TOWN GOLD	1936	REP	55
ROARIN' LEAD	1936	REP	53

THE THREE MESQUITEERS series, continued

THE RIDERS OF THE WHISTLING SKULL	1937	REP	55
(aka THE GOLDEN TRAIL)			
HIT THE SADDLE	1937	REP	57
GUNSMOKE RANCH	1937	REP	56
COME ON, COWBOYS!	1937	REP	57-59
RANGE DEFENDERS	1937	REP	56
HEART OF THE ROCKIES	1937	REP	56

(RAY CORRIGAN, MAX TERHUNE, RALPH BYRD)

THE TRIGGER TRIO	1937	REP	56-60

(ROBERT LIVINGSTON, RAY CORRIGAN, MAX TERHUNE)

WILD HORSE RODEO	1937	REP	56
THE PURPLE VIGILANTES	1938	REP	58
(aka THE PURPLE RIDERS)			
CALL THE MESQUITEERS	1938	REP	55
(aka OUTLAWS OF THE WEST)			
OUTLAWS OF SONORA	1938	REP	55
RIDERS OF THE BLACK HILLS	1938	REP	55
(aka RIDERS OF BLACK HILLS)			
HEROES OF THE HILLS	1938	REP	56

(JOHN WAYNE, RAY CORRIGAN, MAX TERHUNE)

PALS OF THE SADDLE	1938	REP	55-60
OVERLAND STAGE RAIDERS	1938	REP	55
SANTA FE STAMPEDE	1938	REP	56
RED RIVER RANGE	1938	REP	56
THE NIGHT RIDERS	1939	REP	58
THREE TEXAS STEERS	1939	REP	57
(aka DANGER RIDES THE RANGE)			

(JOHN WAYNE, RAY CORRIGAN, RAYMOND HATTON)

WYOMING OUTLAW	1939	REP	56
NEW FRONTIER (aka FRONTIER HORIZON)	1939	REP	57

(ROBERT LIVINGSTON, DUNCAN RENALDO, RAYMOND HATTON)

THE KANSAS TERRORS	1939	REP	57
COWBOYS FROM TEXAS	1939	REP	57
HEROES OF THE SADDLE	1940	REP	56-59
PIONEERS OF THE WEST	1940	REP	56
COVERED WAGON DAYS	1940	REP	56
ROCKY MOUNTAIN RANGERS	1940	REP	58
OKLAHOMA RENEGADES	1940	REP	57

(ROBERT LIVINGSTON, BOB STEELE, RUFE DAVIS)

UNDER TEXAS SKIES	1940	REP	57
THE TRAIL BLAZERS	1940	REP	58
LONE STAR RAIDERS	1940	REP	57
PRAIRIE PIONEERS	1941	REP	58
PALS OF THE PECOS	1941	REP	56
SADDLEMATES	1941	REP	56
GANGS OF SONORA	1941	REP	56-58

(BOB STEELE, TOM TYLER, RUFE DAVIS)

OUTLAWS OF CHEROKEE TRAIL	1941	REP	56
GAUCHOS OF ELDORADO	1941	REP	56

186 / THE THREE MESQUITEERS series, continued

WEST OF CIMARRON	1941	REP	56
CODE OF THE OUTLAW	1942	REP	57
RAIDERS OF THE RANGE	1942	REP	55
WESTWARD HO	1942	REP	56
THE PHANTOM PLAINSMEN	1942	REP	56

(BOB STEELE, TOM TYLER, JIMMIE DODD)

SHADOWS ON THE SAGE	1942	REP	57
VALLEY OF HUNTED MEN	1942	REP	60
THUNDERING TRAILS	1943	REP	56
THE BLOCKED TRAIL	1943	REP	55-58
SANTA FE SCOUTS	1943	REP	55-57
RIDERS OF THE RIO GRANDE	1943	REP	55

SPENCER TRACY (1900 - 1967)

One of the screen's best actors who rarely made westerns. His best-remembered role in the genre is the one-armed World War II veteran in BAD DAY AT BLACK ROCK.

SAN FRANCISCO (cs)	1936	MGM	115
NORTHWEST PASSAGE	(C) .. 1940	MGM	125-126
BOOM TOWN	1940	MGM	116-120
THE SEA OF GRASS	1947	MGM	131
BROKEN LANCE	(C) .. 1954	20T	96
BAD DAY AT BLACK ROCK	(C) .. 1955	MGM	81
HOW THE WEST WAS WON (nr)	(C) .. 1963	MGM	155-165
IT'S A MAD MAD MAD MAD WORLD	(C) .. 1963	UA	175

THE TRAIL BLAZERS series (1943 - 1944)

One-and-a-half seasons of horse operas were in store only for this hard-riding "B" series with that old but peppy Monogram scoring. Hoot Gibson's "great" ideas always aggravated pal Ken Maynard, but the films were a pleasure to watch. Bob Steele joined up with DEATH VALLEY RANGERS, the top feature. Maynard's line of "Well, here we go again" meant swift corralling of the U.S. marshals' intended prey.

(KEN MAYNARD, HOOT GIBSON, BOB BAKER)

WILD HORSE STAMPEDE	1943	MON	59

(KEN MAYNARD, HOOT GIBSON)

THE LAW RIDES AGAIN	1943	MON	58
BLAZING GUNS	1943	MON	55

(KEN MAYNARD, HOOT GIBSON, BOB STEELE)

DEATH VALLEY RANGERS	1943	MON	55-59
WESTWARD BOUND	1944	MON	54-59
ARIZONA WHIRLWIND	1944	MON	59

(HOOT GIBSON, BOB STEELE, CHIEF THUNDER CLOUD, ROCKY CAMRON)

OUTLAW TRAIL	1944	MON	53-55
SONORA STAGECOACH	1944	MON	60

TOM TRYON (1926 - 1991)

Actor-writer whose western films were few, but made some prominence with the "Tales of Texas John Slaughter" hour-long TV episodes—16 in all—for Disney (1958-59). Tryon performed well for WINCHESTER '73.

THREE VIOLENT PEOPLE (s)	(C)	1957	PAR	100
WILD TIMES		1962	BV	77
GUNFIGHT AT SANDOVAL		1963	BV	74
(aka GUNDOWN AT SANDOVAL)				
GERONIMO'S REVENGE		1965	BV	61
THE GLORY GUYS	(C)	1965	UA	112
STAMPEDE AT BITTER CREEK		1966	BV	81
WINCHESTER '73	(C)	1967	UNI-TV	97

FORREST TUCKER (1915 - 1986)

Tall, rugged actor who often played villains early in his film career. By 1950, Tucker had risen to leading man status at Republic Pictures with ROCK ISLAND TRAIL and CALIFORNIA PASSAGE. He enjoyed popularity when in charge of the "F Troop" 30-minute shows on ABC-TV (1965-67) for 65 segments. Forrest and John Wayne did battle with each other effectively in CHISUM.

THE WESTERNER (s)		1940	UA	94-100
THE HOWARDS OF VIRGINIA		1940	COL	122
(aka TREE OF LIBERTY) (s)				
SHUT MY BIG MOUTH (s)		1942	COL	71
RENEGADES (s)	(C)	1946	COL	87
THE YEARLING (s)	(C)	1946	MGM	128-131
GUNFIGHTERS (aka THE ASSASSIN) (s)	(C)	1947	COL	87
ADVENTURES IN SILVERADO		1948	COL	75
(aka ABOVE ALL LAWS) (s)				
CORONER CREEK (s)	(C)	1948	COL	90
TWO GUYS FROM TEXAS	(C)	1948	WB	86
(aka TWO TEXAS KNIGHTS) (s)				
THE PLUNDERERS (s)	(C)	1948	REP	87
THE BIG CAT (s)	(C)	1949	EL	75
THE LAST BANDIT (s)	(C)	1949	REP	80
HELLFIRE (cs)	(C)	1949	REP	90
BRIMSTONE (s)	(C)	1949	REP	90
THE NEVADAN	(C)	1950	COL	81
(aka THE MAN FROM NEVADA) (cs)				
ROCK ISLAND TRAIL	(C)	1950	REP	90
(aka TRANSCONTINENT EXPRESS)				
CALIFORNIA PASSAGE		1950	REP	90
OH! SUSANNA	(C)	1951	REP	90
WARPATH	(C)	1951	PAR	95
FLAMING FEATHER	(C)	1952	PAR	77-78
BUGLES IN THE AFTERNOON	(C)	1952	WB	85
MONTANA BELLE (s)	(C)	1952	RKO	81
RIDE THE MAN DOWN (s)	(C)	1953	REP	90
SAN ANTONE (cs)		1953	REP	90
PONY EXPRESS (s)	(C)	1953	PAR	101
JUBILEE TRAIL (cs)	(C)	1954	REP	103
RAGE AT DAWN (aka SEVEN BAD MEN)	(C)	1955	RKO	87
THE VANISHING AMERICAN (cs)		1955	REP	90

188 / FORREST TUCKER, continued

STAGECOACH TO FURY	1956...20T...76
THREE VIOLENT PEOPLE (s)	(C)..1957...PAR...100
THE QUIET GUN	1957...20T...77-79
THE DEERSLAYER	(C)..1957...20T...75-78
GIRL IN THE WOODS	1958...REP...71
FORT MASSACRE	(C)..1958...UA...80
GUNSMOKE IN TUCSON	(C)..1958...AA...79-80
BARQUERO (cs)	(C)..1970...UA...115
CHISUM	(C)..1970...WB...111
ALIAS SMITH AND JONES	(C)..1971...UNI-TV...90
CANCEL MY RESERVATION (s)	(C)..1972...WB...99
THE WILD McCULLOCHS	(C)..1975...AI...93
(aka THE McCULLOCHS; J. J. McCULLOCH)	
THE WACKIEST WAGON TRAIN IN THE WEST	(C)..1976...TOP...86
INCREDIBLE ROCKY MOUNTAIN RACE	(C)..1977...SCP-TV...100
THE REBELS (s)	(C)..1979...UNI-TV...200
THE ADVENTURES OF HUCKLEBERRY FINN (s)(C)	.1981...SCP-TV..100
TIMESTALKERS (s)	(C)..1987...FE-TV...100

TOM TYLER (1903 - 1954)
Having begun silent sagebrushers in the 1920s, Tom continued as a "B" sound star through 1937 for such studios as Monogram and Victory. He was Stony Brooke in *The Three Mesquiteers* series (1941-43), then concentrated on strong support roles like SAN ANTONIO, RED RIVER, BLOOD ON THE MOON, and SHE WORE A YELLOW RIBBON into 1953 before retiring from such top-grade "A" westerns due to arthritis which prematurely ended his life in 1954.

THE TRAIL OF THE HORSE THIEVES	1929...FBO...54
GUN LAW	1929...FBO...53
IDAHO RED	1929...FBO...53
THE PRIDE OF PAWNEE	1929...FBO...53
LAW OF THE PLAINS	1929...SYN...54
THE MAN FROM NEVADA	1929...SYN...53
THE PHANTOM RIDER	1929...SYN...54
'NEATH WESTERN SKIES	1929...SYN...55
THE LONE HORSEMAN	1929...SYN...55
PIONEERS OF THE WEST	1929...SYN...48
THE CANYON OF MISSING MEN	1930...SYN...53
CALL OF THE DESERT	1930...SYN...54
THE PHANTOM OF THE WEST	(SER)..1930...MAS...10CH
WEST OF CHEYENNE	1931...SYN...56-60
A RIDER OF THE PLAINS (aka THE GREATER LOVE)	1931...SYN...57-61
GOD'S COUNTRY AND THE MAN	1931...SYN...59-67
(aka GOD'S COUNTRY; ROSE OF THE RIO GRANDE)	
BATTLING WITH BUFFALO BILL	(SER)..1931...UNI...12CH
PARTNERS OF THE TRAIL	1931...MON...64
THE MAN FROM DEATH VALLEY	1931...MON...62-64
TWO-FISTED JUSTICE	1931...MON...63
GALLOPING THRU	1931...MON...58
SINGLE-HANDED SANDERS	1932...MON...63
THE MAN FROM NEW MEXICO	1932...MON...60
VANISHING MEN	1932...MON...62
HONOR OF THE MOUNTED	1932...MON...60-62
THE FORTY-NINERS	1932...FM...59
CLANCY OF THE MOUNTED	(SER)..1933...UNI...12CH

TOM TYLER, continued / 189

Title	Year	Studio	Pages
WHEN A MAN RIDES ALONE	1933	FM	60
DEADWOOD PASS	1933	FM	60-62
THE PHANTOM OF THE AIR (SER)	1933	UNI	12CH
WAR ON THE RANGE	1933	FM	59-60
TRACY RIDES	1935	COM	55-60
UNCONQUERED BANDIT	1935	COM	65
COYOTE TRAILS	1935	COM	63-65
BORN TO BATTLE	1935	COM	63
MYSTERY RANCH	1935	COM	55-56
FIGHTING HERO	1935	COM	59
SILENT VALLEY	1935	COM	63
THE SILVER BULLET	1935	COM	58
THE LARAMIE KID	1935	COM	65
RIO RATTLER	1935	COM	63
TERROR OF THE PLAINS	1935	COM	57
RIDIN' THRU	1935	COM	55
POWDERSMOKE RANGE (s)	1935	RKO	71
FAST BULLETS (aka LAW AND ORDER)	1936	COM	57
RIDIN' ON	1936	COM	56
ROAMIN' WILD	1936	COM	55-58
PINTO RUSTLERS	1936	COM	56
TRIGGER TOM	1936	COM	57
SANTA FE BOUND	1936	COM	56
THE LAST OUTLAW (s)	1936	RKO	72
RIP ROARIN' BUCKAROO	1936	VIC	58
THE PHANTOM OF THE RANGE	1936	VIC	57
CHEYENNE RIDES AGAIN	1937	VIC	56
THE FEUD OF THE TRAIL	1937	VIC	56
MYSTERY RANGE	1937	VIC	55
BROTHERS OF THE WEST	1937	VIC	55-58
LOST RANCH	1937	VIC	56-58
ORPHAN OF THE PECOS	1937	VIC	55
STAGECOACH (s)	1939	UA	96
THE NIGHT RIDERS (s)	1939	REP	58
FRONTIER MARSHAL (s)	1939	20T	71
DRUMS ALONG THE MOHAWK (s) (C)	1939	20T	103
GONE WITH THE WIND (s) (C)	1939	SEL/MGM	222
THE GRAPES OF WRATH (s)	1940	20T	129
THE LIGHT OF WESTERN STARS (s)	1940	PAR	67
THE WESTERNER (s)	1940	UA	94-100
CHEROKEE STRIP (s)	1940	PAR	84-86
TEXAS RANGERS RIDE AGAIN (s)	1940	PAR	68
BORDER VIGILANTES (s)	1941	PAR	62
BAD MEN OF MISSOURI (s)	1941	WB	71-74
RIDERS OF THE TIMBERLINE (s)	1941	PAR	59
OUTLAWS OF CHEROKEE TRAIL	1941	REP	56
(starts *The Three Mesquiteers* series for Republic)			
GAUCHOS OF ELDORADO	1941	REP	56
WEST OF CIMARRON	1941	REP	56
CODE OF THE OUTLAW	1942	REP	57
VALLEY OF THE SUN (s)	1942	RKO	79-84
RAIDERS OF THE RANGE	1942	REP	55
WESTWARD HO	1942	REP	56
THE PHANTOM PLAINSMEN	1942	REP	56
SHADOWS ON THE SAGE	1942	REP	57
VALLEY OF HUNTED MEN	1942	REP	60

TOM TYLER, continued

Title	Year	Studio	#
THUNDERING TRAILS	1943	REP	56
THE BLOCKED TRAIL	1943	REP	55-58
SANTA FE SCOUTS	1943	REP	55-57
RIDERS OF THE RIO GRANDE	1943	REP	55
(ends *The Three Mesquiteers* series)			
WAGON TRACKS WEST (s)	1943	REP	55
BOSS OF BOOMTOWN (s)	1944	UNI	56
SING ME A SONG OF TEXAS	1945	COL	66
(aka FORTUNE HUNTER)			
SAN ANTONIO (s) (C)	1945	WB	112
BADMAN'S TERRITORY (s)	1946	RKO	98
CHEYENNE (aka THE WYOMING KID) (s)	1947	WB	100
THE DUDE GOES WEST (s)	1948	AA	86
RETURN OF THE BAD MEN (s)	1948	RKO	90
THE GOLDEN EYE	1948	MON	69
(aka THE MYSTERY OF THE GOLDEN EYE) (s)			
RED RIVER (s)	1948	UA	125-133
BLOOD ON THE MOON (s)	1948	RKO	88
I SHOT JESSE JAMES (s)	1949	SG	81
THE YOUNGER BROTHERS (s) (C)	1949	WB	77
LUST FOR GOLD (s)	1949	COL	90
MASKED RAIDERS (s)	1949	RKO	60
SHE WORE A YELLOW RIBBON (s) (C)	1949	RKO	103
SQUARE DANCE JUBILEE (s)	1949	LIP	79
RIDERS OF THE RANGE (s)	1950	RKO	60
HOSTILE COUNTRY (GUNS OF JUSTICE) (s)	1950	LIP	60
MARSHAL OF HELDORADO	1950	LIP	53
(aka BLAZING GUNS) (s)			
CROOKED RIVER (aka THE LAST BULLET) (s)	1950	LIP	55
COLORADO RANGER (aka OUTLAW FURY) (s)	1950	LIP	54
WEST OF THE BRAZOS	1950	LIP	58
(aka RANGELAND EMPIRE) (s)			
FAST ON THE DRAW (aka SUDDEN DEATH) (s)	1950	LIP	55
RIO GRANDE PATROL (s)	1950	RKO	60
OUTLAWS OF TEXAS (s)	1950	MON	56
TRAIL OF ROBIN HOOD (gs) (C)	1950	REP	67
THE GREAT MISSOURI RAID (s) (C)	1951	PAR	85
THE DALTONS' WOMEN (s)	1951	WA	80
KING OF THE BULLWHIP (s)	1951	WA	59
BEST OF THE BADMEN (s) (C)	1951	RKO	84
MYSTERIOUS ISLAND (s) (SER)	1951	COL	15CH
ROAD AGENT (s)	1952	RKO	60
THE LION AND THE HORSE (s) (C)	1952	WB	83
OUTLAW WOMEN (s) (C)	1952	LIP	75
COW COUNTRY (s)	1953	AA	82
THE ADVENTURES OF THE TUCSON KID	1953	TKP	50

LEE VAN CLEEF (1925 - 1989)

After a long career as a character actor starting with HIGH NOON, he became a leading man in European westerns. Van Cleef made numerous films towards the latter part of his career through the mid-1970s including two with Clint Eastwood.

Title	Year	Studio	#
HIGH NOON (s)	1952	UA	85
UNTAMED FRONTIER (s) (C)	1952	UI	75

LEE VAN CLEEF, continued

Title	Color	Year	Studio	Pages
THE LAWLESS BREED (s)	(C)	1953	UI	83
ARENA (s)	(C)	1953	MGM	71-83
JACK SLADE (aka SLADE) (s)		1953	AA	90
THE NEBRASKAN (s)	(C)	1953	COL	68
TUMBLEWEED (s)	(C)	1953	UI	79-80
GYPSY COLT (s)	(C)	1954	MGM	72
RAILS INTO LARAMIE (s)	(C)	1954	UI	81
ARROW IN THE DUST (s)	(C)	1954	AA	80
THE YELLOW TOMAHAWK (s)	(C)	1954	UA	82
THE DESPERADO (s)		1954	AA	81
DAWN AT SOCORRO (s)	(C)	1954	UI	80
TREASURE OF RUBY HILLS (s)		1955	AA	71
TEN WANTED MEN (s)	(C)	1955	COL	80
THE ROAD TO DENVER (s)	(C)	1955	REP	90
A MAN ALONE (s)	(C)	1955	REP	96
THE VANISHING AMERICAN (s)		1955	REP	90
TRIBUTE TO A BAD MAN (s)	(C)	1956	MGM	95
PARDNERS (s)	(C)	1956	PAR	85-88
THE QUIET GUN (s)		1957	20T	77-79
GUNFIGHT AT THE O.K. CORRAL (s)	(C)	1957	PAR	122
THE BADGE OF MARSHAL BRENNAN (s)		1957	AA	74-76
THE LONELY MAN (s)		1957	PAR	87
LAST STAGECOACH WEST (s)		1957	REP	67
JOE DAKOTA (s)	(C)	1957	UI	79
GUN BATTLE AT MONTEREY (s)		1957	UA	67
RAIDERS OF OLD CALIFORNIA (s)		1957	REP	72
THE TIN STAR (s)		1957	PAR	93
DAY OF THE BAD MAN (s)	(C)	1958	UI	81
THE BRAVADOS (s)	(C)	1958	20T	98
RIDE LONESOME (s)	(C)	1959	COL	75
POSSE FROM HELL (s)	(C)	1961	UI	89
THE MAN WHO SHOT LIBERTY VALANCE (s)		1962	PAR	122
HOW THE WEST WAS WON (s)	(C)	1963	MGM	155-165
FOR A FEW DOLLARS MORE	(C)	1967	UA	130
THE GOOD THE BAD AND THE UGLY	(C)	1967	UA	161
THE BIG GUNDOWN	(C)	1968	COL	90
DEATH RIDES A HORSE	(C)	1969	UA	114
DAY OF ANGER	(C)	1969	NG	109-112
BARQUERO	(C)	1970	UA	108-115
EL CONDOR	(C)	1970	NG	102
SABATA	(C)	1970	UA	106-107
CAPTAIN APACHE	(C)	1971	SI	94-95
THE MAGNIFICENT SEVEN RIDE!	(C)	1972	UA	100
THE RETURN OF SABATA	(C)	1972	UA	106
BAD MAN'S RIVER	(C)	1972	SI	100
BEYOND THE LAW	(C)	1972	WW	91-100
BLOOD MONEY	(C)	1974	HAR	100
THE GRAND DUEL	(C)	1974	CS	92
TAKE A HARD RIDE	(C)	1975	20T	103-108
THE STRANGER AND THE GUNFIGHTER	(C)	1976	COL	107
KID VENGEANCE	(C)	1977	IYC	94
GOD'S GUN	(C)	1977	IYC	93

ROBERT WAGNER (1930 -   )

A debonair feature actor with 20th Century-Fox in the 1950s, Wagner starred in a few "A" oaters, then devoted the 1960s-1980s with two high-rated TV series, "It Takes a Thief" and "Hart to Hart". Rival to Richard Widmark in BROKEN LANCE.

THE SILVER WHIP (cs)	1953	20T	73
BROKEN LANCE	(C).. 1954	20T	96
WHITE FEATHER	(C).. 1955	20T	102
THE TRUE STORY OF JESSE JAMES (aka THE JAMES BROTHERS)	(C).. 1957	20T	92

JIMMY WAKELY (1914 - 1982)

A smooth-voiced singer for five years in other cowboy stars' westerns, Wakely landed his own Monogram Pictures series in 1944 and lensed 28 oatuners through 1949. With the studio forcing him to sing less in each succeeding feature, Wakely departed his "B" days at Monogram to concentrate on a lucrative recordings career.

SAGA OF DEATH VALLEY (s)	1939	REP	58
THE TULSA KID (s)	1940	REP	57
TRAILING DOUBLE TROUBLE (s)	1940	MON	58
PONY POST (s)	1940	UNI	59
TEXAS TERRORS (s)	1940	REP	57
SIX LESSONS FROM MADAME LA ZONGA (s)	1941	UNI	62
BURY ME NOT ON THE LONE PRAIRIE (s)	1941	UNI	61
TWILIGHT ON THE TRAIL (s)	1941	PAR	58
STICK TO YOUR GUNS (s)	1941	PAR	63
HEART OF THE RIO GRANDE (s)	1942	REP	70
COME ON DANGER (s)	1942	RKO	58
THE SILVER BULLET (s)	1942	UNI	61
BOSS OF HANGTOWN MESA (s)	1942	UNI	59
DEEP IN THE HEART OF TEXAS (s)	1942	UNI	62
LITTLE JOE, THE WRANGLER (s)	1942	UNI	64
STRICTLY IN THE GROOVE (s)	1942	UNI	60
THE OLD CHISHOLM TRAIL (s)	1942	UNI	60
TENTING TONIGHT ON THE OLD CAMP GROUND (aka TENTING TONIGHT) (s)	1942	UNI	61
CHEYENNE ROUNDUP (s)	1943	UNI	59
RAIDERS OF SAN JOAQUIN (s) (aka RIDERS OF SAN JOAQUIN)	1943	UNI	59
ROBIN HOOD OF THE RANGE (s)	1943	COL	57
THE LONE STAR TRAIL (s)	1943	UNI	58
COWBOY IN THE CLOUDS (s)	1943	COL	55
COWBOY CANTEEN (aka CLOSE HARMONY) (s)	1944	COL	72
SUNDOWN VALLEY (s)	1944	COL	55
SWING IN THE SADDLE (aka SWING AND SWAY) (s)	1944	COL	69
COWBOY FROM LONESOME RIVER (aka SIGNED JUDGEMENT) (s)	1944	COL	55
SADDLE LEATHER LAW (aka THE POISONER) (s)	1944	COL	55
I'M FROM ARKANSAS (s)	1944	PRC	70
CYCLONE PRAIRIE RANGERS (s)	1944	COL	56
SONG OF THE RANGE	1944	MON	55
SAGEBRUSH HEROES (s)	1945	COL	54

JIMMY WAKELY, continued /193

Title	Year	Studio	Pages
ROUGH RIDIN' JUSTICE (aka DECOY) (s)	1945	COL	58
SPRINGTIME IN TEXAS	1945	MON	55
SADDLE SERENADE	1945	MON	57
RIDERS OF THE DAWN	1945	MON	58
THE LONESOME TRAIL	1945	MON	57
MOON OVER MONTANA	1946	MON	56
WEST OF THE ALAMO	1946	MON	58
TRAIL TO MEXICO	1946	MON	56
SONG OF THE SIERRAS	1946	MON	58
RAINBOW OVER THE ROCKIES	1947	MON	54
SIX-GUN SERENADE	1947	MON	54
SONG OF THE WASTELAND	1947	MON	56
RIDIN' DOWN THE TRAIL	1947	MON	53
SONG OF THE DRIFTER	1948	MON	53
OKLAHOMA BLUES	1948	MON	56
PARTNERS OF THE SUNSET	1948	MON	53
RANGE RENEGADES	1948	MON	54
COWBOY CAVALIER	1948	MON	57
SILVER TRAILS	1948	MON	53-54
THE RANGERS RIDE	1948	MON	56
OUTLAW BRAND	1948	MON	57-58
COURTIN' TROUBLE	1948	MON	56-58
GUN RUNNER	1949	MON	54
GUN LAW JUSTICE	1949	MON	54
ACROSS THE RIO GRANDE	1949	MON	56
BRAND OF FEAR	1949	MON	56
ROARING WESTWARD (aka BOOM TOWN BADMEN)	1949	MON	55-58
LAWLESS CODE	1949	MON	58
THE MARSHAL'S DAUGHTER (gs)	1953	UA	71
ARROW IN THE DUST (s)	(C)..1954	AA	80
THE SILVER STAR (so)	1955	LIP	73
SLIM CARTER (so)	(C)..1957	UI	82
MONEY, WOMEN, AND GUNS (so)	(C)..1959	UI	80

WALLY WALES (1895 - 1980)
(aka HAL TALIAFERRO, WALT WILLIAMS)

A native of Montana, he had a struggle starring in early 1930s independent oaters, but Taliaferro—a name Wales later adopted—did important western parts into the early 1950s, many of which were classics due to his often unshaven, gritty makeup.

Title	Year	Studio	Pages
OVERLAND BOUND	1930	SYN	58
BAR L RANCH	1930	B4	60
CANYON HAWKS	1930	B4	60
TRAILS OF DANGER (aka TRAILS OF PERIL)	1930	B4	60
BREED OF THE WEST	1930	B4	60
RED FORK RANGE	1931	B4	60
WESTWARD BOUND (s)	1931	SYN	60
HELL'S VALLEY	1931	B4	60
SO THIS IS ARIZONA	1931	B4	60
RIDERS OF THE CACTUS	1931	B4	60
FLYING LARIATS	1931	B4	60
LAW AND LAWLESS (s)	1932	MAJ	62

WALLY WALES, continued

Title	Year	Studio	#
DEADWOOD PASS (cs)	1933	FM	62
RUSTY RIDES ALONE (s)	1933	COL	58
FIGHTING TEXANS (aka RANDY STRIKES OIL) (s)	1933	MON	58
THE TRAIL DRIVE (s)	1933	UNI	60
SAGEBRUSH TRAIL (s)	1933	LMO	58
THE MYSTERY SQUADRON (s) (SER)	1933	MAS	12CH
POTLUCK PARDS (aka GUN RIDERS)	1934	REL	28
ADVENTURES OF TEXAS JACK	1934	SEC	17
ARIZONA CYCLONE	1934	IMP	51
CARRYING THE MAIL	1934	IMP	27
BORDER GUNS	1934	AYW	55
DESERT MAN	1934	IMP	20
THE LONE RIDER	1934	IMP	27
PALS OF THE WEST	1934	IMP	29
THE SUNDOWN TRAIL	1934	IMP	20
WEST OF THE LAW	1934	IMP	28
THE WAY OF THE WEST	1934	SPR	52
THE WHEELS OF DESTINY (s)	1934	UNI	64
NEVADA CYCLONE (s)	1934	REL	33
HONOR OF THE RANGE (s)	1934	UNI	61
SMOKING GUNS (s)	1934	UNI	65
THE LAW OF THE WILD (s) (SER)	1934	MAS	12CH
THE OIL RAIDER (s)	1934	MAY	65
FIGHTING THROUGH (s)	1934	KEN	55
MYSTERY MOUNTAIN (s) (SER)	1934	MAS	12CH
THE CACTUS KID (s)	1934	REL	56
THE LONE BANDIT (cs)	1934	EMP	60
UNCONQUERED BANDIT (s)	1935	COM	59
THE RUSTLERS OF RED DOG (s) (SER)	1935	UNI	12CH
SIX GUN JUSTICE	1935	SPE	57
THE PHANTOM EMPIRE (s) (SER)	1935	MAS	12CH
RANGE WARFARE (cs)	1935	KEN	55
THE COWBOY AND THE BANDIT (s)	1935	SPR	57
THE SILVER BULLET (s)	1935	COM	58
THE MIRACLE RIDER (s) (SER)	1935	MAS	15CH
RIDING WILD (s)	1935	COL	56
THE VANISHING RIDERS (s)	1935	SPE	58
HEIR TO TROUBLE (s)	1935	COL	59
POWDERSMOKE RANGE (s)	1935	RKO	71
BETWEEN MEN (s)	1935	SUP	59
WESTERN COURAGE (s)	1935	COL	58
SWIFTY (s)	1935	FD	60
LAWLESS RIDERS (s)	1935	COL	57
DANGER TRAILS (cs)	1935	BEA	55
GUN PLAY (aka LUCKY BOOTS) (cs)	1935	BEA	59
FIVE BAD MEN (s)	1935	SUN	
THE LARAMIE KID (s)	1935	COM	65
SILENT VALLEY (cs)	1935	COM	63
WESTERN RACKETEERS (cs)	1935	AYW	48
TRIGGER TOM (s)	1936	COM	57
THE PECOS KID (s)	1936	COM	56
LUCKY TERROR (s)	1936	GN	61
HEROES OF THE RANGE (s)	1936	COL	51-58
AVENGING WATERS (s)	1936	COL	57
THE PHANTOM RIDER (s) (SER)	1936	UNI	15CH
THE TRAITOR (cs)	1936	PUR	56

AMBUSH VALLEY (s)	1936	REL	57
LAW AND LEAD (cs)	1936	CLY	60
THE UNKNOWN RANGER (cs)	1936	COL	57
RIO GRANDE RANGER (cs)	1936	COL	54
HAIR-TRIGGER CASEY (s)	1936	ATL	59
THE GUN RANGER (s)	1937	REP	56
LAW OF THE RANGER (s)	1937	COL	57
ROOTIN' TOOTIN' RHYTHM (aka RHYTHM ON THE RANCH) (s)	1937	REP	60
THE PAINTED STALLION (s) (SER)	1937	REP	12CH
ONE MAN JUSTICE (s)	1937	COL	59
THE RANGERS STEP IN (s)	1937	COL	58
HEART OF THE ROCKIES (s)	1937	REP	56
THE TRIGGER TRIO (s)	1937	REP	56
THE LONE RANGER (cs) (SER)	1938	REP	15CH
STAGECOACH DAYS (s)	1938	COL	58
THE GREAT ADVENTURES OF WILD BILL HICKOK (s) (SER)	1938	COL	15CH
PIONEER TRAIL (s)	1938	COL	55
SOUTH OF ARIZONA (s)	1938	COL	56
PHANTOM GOLD (s)	1938	COL	56
THE BLACK BANDIT (s)	1938	UNI	57
WEST OF THE SANTA FE (s)	1938	COL	57
GUILTY TRAILS (s)	1938	UNI	57
PRAIRIE JUSTICE (s)	1938	UNI	57
RIO GRANDE (aka RIO GRANDE STAMPEDE) (s)	1938	COL	59
THE THUNDERING WEST (s)	1939	COL	57
FRONTIERS OF '49 (cs)	1939	COL	54
NORTH OF THE YUKON (s)	1939	COL	64
MAN OF CONQUEST (s)	1939	REP	97-105
WESTERN CARAVANS (s)	1939	COL	58
RIDERS OF THE FRONTIER (s) (aka RIDIN' THE FRONTIER)	1939	MON	58
OVERLAND WITH KIT CARSON (s) (SER)	1939	COL	15CH
OUTPOST OF THE MOUNTIES (aka ON GUARD) (s)	1939	COL	63
THE STRANGER FROM TEXAS (aka THE STRANGER) (s)	1939	COL	54
SAGA OF DEATH VALLEY (s)	1939	REP	58
TWO-FISTED RANGERS (s)	1940	COL	62
BULLETS FOR RUSTLERS (aka SPECIAL DUTY) (s)	1940	COL	58
PIONEERS OF THE WEST (s)	1940	REP	56
HI-YO-SILVER (feature version of THE LONE RANGER serial) (cs)	1940	REP	69
DARK COMMAND (s)	1940	REP	94
ADVENTURES OF RED RYDER (s) (SER)	1940	REP	12CH
THE CARSON CITY KID (s)	1940	REP	57
COLORADO (s)	1940	REP	57
CHEROKEE STRIP (s)	1940	PAR	84-86
YOUNG BILL HICKOK (s)	1940	REP	59
TEXAS TERRORS (s)	1940	REP	57
THE BORDER LEGION (aka WEST OF THE BADLANDS) (s)	1940	REP	57
ALONG THE RIO GRANDE (s)	1941	RKO	61-64
THE GREAT TRAIN ROBBERY (s)	1941	REP	61
IN OLD CHEYENNE (s)	1941	REP	58
BORDER VIGILANTES (s)	1941	PAR	62

WALLY WALES, continued

Title	Year	Studio	Page
SHERIFF OF TOMBSTONE (s)	1941	REP	56
LAW OF THE RANGE (s)	1941	UNI	59
UNDER FIESTA STARS (s)	1941	REP	64
BAD MAN OF DEADWOOD (s)	1941	REP	61
RIDERS OF THE TIMBERLINE (s)	1941	PAR	59
ROARING FRONTIERS (aka FRONTIER) (s)	1941	COL	62
JESSE JAMES AT BAY (s)	1941	REP	56
RED RIVER VALLEY (s)	1941	REP	62
BULLETS FOR BANDITS (s)	1942	COL	55
ROMANCE ON THE RANGE (s)	1942	REP	63
TOMBSTONE, THE TOWN TOO TOUGH TO DIE (s)	1942	PAR	79
SONS OF THE PIONEERS (s)	1942	REP	61
KING OF THE MOUNTIES (s) (SER)	1942	REP	12CH
LITTLE JOE, THE WRANGLER (s)	1942	UNI	64
AMERICAN EMPIRE (aka MY SON ALONE) (s)	1942	UA	81
HEART OF THE GOLDEN WEST (s)	1942	REP	65
RIDIN' DOWN THE CANYON (s)	1942	REP	54
IDAHO (s)	1943	REP	70
HOPPY SERVES A WRIT (s)	1943	UA	67
LEATHER BURNERS (s)	1943	UA	58
SONG OF TEXAS (s)	1943	REP	69
SILVER SPURS (s)	1943	REP	68
MAN FROM MUSIC MOUNTAIN (aka TEXAS LEGIONNAIRES) (s)	1943	REP	71
FRONTIER LAW (s)	1943	UNI	55
COWBOY IN THE CLOUDS (s)	1943	COL	55
THE WOMAN OF THE TOWN (s)	1943	UA	88
LUMBERJACK (s)	1944	UA	63
COWBOY AND THE SENORITA (s)	1944	REP	78
FORTY THIEVES (s)	1944	UA	60
THE YELLOW ROSE OF TEXAS (s)	1944	REP	69
VIGILANTES OF DODGE CITY (s)	1944	REP	54
ZORRO'S BLACK WHIP (s) (SER)	1944	REP	12CH
UTAH (s)	1945	REP	78
SPRINGTIME IN TEXAS (s)	1945	MON	55
SAN ANTONIO (s) (C)	1945	WB	112
THE SCARLET HORSEMAN (s) (SER)	1946	UNI	13CH
THE PHANTOM RIDER (s) (SER)	1946	REP	12CH
IN OLD SACRAMENTO (aka FLAME OF SACRAMENTO) (s)	1946	REP	89
HEADING WEST (aka THE CHEAT'S LAST THROW) (s)	1946	COL	56
PLAINSMAN AND THE LADY (s)	1946	REP	87
DUEL IN THE SUN (s) (C)	1947	SEL	130-138
RAMROD (s)	1947	UA	94
WEST OF SONORA (s)	1948	COL	52-55
THE GALLANT LEGION (s)	1948	REP	88
RED RIVER (s)	1948	UA	125-133
BLOOD ON THE MOON (s)	1948	RKO	88
BRIMSTONE (s) (C)	1949	REP	90
THE SAVAGE HORDE (s)	1950	REP	90
COLT .45 (aka THUNDERCLOUD) (s) (C)	1950	WB	74
CALIFORNIA PASSAGE (s)	1950	REP	90
JUNCTION CITY (s)	1952	COL	54

CLINT WALKER (1927 -   )

Huge actor whose early jobs as a deputy sheriff and silver miner added authenticity to his western portrayals. Best remembered for his ABC television series, "Cheyenne" (1955-63) which consisted of 107 hour-long shows.

FORT DOBBS	1958	WB	90
YELLOWSTONE KELLY	(C).. 1959	WB	91
GOLD OF THE SEVEN SAINTS	1961	WB	88-90
THE NIGHT OF THE GRIZZLY	(C).. 1966	PAR.	102-103
MORE DEAD THAN ALIVE	(C).. 1969	UA	101
SAM WHISKEY	(C).. 1969	UA	96-97
THE GREAT BANK ROBBERY (cs)	(C).. 1969	WB	98
YUMA	(C).. 1971	ABC-TV	73
HARDCASE	(C).. 1972	ABC-TV	74
THE BOUNTY MAN	(C).. 1972	ABC-TV	73-74
PANCHO VILLA	(C).. 1973	SI	92
BAKER'S HAWK	(C).. 1976	DD	98-105
THE WHITE BUFFALO (aka HUNT TO KILL) (s)	(C).. 1977	UA	97
THE GAMBLER, PART IV— THE LUCK OF THE DRAW (gs)	(C).. 1991	NBC-TV	200

JAMES WARREN (1913-   )

He was pursuing his New York City art career when a talent scout sent Warren to California for screen testing which resulted in several mid-1940s RKO Radio westerns based on the studio's continued lensing of Zane Grey stories. James had returned full-time to his original profession by the early 1950s. On Maui since 1968, Warren is internationally recognized today for his beautiful watercolor paintings.

GIRL CRAZY (s)	1943	MGM	99
MAISIE GOES TO RENO (aka YOU CAN'T DO THAT TO ME)	1944	MGM	90
WANDERER OF THE WASTELAND	1945	RKO	67
DING DONG WILLIAMS (aka MELODY MAKER) (s)	1946	RKO	62
BADMAN'S TERRITORY (s)	1946	RKO	98
SUNSET PASS	1946	RKO	59
CODE OF THE WEST	1947	RKO	57

JOHN WAYNE (1907 - 1979)

Best-known western film actor of all time who labored in "B" films—he made the Top Money-Making Western Star list in 1936—for almost one decade before becoming a major star in John Ford's STAGECOACH. Wayne's staying power as a dominant "A" oater player outlasted all others until his death. He made many outstanding western films like RED RIVER, RIO GRANDE, and THE SEARCHERS. John's Oscar was won for his portrayal of Marshal Rooster Cogburn in TRUE GRIT, one of only three ever given for western roles as outstanding actor. THE SHOOTIST was a fitting valedictory to Wayne's 50-year movie career.

ROUGH ROMANCE (s)	1930	FOX	55
THE BIG TRAIL	1930	FOX	125
ARIZONA (aka MEN ARE LIKE THAT; THE VIRTUOUS WIFE) (s)	1931	COL	67
THE RANGE FEUD (s)	1931	COL	64

198 / JOHN WAYNE, continued

Title	Year	Studio	Pages
TEXAS CYCLONE (s)	1932	COL	63
TWO-FISTED LAW (s)	1932	COL	57
RIDE HIM, COWBOY (aka THE HAWK)	1932	WB	56
THE BIG STAMPEDE	1932	WB	54
HAUNTED GOLD	1932	WB	58
THE TELEGRAPH TRAIL	1933	WB	55
SOMEWHERE IN SONORA	1933	WB	57
THE MAN FROM MONTEREY	1933	WB	57
RIDERS OF DESTINY	1933	LMO	58
SAGEBRUSH TRAIL	1933	LMO	58
THE LUCKY TEXAN	1934	LMO	55
WEST OF THE DIVIDE	1934	LMO	54
BLUE STEEL	1934	LMO	54
THE MAN FROM UTAH	1934	LMO	54
RANDY RIDES ALONE	1934	LMO	55
THE STAR PACKER	1934	LMO	54-60
THE TRAIL BEYOND	1934	LMO	55
THE LAWLESS FRONTIER	1934	LMO	54-59
'NEATH THE ARIZONA SKIES	1934	LMO	52
TEXAS TERROR	1935	LMO	51
RAINBOW VALLEY	1935	LMO	52
THE DESERT TRAIL	1935	LMO	54
THE DAWN RIDER	1935	LMO	57
PARADISE CANYON	1935	LMO	52
WESTWARD HO	1935	REP	60
THE NEW FRONTIER	1935	REP	54-60
LAWLESS RANGE	1935	REP	59
OREGON TRAIL	1936	REP	59
THE LAWLESS NINETIES	1936	REP	55
KING OF THE PECOS	1936	REP	54
THE LONELY TRAIL	1936	REP	55-58
WINDS OF THE WASTELAND	1936	REP	53-58
CONFLICT	1936	UNI	63
BORN TO THE WEST (aka HELL TOWN)	1937	PAR	66
PALS OF THE SADDLE	1938	REP	55-60
(starts *The Three Mesquiteers* series)			
OVERLAND STAGE RAIDERS	1938	REP	55
SANTA FE STAMPEDE	1938	REP	56
RED RIVER RANGE	1938	REP	56
(halts *The Three Mesquiteers* series)			
STAGECOACH	1939	UA	96-99
THE NIGHT RIDERS	1939	REP	58
(resumes *The Three Mesquiteers* series)			
THREE TEXAS STEERS	1939	REP	57
(aka DANGER RIDES THE RANGE)			
WYOMING OUTLAW	1939	REP	56
NEW FRONTIER (aka FRONTIER HORIZON)	1939	REP	57
(ends *The Three Mesquiteers* series)			
ALLEGHENY UPRISING	1939	RKO	81
(aka THE FIRST REBEL; ALLEGHENY FRONTIER)			
DARK COMMAND	1940	REP	94
THREE FACES WEST (aka THE REFUGEE)	1940	REP	79-81
LADY FROM LOUISIANA	1941	REP	82
THE SHEPHERD OF THE HILLS (C)	1941	PAR	95-98
LADY FOR A NIGHT	1942	REP	88
THE SPOILERS (cs)	1942	UNI	84-87

JOHN WAYNE, continued

Title	Year	Studio	Page
IN OLD CALIFORNIA	1942	REP	88
A LADY TAKES A CHANCE	1943	RKO	86
IN OLD OKLAHOMA (aka WAR OF THE WILDCATS)	1943	REP	102
TALL IN THE SADDLE	1944	RKO	87
FLAME OF BARBARY COAST	1945	REP	91
DAKOTA	1945	REP	82
ANGEL AND THE BADMAN	1947	REP	100
FORT APACHE	1948	RKO	127
RED RIVER	1948	UA	125-133
3 GODFATHERS	(C) 1949	MGM	106
THE FIGHTING KENTUCKIAN	1949	REP	100
SHE WORE A YELLOW RIBBON	(C) 1949	RKO	104
RIO GRANDE	1950	REP	105
HONDO	(C) 1954	WB	83
THE SEARCHERS	(C) 1956	WB	119
LEGEND OF THE LOST	(C) 1957	UA	109
RIO BRAVO	(C) 1959	WB	141
THE HORSE SOLDIERS	(C) 1959	UA	119
THE ALAMO	(C) 1960	UA	161-190
NORTH TO ALASKA	(C) 1960	20T	122
THE COMANCHEROS	(C) 1961	20T	107
THE MAN WHO SHOT LIBERTY VALANCE	1962	PAR	119-123
HOW THE WEST WAS WON	(C) 1963	MGM	155-165
McLINTOCK!	(C) 1963	UA	127
CIRCUS WORLD (aka THE MAGNIFICENT SHOWMAN)	(C) 1964	PAR	135
THE SONS OF KATIE ELDER	(C) 1965	PAR	122
THE WAR WAGON	(C) 1967	UNI	101
EL DORADO	(C) 1967	PAR	126
TRUE GRIT	(C) 1969	PAR	128
THE UNDEFEATED	(C) 1969	20T	119
CHISUM	(C) 1970	WB	111
RIO LOBO	(C) 1970	NG	114
BIG JAKE	(C) 1971	NG	110
THE COWBOYS	(C) 1972	WB	128
CANCEL MY RESERVATION (gs)	(C) 1972	WB	99
THE TRAIN ROBBERS	(C) 1973	WB	92
CAHILL UNITED STATES MARSHAL (aka CAHILL)	(C) 1973	WB	103
ROOSTER COGBURN	(C) 1975	UNI	107
THE SHOOTIST	(C) 1976	PAR	99-100

RICHARD WIDMARK (1914 -)

Wiry, tough actor who began movie acting playing villains and rose to become a versatile leading man. Later in his career, Richard made several westerns. Outstanding were YELLOW SKY and THE LAST WAGON for Widmark.

Title	Year	Studio	Page
YELLOW SKY (cs)	1948	20T	98
RED SKIES OF MONTANA	(C) 1952	20T	89-98
GARDEN OF EVIL (cs)	(C) 1954	20T	100
BROKEN LANCE (s)	(C) 1954	20T	96
BACKLASH	(C) 1956	UI	84
THE LAST WAGON	(C) 1956	20T	99

RICHARD WIDMARK, continued

THE LAW AND JAKE WADE	(C)	1958...MGM	86
THE TRAP (aka THE BAITED TRAP)	(C)	1959...PAR	84
WARLOCK	(C)	1959...20T	121-122
THE ALAMO	(C)	1960...UA	161-190
TWO RODE TOGETHER	(C)	1961...COL	91-109
HOW THE WEST WAS WON (s)	(C)	1963...MGM	155-165
CHEYENNE AUTUMN	(C)	1964...WB	145-160
ALVAREZ KELLY	(C)	1966...COL	116
THE WAY WEST (cs)	(C)	1967...UA	122
DEATH OF A GUNFIGHTER	(C)	1969...UNI	94-100
(aka THE LAST GUNFIGHTER)			
WHEN THE LEGENDS DIE	(C)	1972...20T	104-106
THE LAST DAY	(C)	1975...PAR-TV	100
THE SWARM	(C)	1978...PAR	116
MR. HORN	(C)	1979...LOR-TV	200
BEAR ISLAND (cs)	(C)	1980...COL	118
ONCE UPON A TEXAS TRAIN	(C)	1988...CBS-TV	100
(aka TEXAS GUNS)			

BILL WILLIAMS (1915 - 1992)
Leading man who played both villains and heroes. Best known in westerns for his television series, "The Adventures of Kit Carson" (1951-55), with 104 half-hour segments. Unsuccessful at wooing Jane Russell in SON OF PALEFACE.

WEST OF THE PECOS (s)		1945...RKO	66-68
FIGHTING MAN OF THE PLAINS	(C)	1949...20T	94
OPERATION HAYLIFT		1950...LIP	74-75
THE CARIBOO TRAIL (cs)	(C)	1950...20T	81
CALIFORNIA PASSAGE (s)		1950...REP	90
THE GREAT MISSOURI RAID (s)	(C)	1951...PAR	83-85
THE LAST OUTPOST (s)	(C)	1951...PAR	88
ROSE OF CIMARRON (cs)	(C)	1952...20T	72
BRONCO BUSTER (s)	(C)	1952...UI	80-81
SON OF PALEFACE (s)	(C)	1952...PAR	95-104
RACING BLOOD	(C)	1954...20T	76
THE OUTLAW'S DAUGHTER	(C)	1954...20T	75
APACHE AMBUSH		1955...COL	68
THE WILD DAKOTAS		1956...ASC	73-75
THE BROKEN STAR (cs)		1956...UA	82
THE HALLIDAY BRAND (s)		1957...UA	77-79
THE STORM RIDER (cs)		1957...20T	70
GUNFIGHT AT THE O.K. CORRAL (s)	(C)	1957...PAR	122
PAWNEE (aka PALE ARROW)	(C)	1957...REP	80
SLIM CARTER (s)	(C)	1957...UI	82
OKLAHOMA TERRITORY		1960...UA	67
LAW OF THE LAWLESS	(C)	1964...PAR	88
(aka INVITATION TO A HANGING) (s)			
TICKLE ME (s)	(C)	1965...AA	90
BUCKSKIN (s)	(C)	1968...PAR	97
RIO LOBO (s)	(C)	1970...NG	114
SCANDALOUS JOHN (s)	(C)	1971...BV	113-117

GUINN "BIG BOY" WILLIAMS (1900 - 1962)

He was a rough-and-tumble, happy-go-lucky cowboy. Williams did a few Beacon oaters as star (1934-35), then exclusively supported other movie saddlers like Errol Flynn, Roy Rogers, Ken Curtis, and Randolph Scott over 25 years usually as an opinionated sidekick. Guinn appeared in the NBC-TV "Circus Boys" series (1956-57).

Title	Year	Studio	No.
THE BAD MAN (s)	1930	FN	77
THE GREAT MEADOW (cs)	1931	MGM	78-81
HERITAGE OF THE DESERT (aka WHEN THE WEST WAS YOUNG) (s)	1932	PAR	59-63
MAN OF THE FOREST (s)	1933	PAR	62
THUNDER OVER TEXAS	1934	BEA	61
COWBOY HOLIDAY	1934	BEA	56
THE LAW OF THE 45s	1935	FD	56
BIG BOY RIDES AGAIN	1935	BEA	57
DANGER TRAILS	1935	BEA	55
GUN PLAY (aka LUCKY BOOTS)	1935	BEA	59
POWDERSMOKE RANGE	1935	RKO	71
THE LITTLEST REBEL (s)	1935	20T	70-73
THE VIGILANTES ARE COMING (cs) (SER)	1936	REP	12CH
END OF THE TRAIL (aka REVENGE) (s)	1936	COL	70
NORTH OF NOME (cs)	1936	COL	63
THE BAD MAN OF BRIMSTONE (s)	1937	MGM	89-90
ARMY GIRL (aka THE LAST OF THE CAVALRY) (s)	1938	REP	80
DOWN IN "ARKANSAW" (s)	1938	REP	72
DODGE CITY (s) (C)	1939	WB	104
BAD LANDS (cs)	1939	RKO	70
MUTINY ON THE BLACKHAWK (s)	1939	UNI	68
LEGION OF LOST FLYERS (s)	1939	UNI	63
VIRGINIA CITY (s)	1940	WB	121
WAGONS WESTWARD (s)	1940	REP	69-70
SANTA FE TRAIL (s)	1940	WB	110
BILLY THE KID (s) (C)	1941	MGM	95
RIDERS OF DEATH VALLEY (s) (SER)	1941	UNI	15CH
SILVER QUEEN (s)	1942	UA	80
AMERICAN EMPIRE (aka MY SON ALONE) (s)	1942	UA	81-82
THE DESPERADOES (s) (C)	1943	COL	85
HANDS ACROSS THE BORDER (s)	1943	REP	73
COWBOY CANTEEN (aka CLOSE HARMONY) (s)	1944	COL	72
COWBOY AND THE SENORITA (s)	1944	REP	78
SWING IN THE SADDLE (aka SWING AND SWAY) (s)	1944	COL	69
NEVADA (s)	1944	RKO	62
BELLE OF THE YUKON (s) (C)	1944	RKO	84
SING ME A SONG OF TEXAS (aka FORTUNE HUNTER) (s)	1945	COL	66
RHYTHM ROUND-UP (aka HONEST JOHN) (s)	1945	COL	66-68
SONG OF THE PRAIRIE (aka SENTIMENT AND SONG) (s)	1945	COL	69
THROW A SADDLE ON A STAR (s)	1946	COL	65
THAT TEXAS JAMBOREE (aka MEDICINE MAN) (s)	1946	COL	67
COWBOY BLUES (aka BENEATH THE STARRY SKIES) (s)	1946	COL	65
SINGING ON THE TRAIL (aka LOOKIN' FOR SOMEONE) (s)	1946	COL	69
SINGIN' IN THE CORN (aka GIVE AND TAKE) (s)	1946	COL	65-68
OVER THE SANTA FE TRAIL (aka NO ESCAPE) (s)	1947	COL	63

202 / GUINN "BIG BOY" WILLIAMS, continued

KING OF THE WILD HORSES (s)	1947	COL	79
STATION WEST (s)	1948	RKO	92
SMOKY MOUNTAIN MELODY	1948	COL	61
BAD MEN OF TOMBSTONE (s)	1949	AA	75
BRIMSTONE (s)	(C) 1949	REP	90
HOEDOWN (s)	1950	COL	64
ROCKY MOUNTAIN (s)	1950	WB	83
AL JENNINGS OF OKLAHOMA (s)	(C) 1951	COL	79
MAN IN THE SADDLE (aka THE OUTCAST) (s)	(C) 1951	COL	87
SPRINGFIELD RIFLE (s)	(C) 1952	WB	93
HANGMAN'S KNOT (s)	(C) 1952	COL	81
SOUTHWEST PASSAGE (aka CAMELS WEST) (s)	(C) 1954	UA	82
MASSACRE CANYON (s)	(C) 1954	COL	66
THE OUTLAW'S DAUGHTER (s)	(C) 1954	20T	75
HIDDEN GUNS (s)	1956	REP	66
MAN FROM DEL RIO (s)	1956	UA	82
THE HIRED GUN (s)	1957	MGM	63
HOME FROM THE HILL (s)	(C) 1960	MGM	150
FIVE BOLD WOMEN (s)	(C) 1960	CIT	82
THE ALAMO (s)	(C) 1960	UA	161-190
THE COMANCHEROS (s)	(C) 1961	20T	107

FRED WILLIAMSON (1938 -   )
Black leading man best known for his action roles, including westerns.

THE LEGEND OF NIGGER CHARLEY	(C) 1972	PAR	98-100
THE SOUL OF NIGGER CHARLEY	(C) 1973	PAR	104-109
BOSS NIGGER (aka BOSS; THE BLACK BOUNTY KILLER)	(C) 1974	DP	87-97
TAKE A HARD RIDE (cs)	(C) 1975	20T	102
ADIOS AMIGO	(C) 1975	AP	87
JOSHUA (aka THE BLACK RIDER)	(C) 1977	LSP	75-90

WHIP WILSON (1915 - 1964)
He was a few years' rival (1949-52) to Lash LaRue when the Monogram Pictures' screenplays required him to display that bullwhip prowess. Wilson's "B" western series were enhanced by upgraded music scoring from the studio's Music Department in the late 1940s.

GOD'S COUNTRY (s)	(C) 1946	SG	62
SILVER TRAILS (s)	1948	MON	53-54
CRASHING THRU	1949	MON	58
SHADOWS OF THE WEST	1949	MON	59
HAUNTED TRAILS	1949	MON	58-60
RIDERS OF THE DUSK (aka RIDERS FROM THE DUSK)	1949	MON	57
RANGE LAND	1949	MON	56
FENCE RIDERS	1950	MON	57
GUNSLINGERS	1950	MON	55
ARIZONA TERRITORY	1950	MON	56
SILVER RAIDERS	1950	MON	55
CHEROKEE UPRISING	1950	MON	55-57

OUTLAWS OF TEXAS	1950	MON	56
ABILENE TRAIL	1951	MON	54-64
CANYON RAIDERS	1951	MON	54
NEVADA BADMEN	1951	MON	58
STAGECOACH DRIVER	1951	MON	52
WANTED: DEAD OR ALIVE	1951	MON	59
LAWLESS COWBOYS	1951	MON	58
STAGE TO BLUE RIVER	1951	MON	56
(aka STAGE FROM BLUE RIVER)			
NIGHT RAIDERS	1952	MON	52
THE GUNMAN	1952	MON	52
MONTANA INCIDENT	1952	MON	54
WYOMING ROUNDUP	1952	MON	53
THE KENTUCKIAN (s)	(C) 1955	UA	104

MONTGOMERY WOOD (1938 -)
(aka GIULIANO GEMMA)

Leading man in European western films. Wood is a Rome-based citizen and still active with features.

ADIOS, GRINGO (aka ADIOS AMIGO)	(C) 1965	TLU	87-97
BLOOD FOR A SILVER DOLLAR	(C) 1965	TW	92
THE RETURN OF RINGO	(C) 1965	RF	104
A PISTOL FOR RINGO	(C) 1966	EMB	97
ONE SILVER DOLLAR	(C) 1967	PEACF	95
THE MAN FROM NOWHERE	(C) 1968	GGP	100
(aka ARIZONA COLT)			
WANTED	(C) 1968	COC	104
FORT YUMA GOLD	(C) 1969	GAL	100
DAY OF ANGER	(C) 1969	NG	112

ROBERT WOODS (1936-)

Leading man in European western films. Lives in Los Angeles and is semi-active with the feature business.

BLACK STAR	(C) 1966	AC	93
$5000 ON ONE ACE	(C) 1966	BAL	91
FOUR DOLLARS FOR REVENGE	(C) 1966	GAR	88
PECOS CLEANS UP	(C) 1967	UFA	87
7 GUNS FOR THE MacGREGORS	(C) 1968	COL	97
MY NAME IS PECOS	(C) 1968	GE	83
EL PURO	(C) 1972	FC	89

LORETTA YOUNG (1913 -)

Excellent actress whose versatility in film roles included several western leads, although she is better known for her non-genre roles. Loretta won an Oscar for her performance in THE FARMER'S DAUGHTER, a film that included among its players a very young James Arness.

THE CALL OF THE WILD	1935	UA	81-95
RAMONA	(C) 1936	20T	90-94
THE LADY FROM CHEYENNE	1941	UNI	87
RACHEL AND THE STRANGER	1948	RKO	79-93

ROBERT YOUNG (1907 -   )
A major MGM star—drama- and light-comedy oriented—with endless credits in the 1930s-1940s, Young made several classic westerns. He found a new career in television with NBC-TV's "Father Knows Best" (1953-60) and later on during the 1970s as "Marcus Welby, M.D." for ABC.

SPITFIRE	1934	RKO	88
MAISIE	1939	MGM	72
NORTHWEST PASSAGE	(C) .. 1940	MGM	125-126
WESTERN UNION	(C) .. 1941	20T	94
THEY WON'T BELIEVE ME	1947	RKO	79
RELENTLESS	(C) .. 1948	COL	93
THE HALF-BREED	(C) .. 1952	RKO	81

INDEX OF FILM AND TV STUDIOS

A

AA	Allied Artists
ABC-TV	American Broadcasting Corporation-TV
ABCCF-TV	ABC Circle Films-TV
AC	Ambrociana Cinematografica
ACA	Academy Home Entertainment
ACP	Action Promo
AE	Avco Embassy
AF	Alive Films
AFD	Associated Film Distributors
AFP-TV	Agamemnon Film Productions-TV
AFR	Associated Film Releasing Corporation
AFRC	American Film Releasing Corporation
AGM	Agamemnon Film
AI	American International
AJA	Ajay Films
ALL	Allied
ALP-TV	Alan Landsburg Production-TV
AMB	Ambassador
AME	American
ANE	American National Enterprises
AP	Atlas Productions
APE	Apex
ARC	American Releasing Corporation
ARN	Artists Creation
ART	Artclass
ASC	Associated
ASP-TV	Aaron Spelling Productions-TV
AST	Astor
ATL	Atlantic
AUD	Audible
AYW	Aywon

B

BAL	Balcazar
BAN	Banner
BDP	Booth Dominion Pictures
BEA	Beacon
B4	Big 4
BI	Brentwood International
BIE	Barjul International/Emerson
BJP	Buck Jones Productions
BRC	BRC/Estela Films
BV	Buena Vista

C

CAL	Calendar Corporation
CBS-TV	Columbia Broadcasting Corporation-TV
CCCFK	CCC/Filmkunst
CE	Carmel Enterprises

CFE	Capital Film Exchange
CFE-TV	Cabin Fever Entertainment-TV
CFP-TV	Charles Fries Productions-TV
CHE	Chevron
CIT	Citation
CLY	Colony
COC	Cociemento
COL	Columbia
COL-TV	Columbia-TV
COM	Commodore
COS	Cosmos
COT	Comet
COU	Cougar Productions
CP	Capitol Productions
CRC	Cinerama Releasing Corporation
CRE	Crescent
CRO	Crown
CRP	Crown Productions
CS	CS
CTI	Casey Tibbs, Inc.
CTJ	Constantine-Jolly-Trio Films
CU	Commonwealth Unlimited
CV	Color Vision
CZ	Conrad-Zacharias

D

DD	Doty Dayton
DER	Dynamite Entertainment-Rearguard
DP	Dimension Productions
DWP-TV	David Wolper Productions-TV

E

EE	Ellman Enterprises
EFE	Emerson Film Enterprises
EL	Eagle-Lion
EMB	Embassy
EMP	Empire

F

FA	First American
FAN	Fanfare
FBO	Film Booking Office
FC	Filmar Cinematografica
FD	First Division
FFC	Feature Film Corporation
FE-TV	Fries Entertainment-TV
FHG	Fenix Harold Goldman
FIP	Fipco Productions
FM	Freuler/Monarch
FN	First National
FOX	Fox
4ST	Four Star/Excelsior

FP	Fernando Piazza
FPL	Famous Players
FR	Fox Run
FV	Film Ventures
FVI	Film Ventures International
FW-TV	Filmways-TV

G

GADP	Gad Productions
GAL	Gala
GAR	Gar Films
G-B	Gaumont-British
GC	Golden Circle
GC-TV	Golden Circle-TV
GE	Golden Era
GEA	Golden Eagle
GFE	Goldstone Film Enterprises
GGP	Gadabout Gaddis Productions
GK	Gold Key
GLB	Globe
GN	Grand National

H

HAM	Hampton International
HAR	Harbor Productions
HBO-TV	Home Box Office-TV
HBP-TV	Hanna Barbera Productions-TV
HCF	Hispano Continental Films
HE-TV	Heritage Entertainment-TV
HEX	Hexagon
HI	Howco International
HN	Horschman Northern
HP	Horner Productions
HPI	H.P. International

I

IA	International Amusements
IH	International Harmony
II	Independent International
IMP	Imperial
IPC	International Producers Corporation
IR	Intercontinental Releasing
IRC	International Releasing Corporation
IYC	Irwin Yablans Company

J

JCP-TV	Joseph Cates Productions-TV
JF	Junior Films
JFP	Jensen Farley Pictures
JHH	Jack H. Harris Enterprises

K

KEN	Kent
KI	Key International
KS-TV	Konigsbert-Sanitsky-TV
KSC	Kayson/Screencraft
KTI	K-Tel International

L

LAC	Lacy
LIB	Liberty
LI	Liber Film
LIP	Lippert
LMO	Lone Star/Monogram
LOR-TV	Lorimar Productions-TV
LSP	Lone Star Productions

M

MAJ	Majestic
MAP	Manson Productions
MAS	Mascot
MAT	Mattox
MCB	Miro Cinematografica/Balcazar
MDA	M.D.A. Associates, Inc.
MET	Metropolitan
MGM	Metro-Goldwyn-Mayer
MGM-TV	Metro-Goldwyn-Mayer-TV
MGM/UA-TV	Metro-Goldwyn-Mayer/United Artists-TV
MHV	Monterey Home Video
MON	Monogram
MPCS	M.P.C./Stonehenge
MPC-TV	Metromedia Producers Corporation-TV

N

NBC-TV	National Broadcasting Company-TV
NG	National General
NLC	New Line Cinema
NW	New World

O

OETA-TV	Oklahoma Educational Television Authority-TV
OPT-TV	Operation Prime Time-TV
ORB	Orbita
ORI	Orion

P

PA	Principal Attraction
PAD	Parade
PAL	Palestine
PAR	Paramount
PAR-TV	Paramount-TV
PAT	Pathe-American
PDC	Producers Distributing Corporation

PEACF	P.E.A./Centurio Films
PEN	Penland
PF-TV	Pedernales Films-TV
PI	Pacific International
PIC	Picturmedia
PIE	Premier Productions
PPP-TV	Phoenix Production Partners-TV
PRC	Producers Releasing Corporation
PRN	Principal
PRO	Producers Releasing Organization
PSM	PSM Entertainment
PUR	Puritan

Q

QMP-TV	Quinn Martin Productions-TV

R

RAF	RAF Industries
REA	Realart
REI	Reina Productions
REL	Reliable
REP	Republic
RES	Resolute
REV	Revue
RF	Rezzoli Film
RJH	R.J. Horner
RKO	Radio Keith Orpheum
RMF	R.M. Films
RP	Roundup Pictures

S

SCI	Scotia International
SCP-TV	Sunn Classic Productions-TV
SE	Shapiro Entertainment
SEC	Security
SEL	Selznick
SEL/MGM	Selznick/Metro-Goldwyn-Mayer
SEN	Simitar Entertainment
SG	Screen Guild
SGC	Samuel Goldwyn Company
SGE-TV	Screen Gems-TV
SGP-TV	Spelling/Goldberg Productions-TV
SI	Sun International
SPE	Spectrum
SPF-TV	SPF-TV
SPR	Superior
S&S	Stage and Screen
STE	Stellar IV
SUN	Sunset
SUP	Supreme
SYN	Syndicate
SYT-TV	Syndicated Television-TV

T

TEC	Tecish
TEG-TV	Taft Entertainment Group-TV
TIF	Tiffany
TIM	Times
TIT	Titanus
TKP	Tucson Kid Productions
TLU	Trans-Lux Distribution Corporation
TMP	Triad Motion Pictures, Inc.
TNT-TV	Turner Network Television-TV
TOP	Topar
TP	Transvue Pictures
TS	Tri-Star
TW	Teleworld
20T	Twentieth Century-Fox
20T-TV	Twentieth Century-Fox-TV
21T	Twenty-First Century-Fox

U

UA	United Artists
UF	Universal France
UFA	UFA International
UHC	Ultimate/Hesperia/Cineurope
UI	Universal-International
UNI	Universal
UNI-TV	Universal-TV
USA	United Screen Arts
USA-TV	USA-TV
UV	Unicorn Video

V

VIC	Victory
VIS	Visual Drama

W

WA	Western Adventure
WAS	Western Adventure/Screen Guild
WB	Warner Brothers
WB-TV	Warner Brothers-TV
WC	West Coast
WCP	Wheeler Company Productions
WES	Western World
WME	Walter Manley Enterprises
WRA-TV	Wrather Corporation-TV
WW	World Wide

Y

YUC	Yucca Productions

Z

ZIE	Ziehm, Inc.
ZIV	ZIV International, Inc.

REFERENCES

Aaronson, Charles S. 1961 INTERNATIONAL MOTION PICTURE ALMANAC, 1960, Quigley Publications Company, New York, NY.

Adams, Les and Buck Rainey. SHOOT-EM-UPS, 1978, Arlington House, New Rochelle, NY.

Bartelt, Chuck and Barbara Bergeron. VARIETY OBITUARIES, 1989, Garland Publishing, Inc., New York, NY.

Bond, Johnny. THE TEX RITTER STORY, 1976, Chappell & Company, Inc., New York, NY.

Carman, Bob and Dan Scapperotti. THE ADVENTURES OF THE DURANGO KID, 1983, Privately published.

Cocci, John. SECOND FEATURE, 1991, Carroll Publishing Group, New York, NY.

Copyright Office, The Library of Congress. MOTION PICTURES (1930-1939), (1940-1949), (1950-1959), Washington, DC.

Fitzgerald, Michael G. UNIVERSAL PICTURES, 1977, Arlington House, New Rochelle, NY.

Gottschalk, Earl C., Jr. "John Carpenter and His Miracle Ranch", August 1982, Reader's Digest, Pleasantville, NY.

Hardy, Phil. THE WESTERN, 1983, William Morrow and Company, New York, NY.

Magers, Boyd. WESTERN CLIPPINGS, July 1990, July, 1991, and September 1991, *Big Reel* magazine, Madison, NC.

Maltin, Leonard. LEONARD MALTIN'S TV MOVIES VIDEO GUIDE 1991 EDITION, 1990, Penguin Books, New York, NY.

Maltin, Leonard. LEONARD MALTIN'S MOVIE AND VIDEO GUIDE 1992, 1991, Penguin Books, New York, NY.

Martin, Len D. THE COLUMBIA CHECKLIST, 1991, McFarland & Company, Inc., Jefferson, NC.

Martin, Mick and Marsha Porter. VIDEO MOVIE GUIDE 1991, 1990, Ballantine Books, New York, NY.

Mathis, Jack. REPUBLIC CONFIDENTIAL (THE PLAYERS), Volume 2, 1992, Jack Mathis Advertising, Barrington, IL.

Mathis, Jack. VALLEY OF THE CLIFFHANGERS, 1975, Jack Mathis Advertising, Northbrook, IL.

Michael, Paul. THE AMERICAN MOVIES REFERENCE BOOK THE SOUND ERA, 1969, Prentice-Hall, Inc., Englewood Cliffs, NJ.

Montgomery, George and Jeffrey Millett. THE YEARS OF GEORGE MONTGOMERY, 1981, Taylor Publishing Company, Dallas, TX.

Nash, Jay Robert and Stanley Ralph Ross. THE MOTION PICTURE GUIDE, 1985-1990, Cinebooks, Inc., Chicago, IL.

Nevins, Francis M. THE FILMS OF HOPALONG CASSIDY, 1989, The World of Yesterday, Waynesville, NC.

Parrish, James Robert and Vincent Terrace. THE COMPLETE ACTORS' TELEVISION CREDITS (1948-1988), 2nd edition, 1989, The Scarecrow Press, Metuchen, NJ.

The Philadelphia Inquirer. MOVIE GUIDE FOR VCRs, 1988, 1988, Bart Books, New York, NY.

Pitts, Michael R. WESTERN MOVIES, 1986, McFarland & Company, Inc., Jefferson, NC.

Quinlan, David. THE ILLUSTRATED GUIDE TO FILM DIRECTORS, 1983, Barnes & Noble Books, Totowa, NJ.

Rainey, Buck. HEROES OF THE RANGE, 1987, The World of Yesterday, Waynesville, NC.

Rainey, Buck. SADDLE ACES OF THE CINEMA, 1980, A.S. Barnes & Company, Inc., New York, NY.

Rainey, Buck. THE SHOOT-EM-UPS RIDE AGAIN, 1990, The World of Yesterday, Waynesville, NC.

Scheuer, Steven H. MOVIES ON TV AND VIDEOCASSETTE, 1991, Bantam Books, New York, NY.

Thornton, Chuck, and David Rothel. LASH LARUE, THE KING OF THE BULLWHIP, 1988, Empire Publishing, Inc., Madison, NC.

Truitt, Evelyn Mack. WHO WAS WHO ON SCREEN, 1983, R.R. Bowker Company, New York, NY.

Weiner, David J. THE VIDEO SOURCE BOOK (10th edition), 1989, Gale Research, Inc., Detroit, MI.

Witt, Paula Simpson and Snuff Garrett. THE ARIZONA COWBOY: REX ALLEN, 1989, RexGarRus Press, Scottsdale, AZ.

THE AUTHORS

John A. Rutherford

John A. Rutherford is a college instructor at Radford University where he has taught for nearly 30 years. He has been a "B" western film fan ever since he began going to see them at the Visualite and Strand theaters in Staunton, Virginia in the 1930s.

John has been a regular contributor to several western film magazines, including THE BIG REEL, UNDER WESTERN SKIES and CLIFFHANGERS. He has done a series of articles in those periodicals on the western comic sidekicks.

Since 1981 he has been a film collector of western and other films. At present his collection contains films of Bill Elliott, Buster Crabbe and John Wayne. Along with other film collectors in his home area, he began the Nickelodeon Films, shown monthly at Radford University since 1980. He has also attended just about every western film festival in the eastern United States and estimates that he has seen almost 2000 "B" western films in the last 12 years.

This book is an outgrowth of his continued interest in the western film. More than five years of research went into the preparation for this book. It is the culmination of a lifelong love of western films.

■■■■■■■■■■■■■■■■■■■■■■■■■■■■■■■■■■■■■■■

Richard B. Smith, III developed an ongoing fascination with the sound "B" western around 1948 when he started attending Saturday oater matinees at the now-razed Pitts-Clarco Theater in Berryville, Virginia. He also saw "A"s at both the once-active Hable's Palace and Stanley Warner Capitol Theaters at nearby Winchester.

Interest in this particular genre was greatly accelerated for young Smith in 1951 as television had begun showing the 1930s-1940s low-budgeters which he was able to view over stations from Baltimore, Maryland, and Washington, D.C.

In 1958, Smith commenced continuing research on the "B" western with completions of filmographies by perusing old movie display ads from newspaper morgues of northwestern Virginia and the eastern panhandle of West Virginia. Further knowledge for him in recent years has come through scanning files, books, and other publications such as DAILY VARIETY, VARIETY, and THE HOLLYWOOD REPORTER in bound volumes and microfilm, mainly at the Motion Picture Division and main stacks of the Library of Congress.

Having authored personality articles, tributes, and various reviews for THE WORLD OF YESTERDAY and THE BIG REEL, Smith also has a continuing, semi-regular column in UNDER WESTERN SKIES entitled "B-Westerns in Perspective." Each feature is highlighted with technical data on filming dates, locations, running times, release dates, comments, evaluations, synopses, etc.

Smith assisted Jack Mathis with compilation of the Super-Index of Republic Pictures' players for REPUBLIC CONFIDENTIAL (Volume 2), which was published in 1992.

He is a 1963 Bachelor of Arts degree graduate in English/Journalism from Shepherd College, Shepherdstown, West Virginia, and is currently employed as a printer proofreader with the United States Government Printing Office in Washington.

Richard B. Smith, III